The

Heirloom

Garden

The
Heirloom
Garden

Selecting & Growing
Over 300 Old-Fashioned Ornamentals

Jo Ann Gardner

A Garden Way Publishing Book

Storey Communications, Inc.
Pownal, Vermont 05261

Cover painting by Kathleen Kolb
Illustrations by Mallory Lake
Illustrations on pages 12,16,49, 62, and 207 by Judy Eliason
Designed and produced by Cindy McFarland

Copyright © 1992 by Jo Ann Gardner

The name Garden Way Publishing is licensed to Storey Communications, Inc. by Garden Way, Inc.

The information in this book is true and complete to the best of our knowledge.
All recommendations are made without guarantee on the part of the author or Storey Communications, Inc.
The author and publisher disclaim any liability incurred with the use of this information.

Printed in the United States by The Book Press
Color signature printed by Excelsior Printing Company

First Printing, January 1992

Library of Congress Cataloging-in-Publication Data

Gardner, Jo Ann, 1935-
      The heirloom garden : selecting & growing over 300 old-fashioned ornamentals / Jo Ann Gardner.
            p.   cm.
      "A Garden Way Publishing book."
      Includes bibliographical references and indexes.
      ISBN 0-88266-752-1 — ISBN 0-88266-751-3 (pbk.)
      1. Plants, Ornamental—Heirloom varieties.   2. Flowers—Heirloom varieties.   3. Plants, Ornamental—North America—Heirloom varieties.   4. Flowers—North America—Heirloom varieties.   I. Title.
      SB407.G345   1992
      635.9—dc20   91-55487

To my grandparents,
who never had a garden:
Rebecca, Isaac, Rose, and Sam .

This is how preservation comes about . . . the old friends remain in our gardens because we love them and because they are survivors.

HISTORIC IRIS PRESERVATION SOCIETY,
VOL. 2, NO. 2, 1989

Contents

Acknowledgments

My thanks to the following enthusiastic gardeners and organizations for their generous help: Heather Apple, Heritage Seed Program; Verna Lauren, Historic Iris Preservation Society; Grant Wilson, general editor, Canadian Gladioli Society; Walter Oakes and Charles Holetich, International Lilac Society; Lily Shohan, Heritage Rose Group; Jeanette Lowe, Marigold Society of America; Arthur Haskins, Nova Scotia Dahlia expert; John Moe, Washington State Lily connoisseur; Audrey O'Connor, retired editor, *Cornell Plantations*, and discerning gardener; Meg Yerger, Maryland Poeticus Daffodil collector.

Thanks, too, to Ben Watson, my editor at Storey Communications,
for his support and encouragement,
and thanks is insufficient for my husband, Jigs, partner-in-all-things,
whose double duty in the barn, the field, the buttery, and the study (sans computer)
enabled me to write this book.

Credits

The recipe for Currant Jam was adapted from my book, *The Old-Fashioned Fruit Garden* (Nimbus Publishing, 1989).

Directions for making a child's arbor were adapted from directions courtesy of Christie White, lead interpreter for horticulture, Old Sturbridge Village, Sturbridge, Massachusetts.

Quiggly fence directions were adapted from directions courtesy of Bernard S. Jackson, curator, Memorial University Botanical Garden.

Brief quotes throughout the book from Louise Beebe Wilder and Mrs. Francis King come from the following sources, unless otherwise indicated:

Louise Beebe Wilder, *The Fragrant Garden* (Dover, 1974); *The Garden in Color* (Macmillan, 1937).

Mrs. Francis King, *From a New Garden* (Alfred A. Knopf, 1930).

PART I

An Introduction to Heirlooms

An heirloom
is a valued possession passed down . . .
through successive generations.

—THE AMERICAN HERITAGE DICTIONARY, 1975

The Education
of an
Heirloom Gardener

IN 1970 WE MOVED a Noah's Ark of animals — two horses, two cows, miscellaneous chickens, cats, and a dog — 750 miles northeastward to a 100-acre farm at the end of a dirt road on a remote peninsula in Cape Breton Island, Nova Scotia. After we had rebuilt the barn, plowed and planted the fields, restored the fences, and established vegetable and fruit gardens, I turned my attention to the ornamentals I'd inherited with the property: herbs, flowers, and shrubs planted close to the house on a knoll just beyond the front door. There were Lilacs, purple and white, their aging limbs spread over a wide area, almost touching one another. At the base of one, the ground was entirely covered with spotted-leaved Lungwort (*Pulmonaria officinalis*) — clusters of small pink and lilac-blue trumpets in the early spring — and nearby was an impressive clump of Tawny Daylilies (*Hemerocallis fulva*), once described as the floral symbol of our gardening past.

Struggling to survive on the same piece of ground were a few Mock Orange bushes and a group of Daffodils, known locally as the "French Lily" or "White Lily," most of whose buds never opened but expired within their papery covering. The few flowers I saw, though, were unforgettable: tight clusters of intensely fragrant, double white blooms.

A Rose bush sprawled in front of the house, just under a window, its suckers spreading in every direction. I knew virtually nothing about Old Roses then (this, I later learned, was a Banshee, also known as the "Loyalist Rose," one of the most common at colonial sites all over the Northeast). When the flowers opened, I discovered Old Rose essence for the first time, deep within the layers of blush pink petals.

Yellow Flag Iris (*Iris pseudacorus*) flourished in a large colony by the back door — swordlike green leaves and small fleur-de-lis blossoms in a classic design I'd never seen before. I'd never seen the likes of *any* of these plants, having grown up in the suburbs and spent my gardening time hoeing rows of string beans to feed our family. This small collection of ornamentals opened up a new world to me. I was attracted to the plants' pronounced scents, variety of forms (somewhat on the wild side), and charming, often quirky ways. Gradually I began to explore the area for other remnants of old gardens and plants.

The peninsula proved to be a rich hunting ground. Because of its isolation from the mainstream, untouched by fashion or development until relatively recently, old plantings here have remained undisturbed for many years. On deserted farms, up lonely glens and mountainsides named for the places the early nineteenth-century Highland Scottish settlers had left behind — Lewis, Skye, Barra — I found Foxglove, naturalized at the edge of woodland roads where no one had lived for at least fifty years; Peonies, growing among old spruce trees; the double-flowered Bouncing-bet (*Saponaria officinalis* 'Flore Plena'), once a garden plant, now a roadside weed.

One midsummer day, a friend came by to tell me I'd better get over to see his folks' place before it was leveled by the 'dozer. (Even as I was discovering them, old gardens and plants were beginning to disappear.) Rounding a bend past Blackberries, wild Roses, and Jerusalem-artichokes, I found the house, built in 1878, the third one for a family of settlers from the Isle of Lewis in the early 1800s. The first settlers had spent the winter under a boat by the shore of the nearby lake. I stood on the falling-down porch and looked at the clear signs of a garden: Daylilies, Yellow Loosestrife, Lilacs, Roses, the inevitable Rhubarb, and, at my feet, mats of Forget-me-nots and Columbine, long past blooming. Looking up, I saw the luxuriant Virginia Creeper adorned with clusters of small purple berries, the vine soaring to the peak of the house, past broken windows through which no one would ever look again, the house of my

friend's parents, who had flailed oats till midnight and milked cows at dawn yet had planted gardens of "use and delight."

These early experiences shaped my ideas about heirloom plants, which I then defined in a general sort of way as "the ones our ancestors grew." These plants, I thought, with their simple grace and charm, were close to the wild, unspoiled by human intervention. But as I became more involved with the subject of old ornamentals, I realized that curious gardeners had been tinkering with nature for centuries, that the subject was much broader and more complex than I had imagined. It was, ironically, the plight of a modern Hybrid Rose that put the designation "heirloom ornamental" in perspective for me, that made me confront the word *old* when applied to plants. What is old in this context? We have no trouble with plants introduced before the modern era, say 1900. But in the modern era, plant breeding, burgeoning as never before, has created thousands of new plants, and the pressure for their survival has been enormous. The market, in responding to ever-new offerings, tends to cast aside many worthy plants. In a way, we can say that the aging process in plant longevity has been speeded up. Plants enjoying tremendous popularity today may be on the preservationist list thirty years hence.

'Ma Perkins' was introduced to the world in 1952, the creation of the well-known plant breeder Gene Boerner. It is described in Peter Beales's English Rose catalog as "superb Floribunda which must not be lost. Globular buds opening to cupped flowers of shell pink with salmon shading in well-spaced clusters on a bush with good and ample dark green foliage," and fragrant to boot.

I asked Mr. Beales, a noted Rose authority and author of *Classic Roses* (Collins/Harvill, 1985), if there was anything wrong with 'Ma', any blemish on her evident beauty that would explain why such a quintessential American Rose (bred in America, AARS winner, named after the 1940s folksy soap opera) had vanished from the American marketplace. Was 'Ma' a carrier of some dread disease, a poor performer in American gardens?

Mr. Beales responded that he was frequently baffled as to why Roses of such caliber disappear from commercial circulation. The only possible explanation, he suggested, is that with sharpened marketing techniques, the public is led to believe that anything new must be better, and when sales drop off to a certain level, the older introduction is quickly dropped.

I began to understand that what constitutes an heirloom ornamental is open to interpretation. Heirlooms change over time and are not fixed absolutely, but represent valued possessions at different periods in history. Those plants that deserve our attention as heirloom gardeners can be as varied as the truly antique sixteenth-century double-flowered Dame's-rocket (where is it now?) — a naturally occurring sport of nature probably selected and reselected by generations of keen-sighted gardeners — as well as hybrid creations such as 'Ma' — deserving of attention, increasingly rare, and in danger of being lost to future generations of gardeners.

As I was drawn into the effort to find and preserve heirlooms, I met extraordinary heirloom gardeners such as Verna Lauren, secretary of the Canadian Iris Society, who never intended to collect older Iris, she wrote, but "just grow ones that I like," which turned out to be more than one hundred varieties in a city backyard. From Maryland, I learned about Meg Yerger, who began growing Daffodils for an all-white garden many years ago and now has what is probably the largest collection of Poeticus types in the world. "It would be nice if you could mention the names of the older Poets, so people will ask for them by name at specialist nurseries and so those places may unearth sources — 'Dulcimer' (1913), 'Hexameter' (1927), 'Homer' (1898), 'Lights Out' (1938)" — all of which she describes as beautiful and fragrant.

Locally, I found lovely Garden Phlox, developed from our native species, some of which couldn't have been more than thirty or forty years old. They were carefully tended, regarded as one of the family. I found Dahlias, passed around from hand to hand, from garden to garden, whose names were long forgotten but whose fat, homely roots were cherished by people who regarded them as "survivors," although they were probably introduced no earlier than the 1960s.

Just as my earlier experiences had shaped my idea of *heirloom*, my expanded knowledge contributed to a new vision, aptly summed up in Edward Hyams' description of worthy Lilies: easy, tolerant, robust, and enduring — to which I would add beautiful in some irreplaceable way, like 'Ma Perkins'.

This is the vision that stands behind the wide selection of plants I have chosen to describe. I hope that those just becoming interested in the subject of heirloom ornamentals can experience its diversity as I have and make informed choices about what to grow and which aspects of heirloom plants to explore in more depth.

I believe that qualities such as easy, tolerant, robust, and enduring are virtues in which many gardeners are interested and that these values are most in tune with the kinds of gardens they want to create: informal, low-maintenance, attractive landscapes in harmony with the surrounding environment. As I have learned, the plants that fit that description include the silver-leaved Lungwort, tending to itself under the filtered shade of my old Lilac tree; the broad border of colorful Hybrid Dahlias that thrive at the edge of my neighbor's potato patch; and the 1942 'Blue Shimmer' Iris, an indestructible Bearded type that I acquired in the 1970s and have moved more times than I care to remember, now regarded as an "old favorite" and "antique" in the world of Iris fanciers.

If one of the greatest pleasures of gardening is sharing, then how much greater is that pleasure when the sharing includes such a rich world of interesting and varied plants, our collective valued possessions.

The Heirloom Garden Book

This book is designed to define the world I discovered — its language and its plants — and thereby make it accessible to ordinary gardeners, while also enlarging the possibilities for the committed enthusiast. Both will enjoy meeting old garden friends and getting to know new ones.

The definition of *heirloom ornamentals* here is as follows: those plants introduced to American gardens from 1600 to 1950 (and a little beyond to accommodate Iris and other plants defined as "antique" if they have been introduced in the past thirty years). This is a diverse group of herbs, flowers, shrubs, and vines, native flora and plants from around the world. It is broken down into two categories: (1) *Ancient* and *antique* types (the terms are almost synonymous, with *ancient* suggesting older), known and described as early as Classical times. The plants in this group include many very hardy, nearly wild types that we associate with English cottage gardens. (2) *Middle-aged* types. These are hybrid variations on ancient and antique themes that began to appear in great numbers as the result of expanded knowledge about plant breeding toward the end of the

nineteenth century.

Strictly speaking, *hybrids* are the result of cross-fertilization between two plant species, sometimes occurring naturally but usually on purpose. The horticulturalist uses the term more loosely to apply to any cross-fertilization between variant parents, such as the thousands of Glads and Iris created by crossing and recrossing cultivars. A *cultivar*, or *variety*, is any plant that arises from cultivation and is significant enough to name, as distinct from naturally occurring variations. You've probably heard the term *open-pollinated* (OP to the initiated). This means that the blossoms from those plants have been pollinated "in the open" by nature. Plants from any of the groups I have described are variously referred to as "antique" or "old-fashioned."

If you've grown only tamed types in your garden, you might like to become familiar with easily naturalized wild (OP) species, which, as I show, constitute a large and varied group of garden-worthy plants. If you've grown only the latest Hybrid Tea Rose, a whole world of ancient, antique, and modern classic Roses awaits you. If you're interested in edible landscapes, heirloom plants supply plenty of material for making delicious and useful products — from salt substitutes and jellies to homemade detergent. Directions for making a few such products are sprinkled throughout the book.

In the next chapter on planning, you will find a way to plunge into creating an heirloom garden by following the suggested plantings, which have been organized into historical groupings. Here the gardener can explore superhardy and OP plants typical of early settlers' gardens, as well as the tender vine-covered arbors and Hybrid Roses, Daffodils, and Lilies of later periods. These are not meant to suggest the strict period gardens of authentic restorations, although those interested in such undertakings may find useful material here. In addition to the suggestions for planting in this chapter, Part II contains a wealth of ideas for plant combinations and mixed plantings.

Also in the following chapter you will learn some simple techniques for plant propagation, especially important to know for sharing heirlooms with others. A guide for collecting ornamentals from noncommercial sources (old gardens, the wild, and threatened habitats) is based on my own and others' knowledge of such procedures and is among the first such guides offered specifically for collecting ornamental plants. Organizations devoted to preserving heirlooms are described in Part III.

At the heart of the book are the seventy-five plant portraits in Part II. I have tried to balance historical information (to inform rather than overwhelm) with down-to-earth gardening instructions. These practical instructions appear near the end of each portrait under the heading "To Grow." Readers wanting more gardening information are referred to the bibliography, where I have noted especially helpful books.

Latin names throughout are based on common usage, mainly drawn from *Hortus Third*. In such matters, I follow Donald Wyman, who in discussing *Clematis paniculata* (Sweet Autumn Clematis) points out that its correct name — *C. dioscoreifolia robusta* — has not been used during the past two decades, and those who wish to be meticulously correct should note the change (*Shrubs and Vines for American Gardens*, Macmillan, 1969). It is most important for gardeners to have a rough familiarity with Latin names because common names, while charming, are unreliable for identification, and you may want to know the precise name of the plant you admire so you can order it from a plant or seed source. Where I live, several different plants are known as "London-pride,"

but none is the lovely little Saxifrage (*Saxifraga umbrosa*) that most people associate with Gertrude Jekyll's cherished London-pride.

Common names are more than charming, which is why I have included so many of them. They, too, are part of our plant heritage, the stored wisdom and wit of countless generations of ordinary gardeners. They preserve interesting bits of history and often refer to a plant's outstanding physical characteristics in memorable images. Hurt-sickle, for instance, describes the way a mower's sickle was often caught in the wiry stems of *Centaurea cyanus* as it mingled with grain in the fields of Europe. Today we know this plant mainly by its Victorian name — Bachelor's-button — from its use as a boutonniere.

The dates of introduction represent the general period when a plant or group of plants was introduced to American gardens. The dates are drawn mainly from *Landscapes and Gardens for Historic Buildings* by Favretti and Favretti (American Association for State and Local History, 1978) and from the three-volume Leighton work (see Bibliography), supplemented, where necessary, with information from period literature, old plant lists, and assorted reference works. Specific dates of introduction may appear in the text or in the "Collector's Choice" section at the end of each portrait. Sometimes the date range covers several hundred years — for instance, 1600 to 1900 for Old Garden Roses.

Growing zones can be as difficult to ascertain as dates of introduction, since authorities do not always agree. The lower figure represents the growing zone where the plant can be expected to survive the winter without protection; the higher number represents the warmest growing zone where a plant can be expected to perform satisfactorily. Growing zone figures are based on the U.S. Department of

Agriculture's (USDA) Hardiness Zone Map (see p. 210). As experienced gardeners know, you can push these limits by planting in microclimates (protected sites where extra moisture, protection from the wind, exposure to sun, and so on, are provided) depending on the requirements of the situation.

"Collector's Choice" lists the choicest cultivars and strains available (based on the opinions of experienced gardeners and experts), as well as any additional information (such as plant height, bloom season, and hardiness) not discussed in the text. *Strains*, by the way, are plant types resulting from carefully selected seeds from desirable variants (*sports*) in any plant population, the most famous examples of which are Reverend Wilkes's Shirley Poppies and 'Giant Shirley' Foxglove, both created from such variants. "Collector's Choice" is in many instances a much-needed guide for choosing among the wide variety of heirloom plants available in groups such as Iris and Daffodils, as well as a guide to their classification systems. You may need to know, for instance, what an FD Dahlia is, a Div. 3 Narcissus, or an IB Iris. Specialty catalogs and plant organizations often assume such knowledge. All of the choices in this section reflect a concern for the varied growing conditions with which gardeners must contend. If, for instance, you're looking for an heirloom Lilac that is drought-resistant or extraordinarily hardy, you will find it here.

I have indicated, where possible, which choices are authentic heirlooms (usually dated) and which are in the spirit of heirlooms (designated *old style*). In the latter category is the list of Russell Hybrid Lupine cultivars, the originals of which wowed the Royal Horticultural Society judges in 1937, when Mr. Russell introduced them. Frankly, I don't know when those I list were introduced, but they certainly are in the spirit of the originals. Clearly, this is not a purist's approach to heirlooms.

Throughout the book I have noted especially fragrant or scented plants (flowers or leaves) with a floral symbol. Fragrance is a characteristic that many heirloom gardeners prize, for it almost guarantees the presence of birds, bees, and butterflies in the garden for pollination and enjoyment.

Plant and seed sources are represented by numbers following each selection in "Collector's Choice." They are listed alphabetically by state in the source section of Part III. Collectively, they represent state-of-the-art sources in the field, aside from very specialized listings, and they range from mimeographed sheets to fat, glossy catalogs. They are a world unto themselves and often worth ordering just to read.

Despite the large number of plants included in this book, I was not able to include the many fine heirlooms that would have required at least another volume — Tulips, Hyacinth, Sweet Woodruff, and Silver-pennies, among others. Contrary to accepted wisdom, ours is a tradition rich in plants if not in grand gardens.

I have often been asked whether a cottage garden is an heirloom garden. The term *cottage garden* has been used in a variety of contexts, most of which have very little to do with the historic cottage gardens of the English rural poor. Our conception of them has been largely idealized, but the current preoccupation with cottage gardens in America reflects a yearning for freer, more bountiful, and more varied plantings than the suburban ideal of the past fifty years. If you create a garden or a planting, no matter how small, with even a few of the extraordinarily varied plants described in this book, you will also create an heirloom cottage garden that answers the needs of contemporary American gardeners.

Planning & Preserving the Heirloom Garden

The love of flowers brings surely with it the love of all the green world.
—Mrs. Francis King (*The Well-Considered Garden*, 1915)

THE SUBJECT OF heirloom plants is broad enough to include the nearly wild, open-pollinated (OP) herbs and flowers of old English cottage gardens and early American gardens as well as the relatively new hybrid forms that poured forth in great numbers around the end of the nineteenth century, especially among Roses, Iris, and Daffodils. If your tastes run to the former category and you think hybrids have no place in the heirloom garden, you can choose from a wide variety of plants introduced from the seventeenth to the nineteenth centuries in America, among them many wonderful natives.

I have organized the following groupings historically so that you may choose to plant those types that most satisfy the varied meanings of *heirloom*. For the eclectic gardener interested in beautiful and deserving plants from any era, I have included a wide-open garden with plants from all periods.

Plant Categories

Perennials: Live for more than three years.

Short-Lived Perennials: Need to be replaced every few years.

Biennials: Take two seasons to flower from seed; may self-seed from year to year.

Annuals: Tender annuals are damaged by frost; hardy annuals are frost-hardy in varying degrees and often self-sow from year to year.

Bulbs: Hardy bulbs (such as Lilies and Narcissus) are perennials. They are left in the ground from year to year except in warm-winter areas, where they may need to be grown as annuals and prechilled). Tender bulbs (such as Dahlias) are usually treated as annuals, except where winters are mild and they can be left in the ground from year to year.

Vines: Twining (such as the Scarlet Runner Bean); tendril (such as Sweet Pea and Clematis;

it climbs by tendril-like leaves); and clinging (such as the Virginia Creeper). The first two types need support, such as a fence, post, wire, or trellis; the last type will climb on its own if planted close to a wall or tree trunk. If not given any support, most vines make a good ground-cover. Although Roses aren't vines, those with long enough canes (six feet or over) can be so treated if given means of support — that is, trained along fences or arbors.

Note: Check the "Gardens to Visit" section in Part III. These have been carefully chosen for their displays of heirloom plants mentioned throughout the book. Growing directions and bloom periods for all the plants listed in the following section can be found in Part II.

An Early Settler's Cottage Garden: 1600-1699

It is surprising how many ornamental plants turn up on lists of those grown in the seventeenth century, especially since we have been told so often about the Puritan gardens of utility. I rather think that these gardens, like most of those planted since the beginning of horticulture, were "compounded of both dreams and utility." How else can we explain the appearance of Lilies-of-the-valley, Sweet-William, Canterbury-bells, Dame's-rocket, Lilacs, and Mock Orange, whose herbal virtues are almost nonexistent?

As might be expected, these gardens are characterized by sturdy, reliable plants able to survive in a variety of habitats, adaptable and extremely hardy, and almost all from the Old World, with the exception of the native Canada Lily (*Lilium canadense*), the Wild-bergamot (*Monarda fistulosa*), and the flamboyant Scarlet Honeysuckle (*Lonicera sempervirens*).

If you're just becoming interested in herbs, a settler's herb garden is a good way to start, since these plants are easy to grow and have many uses that speak to us today. All love the sun and can be grouped by the kitchen door within easy reach: Chives for chopping into salads; Southernwood sprigs for adding to pot-pourri or sachets, pebbly leaved Sage for flavoring; Wild-bergamot for tea; Calendula petals for decorating cakes; at least one Old Garden Rose for rose petal jelly.

Train a Hop, Honeysuckle, or Everlasting Pea vine on an old-fashioned quiggly fence (perhaps the kind the settlers built), and you will also have support for the tall, single-flowered Hollyhock and a variety of settler plants we value primarily for their good looks: Bell-flowers, Feverfew, the bright red Jerusalem-cross, and the soft pink Musk Mallow (don't be afraid to pair them), the exquisite pearly Florentine Iris, and, rising here and there, the flower-laden spikes of the White or Madonna Lily (*Lilium candidum*) and the pastel clusters of Dame's-rocket, both to perfume the early evening air. Sow dark blue Bachelor's- button among these and add a double-flowered Peony or two on the other side of the doorway. Before you know it, you will have the proverbial cottage garden.

You can carpet the ground beneath nearby Lilacs and Mock Orange with spotted-leaved Lungwort, to be followed by plants that appreciate the partial shade and moist ground they provide: Lilies-of-the-valley, Sweet Cicely, Columbine, Daylilies, Canada Lilies, and little Johnny-jump-ups. All of these plants will thrive with very little attention.

You can choose from the plants listed below to create your own settler's garden. Consult the individual plant portraits in Part II to find those best suited to your area's particular growing conditions.

(* indicates fragrant plants)

Hardy Perennials (hardy to Zone 3)

Chives (*Allium schoenoprasum*)
Columbine, single and double (*Aquilegia vulgaris*)
*Cowslip (*Primula veris*)
*Florentine Iris (*Iris* x *germanica* 'Florentina')
*Garden Sage (*Salvia officinalis*)
*Grandma's Peony (*Paeonia officinalis*)
Jerusalem-cross (*Lychnis chalcedonica*)
*Lemon Lily (*Hemerocallis lilioasphodelus*)
*Lily-of-the-valley (*Convallaria majalis*, hardy bulb)
Lungwort (*Pulmonaria officinalis*)
*Madonna Lily (*Lilium candidum*)
Monkshood (*Aconitum napellus*)
Musk Mallow (*Malva moschata*)
Peach-leaved Bellflower, single and double (*Campanula persicifolia*)
*Southernwood (*Artemisia abrotanum*)
Tawny Daylily (*Hemerocallis fulva*)
*Wild-bergamot (*Monarda fistulosa*)

Biennials and Short-Lived Perennials

Canterbury-bells, single and double (*Campanula medium*)
*Clary Sage (*Salvia sclarea*)
*Dame's-rocket (*Hesperis matronalis*)
Feverfew, single and double (*Chrysanthe mum parthenium*)
Hollyhock (*Alcea rosea*)

Hardy Annuals

Bachelor's-button (*Centaurea cyanus*)
Calendula (*Calendula officinalis*)
Johnny-jump-up (*Viola tricolor*)

Shrubs (hardy to Zone 3)

*Lilac (*Syringa vulgaris*)
*Mock Orange (*Philadelphus coronarius*)
*Roses: Apothecary, Cabbage, Damask

Perennial Vines (twining, hardy to Zone 3)

Everlasting Pea (*Lathyrus latifolius*, nearly evergreen in the South)
*Hop Vine (*Humulus lupulus*)
*Scarlet Honeysuckle (*Lonicera sempervirens*, evergreen in the South)

A Native Flora Garden: 1700-c. 1850

The period from the eighteenth century through the early to mid-nineteenth century was characterized by a slow but growing awareness of our native plant treasures. Through the efforts of people like John Bartram — farmer, plant collector, and curious gardener extraordinaire — who established his own plant nursery in 1728, Americans for the first time had a commercial source for a variety of native plants, especially shrubs. He, for instance, was responsible for introducing Mountain-laurel and the Catawba Rhododendron (considered to be among our finest native shrubs). In the early nineteenth century, Bernard M'Mahon introduced some of the plants discovered during the 1803 Lewis and Clark Expedition — flowering Currants (Golden and Clove), for instance. Thomas Jefferson grew many of these native shrubs at his home, Monticello.

If you're interested in native flora, an heirloom garden is an excellent starting point, as well as a good introduction to shrub growing in general. While some of these plants are quite specific in their growth requirements — preferring sun or shade, moist or dry soil — all are

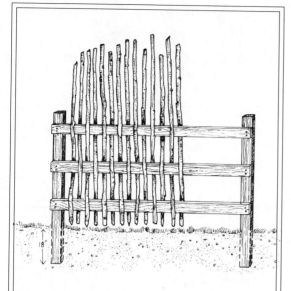

How to Make a Quiggly Fence

Build a three-rail fence by driving treated six-foot posts eighteen inches into the ground as far apart as the length of the fence. If the fence is longer than twelve feet, drive a post in the middle. Nail rails (use treated wood or peeled hardwood saplings) across the posts at eighteen inches, thirty-six inches, and forty-eight inches. Weave young, unpeeled, *fresh-cut* saplings (black spruce or larch are best), no bigger around than two inches, vertically through the rails (behind the bottom rail, in front of the middle one, and behind the top rail). Every other sapling should be woven in reverse (in front of the bottom, behind the middle, and in front of the top). Space the saplings an inch or two apart. You may cut them at a uniform height of seven or eight feet or vary them for a more natural effect. This type of fence also acts as an effective windbreak.

easy to grow once these conditions have been met. They are especially recommended for low-maintenance gardens that complement and blend in with their natural surroundings. Since many of these plants are fragrant, you will also have an attractive habitat for birds and butterflies.

For a garden in partial shade with moist, humusy soil, choose among several native Rhododendrons and Azaleas (the former have nearly evergreen leaves, the latter deciduous ones that turn bronze or scarlet in the fall). Underplant them with native wildflowers such as Virginia-bluebells, Scarlet Bee-balm (really brilliant in partial shade), and Bleeding-heart (*Dicentra eximia* and *D. formosa*), and among them plant Maidenhair Fern for all-season dainty green foliage.

Shrubs that will grow almost anywhere, resisting both drought and damp conditions, include the flowering Golden and Clove Currants (*Ribes aureum* and *R. odoratum*, respectively), Mountain-laurel, and Highbush Cranberry (this will give you creamy white flower clusters in early summer and bright red berries and foliage in the fall). If planted in full sun, Mountain-laurel will reward you with masses of cup-shaped white flowers in late spring or early summer, but its handsome glossy leaves remain green all season and will provide a background for sun-loving plants such as Eastern Columbine (*Aquilegia canadensis*), Butterfly Weed, Black-eyed-Susan, the yellow-whorled Horsemint (*Monarda punctata*), and the bright orange-red Leopard Lily (*Lilium pardalinum*).

A sunny rock garden should include low-growing Moss Phlox spilling over and between the rocks — a mass of little blue flowers with drought-resistant needlelike green foliage; Rhodora, a diminutive Rhododendron with rose-colored flowers and attractive foliage; and Crested Iris, just three to four inches high — a mass of violet and gold in the spring. All of these could be followed by the colorful Drummond Phlox for a long season of bloom and interest.

In that damp spot in the sun where nothing else will grow, you can plant the wild Blue Flag Iris (combine it with the European Yellow Flag Iris). The native Elderberry (*Sambucus canadensis*) is adaptable to damp as well as dry soil, and its thinly branched form won't block out the sun. At its feet you may encourage a colony of the magnificent Turk's-cap Lily (*Lilium superbum*), which is bright orange and heavily spotted. "A plant of so much beauty," Jefferson declared, "will be a valuable addition to our flower gardens."

If you're looking for an easy-to-grow vine for damp conditions, try American Virgin's-bower, a woody twining vine that can be trained over an arbor, where it will produce masses of small white flowers in the spring, followed by unusual fluffy fruits in the fall. You can establish a groundcover at its feet with two fine eighteenth-century introductions "from away": the azure Blue Lungwort (*Pulmonaria angustifolia*) and variegated Goutweed. If you also let the old-fashioned Bouncing-bet grow in a wide mat as it likes to do, its pink flowers will perfume the air in the early evening. Forget-me-nots should be added to any planting where the soil is moist, either in sun or shade. The popular Virginia Creeper (*Parthenocissus quinquefolia*) not only can be trained up the side of a building (it's a clinging vine), but when grown over an arbor, its side shoots will trail downward, creating a graceful effect anytime and a dramatic effect in the fall, when its foliage turns scarlet red.

Choose from among these native plants those that are best suited to your area's growing conditions. All plants are hardy to Zone 3 or 4 except as noted.

(* indicates fragrant plants)

Perennials

*Bee-balm (*Monarda didyma*)
 Blue Flag Iris (two species; one, *Iris virginica*, is hardy to Zone 7)
*Butterfly Weed (*Asclepias tuberosa*)
 Crested Iris (*Iris cristata*)
 Eastern Columbine (*Aquilegia canadensis*)
*Horsemint (*Monarda punctata*, Zone 6)
 Leopard Lily (*Lilium pardalinum*)
 Lupine (*Lupinus polyphyllus*)
 Maidenhair Fern (*Adiantum pedatum*)
 Moss Phlox (*Phlox subulata*)
 Turk's-cap Lily (*Lilium superbum*, bulb hardy to Zone 5)
 Wild Bleeding-heart (*Dicentra eximia* and *D. formosa*)

Biennial or Short-Lived Perennial

Black-eyed-Susan (*Rudbeckia hirta*)

Annuals

Clarkia
Drummond Phlox (*Phlox drummondii*)
Godetia (*Clarkia amoena*)

Shrubs

*Catawba Rhododendron (*Rhododendron catawbiense* 'Album')
*Clove and Golden Currants (*Ribes odoratum* and *R. aureum*, respectively)
*Elderberry (*Sambucus canadensis*)
*Flame Azalea (*Rhododendron calendulaceum*, Zone 5)
*Highbush Cranberry (*Viburnum trilobum*)
 Mountain-laurel (*Kalmia latifolia*)
 Oregon Holly-grape (*Mahonia aquifolium*, Zone 5)

*Pink-shell Azalea *(Rhododendron vaseyi)*
*Rosebay Rhododendron *(Rhododendron maximum)*
*Swamp Azalea *(Rhododendron viscosum)*
*Winter Currant *(Ribes sanguineum, Zone 6)*

Perennial Vines

*American Virgin's-bower *(Clematis virginiana)*
Virginia Creeper *(Parthenocissus quinquefolia)*

An Old-Fashioned Mix: 1800-1900

The term *old-fashioned* conjures up different images: a rustic, vine-covered arbor or a Bleeding-heart laden with dangling rosy hearts. Both fit the description of nineteenth-century plants: tender annuals from the Tropics (Morning-glories and Nasturtiums) and sturdy perennials from the Orient. This period offers great scope, for the heirloom gardener can become acquainted with early hybrids — lush-flowered Bourbon and Hybrid Perpetual Roses, whose generous, untailored forms evoke the past, blooming almost the entire summer or intermittently rather than all at once like the ancient Old Garden Roses.

These are mixed plantings, a far step from the early settler's cottage garden of dreams and utility and a bridge to the new world of hybrids, where art and science combine to produce new forms never before known, such as the large-flowered 'Jackman Clematis' introduced in 1860 and still popular. Here you can also find the increasingly rare OP "Essential Petunia," a little sweet-scented pure white or dark purple velvet trumpet. This period offers a fine introduction to the whole concept of *heirloom*, saving the best from the period prior to the modern era.

A child's rustic arbor (see directions on p. 16) can be clothed in Morning-glories, Moon-flowers, and Sweet Pea and Scarlet Runner Bean vines, all quick-growing plants. Around three sides — leaving room for an entrance path — plant a colorful annual border for all-season bloom from early summer into the fall: Cosmos, double-flowered Balsam, Nicotiana, Shirley Poppies or Corn Poppies, Petunias, Marigolds (single French and dwarf Signets). This is certain to be a popular place for children in summer. Even if you have only a little room, several of these can be planted in containers. The heirloom strain Nasturtium 'Empress of India', for instance, is gorgeous in a hanging basket, with its cascading orange-red spurred flowers. The seldom-grown fern-scented Signets, a mound of orange or yellow bloom until frost (and even beyond if sheltered), fit into the landscape almost anywhere. If you plant in containers, remember that the wider the surface area, the less the soil will dry out, especially if the plants are mulched and protected from the glare of the sun at least part of the day where summers are very hot.

If you think Hostas are boring, this is the opportunity to learn more about them. The types here were introduced from the Far East before the end of the nineteenth century. Try them in filtered shade (a good place for Bleeding-heart, too) and group them for contrast of foliage — broad and glossy, undulating, narrow, or variegated. Most Hostas sport attractive, and sometimes quite fragrant, flowers. These plants, when given the right accommodations — moist and cool — will spread out and look as if they mean to stay a long time (they will), and you won't be sorry you planted them.

The spectacular wild Goldband Lily and the Rubrum Lily from the Orient — fragrant and free-flowering with large, waxy white, re-curved pendant blooms — will do best among shrubbery, especially Rhododendron, which also enjoy rich, humusy soil that is heavily mulched.

Plant Hybrid Roses on a sunny bank and edge them generously with furry gray, drought-resistant mats of Lamb's-ears interplanted with the indispensable Sweet-alyssum, a border that will take care of itself all season.

For a hardy perennial vine to climb up a tree (use chicken wire), Jackman Clematis puts on a good show all summer, but all of the vines below have proven their worth. To cover the side of an old shed, there is no better vine than the Sweet Autumn Clematis.

Following are suggested plants for the old-fashioned mix.

(* indicates fragrant plants)

Perennials (hardy to Zone 3 or 4 except as noted)

Bleeding-heart (*Dicentra spectabilis*)
Daffodils (hardy bulbs):
   Angel's-tears (*Narcissus triandus albus*; inquire if nursery-propagated)
   Hoop-petticoat Daffodil (*N. bulbocodium* 'Conspicuous', Zone 6; inquire about zone if nursery-propagated)
   *Old Pheasant's-eye (*N. poeticus recurvus*)
Hostas:
   Blue Plantain Lily (*Hosta ventricosa*)
   Fortune's Plantain Lily (*H. fortunei* 'Hyacinthina')
   *Fragrant Plantain Lily (August or Corfu Lily) (*H. plantaginea*)
   Siebold Plantain Lily (*H. sieboldiana* 'Elegans')
Lilies:
   Goldband Lily (*Lilium auratum*)

   Rubrum Lily (*L. speciosum* 'Rubrum')
Balsam (*Impatiens balsamina*)
Cosmos (*Cosmos bipinnatus*)
*Marigolds (*Tagetes patula* and *T. tenuifolia*)
*Moonflower (*Ipomoea alba*, quick-growing twining vine)
*Nasturtiums (*Tropaeolum majus*, flower and quick-growing twining vine)
*Nicotiana (*Nicotiana alata*)
*Petunia (*Petunia* x *hybrida*)
Scarlet Runner Bean and White Runner Bean (*Phaseolus coccineus* and *P. coccineus* 'Albus', respectively, quick-growing twining vines)
Shirley or Corn Poppy (*Papaver rhoeas*)
*Sweet Pea (*Lathyrus odoratus*, twining vine)
*Sweet-alyssum (*Lobularia maritima*)

Shrubs

Roses
   Bourbon: *'Louise Odier' (Zone 6)
    *'Mme. Isaac Pereire' (Zone 6)
   Hybrid Perpetual:*'Baronne Prevost' (Zone 5)
    'Frau Karl Druschki' (Zone 5)
   Rugosa: *'Blanc Double de Coubert' (Zone 3 or 4)
    *'Roseraie de l'Hay' (Zone 3 or 4)

Vines (hardy to Zone 3 or 4; twine like grapes; need horizontal support)

Clematis:
   *Anemone Clematis (*Clematis montana rubens*)
   *'Elsa Späth'
   *Jackman Clematis (*C.* x *jackmanii*)
   *'Lord Neville'
   *'Nelly Moser'
   *Sweet Autumn Clematis (*C. paniculata*)

A Child's Arbor

To make this charming structure, you need half a dozen freshly cut saplings (alder, willow, or birch are good), two inches thick at the butt and twelve feet long. Leave the twigs on. Mark a circle with a six-foot diameter on the ground. Sharpen the saplings' butts. Thrust two saplings into the ground opposite each other at six and twelve o'clock and arch them over each other, leaving enough room to walk underneath. Tie the saplings together securely with inconspicuous twine or wire at two or three places where they overlap on both sides. Do the same with two more saplings at two and eight o'clock, then with two more at four and ten o'clock. Plant quick-growing annual vines all around the base of the arbor, except at the low entranceway.

The Eclectic Garden: 1600-1950 Plus

This is the place to put it all together — cottage garden herbs and flowers on the wild side with 'New Dawn', the 1930 Hybrid Climbing Rose, which puts forth clusters of blush pink flowers all summer. The eclectic garden is also the place to explore the diverse world of heirloom Glads, Daffodils, Iris, and Lilies (so defined if they were introduced more than thirty years ago). These hardy plants have endured in the marketplace or in the hearts of gardeners because of their superior qualities: adaptability, beauty, and an undefinable essence that elevates them to the status of legend. Did you ever think a Glad could fall into this category? Many enthusiasts feel that way about 'Picardy', a 1931 creation with soft pink blooms that has vanished from the marketplace but is perhaps still growing in a garden somewhere. Some heirloom gardeners feel as strongly about preserving 'Amigo', a 1938 Bearded Iris with extraordinary pansy coloring and generous form, as others feel about preserving eighteenth-century laced pinks. There is room in the eclectic garden for the simple, unadorned beauty of the wild Cowslip (*Primula veris*) and Jan de Graaf's 1947 'Enchantment' Lily, an introduction that set the standard for Hybrid Lilies: reliable, free-flowering, and disease-resistant. Wherever they are planted, ancient, antique, and middle-aged heirlooms enjoy and thrive in each other's company.

In full sun, plant early settlers' flowers and herbs such as Musk Mallow, Bellflower, Sweet-William, Jerusalem-cross, Dame's-rocket, Sweet Cicely, Sage, and Feverfew. Add to these the outrageous but indispensable Oriental Poppy, fortified by the Mountain-bluet to help prop up its sprawling stems. Also add Mr. Russell's late 1930s luscious Hybrid Lupines in every shade you can get, the tall spires of Foxglove, and the sunny daisylike Golden-Marguerite (through which the gray-green Sage foliage will appear to advantage). Among these sow tall, white Nicotiana and Cosmos, dark blue Bachelor's-button, and annual Poppies and Calendula. To this generous all-season border, add Bearded Iris (all sizes and colors), vintage large-flowered Glads — grouped together near the middle of the border, where just their blooms will be exposed — and an heirloom Lily or two. The fragrant Regal Lily, with large white trumpets, is a good substitute for the White or Madonna Lily.

Did you know that there are wild Glads for naturalizing, some so hardy that you need not dig up their corms in the fall (Hardy Glad)? These can be grown with wild Sweet Flag Iris, which have fragrant lavender-blue flowers and striped foliage. In the rock garden, add 'Little Witch', a 1929 Cyclamineus Daffodil (only eight inches high) with yellow flared-back petals, and 'Louisa', a lovely variation on the Narrow-leaved Plantain Lily with its narrow, white-edged leaves and white flowers. In partial shade, plant the first pink-apricot trumpeted Daffodil, 'Mrs. R.O. Backhouse', with Virginia-bluebells. ('Louisa' will enjoy growing here, too.)

In that damp ground where nothing else will grow, establish Siberian Iris to naturalize with the ancient and native Yellow and Blue Flag Iris.

Of course, you must have Roses — for making hedges, arbors, adding to the shrubbery, and even planting in containers. Investigate the middle-aged classics such as 'Buff Beauty', a 1939 Hybrid Musk shrub with a strong fragrance and an equable disposition, producing gold-cream flowers all summer long, even in drought conditions. The everblooming Polyantha 'The Fairy', with masses of light pink double blossoms that last all summer, will make a low hedge or even a container plant. For a bushy hedge, grow 'Betty Prior', which has bright, single-petaled pink blooms all summer and is spectacular when massed. As for 'Blaze', tie it to a post for full vertical bloom and train it along a fence (pegging down the long, supple canes), or over an arbor, where it will provide a fitting entrance to the eclectic garden.

(* indicates fragrant plants)

Perennials (hardy to Zone 3 or 4 except as noted)

Daffodils:
  'Beersheba'
  'Little Witch'
  'Mrs. R.O. Backhouse'
  *'Silver Chimes' (Zone 6)
  *'Thalia'
Foxglove (*Digitalis purpurea*)
Glads (for naturalizing):
  *Colville Glad (*Gladiolus* x *colvillei* 'Albus', Zone 7)
  *Hardy Glad (*G. byzantinus*, Zone 4)
  *Hybrid Glads (treat as annuals):
    'Dawn Glow'
    'Glacier'
    'Peter Pears'
Golden-Marguerite (*Anthemis tinctoria*)

Hosta:
  'Louisa'
Iris, Bearded:
  'Amigo'
  'Black Forest'
  'Blue Denim'
  'Honorabile'
  'Wabash'
Iris, Siberian *(Iris sibirica):*
  'Eric the Red'
  'Helen Astor'
  'White Swirl'
*Sweet Iris *(Iris pallida,* Zone 5)
*Regal Lily *(Lilium regale)*
Lupines (Russell Hybrids)
Mountain-bluet *(Centaurea montana)*
Oriental Poppy *(Papaver orientale)*
Roses (shrubs, ramblers, and climbers used
  as vines; hardy to Zone 5 except where
  noted):
    'Betty Prior'
    'Blaze'
    *'Buff Beauty'
    *'Crimson Glory'
    'Paul's Scarlet Climber'
    'The Fairy' (Zone 4)
    *'Therese Bugnet' (Zone 4)

Preserving the Heirloom Garden

It is important for heirloom gardeners to understand the principles behind plant propagation — seed saving, root division, and cuttings — because mastery of these methods ensures the survival of rare or choice strains that may not be readily available. With an assured surplus of such plants in whatever form, the heirloom gardener will be helping to preserve our horticultural heritage. This bounty can be shared with others, another strategy in the effort to preserve heirloom ornamentals.

Brother Gilbert Koster, a gardening friend who has taught me a great deal, embodies the ideals of heirloom gardening. He not only knows how to preserve and propagate his treasures (some very old strains), but he achieves results with the utmost simplicity and economy — the kind that underlies conservation in its fundamental sense.

I once asked him how he created his flower gardens more than twenty years ago, carved by hand out of scrub woodland. He said that someone had given him a few Dahlia tubers. He made stem cuttings from them in late winter, thus creating dozens more identical plants (see the Dahlia plant portrait in Part II for directions). He sowed annual and biennial seeds among them and saved the annual seeds at the end of the first season. By the following spring, he had hundreds of robust seedlings growing in an improved cold frame. (He had enclosed a small area on a southern slope with boards and had covered it with a sheet of clear plastic attached to a stick so it could be easily unrolled; on cold nights, he covered the cold frame with an old blanket.)

Brother Gilbert's garden — like a picture book — overflows with flowers of all kinds, as well as shrubs (even trees) and vines, almost all grown from seeds acquired here and there. Follow this simple seed-saving guide based on his sound principles, and it will help you to preserve your heirloom plants by the easiest means.

Seed Saving

Use this method for annuals and biennials. Perennials are easier to propagate by root division. Where necessary, follow the directions for stem cuttings under "Wintering Annuals" (p. 20).

Plants vary in their fruiting habits. Some

fruits ripen and spill their contents before you know it (Johnny-jump-ups and Foxglove); other seeds are held tightly within heads (Black-eyed-Susans), disk-shaped rounds (Mallows and Hollyhocks), or shaker-type holders (Poppies and Columbine). You will learn about these differences by observing the plants in your garden.

1. Choose several plants of the same type whose seeds you want to save (insurance in case one of the plants meets with misfortune). You thereby increase the likelihood of discovering worthwhile sports. Don't hesitate to save seeds from hybrids. Brother Gilbert has been doing so for years. These may differ from their parents, but they often do so in interesting and desirable ways.

2. Harvest seeds when the capsules have turned light brown but before they have opened. Put heads or seeds in individual paper bags — one type to each bag — making sure the bags are labeled clearly.

3. Spread out the seeds to dry indoors in a sunny spot, being sure to separate seeds from chaff as much as possible. In the case of the tightly packed Hollyhock or Mallow capsules, separate the moist seeds and spread them out.

4. Don't crowd groups of seeds, since one type can easily mingle with another (if Johnny-jump-ups are left in their capsules, they will literally jump all over the place). Put each type in a separate labeled tray (paper plates work well). Mark each with a felt-tip marker rather than a pencil, which may fade in the sun. Crayon works well, too.

5. When the seeds are completely dry (in a week or so), sort and pack them. You can tell if some seeds, such as Marigolds, are likely to be fertile by rolling them between your fingers. If

you feel a hard little kernel, the seed will probably germinate.

6. Store the seeds in sealed envelopes, labeled in the upper left-hand corner. File them in an old shoe box for easy access. Place the box in a cool, dry place until you need them the following season. For storage over longer periods, use airtight jars (check every so often to make sure no moisture is collecting in them). The temperature of your storage area should never exceed 95°F. (35°C.). Even imperfectly stored and harvested home-saved seeds usually germinate better than store-bought ones, and they will keep well for several years. Always share seeds as much as possible, not only to be generous and neighborly but also to ensure the plant's survival somewhere else besides your garden.

Note: Some seed savers use hand-pollination to ensure that heirloom strains are kept pure. Brother Gilbert takes a more casual approach, gathering naturally pollinated ripened seeds from the strains he wants to keep, then storing and sowing them separately from other types.

To Hand-Pollinate

Cover the buds with cheesecloth bags before they open. Do this on different plants of the same strain. When the buds open and the pollen is being released, remove the bags, and with a small paintbrush, rub the pollen from one flower onto another. If the plants being pollinated are close to each other, rub one flower against another. Then bag the blossoms again so that no bee can visit them. Don't remove the bags until the seeds have ripened. Soak the paintbrush in alcohol for five to ten minutes and wash and dry it before reusing.

Wintering Annuals

Another way to preserve annuals is to winter them over indoors and replant them the following season. This works with Petunias, Nasturtiums, Sweet-alyssum, and Nicotiana — plants that are short-lived perennials in their native habitat. Wintering gives you a head start on blooming the following season.

1. Cut back and pot up garden plants four to six weeks before the last frost.

2. Put the potted plants in a shed before bringing them indoors so they can soften up (the reverse of plant hardening). Place them in a cool, sunny window and water them as little as possible without causing wilting. (The point is to conserve energy for the spring push.)

3. In late winter, when the plants begin to show signs of new growth, start watering them more regularly and fertilize them weekly with a dilute (half strength) solution of plant food.

4. Replant them in early spring or when appropriate by tapping on the bottom of the plant container so the whole plant slides out without disturbing its roots. It will probably be pot-bound and slide out easily, especially if the soil is damp (not wet).

An alternative method of wintering annuals is to take *stem cuttings* in late summer (six to eight weeks before the last frost) or anytime when there is sufficient stem growth and steadily increasing temperatures of 70°F. to 80°F. (21°C. to 28°C.) for about ten days. Since the "annuals" become woody after their second season, you will eventually need to preserve them this way.

To Make Cuttings

1. Pick healthy lateral stems. Make a clean, sharp cut at an angle just below a node where the plant's leaves are joined to the stem. The cutting should be four to six inches long. Remove all the lower leaves, leaving the upper ones to encourage rooting.

2. Dip the stems in water, then in rooting hormone. Shake off excess powder. Plant the stems deeply and firmly in a moistened soil-less mix or a sand-vermiculite mixture in a clean cottage cheese container (or something similar) with a slit cut in the bottom for drainage. Stem cuttings root best when crowded together. Those placed on the outer edges also seem to do best.

3. Cover the container with thin, clear plastic to create a moist mini-greenhouse. Check the container daily to make sure excess moisture isn't collecting. If it is, lift the plastic a bit. When the cuttings are growing well, gradually remove the plastic over the period of a couple of days, first untucking it from around the container, then lifting it halfway off, then all the way, so the cuttings gradually become accustomed to normal growing conditions. If they are well-rooted, they should respond favorably to this treatment. Leave the cuttings in the container about two weeks after they have started growing.

4. Repot the well-rooted cuttings in regular potting soil and plant them out as usual with other annuals when all danger of frost has passed.

Division

This is the simplest way to increase perennials (and be assured that your new plants will be identical to the old ones). Some plants need dividing every three years, while others, such as Bleeding-heart, can be left undisturbed indefinitely. A general rule of thumb is that if you find you have to divide a plant every year because of its vigor, plant it in a naturalized setting where it can let go and enjoy itself.

Division is very simple. Cut up (most likely chop) the plants into the desired number of pieces, making sure each piece is vigorous (that is, it has plenty of roots and growing tips). Plants that bloom in the spring should be divided in the fall; those that bloom in the fall should be divided in the spring. Always discard woody pieces.

Any growing medium that encourages root formation can be used for all the propagation methods that follow. You can use sand, a sand and peat mixture, potting soil, or some other medium.

Softwood and Hardwood Stem Cuttings

Use this method to propagate shrubs and vines outdoors in a trench or cold frame. You can use rooting hormone or not, as you choose. Many plants will root well without it.

Softwood Stem Cuttings (take in summer)

Use a sharp knife to cut a three- to eight-inch length at the node, where the leaves join the stem. Remove the lower leaves and insert the cutting in moist sand up to half its length. Rooted plants can be removed to a cold frame or nursery bed for at least one growing season before being planted in their permanent site. It takes two years from cutting the stem to planting it out permanently in the garden. Exceptions are very vigorous plants.

Hardwood Stem Cuttings (take in the fall)

1. Take six- to ten-inch stem cuttings with a sharp knife or clippers. The cut should be half an inch below the lowest bud and half an inch or more above the uppermost bud. Tie these stems in bundles (as many as two dozen is O.K.) and bury them horizontally in moist sand. This is a good way to establish many plants to make a hedge.

2. In the spring, plant the stems two to four inches apart in a trench almost covered with soil so that the top bud is at ground level. Water the soil during dry spells. Cuttings should be well established by the end of their second season in the trench. They can then be planted in their permanent site.

A Simple Way to Propagate Old Garden Roses

This method can be used to propagate Old Garden Roses that you find growing neglected in abandoned gardens or other sites.

1. Take twelve- to eighteen-inch side shoots from stems anytime in the summer after they have flowered. Pull, rather than cut, these off the bush, so that each stem has a "heel" from the cane from which it was growing.

2. Remove the bottom leaves and stick the cuttings in rooting hormone, then in soil in your cold frame. Set them four inches deep and six inches apart, cutting back the tops so that each has at least three leaves. Do not let the soil dry out.

3. In the fall, cover each cutting with a mason jar and leave it in place until the following spring, when the cutting should be rooted. Harden it gradually by tipping the jar to let in air. Remove the rooted plants to a nursery bed and plant them out the following season in their permanent site.

Layering

Use this method with shrubs or vines. Some of these will layer themselves, forming roots where branches or vines touch the ground. When the offshoots are rooted, sever them from the mother plant and replant them in a nursery bed for another season unless they are especially vigorous. To layer a branch or vine, follow these directions:

❦ Make a slit on the point of the branch or cane you want to root. Bury it in three to four inches of soil, pegging it down securely so it will stay in place. During the following growing season, sever the rooted plant from its parent and proceed as described.

❦ To make many plants from one branch, make slits along it, then peg it down and bury the whole branch or cane in three to four inches of soil, leaving the growing tip exposed. Proceed as described.

Propagating and Preserving Bulbs

Bulbs of various types, hardy or tender, produce offspring in the form of bulblets. These can be replanted in a nursery bed for at least two seasons, then planted out permanently. If you need to dig up bulbs you find growing in neglected gardens or elsewhere, follow this general procedure:

❦ It's very important to wait until the leaves have died down after the plant has flowered (this could take four to six weeks with Daffodils). Carefully loosen the soil in a small area of the planting, using a spading fork so you won't damage the bulbs. Carefully lift out each bulb, put it in a sunny spot to dry, and then replant it in the appropriate season.

❦ Alternatively, dig up the bulb with a good ball of dirt around the roots, then replant it immediately. Water it well.

Another method of plant preservation is rejuvenation. To rejuvenate a shrub or vine,

follow the directions under the plant portrait for Lilacs in Part II (see p. 199). To revive an old perennial bed, see Lewis and Nancy Hill's excellent directions in *Successful Perennial Gardening* (Garden Way Publishing, 1988)

Plant Collector's Guide

Most gardeners buy their heirloom plants from the many established plant and seed sources listed in Part III. But discovering and collecting plants from neglected or abandoned gardens, old farm sites, roadsides, or graveyards (a great place to find Old Roses, I'm told) can be a fascinating and rewarding hobby: "It's like finding buried treasure," one enthusiast told me. You may find a rare plant hitherto unavailable in commercial trade, and you may be the means of reestablishing it in the plant world. Or you may find an old-time favorite languishing from neglect and feel the need to provide it with a new home where you can care for it and carry on the work of some unknown gardener.

These are praiseworthy goals, but even plant lovers are not immune to greed. Once when I returned to a well-cared-for older garden to take a few roots of a nice old Phlox after receiving permission from the elderly owner to do so, I was taken aback to find that someone had ruthlessly dug in his or her shovel to the hilt and taken away at least half of the planting, along with much of the soil. Other ornamentals nearby had been treated similarly. Hardy types may endure such mishandling, but that's no way to go about saving plants for posterity. Being an heirloom gardener means having a responsibility to both the plants themselves and the world they inhabit. It's very important to offer gardeners sound advice about collecting heirloom plants at the same time we encourage them to grow these plants in their gardens.

The following guide, based on my own experience and that of other collectors, deals wholly with collecting ornamentals. The same principles should be followed in collecting any plants in similar situations.

❦ Look for plants in overgrown, neglected gardens, at abandoned farms, along undisturbed byways, in graveyards, and in well-cared-for older gardens in the area. Ask people in the area about old gardens and gardeners interested in growing old ornamentals, and you'll soon have a plant collectors' network. *Always ask permission for exploring an area.* Someone owns that abandoned farm; your graveyard explorations might not be welcome. When you seek permission, ask if it's O.K. to take a small sample of what you find.

❦ Start your search in the spring (earlier in warmer regions) when many plants break their dormancy. This is when you might find very old types of Daffodils, for instance. If you find something on the first trip, be sure to return to the same place at intervals during the growing season. Chances are you will find something else of value.

❦ Take several photos of the plant — a few close-ups and some of the general area. These may help in plant identification and shed some light on the plant's history. This is important if you are a researcher interested in creating historical landscapes, for instance. Take brief notes, too, as you're sure to forget some important details.

❦ *Unless threatened with destruction, never dig up the whole plant.* If it grows in a clump, take a piece of root from the *back* of the clump, especially if the plant is growing in an established garden. Carefully dig out a piece of root and put it in a plastic bag moistened with damp moss or a similar substance. Root collecting is

the quickest and surest way to establish a clone of the original planting that may be traced back many years. This is important if you are creating a garden of authentic descendant plants of old-time species. Plants established in this way are living links with the past, since they are actually part of the original plant.

❦ When dealing with Old Roses, the established procedure is to take a stem cutting. Stem cuttings also can be used for any plant not large enough to divide or for one of hybrid origin that may be difficult to establish from root division (*Lythrum* hybrids, for instance). Seeds of annual and biennial flowers such as Calendula, Hollyhock, Foxglove, and Sweet-William may be gathered after they have ripened on the plant. Take only a small handful of seed capsules, keeping different colors separate. Bulbs should be dug up only after the leaves have turned brown and returned their nutrients to feed the bulb, the source of next year's flowers. *However you take your plant material, the original planting should look undisturbed.*

❦ Establish your "find" in a specially prepared seedbed, nursery bed, or cold frame. Never plant your treasure directly in the garden (unless you have a staff to tend to such matters), or it may be swamped by lush growth in the vicinity.

❦ If you are concerned about the plant's hardiness, grow it in a cold frame for at least three seasons. If, during that time, you manage to divide it, plant the clones in several places in your garden, leaving at least one plant in the cold frame as insurance. Store dried seeds to plant the following season or plant them in a cold frame or specially prepared fine soil. Since some seeds need freezing temperatures to break their dormancy, you may not see growth until the following season. Store dried bulbs in a dry place until it is time to plant them out in your garden. *Label all plants, seeds, and bulbs.* Keep a written account as well; labels have a way of getting lost.

❧ Contact the botany department at your local college or university if you need help with identification. You may need to find a specialist in old plants to help determine the precise variety or cultivar (this is where a clear photograph or slide comes in handy). Contact local plant societies and garden clubs. They may help identify or be interested in heirloom plants. Contact plant nurseries interested in heirloom or choice plants. They may be interested in propagating your treasure, eventually returning it to commercial trade or introducing it for the first time.

❧ Contact seed exchanges (see Part III). By sending your seeds out to other gardeners, you open the door to a world of unknown plants whose seeds you will receive in exchange.

PAUL MARTIN BROWN: PHOTO/NATS

Rhodora (*Rhododendron canadense* 'Album').

BETH POWNING

Rosa 'Blanc Double de Coubert'; rugosa hybrid rose.

HAL HORWITZ: PHOTO/NATS

Bee-balm
(*Monarda didyma*).

Color in the Heirloom Garden

Sweet Autumn
Clematis
(*Clematis paniculata*).

JOHN A. LYNCH: PHOTO/NATS

Johnny-jump-up
(*Viola tricolor*).

Golden-glow (*Rudbeckia laciniata* 'Hortensia').

Regal Lily (*Lilium regale*).

Poet Narcissus (*Narcissus poeticus* 'Actaea').

JERRY HOWARD: POSITIVE IMAGES

Yellow Dahlia (*Dahlia* hybrid).

HAL HORWITZ: PHOTO/NATS

Butterfly Weed (*Asclepias tuberosa*).

ROBERT E. LYONS: PHOTO/NATS

Flame Azalea *(Rhododendron calendulaceum)*.

Jerusalem-cross *(Lychnis chalcedonica)*.

Eastern Columbine *(Aquilegia canadensis)*.

Rosa 'Blaze'; large-flowered climbing rose.

Mountain-laurel *(Kalmia latifolia).*

Old-fashioned Bleeding-heart *(Dicentra spectabilis).*

Rosa Mundi *(Rosa gallica versicolor).*

Rosa 'Betty Prior'; floribunda hybrid rose.

Clematis 'Nelly Moser'.

Purple Lilac *(Syringa vulgaris)*.

ROBERT E. LYONS: PHOTO/NATS

Chives *(Allium schoenoprasum)*.

DAVID M. STONE: PHOTO/NATS

Moss Phlox *(Phlox subulata)*.

ANN REILLY: PHOTO/NATS

Sweet Pea *(Lathyrus odoratus)*.

Morning-glory
(Ipomoea purpurea).

Oregon Holly-grape *(Mahonia aquifolium).*

Maidenhair Fern *(Adiantum pedatum).*

Wild Lupine *(Lupinus polyphyllus).*

PART II

A Treasury of Heirloom Ornamentals, 1600-1950:

Flowers, Herbs, Shrubs & Vines

"There were Lupines, Sweet Peas, Phlox, Bluebells, Day and Tiger Lilies, Monkshood, Peonies, Columbine, Daffodils, single and double, a Bleeding-heart bush in the front yard, and vines at each corner, which at times nearly covered the house. And always there was Golden-glow by the kitchen door."

— AN OLD-TIME GARDENER

PLANT PORTRAIT EXAMPLE

Latin names: genus, species, family; ✿ *indicates a fragrance or scent in the flowers or foliage*

Dates of introduction   Growing zones   Native/ Naturalized

Common names: one used in portrait appears first in **boldface** *type*

TYPE: PERENNIAL, BIENNIAL, HERB, FLOWER, BULB, ETC.
HEIGHT: BLOOM/SEASON OF INTEREST:
PREFERRED SITE: SUN; PARTIAL SHADE; SHADE

Collector's Choice: recommended plants and sources; P-plants, S-seeds (numbers are keyed to list of sources in Part III beginning p. 211.)

✿ *Asclepias tuberosa* (Cultivar if any)

Asclepiadaceae

1776-1850   ZONES 4-10   NATIVE

Butterfly Weed

Butterfly Flower, Butterfly Milkweed, Chigger Flower, Indian Paintbrush, Pleurisy Root, Swallowwort

---

PERENNIAL WILDFLOWER/HERB
HEIGHT: 2-3'   BLOOM: SUMMER-FALL
SITE: SUN/PARTIAL SHADE

Text description

To Grow:

Asclepias tuberosa, Butterfly Weed.73(p & s); 35(p & s); 5(s); 15(s).

❀ *Abelia* x *grandiflora*

Caprifoliaceae
1850-1900   ZONES 6-10

Glossy Abelia

TYPE: SHRUB
HEIGHT: 5'   BLOOM: SUMMER
SITE: SUN/PARTIAL SHADE

Glossy Abelia is one of thirty species of shrubs originating in Asia,
Mexico, and India. A hybrid of
exceptional vigor and beauty, it is
widely cultivated in the mid-South,
Mid-Atlantic states, and Midwest.
It is valued for its season of bloom
— intermittently throughout most
of the summer — and glossy, almost evergreen leaves. Of medium height and neat habit, it bears
showy white, delicately fragrant,
bell-shaped flowers tinged with
pink. These grow in terminal clusters at the tip of the shrub's
branches, creating a mass of bloom.
In the fall and winter months where
winters are mild, the leaves turn
bronze, thus adding another season of interest
to this valuable ornamental. The genus is named
for Dr. Clark Abel, a doctor and writer who
lived in China in the nineteenth century.

This is a shrub of late nineteenth-century
gardens bred in Italy (*Abelia chinensis* × *A.
uniflora)* sometime before 1880, and like many
plants that attained popularity then, it is regarded as old-fashioned. It was well established by the 1930s and highly recommended
by Mrs. Francis King, well-known arbiter of
horticultural taste of the period, who advised
its use as a formal hedge, noting that "its

Abelia x *grandiflora*

charming bronzy leaves clip well." More than
thirty years later, it was selected as a "Rembrandt
among shrubs" by a distinguished committee
of experts headed by Donald Wyman in *One
Hundred Finest Trees and Shrubs for Temperate
Climates* (BBG Record Plants & Gardens, 1957).
In 1962 it was given the Royal Horticultural
Society Award of Garden Merit, "an accolade
well deserved by such an admirable plant,"
according to Will Ingwersen, who considers it
a classic.

A shrub of such virtues surely
has a place in any garden where
conditions permit. It may be used
as an all-season hedge, clipped or
unclipped; for a mixed foundation
planting among evergreens; or as a
specimen bush behind early-flowering bulbs. The rub is *where conditions permit*, for, though easy to
grow, Glossy Abelia likes heat. Its
neat habit recommends its use in
small gardens.

To Grow: Plant in well-drained,
light, peaty soil — pH 6.0 to 8.0 —
enriched with leaf mold, in a sunny
spot, preferably one that is protected from bright sun and wind.
Light shade is especially welcome where summers are very hot. Prune the plant in the spring
to maintain its shape (blossoms are formed on
new wood, so early pruning is O.K.) and propagate it by four-inch softwood cuttings taken in
the fall and wintered over in a cold frame. This
Abelia is relatively hardy — to New York City
(Zone 6) and possibly farther north to Boston
if it is well protected and planted in a favorable
spot (near a building and away from wind).
Like all Abelias, though, it thrives in heat,
which helps to mature its wood. Mature wood
is more resistant to frost, so the secret of

maintaining a healthy, frost-resistant shrub is to ensure that it receives steady heat for as long as possible.

Collector's Choice:

Abelia × *grandiflora*, Glossy Abelia. 114(p); 134(p).

Achillea ptarmica

Asteraceae

1776-1850   Zones 3-9   Naturalized

Sneezewort

Bride's-bouquet, Nosebleed, Shirtbuttons

A. ptarmica   'The Pearl'

1850-1911

Type: Hardy Perennial Flower/Herb
Height: 2½'   Bloom: Summer
Site: Sun

Sneezewort is an Old World weed naturalized in damp fields and roadsides from eastern Canada to Michigan. It grows by creeping roots that send up stems to two feet or so with narrow, sawtooth leaves and white-petaled flowers in loose clusters. In the single form, a dull greenish center is apparent, but there is a great deal of variability in the wildflowers; some are semidouble, with more than one layer of petals, while others are almost double, with the center just evident. In the cultivar 'The Pearl', the flowers are fully double, with the center almost entirely hidden.

The uses of Sneezewort are preserved in

Achillea ptarmica

sixteenth- and seventeenth-century herbals. Gerard advised mixing its juice with vinegar and "holden in the mouth, easeth much the pain of tooth-ache," while Culpeper spoke of using it dried and powdered as snuff (to cause sneezing) against headaches. Its flowers also yield a greenish dye.

Sneezewort's bouquetlike sprays of flowers also suggested its use in bride's bouquets (a common name still used locally) and dried-flower bouquets popular in the eighteenth century (as they are today). In the nineteenth century, the seedsman Joseph Breck described Sneezewort as a "desirable border flower, especially the double." The double form, known to Gerard, was listed as *A. ptarmica flore pleno*. (*Flore pleno* and its variants — *flora-plen, florepleno, flore-pleno, flo-plen, pleni flora*, and *pleno* — all describe double flowers; the terms turn up on old seed lists. Nowadays such variants are considered cultivars and are usually described with a modern-language name rather than a Latin tag.)

By the late nineteenth and early twentieth centuries, the French nurseryman Lemoine had developed the cultivar known in French as 'Boule de Neige', or 'The Pearl'. It differs significantly from the wild form in that its flowers are of the purest white, fully double, and fluffy with barely a hint of a central disk. They grow in larger clusters — three to six inches across — and are especially long-lasting cut flowers, for which they were in great demand by florists at the time.

My adventures with Sneezewort began in 1978 when I bought a forty-cent packet of seeds described as 'The Pearl'. The flowers were supposed to be fully double, pure white baby pom-

poms. This plant and its numerous descendants grew for many years in and out of my garden (I naturalized it along our lane), and I was content until I found the real thing, quite by chance, growing untended in an old abandoned garden in a tangle of weeds. There could be no mistaking the difference between the flowers of my small, semidouble, creamy white wildflower, Sneezewort, and this elegant plant before me, described by Roy Genders as "the whitest of all flowers." Not only were the flowers of 'The Pearl' larger, but the whole plant was taller and more erect than mine (and this after no attention for decades). I also compared each as a cut flower and found that 'The Pearl' showed no diminution of its beauty after several weeks in a glass of water, while my interloper passed its peak of freshness after seven to ten days (not bad either). The moral of this story is that when you want a choice cultivar, such as 'The Pearl', buy the plant rather than a packet of seeds, which is more than likely to produce an inferior strain.

The wildflower Sneezewort and 'The Pearl' are both useful in the garden where Baby's-breath is hard to grow. They offer an alternative overplanting for the Oriental Poppy (*Papaver orientale*). The bright pink spikes of a Morden Loosestrife cultivar are perfect foils for the rounded form and pure white clusters of 'The Pearl'. Sneezewort is easy to naturalize, being already on the wild side, so take advantage of its nature and let it go if you have a bit of meadow or patch of ground to devote to a wild garden. ("To naturalize" any plant or planting means to establish it artfully in the landscape and allow it to grow with little or no further attention.) And by all means, cut the flowers of either variety for summer bouquets. 'The Pearl' is especially effective when dried for winter bouquets.

To Grow: Plant roots of either Sneezewort or 'The Pearl' in well-drained, humusy soil, in full sun. Both are drought-tolerant, but wind will cause them to sprawl (especially Sneezewort). Both must be divided every two to four years. 'The Pearl' can be propagated by stem cuttings taken anytime during the summer and wintered over in a cold frame. Sneezewort seeds can be planted in a cold frame during the summer, and the seedlings can be planted out the following spring, one to two feet apart, as for 'The Pearl'.

Collector's Choice:

Achillea ptarmica, Sneezewort. 177(s); 155(p).
'The Pearl'. 167; 137; 133; 120; 155 (all plants).

Aconitum spp.

Ranunculaceae
1600-1900   Zones 2-8

Monkshood

Blue-rocket, Cupid's-ear, Friar's-cap, Helmet Flower, Queen-mother-of-poisons, Soldier's-cap, Turk's-cap, Venus's-shell, Wolfsbane

---

Type: Hardy Perennial Flower
Height: to 6'   Bloom: Summer-Fall
Site: Partial Shade/Shade

One hundred or more species of *Aconitum* are native to Europe, Asia, and North America, growing on tall stalks similar in form and flower to Delphinium, except their flowers are quite distinctive upon close examination. Blue, amethyst, violet, purple, and even yellow or pinkish white in wandlike panicles, each flower has a pronounced "hood," actually a sepal, either fitting closely over the rest of the flower or standing up. The cut-up fernlike foliage, similar to that of the Buttercup, to which family it belongs, is widest nearer the stem and glossy, as if warning passersby of the plant's dangerous properties (strong alkaloids in its roots, a characteristic that has given rise to its many and varied folk names). Wolfsbane was derived from the idea that arrows tipped in the plant's juice were supposed to have killed wolves. The genus name is based on the Latin *aconitum*, which for centuries has been synonymous with this poisonous herb (the one with which Romeo poisoned himself). *Aconitum*, or Monkshood, turns up so early in gardening lists that it must have been used as a poison against predators,

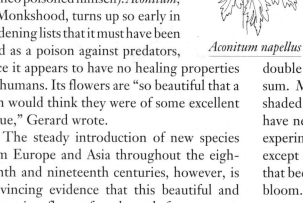

Aconitum napellus

since it appears to have no healing properties for humans. Its flowers are "so beautiful that a man would think they were of some excellent virtue," Gerard wrote.

The steady introduction of new species from Europe and Asia throughout the eighteenth and nineteenth centuries, however, is convincing evidence that this beautiful and interesting flower found much favor among American gardeners, who valued it for its ease of culture, hardiness, midsummer to fall bloom, and long-lasting flowers. As far as I know, the plant's poisonous properties have never caused gardeners any trouble, but it is a good idea to wash your hands after handling the roots.

Monkshood, like the Daylily, is a hardy survivor of neglect, and I have often found it on the peninsula in abandoned gardens, growing in great clumps among Daylilies *(Hemerocallis fulva)*. Contrary to most gardening advice, I have found that clumps can be dug up and replanted right away, with no setback, if a good amount of earth is taken with them around their roots. I have seen Monkshood grown as a stunning, low-maintenance hedge — a "room divider" in a garden designed in the 1920s. The hedge was given no special care, just allowed to grow up naturally every year, then die back in the fall, enriched only by its decaying leaves. Some of the most desirable old types here have bright blue flowers; others have distinctive long-lasting bicolor blooms—white edged with purplish blue — especially if planted in the shade or partial shade.

In my own garden, I grow violet Monkshood in a partially shaded pastel garden with gray-leaved Lamb's-ears, pure white Nicotiana, mauve-flowered Chives, and pink double Poppies, edged with white Sweet-alyssum. Monkshood would do well in a more shaded site, too, among Hostas and Ferns. I have never had any desire, as an herbalist, to experiment with using Monkshood in any form except as a cut flower, although I have noted that bees are drawn to its nectar in its season of bloom.

To Grow: Plant Monkshood in deeply prepared, well-drained, moist soil on the heavy side, in partial shade or shade. It will grow in moist soil in the sun, but the foliage will spoil and the flowers will fade fast. Space plants twelve to eighteen inches apart, with the crowns just below the soil's surface. Where winters are severe, young plants should be protected until they are established. Fresh seeds can be sown in a cold frame to germinate over the winter. Propagation is simple if enough soil is taken with the roots and the reset plants are watered well and protected from the wind and hot sun.

Aconitum carmichaelii, Azure Monkshood (1850-1900); medium blue blooms; 4'; September to October. 6(s); 92(s); 164; 138; 78; 45 (all plants).

A. lycoctonum, Great Yellow Monkshood (1776-1850); light yellow blooms; 2½'; summer; Zone 3. 18(s); 36(p).

A. napellus, Monkshood (1600-1699); violet-blue or purplish blooms; 4'; summer. 6(s); 169(p); 177(s); 153(p); 15(s); 157(p).

A. × bicolor (by 19th century); white-edged, purplish blue blooms; 4'; late summer. 153; 61; 138; 157 (all plants); 92(s).

Adiantum pedatum

Polypodiaceae

1700-1776   Zones 3-9   Native

Maidenhair Fern

American Maidenhair, Five-finger Fern, Northern Maidenhair

Type: Hardy Fern
Height: 12-28" Season of Interest:
                    Summer-Fall Foliage
Site: Partial Shade/Shade

The native Maidenhair Fern, the most delicate and highly prized of our native species, grows on shaded slopes and in old woods wherever the soil is humusy and moist but well drained. Its range extends from Nova Scotia west to Minnesota and south to Georgia and Oklahoma. Its emerald green, deeply divided leaves, or fronds, radiate from glossy stems — dark reddish to ebony — al-

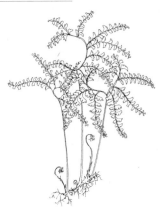

Adiantum pedatum

most forming a halo that flutters gracefully in even a slight breeze. The genus name, from the Greek *adiantos*, meaning "dry," refers to the way the fronds shed water in the rain.

The beauty of this native fern became known to our earliest naturalists and plant collectors. John Bartram, a farmer and naturalist with a deep interest in native flora, grew these plants in his gardens on the Schuylkill River (one of America's first botanical gardens), where people came from all over the world to see the native plants that would soon be growing in the gardens of Europe. Bartram's plant nursery also was one of the country's first, established in 1728. His listings were eagerly perused by such curious gardeners as George Washington and Thomas Jefferson. (For more information on Bartram's gardens, see the listing in "Gardens to Visit" in Part III.)

Although gardening trends change over time — with the "wild garden" enjoying great popularity, then fading into almost total eclipse — the Maidenhair Fern has remained popular for its ability to combine well with many types of flowering plants (bulbs, perennials, and shrubs). It is neither rampant nor overbearing like other fern species, so it is far easier to incorporate into a garden setting (especially a small garden), whether the garden is on the wild side or wholly under the gardener's control in a semiformal landscape.

Maidenhair Fern is most refined, radiating its lovely grace over the entire growing season when planted among rocks and clumps of naturalized Daffodils (so many heirloom types to choose from), later covering up the latter's decaying leaves, or at the woodland's edge, a bridge planting between the garden proper and the wild, thriving in the dappled shade among other native plants such as Bee-balm, Fringed Bleeding-heart, and Columbine (*Aquilegia canadensis*). This fern is even adaptable to container planting, so you can move it where needed, as long as its delicate fronds are protected from the wind. Altogether, Maidenhair Fern is especially recommended to gardeners who think a plant without bright flowers has nothing to offer.

Because Maidenhair Fern is such an admirable plant and grows wild over many parts of the country, it has long been dug up by both gardeners and commercial collectors. Native populations should be left undisturbed (although spore collection, described below, won't hurt the plant). In areas slated for development, these ferns could be rescued from destruction by following the instructions in the "Plant Collector's Guide" (p. 22) and the cultural directions below.

To Grow: The easiest way to establish ferns is by ordering plants from a reputable nursery, such as the ones I have listed. The roots or rhizomes should be planted about one foot apart in moist, humusy, well-drained soil, in partial or full shade, and protected from the wind. Mulch the plants for a year or so until they are well established. When digging up wild plants to rescue, handle them carefully, since the rhizomes are brittle and break apart easily. Clumps can be divided if at least one bud or frond, two inches long, is growing from each section. Plants also can be propagated by collecting the spores that form under the curled-back edges of the leaves. Wait until midsummer or early fall when the spores are dark, then gently shake them into an envelope. Leave the envelope, unsealed, in a warm dry place so the spores can dry. Then sow the spores over moist, well-drained, sterile potting soil. Cover

the soil with clear glass and keep it at 65°F (18°C.). When a thin green tissue develops on top of the soil, begin misting it twice a week (return the cover each time), to encourage fertilization, the first sign of which is a tiny frond. It is important to keep the frond moist, not wet, in a covered situation (clear plastic or glass) and in a warm place. The little plants should be transplanted, one inch apart, to encourage root formation. Leave them indoors (eventually in uncovered pots) until they are well established. Then plant them out as described. The whole process may take eight to twelve months or longer.

Collector's Choice:

Adiantum pedatum, Maidenhair Fern. 169; 118; 67; 35; 138; 20 (all plants).

Aegopodium podagraria

'Variegatum'

Apiaceae
1850-1900?   ZONES 3-9

Goutweed

Bishop's Weed, Ground-ash, Ground-elder, Youth-before-old-age

TYPE: HARDY PERENNIAL GROUNDCOVER
HEIGHT: 6-24"   SEASON OF INTEREST:
                          ALL-SEASON FOLIAGE
SITE: SUN/PARTIAL SHADE/SHADE

The wild form, *Aegopodium podagraria*, or Goutweed, is a native of Europe, an ancient medicinal associated with monasteries and church buildings. An invasive plant with shiny green serrated leaves, it grows by creeping roots. The cultivar 'Variegatum' is far less invasive and more attractive, with mounds of soft emerald green leaves irregularly edged with white. Another common name, Youth-before-old-age, doubtless refers to the plant's habit of sending forth all-green leaves that become variegated as they mature.

The green-leaved Gout-weed is an herb whose healing properties are associated with sore joints, as the common name suggests. Culpeper observed that this was not an idle fancy, adding that besides relieving gout, sciatica, and joint aches, it also relieved "cold griefs." It would seem to have been indispensable in the settlers' pharmacopoeia, but it does not turn up in any list of settlers' herbs. Its variegated-leaf form, however, is often found thriving around old homesteads, where it was favored as a groundcover because of its ease of culture, lovely leaves, and ability to grow just about anywhere, in any soil and in either sun or shade.

It's true, I think, as has been observed, that in the pursuit of rarity, invaluable garden plants are apt to be overlooked. The ornamental Goutweed is rarely mentioned in garden books, even where groundcovers are considered, perhaps because it is so easy to grow that it is taken for granted. Its vigorous, rampant nature is deplored, and gardeners are forewarned about its invasive nature. When it is well handled, however, it is a lovely addition to an heirloom garden, a useful tool that can be used to create different effects, all with great ease.

I first saw 'Variegatum' as a neatly trimmed hedge defining the boundaries of an older backyard planting. It had been part of a rather elaborate scheme devised by a landscape archi-

Aegopodium podagraria

tect around the 1920s that involved shrub-lined "rooms" of Monkshood, Astilbe, and Garden Phlox. The groundcover had been used ingeniously — not like a groundcover at all, but as a stalwart and attractive low wall maintained by mowing both the grass in front of it and the plants themselves, the first time early in the summer when the little umbels of tiny white flowers appear on thin stalks.

A local gardener in the folk tradition added to my knowledge of other ways to grow the accommodating 'Variegatum'. He makes holes in the canopy of leaves, established as a groundcover to light up a shady nook, and in them sinks potted Impatiens or any bright-flowered plant that tolerates shade, such as Nicotiana. The leaves quickly grow back, and the brilliant annuals rise from them — coral, pink, and scarlet amid a sea of emerald and white, as striking a combination as the most discriminating gardener could desire. Potted plants, moreover, need not be sunk in the soil, just placed where you want them.

To Grow: Cultural directions seem superfluous. Just plant the roots in ordinary soil, in sun, partial shade, or shade. Water them and watch them grow. Twelve plants will cover about ten square feet over two seasons. Be sure to mow down the flowers in early spring or whenever they appear, as well as the area around the planting all season, to contain 'Variegatum's rambunctious growth.

Collector's Choice:

Aegopodium podagraria 'Variegatum', Gout-weed. 136, 106; 62; 99; 167; 114 (all plants).

Alcea rosea

Malvaceae

1600-1699   ZONES 3-10

Hollyhock

Chinese Hollyhock, Garden Mallow, Holyoke, Outlandish-rose

TYPE: BIENNIAL FLOWER/HERB
HEIGHT: 8'   BLOOM: SUMMER
SITE: SUN

Hollyhocks are native to China and were cultivated in Asia and the Middle East for many centuries before they were introduced to the West, perhaps by returning Crusaders. These are true biennials, the first year producing clumps or mounds of rough, almost heart-shaped lobed foliage close to the ground, and the second year sending up stems — three to six per clump — that can grow as tall as thirteen feet, with wide-open, overlapping, five-petaled flowers all along their length in shades of rose and pink. The wider range of colors associated with Hollyhocks is the result of selection as well as crossbreeding with other species.

The Englishman John Josselyn, who left a detailed description of the plants he saw growing in early New England gardens, lists Hollyhocks as garden herbs among "Marygolds" (*Calendula*), "French Mallowes" (*Malva sylvestris*), and "Gillyflowers" (*Dianthus*). This should not be surprising, since Hollyhocks belong to a family of plants renowned for their healing properties, based on the mucilaginous materials, found in all of their parts, that were thought to be soothing. The Latin name *Malvaceae* is derived from the Greek word *malakos*, meaning "softening."

Alcea rosea

While the Puritan settlers were, perhaps, drinking brews from dried and powdered Hollyhock flowers to prevent miscarriages and ruptures and to dissolve coagulated blood, early Dutch settlers apparently were growing the double-flowered form — Gerard called them "Outlandish Rose" — for their beauty alone.

Hollyhocks were valued highly by gardeners in later generations for their long season of bloom from early summer to fall — as long as it took each tightly wrapped bud to unfold, starting at the bottom of the stalk and working upward to the tip. In 1845 the Breck catalog listed eight different Hollyhock colors, including black and a mottled type. Mature plants, with their great clusters of spikes — "buxom in character," one writer noted — were grown at the back of the border or planted against trellises, fences, and stone walls.

Beginning in the 1930s, the tall, stately Hollyhock in the single-flowered classic form gave way to ever-shorter types (no staking required) with fat double blossoms — "like rolled-up Kleenex," a gardening friend complained. However fashion depreciates the value of a plant, "it cannot enhance or depreciate the beauty of a single flower," as nineteenth-century gardener Shirley Hibberd wisely observed. When we moved to a rented farm in 1962, I saw the tall type for the first time, growing against the stone wall that sheltered our vegetable patch. I vowed that one day I'd have such beauties in my own garden. Even then, seeds of this type were becoming difficult to find from commercial sources.

In 1970 we moved to Cape Breton, and here, on a spit of land isolated from the modern world and its changing tastes, I came across very old strains of Hollyhocks, some quite close to the wild kind, with pale pink single blooms on thirteen-foot stalks. Inevitably, the color range had narrowed to shades of pink and rose, except for the gorgeous dark purple Black Hollyhock I found growing in one garden in the area. Its flowers were enormous — five to six inches across, with the petals rolled back — on manageable six- to eight-foot stalks: the flowers of my dreams. I traced their origin back three generations to Elizabeth MacDonald, whom I later saw in a faded photograph, still handsome at age ninety and standing beside a great stand of her favorite flowers.

Although they had been growing on their own in the same site for the past fifty years, their habitat had been disturbed recently by the construction of a deck (a recent phenomenon in the area that has been responsible for the displacement of many heirloom flowers and shrubs), under which seedlings still sought the light of day. I saved seeds from mature plants and passed them along to ensure that Elizabeth's strain would not be lost. Fortunately, tall, single-flowered Hollyhocks, including the Black Hollyhock, are once again in favor, and seeds and plants are both available.

Hollyhock Dollies

Dr. Graham Bell Fairchild, now in his eighties, remembers summers at Beinn Breagh, his famous grandparents' turn-of-the-century estate about twenty-five miles from our farm. Alexander Graham Bell's wife was very fond of the tall, single-flowered Hollyhocks, and they were planted along the pergola on the way to the gardener's cottage. The grandchildren, including little Graham, made Hollyhock dollies in the summer from the red, pink, white, and yellow blooms.

To make a dolly, pluck a bud and carefully peel off the sepals that enclose it. Then push the little stem of an opened flower into one of the holes at the base of the bud's folded petals. Voilà: a dolly (the bud) with a lovely billowing skirt (the opened flower).

To Grow: In Zones 3-8 Hollyhocks may grow as short-lived perennials, with new plants growing up from the base of the mother plant to survive another year or two, while self-sown seedlings grow to maturity in the vicinity. Thus the gardener will regard them as perennials. To establish this desirable condition, Hollyhocks require well-drained, moderately rich soil in a warm location. To start, sow the seeds in late summer in a cold frame, where they should germinate in about ten days at 70°F. (21°C.). Early the following spring, before the plants develop a long taproot, set them out two feet apart.

To ensure the survival of mature plants, take cuttings in late summer from the bottom of the spent flower stalks (these should be cut back), removing "daughter" plants with their auxiliary roots to a cold frame for the winter. Then plant them out early the next season. Even if tall Hollyhocks are planted in a sheltered spot, they generally need staking, a small price to pay for such beauty. In Zones 9 and 10 Hollyhocks are grown as biennials, with new plants set out every year, usually in the fall, for continuous bloom.

When saving seeds, separate them from the fruit capsule in which they are tightly packed and allow them to dry thoroughly before storing.

Alcea rosea, Hollyhock; carmine, pink, rose, cream, and white blooms; 5-7'. 5; 87; 92; 18 (all seeds); 20(p).

'Indian Spring' (by 1939); single or semidouble white or pink blooms; 6'. 3(s); 31(p); 96(s); 114(p); 126(s); 164(p).

A. rosea nigra, Black Hollyhock (1800-1825); 8'. 6; 177; 92; 147 (all seeds).

Allium schoenoprasum

Amaryllidaceae
1600-1776   Zones 3-10

Chives

Chebols, Chibolls

❀ *A. tuberosum*

1776-1850   Zones 3-10

Garlic Chives

Chinese Chives, Oriental Garlic, Sweet-scented Garlic

Type: Hardy Herbs/Flowers
Height: 1-2'   Bloom: Early Summer-Fall
Site: Sun

Both Chives and Garlic Chives are herbs that grow from bulbous roots, like onions. Chives, native to Europe and Asia, quickly form tight clusters that sprout grasslike, onion-flavored leaves growing to one foot, breaking through even semifrozen ground with the first hint of spring. Later, the flowering stalks produce lovely ball-shaped, lavender-pink heads composed of many small florets that in maturity open to spill out their tiny black seeds, ensuring the prolific production of new generations of bulbs.

Garlic Chives, native to Asia, are more stately plants, growing to two feet from stout rhizomes. Their leaves, unlike those of Chives, are flat, grow to one-quarter inch wide, and are garlic-flavored. The flowers, produced in late summer, are sweetly scented, growing in round umbels of star-shaped blossoms. They are white with a greenish flush and gradually fall off to reveal distinctive green fruiting knobs.

Chives were universally grown in early American kitchen gardens. They were highly valued as an early spring green or vegetable after a long winter's diet of stored root crops such as carrots, beets, and potatoes. They were probably also eaten as a spring restorative in a salad of bittersweet greens (Dandelions) — a country custom still in practice.

I found one clump, among several examples of Chives used as a pioneer herb on our remote peninsula, where the original plant had been removed to the new farmstead up the road, apparently considered an integral and invaluable part of the household. It had been used in the past to flavor potatoes in the spring, and the old clump, now seldom used for anything but its ornamental flowers, remained in a corner of the herbaceous border that had grown up around it, its outer leaves cut now and then for salad, its girth checked by seasonal digging up of the extra bulblets around it. Treated in this way, it was able to renew itself from its decaying leaves, the source of nutrients for further growth.

Elsewhere on the island, Chives (often called by its older name, Cives) are naturalized in wet meadows near French settlements, where they are used, after being pickled in brine, in Frico, a unique Acadian dish. Among large populations of Chives, as in the wild, there are variations of color and form: rosy globes of flowers, dwarf or taller types, even white-flowered sports (a plant of which was collected from an old garden for the Heritage Garden of the Memorial University Botanical Garden in St. John's, Newfoundland).

You can naturalize Chives if you have the room. They are particularly partial to wet ground — even standing water if it's not too deep — where they will form a beautiful drift of mauve-rose in the spring, followed by Blue and Yellow Flag Iris. They can be massed to edge a bed or grown in clustered clumps among early-blooming flowers such as Columbine, Mountain-bluet, Lupines, and Dame's-rocket, all soft shades of blue, lilac, and rose, and the spreading white umbels of Sweet Cicely. I like to plant a few clumps of Chives by the kitchen door, close at hand for use, where the sprawling mats of Lamb's-ears help to cover the Chives after they have been ravaged by my scissors to flavor salads or cottage cheese. I also use dried bundles of flowering stems in dried bouquets, where they make a splash among the white clusters of 'The Pearl' (Sneezewort), and the felty leaves and stalks of Lamb's-ears.

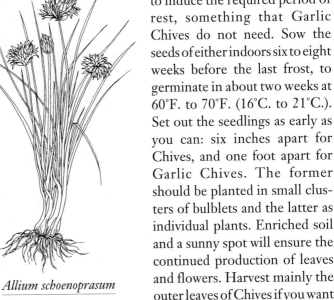

Allium schoenoprasum

Garlic Chives, introduced in the eighteenth or nineteenth century from Asia, apparently were regarded as an ornamental, as well they might be, for in my opinion the plant's value in the flower border outweighs its use in the herb garden. In my gardens of mixed herbs and flowers, I look forward to its late summer appearance when fresh blooms are a novelty and very welcome. Then the white-starred Garlic Chives, rising tall, stately, and unexpectedly behind a spreading colony of purple and white Annual Clary Sage (*Salvia viridis*) and chartreuse Nicotiana ('Limelight') put on a good show until frost (and even a little while beyond).

To Grow: Chives and Garlic Chives can be grown in Zones 3-10, but Chives need to be exposed to freezing temperatures to induce the required period of rest, something that Garlic Chives do not need. Sow the seeds of either indoors six to eight weeks before the last frost, to germinate in about two weeks at 60°F. to 70°F. (16°C. to 21°C.). Set out the seedlings as early as you can: six inches apart for Chives, and one foot apart for Garlic Chives. The former should be planted in small clusters of bulblets and the latter as individual plants. Enriched soil and a sunny spot will ensure the continued production of leaves and flowers. Harvest mainly the outer leaves of Chives if you want to save the flowers. In any case, cut the plant back after flowering, but not severely, so it will have nutrients to produce fresh leaves and flowers in the fall (make sure the ground is rich). Divide Chives and Garlic Chives as needed, about once every three to five years.

Collector's Choice (all sold as both plants and seeds):

Allium schoenoprasum, Chives. 133; 114; 126; 177; 95.

A. tuberosum, Garlic Chives. 126; 177; 116; 121; 36; 49.

Anthemis tinctoria

Asteraceae
1850-1900?   ZONES 3-10

Golden-Marguerite

Dyer's Chamomile, Golden Anthemis, Ox-eye Chamomile

TYPE: SHORT-LIVED PERENNIAL/BIENNIAL
    FLOWER/HERB
HEIGHT: 2½-3'   BLOOM: SUMMER-FALL
SITE: SUN/PARTIAL SHADE

Golden-Marguerite is a bushy and somewhat sprawling short-lived perennial native to central and southern Europe and western Asia. It has profuse golden yellow, daisy-shaped blooms, two or more inches across, complemented by distinctive feathery foliage that is dense, aromatic, gray, and downy on the underside. The genus name comes from the Greek *anthemon*, meaning "flower" (used here to describe the plant's free-flowering nature), and the epithet comes from *tinctor*, meaning "dyer." These combine well to sum up Golden-Marguerite's outstanding physical characteristic and its use as a dye plant since antiquity. Golden-Marguerite was indispensable in any self-respecting medieval household, where it was used to make a yellow, gold, or buff dye. Yet it is wholly overshadowed in the literature by its former cousin, *Anthemis nobilis* (now *Chamaemelum nobile*), of fabled chamomile tea and aromatic lawn carpets.

Golden-Marguerite has a strange history

Anthemis tinctoria

as an heirloom ornamental in the New World, seemingly coming from nowhere in the mid-nineteenth century, with no record of prior herb use. Favored for perennial borders, and especially recommended to inexperienced gardeners for its ease of culture, the plant is literally smothered in golden daisies for much of the summer and into the fall, with the lovely, almost evergreen foliage an advantage all season long. The flowering plant is both frost- and disease-resistant.

Garden historians do not come to our aid with tidbits about its culture and lore. Even Margery Fish, usually enamored of any sprawling plant, could work up no enthusiasm for Golden-Marguerite, which she claimed even the cottage folk would not allow in their gardens, noting that it grows profusely, especially where chickens have been (as do most plants).

Both cottagers and Mrs. Fish have missed out on a good thing, one that other gardeners in North America have long valued. I suspect that Golden-Marguerite is especially appreciated in North America because it thrives in the sunny, dry conditions that often prevail in our summer months. 'Kelwayi' is an improved form, with more finely cut foliage and lovely golden yellow daisies, from the nineteenth-century British nurseryman and breeder James Kelway.

Cottagers could have grown this obliging plant among their favorite flowers in the sun: Calendula, Feverfew, Elecampane, Rose Campion, Bouncing-bet, and Daylilies. The golden flowers combine nicely with the brilliant orange Butterfly Weed, the gray-leaved Garden

Sage, and the gray-fringed Southernwood, for an herby touch to the flower border. Golden-Marguerite also can be used as a tall ground-cover for a sunny, dry bank. The flowers are excellent for fresh bouquets, a convenient and far less tedious way to deadhead spent blooms in order to prolong the plant's blooming season.

To Grow: Golden-Marguerite can be grown in Zones 3-10 except in southernmost Florida and along the Gulf Coast. Sow the seeds indoors four to six weeks before the last frost to readily germinate at 68°F. to 78°F. (20°C. to 26°C.), or sow them outdoors in early spring in well-drained soil and full sun. Thin the seedlings to nine inches apart. Poor soil and full sun produce more flowers than enriched soil and shade, but a little shade is appreciated where summers are hot. These are short-lived perennials, so remember to divide the plants about every two years or take stem cuttings, which can be readily rooted in sand to bloom the first summer.

Collector's Choice:

Anthemis tinctoria 'Kelwayi', Golden-Marguerite (probably 1860s). 133(p & s); 177(p & s); 155(p); 15(p); 126(s); 137(s).

Aquilegia canadensis

Ranunculaceae
1700-1850   ZONES 3-10   NATIVE

Eastern Columbine

American Columbine, Canadian Columbine, Meetinghouses

A. vulgaris

1600-1699   ZONES 3-10   NATURALIZED

European Columbine

Columbine, European-crowfoot, Garden-honeysuckle, Granny's-bonnet

---

TYPE: PERENNIAL FLOWER
HEIGHT: 1-2½'   BLOOM: SPRING-EARLY
SUMMER
SITE: SUN/PARTIAL SHADE

Eastern Columbine is a native perennial flower of rocky, wooded, or open slopes from Manitoba and Quebec south through New England to Georgia and west to Wisconsin. The genus name comes from the Latin *aquila*, meaning "eagle," a reference to the flowers' talonlike spurs. Wild Columbine flowers are composed of five petal-like, brilliant red sepals alternating with yellow petals and surrounding a column of bright yellow stamens. The backs of the petals are elongated to form a hollow nectar-bearing spur that curves inward and ends in a decisive knob. The fragile-seeming flowers, sitting atop slender stems that grow to almost three feet, are firmly anchored to the ground by a long taproot from which grow attractive green rounded and lobed leaves, mostly close to the ground. This species is the parent of many modern hybrids.

Aquilegia vulgaris, a native of Europe growing to two and a half feet, bears less brilliant and more varied flowers, usually in soft shades of blue, purple, rose, or white. These flowers have less pronounced spurs or none at all, as in the fully double types. The European Columbine is naturalized locally in North America as a garden escape.

The showy flowers of the native Eastern

Columbine did not long escape the notice of visitors to the New World, and by 1635 Jesuit missionaries in Canada had introduced it to France. In the early 1700s, Eastern Columbine was being grown in American gardens in Pennsylvania and elsewhere with natives such as the Cardinal Flower (*Lobelia cardinalis*), Black-eyed-Susan, and Blue Boneset (*Eupa-torium coelestinum*). By the middle of the nineteenth century, the native Columbine was one of the most popular garden flowers in America, though it later declined significantly with the introduction of hybrids with larger, showier flowers.

The European Columbine was grown in the earliest American gardens, having been a favorite garden flower of variable form (singles and doubles) for centuries in Europe. I traced back a surviving population 120 years. Growing virtually untended, this group produced beautiful double blossoms in a range of colors — purple, blue, pink, and white — a testimony to the plant's endurance. Unlike hybrid forms, these come remarkably true from seed and do not deteriorate in beauty over the years. Though classified as a perennial, Columbine appears to replenish itself by self-seeding, so individual plants are not very old.

A few years ago, friends bought a house in the country built in 1865. They were delighted to find the remnants of an old garden lingering by a stone wall. Among them they discovered Hostas, Cinnamon Fern, and the loveliest semidouble Columbines — pure white and rich pink, one flower set within another, nodding on graceful stems — growing unaided for at least the past sixty years.

Aquilegia canadensis

Both Columbines attract hummingbirds, so you should plant them where they can be easily seen — in rock gardens, near the front of a perennial border, in the semishade of a shrubbery, or on a nearby rocky slope. I grow the Eastern Columbine at the edge of a thinly wooded ravine, where they can receive a few hours of direct sun a day — all they need to thrive if soil conditions are right. I grow European Columbine beneath the dappled shade of an old fruit tree underplanted with Daffodils, among Bleeding-heart, Virginia-bluebells, Hostas, and Forget-me-nots.

Columbines are long-lasting cut flowers. 'Nora Barlow' is a favorite with flower arrangers for its striking form and colors: clusters of white-tipped, carmine-pink petal layers, suffused with lime green, and no spurs evident. Apparently this is a renamed ancient strain.

To Grow: Of the two, European Columbine is the easier to establish and the more adaptable. It does well in moist, well-drained soil to which a little bonemeal or rotted manure has been added. The site can be partially shaded or sunny except in hot, dry, windy areas, where some shade is appreciated. Eastern Columbine requires a lighter, sharply drained soil — thin and gravelly is best.

Seeds of both Columbines should be prechilled for three to four weeks and sown in the summer in a cold frame, where germination will take twenty-one to twenty-five days (or more) at 70°F. to 75°F. (21°C. to 24°C.) Set out plants twelve to twenty-eight inches apart in the fall or very early spring before they have developed a long taproot. Both types can be divided if they seem to need it, but letting new seedlings develop or starting a new colony from seed is best.

Collector's Choice:

Aquilegia canadensis, Eastern Columbine. 20(p); 68(p); 26; 87; 35 (all seeds); 139(p).

A. vulgaris, European Columbine. Mixed colors — 147-8; 18; 87 (all seeds); blue — 5(s).

A. v. plena. 5; 18; 147-8 (all seeds).

'Nora Barlow'. 3; 92; 87; 6 (all seeds); 61(p); 20(p).

'Old-Fashioned Red' (19th century); double maroon-carmine blooms. 92(s).

❧ *Artemisia abrotanum*

Asteraceae
1600-1776   Zones 3-9

Southernwood

Lad's-love, Maid's-ruin, Old-man, Old-man's-love, Old-man Wormwood, The Lovers Plant

Type: Perennial Herb/
    Subshrub
Height: 3-4'
Season of Interest:
    All-Season, Almost-
    Evergreen Foliage
Site: Sun

Southernwood is a very hardy herb and subshrub with almost-evergreen leaves — threaded or fringed and lemon-scented — growing on slender stems to three to four feet. It is often

Artemisia abrotanum

clipped to use as a neat border around herb gardens. Its common name, Southernwood, distinguishes this *Artemisia*, native to southern Europe, from Wormwood (*A. absinthium*), both of which contain the substance absinthum in some degree. Southernwood's Latin epithet, *abrotanum*, meaning "elegance," aptly describes both the form and fragrance of this ancient herb.

Ancient herbals record a wide range of complaints for which Southernwood, in some form, was the answer: inflamed eyes, an outbreak of pimples, ulcers, splinters, thorns, even talking in one's sleep. One of the more persistent claims was its ability to relieve baldness in old men and promote beards in young men, hence several of its common names.

Like any plant that has a long history of association with people, Southernwood was invested with magical powers. According to country wisdom, a few sprays slipped under a young woman's pillow, down her back, or into her bouquet would cause the first man she met to fall in love with her, leading ultimately to her ruin. Herbal lore of this type probably had little influence on its use in early gardens.

Southernwood was included in the medicinal gardens of early Moravian settlers in North Carolina and in the formal gardens of William Paca, one of the signers of the Declaration of Independence, in Annapolis, Maryland, where it hedged in the kitchen garden. The Plymouth colonists knew Southernwood, too, and most likely used it to scent linens (easier to grow for them than Lavender) and to make a yellow dye. In their informal but neat cottage garden-type plantings, perhaps Southernwood spread out from its usual mounded, clipped form to grow as it liked, a greenish gray foil for the more colorful flowering herbs of a dooryard garden.

Such enduring plants naturally lend themselves to becoming family heirlooms. I found a ninety-year-old specimen that had been grown from a slip taken from Boston around the turn of the century and carefully passed down from great-grandmother to great-granddaughter, who gave me a piece of it. Now "it groweth in my garden" among purple-flowering stalks of Foxglove and pink Mallow.

It's a nice idea to establish a plant or two near a well-used entranceway, where sprigs may be conveniently harvested to use in nosegays (tussie-mussies), potpourri, or sachets. To harvest Southernwood, cut the tops or branches during the summer and spread them on newspaper indoors away from the light. When the leaves feel quite dry, run your hands along the hard stems, and the leaves will drop off in a heap. Their scent lasts six months in sachets. Southernwood branches can be used to make wreaths, too. They should be bent into shape when they are green and pliant.

To Grow: Since Southernwood rarely produces flowers, it is usually grown from roots, which are easily established in ordinary garden soil, even clay, on the compost side, in full sun. Place them one to two feet apart or more depending on how you want them to grow (as a clipped hedge or more sprawling bush). Southernwood will tolerate partial shade, but the leaves will not flourish and some may turn yellow. In early spring, clip back an established plant to about six inches to encourage fresh growth. Clip it again during early summer if you want it to grow as a neat mound. Do not clip the plant in late summer, since the new growth will be too weak to winter over. By late fall in colder areas, the leaves will finally drop off, to return slowly the following spring. The time to divide is early fall or spring. Break off a stem with lateral roots and little rootlets, and plant it. Or take three-inch tip cuttings in the spring and plant those.

Collector's Choice:

Artemisia abrotanum, Southernwood. 93; 110; 177; 16; 116; 104; 49 (all plants).

❦ *Asclepias tuberosa*

Asclepiadaceae
1776-1850   ZONES 4-10   NATIVE

Butterfly Weed

Butterfly Flower, Butterfly Milkweed, Chigger Flower, Indian-paintbrush, Pleurisy Root, Swallowwort

---

TYPE: PERENNIAL WILDFLOWER/HERB
HEIGHT: 2-3'   BLOOM: SUMMER-FALL
SITE: SUN/PARTIAL SHADE

Butterfly Weed is a conspicuous wildflower that grows in dry fields and along woodlands and roadsides from New Hampshire to Florida, as well as on the plains of Minnesota, Colorado, Arizona, and Texas — a reflection of its wide-ranging adaptability. It grows from a deep taproot but, unlike other milkweeds, lacks any juice in its stems. These grow from one to three feet and have narrow, lance-shaped leaves. At their tops they bear two-inch clusters of waxy orange, nectar-rich, fragrant flowers and, later, spindle-shaped seedpods that pop open to disperse flat brown seeds with long, silky hairs. The flat-topped clusters present perfect landing pads for the Monarch butterfly in the summer and fall.

This beautiful native flower drew attention to itself very early. It was officially discovered by 1690, but it is quite likely that the settlers learned about its medicinal uses earlier from the Indians, who used it as a remedy for lung and throat troubles and to soothe wounds and sores. The young shoots, boiled in the spring, were eaten as a vegetable, as were the seedpods.

Butterfly Weed is one of the few native plants favored by gardeners from New England to Alabama. To satisfy the great demand, plants were dug up from the wild in great numbers. S.N.F. Sandford, writing for the New England Museum of Natural History in 1937, remarked that "even on Cape Cod, where it was formerly abundant, it is no longer common, and there is not much on Martha's Vineyard, while on Nantucket it is now rare" (*New England Herbs*, New England Museum of Natural History, 1937). Fortunately, Butterfly Weed is difficult to destroy, for a piece of its long taproot ensures renewed life, as do its abundant seeds, blown far and wide.

As a garden plant, it is extraordinarily adaptable, growing in a city garden as well as in a wildflower meadow or border of herbs and flowers. It is especially striking when paired with Wild-bergamot, another active herb, which, like Butterfly Weed, loves the sun and is happy in dry soil. Established where it can form a large clump, it is striking against any shrubbery or expanse of lawn. The broad, colorful heads add interest to any garden, and the plant's season of interest is extended by the ornamental seedpods. As a bonus, Butterfly Weed is a long-lasting cut flower, and its dried pods are useful in winter bouquets. The question is, why is this lovely flower called a weed?

Asclepias tuberosa

To Grow: Butterfly Weed is especially valued where conditions are hot and dry. Seeds (preferably fresh) germinate in about three weeks at 70°F. (21°C.). They should be sown where you want the plant to bloom because, once it develops its root, it is difficult to move. Space plants eight to twelve inches apart. Butterfly Weed requires perfectly drained, sandy soil and tolerates light shade, but it does best in full sun. Three- to four-inch cuttings can be taken from the ends of the stem (tips) before flowering. The root can be cut into two-inch sections and rooted in sandy soil if kept moist. To collect the wispy seeds, pull them out from the pod when it begins to split. Sow them at once, or dry them and store them in the refrigerator until needed.

Collector's Choice:

Asclepias tuberosa, Butterfly Weed. 73(p & s); 35(p & s); 5(s); 15(s); 169; 166; 94 (all plants).

Calendula officinalis

Asteraceae
1600-1699

Pot-marigold

Cape-marigold, Marygold, Merrigould, Winking-Mary-budde

TYPE: HARDY ANNUAL FLOWER/HERB
HEIGHT: 1-2'   BLOOM: SUMMER-FALL
SITE: SUN/PARTIAL SHADE

The Pot-marigold, an annual flower native to the Mediterranean and southern Europe, grows to two feet in the wild. It has single- or double-petaled daisylike blooms that can be as large as four inches across and range in color from pale yellow to deep orange. Some have dark centers. The stems are sturdy yet brittle, and the long, pale green leaves are mostly in evidence near the bottom of the plant. The genus name is derived from the Latin *calendae*, meaning "the first of the month," a reference to the fact that, in its native habitat, the Pot-marigold is almost everblooming. It has long been noted that "the flower goes to bed w' the sun/And with him rises weeping" (*A Winter's Tale*), a habit more precisely defined by Linnaeus

Calendula officinalis

as the flower that opens by nine in the morning and closes by three in the afternoon (though very double-flowered types don't quite fit this description).

Calendula officinalis — as its epithet "from the apothecary" indicates — was first considered an herb. As early as the thirteenth century, its medicinal and culinary uses were described in detail. Its flowers were steeped or dried and used primarily in ointments (still available today); the dried petals were stored in barrels and sold by the ounce to flavor soups and stews. In the New World, the flowers were often used to color cheese and butter (the plant yields a yellow dye).

Jefferson grew "Marygolds" at Monticello in 1764 (Calendulas were called "Marygolds" well into the eighteenth century; later they were referred to as Pot-marigolds to distinguish them from the *Tagetes* species, African and French Marigolds). These were probably the single-petaled form, but double flowers

have been known at least since the sixteenth century, when Gerard referred to one as "the greatest double Marigold . . . beautiful round, very large and double . . . like pure gold," a description that could fit many modern types. He described an ancient strain known as 'Hens and Chicks' as *prolifera* and called it "Jack-an-apes-a-horsebacke": "At the top of the stalke one floure like the other Marigolds; from the which start forth sundry other small flowers, yellow likewise, and of the same fashion." If you grow Pot-marigolds long enough, sports like this sometimes turn up among double-flowered types.

Gradually, the beauty of Calendula flowers, their ease of culture, and their adaptability to extremes of heat and cold (surviving successive frosts to 25°F. or -4°C.) recommended them as a subject for breeding. Many cultivars that played on the plant's form and size and the color of the flowers were developed. By 1930 'Orange Shaggy' was offered as a "very distinct break in Calendulas," with long and deeply fringed petals resembling some types of Chrysanthemums, but not all gardeners approved of this meddling with the classic design. "'Orange Shaggy'," Louise Beebe Wilder noted scornfully, "is very well described by its name . . . an unsightly and unseemly flower, not fit to consort with such beauties as . . . 'Apricot', 'Chrysantha', 'Golden Beam', 'Radio', 'Campfire' . . . 'Ball's Orange', 'Ball's Gold', 'Ball's Masterpiece', and 'Lemon Queen'."

Two of these older strains have survived. 'Radio', according to Roy Genders in his book *The Cottage Garden* (Viking Penguin, 1987), is "one of the finest cut flower plants ever raised. The habit is ideal, never becoming tall and 'raggedly', whilst the flowers with their attractive quilled petals are of the clearest orange." 'Orange King' is a vigorous plant, almost two feet tall with large flowers whose double rows of deep orange petals do not obscure the central disk, which is sometimes dark but more often pale green. 'Radio' is very useful in the border, with its Cactus Dahlia-shaped blooms as an easy-to-grow Mum stand-in for fall color. I plant 'King' everywhere for late fall color, often alongside dark blue Bachelor's-button. The brightness of bloom of both these plants is astonishing, deepening in cold weather (or so it seems). The unimproved single-petaled type is allowed to self-sow from year to year, especially in the vicinity of spring-flowering Daffodils. In *Plants from the Past* (Viking, 1987), garden historians Stuart and Sutherland note that in the eighteenth century, the single-flowered type was the one used as a cooking herb and to flavor butter, while the doubles were kept in the flower garden. In my experience, doubles are more useful, for the simple reason that they have more petals. Both types, particularly those with dark centers, are highly prized cut flowers.

To Grow: You can sow the boat-shaped seeds in the fall or spring. Be sure to cover them with one-quarter inch of soil, since they need darkness to germinate. This should occur in four to ten days, or possibly a little longer, if the soil temperature is 70°F. (21°C.). Sow seeds a second time in early summer for late bloom. The soil should be moderately rich — though the plants will tolerate poor soil if the drainage is good — and the site fairly sunny (partial shade is O.K. as long as it receives morning sun). In Zones 8-10 sow seeds in late summer for winter bloom by Christmas. Thin the plants to eight to ten inches apart, and if you want to transplant some, do so when they are in the seedling stage, taking care to plant them deeply and water them well. For winter bloom indoors, cut back the most immature plants in the fall and pot them.

Collector's Choice:

Calendula officinalis, Pot-marigold; 18". 6; 177; 5; 18 (all seeds); 110(p).

'Cottage Charm' (old style); single orange bloom with dark center. 3(s).

'Hens and Chicks'. 6(s); 5(s).

'Orange King' (late 19th century). 5(s); 171(s).

'Radio' (by 1930); 18-20". 92(s).

Callistephus chinensis

Asteraceae
1700-1776

China Aster

German Aster

TYPE: TENDER ANNUAL FLOWER
HEIGHT: 2½'   BLOOM: SUMMER-FALL
SITE: SUN/PARTIAL SHADE

In the wild, the China Aster (native to China, of course) is an erect, branching annual with stems to two and a half feet. It has showy, daisylike flowers as big as five inches across in shades of violet to rose and white. This form has been widely developed to include fully double flowers and dwarf types with an extended color range. "China" distinguishes this flower from the native perennial Asters (*Aster novae-angliae* and *A. novi-belgii*).

The China Aster began its journey to the West when a Jesuit missionary noticed it growing in a field near Peking around 1730. He must have been astonished and delighted to find such a beautiful flower growing in the wild. By 1735 the Englishman Peter Collinson, a leading spirit in transatlantic seed exchange, had sent seeds to John Bartram, America's first botanist-horticulturalist, to whom we (as well as the British) owe so many plant introductions. Collinson observed that the purple and white flowers were "the noblest and finest plant thee ever saw," a judgment that must have been shared by many Americans, for China Asters were among the most cultivated flowers of the eighteenth century.

By the early 1800s, Germany had become the center of seed production — especially for the quilled or "hedgehog" type, which has long, curved petals — hence the then-popular name "German Aster." By 1865 the China Aster had been so changed from its original daisy form that James Vick, proprietor of a New York seed firm, observed with approval, "They are now as double as the Chrysanthemum or the Dahlia and almost as large and showy as the Peony," a sentiment not shared by William Robinson, the English gardener and writer (contemporary of Gertrude Jekyll), who especially deplored the stocky, double dwarf form popular in stiff Victorian gardens, which he called "dumpy."

By the late 1800s, fashions in flowers had changed considerably, and the return to "grandmother's garden" required a freer, more classic flower design, as in some of the cultivars developed for the florist trade, such as 'Boston Florists' White', a snowy white, long-stemmed beauty introduced in 1884. As with many plants, I came to the classic shape by the back door, after first growing every other form, from

Callistephus chinensis

double dwarf pom-poms to frilled and feathery concoctions. Then I discovered 'Heart of France', and I knew at once what I wanted in a China Aster.

'Heart of France' is (or was) a carmine-rose single-petaled flower, four inches across, with a yellow center. It grows to about two and a half feet and is spectacular in the fall among Marigolds and other late bloomers, such as tall white Garden Phlox. It was probably introduced sometime in the late 1920s, for it is described in a 1930 seed catalog as "New! . . . a large full aster with never a trace of hollow center, branching and robust." (But as anyone familiar with seed catalog hyperbole knows, "New!" could mean decades old.)

I began growing single China Asters in 1973 and 'Heart' by 1975. The last time I saw it offered was in the 1980s. Had I known that someday it would disappear from the market, I could have saved its seed to keep the strain alive, but I didn't think about plants as heirlooms then. I thought this lovely flower would always be around. Fortunately, the single-flowered type in the classic form and color range, sold as a mix, is still available, and the heirloom gardener can selectively save seeds of ruby-colored flowers similar to my favorite.

To Grow: For July and August bloom, start seeds indoors in March or April; germination takes ten to fourteen days at 70°F. (21°C.). I have found China Asters easy to raise if temperatures are kept steadily warm. Be sure to transplant the seedlings when the first true leaves appear, because the developed roots don't like being disturbed. For this reason, I usually transplant them into plant cells, which encourage roots to grow as a block that is easy to transplant into the garden. Garden soil should be rich, well drained, and on the sweet side. The site should be sunny, though light shade is acceptable in warmer regions. Plant the seedlings when all danger of frost has passed. Place them about twelve inches apart and mulch the shallow roots with one inch of grass clippings. Avoid fresh manure or compost, which might encourage wilt, a dreaded fungus. Resistance to this disease is not always noted in catalogs, so to be on the safe side, plant China Asters in a different location every year to avoid any buildup of the fungus in the soil.

Collector's Choice:

Callistephus chinensis, China Aster; single blooms; mixed colors:
  'California Giant' (old style). 101(s).
  'Madeleine' (old style). 160(s).
  'Single Rainbow Hybrids' (old style). 96(s).

Campanula spp.

Campanulaceae
1600-1900   ZONES 3-10

Bellflower

TYPE: BIENNIAL/PERENNIAL FLOWER
HEIGHT: TO 4'   BLOOM: LATE SPRING-
                SUMMER
SITE: SUN/PARTIAL SHADE

Bellflowers belong to an extraordinarily large genus of more than fifteen hundred annual, biennial, and perennial species that are widely distributed across the Northern Hemisphere. Several of these are highly regarded as ornamentals for their showy, five-petaled, bell-shaped flowers, which grow in racemes, or terminal spikes, on creeping or tall wandlike stems to four feet or more. The blue, violet, mauve, pink, or white blooms emerge from a rosette of long basal leaves. The genus name is Latin for "little bell."

Two species of Bellflowers were grown in seventeenth-century American gardens: the biennial Canterbury- or Coventry-bells and the hardy perennial Peach-leaved Bellflower, both English cottage garden favorites. The former was named for the two English cathedrals near where it grew wild, perhaps a Roman introduction. The fleshy taproot is reportedly edible, but there is no indication that it was grown on this side of the Atlantic for any reason other than aesthetic appeal and as a living keepsake of the home country. Early strains, closest to the wild, were purplish blue (known since medieval times) and white; their bells were fairly slender rather than inflated (the kind we know today). In the eighteenth century, Jefferson sowed this Bellflower with African Marigolds *(Tagetes erecta)* and White Poppies *(Papaver somniferum)*. Early nineteenth-century seedsmen and nurserymen offered nine types of Bellflowers, among them Peach-leaved, Creeping *(Campanula rapunculoides)*, and Clustered *(C. glomerata)*.

The Peach-leaved Bellflower, or Paper Flower (named after the transparency of its petals), was more on the order of an herb in early American gardens. Introduced to England in the fifteenth century, the plant was used in its entirety, especially the flowers, which, when distilled in water, yielded a medicine to soothe sore throats and cleanse the skin. The roots were boiled and served as a vegetable, as were so many flower roots when other vegetables were scarce. It soon became a valued garden flower, loved for its slightly flaring bells all along its towering stems, as well as its ease of culture. In the eighteenth century, double forms were widely grown, almost displacing the singles in the public's favor, but by the nineteenth century, the crisp, elegant singles were back in fashion, heralded as "new."

Also in the nineteenth century, the harder-to-grow but much-admired Canterbury-bells were offered in the double "cup-and-saucer" and "hose-in-hose" forms. In these types, the flower sits in an enlarged calyx of the same color — cup-and-saucer — or the calyx appears as another row of petals, creating the effect of a double flower with one flower growing inside and from the other — hose-in-hose. Not all gardeners saw these as improvements over the older, daintier form. "A monstrous variety," Mrs. Wilder called the cup-and-saucer. "Who wants a stalk of cups and saucers in his garden!" Apparently many gardeners did and do, as this is the type of Canterbury-bells most widely grown today.

Among popular Bellflowers, two are of special note for their respective histories, both claiming the same title of "Scottish Blue-bell" or "Bluebell of Scotland." The most accepted is *Campanula rotundifolia*, also known as Hare-bell and Witch's-thimble. Gardeners at Old Sturbridge Village, a reconstructed early nineteenth-century village in Massachusetts, grow this Bellflower in the Fenno House garden among Phlox, Golden-glow, and Daylilies (combinations that still speak to us today) and at the Fitch House as part of a low-maintenance garden plan based on a description in Joseph Breck's 1833 garden book for children, *The Young Florist*. This Bellflower is distinguished by its rounded leaves and delicate, drooping pale blue flowers growing in small racemes.

Campanula persicifolia

Another Bellflower, *Campanula rapunculoides,* or Creeping Bellflower (offered by M. Mahon, a nineteenth-century Scotsman), is the undisputed holder of the title "Scottish Bluebell" in New Scotland (Nova Scotia) and on Cape Breton Island where we live. Who, after all, should know better than the Scots themselves? The plants in my garden came from a friend whose own flowers are descended from the ones that grew in her great-grandmother's garden on our remote peninsula, settled by her forebears from the Scottish Highlands. Although this irrepressible black sheep of the Bellflower family is dismissed everywhere in the plant world as a weed to be avoided in the garden *(Hortus Third)* — for if it is admitted, "you will never know peace again" (Reginald Farrer) — it is cherished here for its association with the early settlers and with the old country itself. Its roots can grow between cracks in cement and come up through gravel, bearing delicate light purple bells all along their length — a lovely weed. Around here, it is a sure sign of a former homestead and is still valued as a garden plant despite its vigorous growth.

There should be room in every heirloom garden for a selection of Bellflowers. They say "old-fashioned" in a very appealing way. A most desirable and seldom-grown type, Clustered Bellflower or Danesblood *(Campanula glomerata)*, deserves more attention. Its straight spikes, with long-lasting purple or pure white blooms into midsummer, grow on sturdy stems that never need staking, in any soil (dry or moist), and in sun or partial shade. The Peach-leaved Bellflower is a back-of-the-border plant, indispensable in early summer among Lupines and Foxglove, Mallows and Dame's-rocket. Canterbury-bells are most effective when grown in groups of one color in places where their pretty bells won't be lost among other lush growth during the summer: either toward the front of the border or in a small bed by themselves, edged with Sweet-alyssum and Lamb's- ears — an unbeatable, easily maintained combination.

Either contender for the title "Scottish Bluebell" can be left to roam in a wild garden or wherever you want an irrepressible groundcover to shade out *real* weeds — say, around deciduous shrubs. The daintier *Campanula rotundifolia*, or Harebell, deserves a place in a sunny rock garden. As for the Creeping Bellflower, put it where you want it to creep — along a gravel walk or against a cement foundation — and you won't suffer from its vigorous nature. Actually, it is no problem to grow in a border because unwanted growth is easily controlled by pulling it out, just as you would a weed. The stems insinuate themselves among other flowers, creating masses of bells where you did not expect them. All the Bellflowers are exceptional cut flowers.

To Grow: Bellflowers grow well in full sun or light shade in ordinary, well-drained garden soil. The plants should be set twelve to eighteen inches apart. Seeds of the perennial type can be sown in late summer in a cold frame to germinate early the following spring. The plants should remain in the cold frame until the following season, then be planted out as early as possible. Seeds of the biennial Canterbury-bells should be sown in a cold frame in early summer and planted out early the following spring, when they will flower early (unlike the modern strains that may flower the first year from seed). Seeds germinate in six to twelve days at 70°F. (21°C.); since they need light to germinate, you should barely cover them. If the plants are cut down before they set seed, they may survive to bloom another year, but you should seed annually to be sure of continual bloom. Divide perennials as needed, about every three to five years. The Peach-leaved Bellflower may need staking in a windy, exposed location.

Collector's Choice:

Campanula glomerata, Clustered Bellflower, Danesblood (1700-1850); deep purple clustered flowers on 2' spikes; early summer-midsummer; Zone 2. 3; 6; 92 (all seeds); 63(p); 62(p).

'Alba'; white. 109; 133; 45 (all plants).

C. medium, Canterbury-bells (1600-1699). Single; old style; clear blue, 2-3'; late spring-midsummer. 3; 5; 18; 147-8; 6 (all seeds).

Single; rose. 3(s).

Single; white. 3(s).

Single; mixed. 3; 6; 87 (all seeds); 66(p); 96(s).

Double; mixed. 19(s).

'Calycanthema' (cup-and-saucer) (1850-1900); mixed. 3; 6; 5; 137 (all seeds); 164(p); 168(s).

C. persicifolia, Peach-leaved Bellflower (1600-1699); blue or white; 3'. early summer; 'Alba'; pure white. 45; 116; 120; 164; 149 (all plants); 92(s).

'Grandiflora'; mixed. 18(s); 104(p); 149(p).

'Telham Beauty' (old style); large single blooms; china blue. 45(p); 6(s); 39(p); 92(s); 20(p); 120(p).

C. rapunculoides, Scottish Bluebell, Creeping Bellflower (1776-1850); summer; 3'. 6(s).

C. rotundifolia, Scottish Bluebell, Harebell, Witch's-thimble (1850-1900); summer; 1-2'; Zone 2. 95(s & p); 24(s); 36; 20; 109; 68 (all plants).

Centaurea cyanus

Asteraceae

1600-1699   ZONES 2-8

Bachelor's-button

Blew-bottle, Cornflower, Hurt-sickle, Ragged-sailor

C. montana

Mountain-bluet

Mountain-bluebottle, Perennial Bachelor's-button, Perennial Cornflower

TYPE: HARDY ANNUAL/PERENNIAL FLOWER
HEIGHT: 1-3'   BLOOM: EARLY SUMMER-
                 FALL
SITE: SUN

The annual and perennial Bachelor's-buttons belong to the very large knapweed genus, mainly native to the Mediterranean region, Near East, and Europe. The annual Bachelor's-button or Cornflower is a branching plant that grows to three feet. Its wiry, silver-leaved stems bear many fringed, brushlike deep blue flowers with prominent white-tipped stamens enclosed in distinctive bracts of tightly over-lapping scales. The perennial Mountain-bluet, as the name sug-gests, is native to mountainous regions of cen-tral Europe. Its broader, tapering leaves are also silvery gray in their early growth, while the deep blue feathery flowers — twice the size of the annual at three inches across — are thinly rayed and spidery, touched with dark red at the center, and somewhat black at the edges. The

Centaurea montana

flowers are variable in color, from blue to shades of pink and white, as are those of the annual Bachelor's-button.

Once known as the Cornflower and Hurt-sickle because it grew among corn and its wiry stems could blunt a sickle during mowing time, annual Bachelor's-button has been grown in gardens for many centuries. Its herbal use was confined mainly to making a blue ink from the expressed juice of the petals. Long a favorite in English cottage gardens, it was planted in the earliest New World gardens, perhaps as a source of ink to write letters back home. Under the right conditions, light snow in late fall draws the "ink" from the deep blue flower heads, a graphic illustration of its older name, Blew-bottle.

The Bachelor's-button has always been appreciated for its bright, long-lasting, frost-resistant blooms and its ease of culture (a child's first garden flower). Jefferson grew it at Monticello, where it began to flower in late spring, probably from fall-sown seeds, among Marygolds (*Calendula*), Yellow Flag Iris, and Sweet Peas — a lovely enough com-bination to repeat in any garden today.

Not the least of its charms was its ability to stay fresh in a bouton-niere, a Victorian-era use preserved in the name by which it is now primarily known — Bachelor's-but-ton. Double and single red, violet, pink, and white types, probably taken directly from natural variations, were grown as early as the seventeenth century in England, but as Stuart and Sutherland point out, "some of the simple but intense blue ones are so handsome that there is rarely any point in using anything else," an opinion well taken in my own garden once I had gone through the color range to my satisfaction. 'Jubilee Gem', a 1937 Silver Medal AAS Winner, is a deep blue dwarf form with double flowers—still popular, I suspect, because of its unequivocal blue, a color "unmatch'd" in any other flower, according to no less a source than the great first-century naturalist Pliny the Elder.

"I expect all gardeners have been offered the blue *Centaurea montana*, when they first started making their gardens," Margery Fish observed. "I was given it from a neglected rectory garden and although I have given it away, pulled it up and treated it brutally, I still have it." So do I (after the same treatment), but I have not only become accustomed to it, I have learned to use it to advantage, perhaps in the same way the English cottagers did when they grew it in their overflowing gardens. I find that when three clumps are grown together, they act as support for floppy-stemmed Oriental Poppies and Garden Lupines, whose mixed colors — flaming reds, blues, and various purples — blend together in early summer, highlighted by the white umbels of Sweet Cicely. If Mountain-bluet is cut back after flowering, its fresh mound of silvery gray leaves will provide interest all season, and the plant will bloom again in the fall, when its deep blue is much valued among the tall white globes of Garlic Chives and 'Orange King' Calendula.

Both Bachelor's-buttons make fine cut flowers. The annual also can be used in dried bouquets, where the deep blue is welcome among the usual understated tones. For this purpose, they should be harvested when the flowers are just beginning to open (they'll open up more as they dry).

To Grow: In warm winter regions, sow seeds of annual Bachelor's-button (lightly covered) in late summer for winter or early spring bloom. Elsewhere, sow seeds outside in fall or early spring for continuous bloom through the late fall months. Space plants ten to fifteen inches apart, with the greater distance producing larger flowers. The process of germination may be speeded up by refrigerating the seeds for five days. Sun and any well-drained, not overly rich soil should produce good results, especially if spent flowers are picked off.

Sow seeds of Mountain-bluet in a cold frame during the spring or summer. Set out the seedlings, twelve to eighteen inches apart, early the following spring, when growing conditions are cool. Cut the plants back after flowering for bushy growth, and divide them at least every two to four years, as the clumps will become crowded.

Collector's Choice:

Centaurea cyanus, Bachelor's-button; deep blue wildflower type; 2-3'. 147-8; 5; 166 (all seeds).

'Emperor William' (described by J.L. Hudson as "the last of the old, tall, single-flowered varieties in existence . . . the closest to the wild plant. . . . Long-blooming, unlike modern types"); deep blue. 6(s); 3(s).

'Jubilee Gem' (pre-1937); double deep blue blooms; 12". 133; 96; 42; 101; 92; 173 (all seeds).

C. montana, Mountain-bluet; deep blue blooms; 2'. 6; 137; 177 (all seeds); 109(p); 20(p).

'Alba'; pure white blooms. 61(p).

❀ *Chrysanthemum parthenium*

Asteraceae
1600-1699   ZONES 3-9   NATURALIZED

Feverfew

Featherfoil, Fether-few, Flirtwort

TYPE: SHORT-LIVED PERENNIAL FLOWER/
    HERB
HEIGHT: 1-3'   BLOOM: SUMMER-FALL
SITE: SUN/PARTIAL SHADE

Feverfew is an upright bushy plant that can grow to three feet but is usually shorter. It has abundant light green, broadly segmented, pungent foliage growing along many branched sprays bearing masses of small daisy-like flowers — yellow button centers, rimmed by a layer of stubby white petals — three-quarters of an inch across. Native from southeastern Europe to the Caucasus, it has

Chrysanthemum parthenium

been naturalized throughout Europe and also grows as a roadside weed in North America. The common name is a corruption of *febrifuge*, from the Latin *febris*, "fever," and *fugere*, "to chase away," a reference to Feverfew's long history of treating fevers and headaches. Garden catalogs may still list this plant under the genus *Matricaria*, from whence it was moved to *Chrysanthemum* (residing before that under *Pyrethrum*); more recently it has been moved to the genus *Tanacetum*. For now, we'll stick with the slightly outmoded nomenclature for simplicity's sake.

It is no wonder that Feverfew was among the herbs grown in early American gardens. It was so highly regarded as an antidote to headaches that it was called "the housewife's aspirin." It was used to ward off melancholy, too. An old cookbook recipe for "the dumps" includes Feverfew, Roses, Violets, Saffron, Rosemary, wine, and cider (the last two presumably in large doses).

Into the nineteenth century, Feverfew was still grown as a medicinal by the Shakers, who by 1850 had two hundred acres of various herbs under cultivation for seed at Harvard, Massachusetts, and Mount Lebanon, New York. Theirs was the first commercial enterprise devoted wholly to herbs and, for many years, the only seed source, as interest in "simples" declined until the herb revival of the 1930s. By 1881 Feverfew was in general circulation as a garden flower, with no reference to its herbal properties except to note that it resembled Chamomile.

The golden-leaved variety known as Golden-feather was used extensively for mass displays in Victorian bedding-out schemes, at least in England — a practice deplored by Gertrude Jekyll in the early 1900s. She warned fellow gardeners, though, not to neglect this fine plant just "because it is so common and so easy to grow." By removing its flowering stems, she dwarfed it and enjoyed the interesting foliage along the front of the border.

The double-flowered white variety, 'Flore Pleno', was described by the late sixteenth century. It smothers the plant in fluffy little pom-poms, with the yellow centers barely evident. I first saw it growing at the Heritage Garden in St. John's, Newfoundland (Memorial University Botanical Garden). The pungent, rather medicinal aroma of the leaves of all types is said to discourage bees, but this does not seem to hamper the production of flowers, produced in masses from early summer to fall whether or not the spent blooms are picked off.

Feverfew is useful in the border to fill in over early-flowering bulbs, as an edging plant (especially if you dwarf Golden-feather as Miss Jekyll did), or in a mixed border among massed deep orange Calendula, Garden Sage (*Salvia*

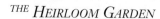

officinalis), and the purple bracts of Annual Clary Sage *(S. viridis)*. All the Feverfews make splendid cut flowers (try 'Flore Pleno' in bouquets with the classic single Calendula); Golden-feather's foliage is especially attractive in arrangements.

To Grow: Sow seeds indoors four to six weeks before the last frost, just pressing them into the soil. Light speeds germination, which should occur in ten to fifteen days at 70°F. (21°C.). Plant the seedlings one foot apart as soon as they have four true leaves, since they are difficult to transplant in maturity. You also can sow the seeds outside in early spring, as soon as the ground can be worked, and again in midsummer. Feverfew grows best in cool weather, so two sowings ensure an early and late crop. In northern growing regions, where summers are cool, the plants will bloom at least by midsummer and well into the fall, so two sowings are unnecessary. The site should be sunny (though Feverfew tolerates partial shade) and the soil fairly fertile and moist but well drained. If drainage is inadequate, the plants may not return the following year. To propagate Feverfew, divide the plants in the spring or cut young shoots from their base in early spring — each with a heel from the old stem — and root them in sandy soil for bloom the first year. When well established, this short-lived perennial should self-seed, ensuring a steady supply of plants.

Collector's Choice:

Chrysanthemum parthenium, Feverfew; 18". 110(p); 177(p & s); 36(p & s); 49; 121; 155 (all plants); 26(s).

'Aureum', Golden-feather (19th century); 12". 110(p); 111(p); 177(p & s); 15(s).

'Flore Pleno'; double white blooms; 2'. 126; 121; 36 (all plants).

Clarkia amoena (*Godetia amoena; G. grandiflora*)

Onagraceae
1800-1850   NATIVE

Godetia

Farewell-to-spring, Satin Flower

C. pulchella

Beautiful Clarkia

C. unguiculata (*C. elegans*)

Rocky Mountain Garland

Clarkia

TYPE: ANNUAL FLOWER
HEIGHT: 1-3'   BLOOM: SPRING-FALL
SITE: SUN/PARTIAL SHADE

Clarkias, annual flowers of the American West, grow from the Rocky Mountains to the Pacific coast and were mostly discovered during the Lewis and Clark Expedition, after whom the genus is partly named. While most gardeners (and seed catalogs) have resisted regarding Godetia as belonging to the Clarkias, it will be so treated here for convenience.

The *true* Clarkia (according to gardeners) is *C. unguiculata* (formerly *C. elegans,*) or Rocky Mountain Garland, aptly named for the plant's habit of producing showy racemes of delicate rose or purple flowers about one inch across all along its long stems, which grow to about three feet. The Beautiful Clarkia is shorter (twelve to fifteen inches), with the same triangular petals ranging in color from bright pink to lavender.

Cultivated forms of both may be double-flowered, with notched or blotched petals, in an extended color range.

Two Godetias are familiar to gardeners. The taller type (to three feet) is Farewell-to-spring, which has rosy purple, satin-petaled cuplike blooms three to five inches across clustered along the stems. The shorter form, Satin Flower, grows to about one foot and has rose-red, satin-petaled cup-like flowers that are blotched at the center. Cultivated forms of these two types may have double flowers and come in varying heights and colors.

All of the Clarkias, whatever their vexing nomenclature, are lovely flowers, sharing narrow-pointed foliage and distinctive pointed buds and seedpods (the latter prized for dried arrangements). Clarkias and Godetias complement each other's blooming period: Clarkias bloom in early summer and Godetias from midsummer through fall.

Clarkias dislike the summer weather that prevails over much of North America, but they continue to be grown and enjoyed because gardeners have been unable to resist their beauty and because late nineteenth-century cultivars from Europe (where most of the breeding of Clarkias is done because of favorable climatic conditions) provided gorgeous variations on the simple wildflower. In 1861, for instance, the French firm Vilmorin introduced Americans to the 'New Double White Clarkia Elegans', which, unlike the sterile-flowered double Petunia, could be reproduced true to form from seed. Between 1890 and 1914, the luscious 'Salmon Queen' was introduced, described in the most glowing terms by Louisa

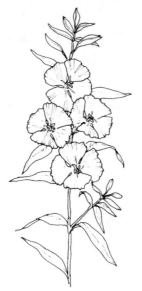

Clarkia amoena

(Mrs. Francis) King, one of the founders of the Garden Club of America, who drew on her own gardening experiences when evaluating various flowers and shrubs for her American audience: "One of the most graceful and remarkably pretty annuals which has ever come beneath my eye" (*The Well-Considered Garden*, 1915).

Until recently, named cultivars enjoyed by gardeners in decades past were unavailable, but the situation is changing with the renewed interest in cut flowers and choice plants from our past. All Clarkias have much to offer on both counts. By growing them carefully with their special needs in mind (protection from very hot summer temperatures), we, too, can have "fields ablaze" with their beauty all season, a phenomenon observed with envy by American visitors abroad in the nineteenth century.

Clarkias (the *real* Clarkias) yield sprays and sprays of flowers for cutting. If you are lucky enough to have a cool greenhouse, they will bloom magnificently all winter long. Consider a cutting bed just for them, but also plant them for early summer bloom in the vicinity of spent bulb plants (Daffodils), where they will cover up nicely. Godetias are highly valued in the light shade of a shrubbery, a welcome change from the ubiquitous Impatiens one so often sees. In my Zone 4 garden, the shimmering mass of satiny blooms never fails to elicit favorable comment and the inevitable question: "What's the name of those pretty flowers?"

To Grow: Clarkias and Godetias should be sown where they are to bloom because they don't transplant well. Just scatter the seeds on top of the soil (they need light to germinate) in early spring, as soon as the ground can be worked. Germination occurs in about a week at 60°F. (16°C.); thin the plants to six to twelve inches apart, depending on their height, and give taller species some support with twiggy brush. For larger sprays of flowers, the taller Clarkias need more room to spread out. The soil should be thin (not too rich or high in nitrogen), somewhat sandy, and well drained. Godetias, especially, enjoy light shade. All Clarkias should be mulched and kept moist during the heat of summer. In Zones 8-10, sow both Clarkias and Godetias in the fall for abundant spring bloom.

Collector's Choice (all sold as seeds):

Clarkia amoena, Godetia, Farewell-to-spring; single blooms; 1½'. 49; 3. Double blooms; mixed colors; 30". 3; 92; 101.

C. amoena, Godetia, Satin Flower; double blooms (old style); 18". The following cultivars in single colors are all available as seeds from the same source (3):

    'Cattleya'; lilac.

    'Maidenblush'; bright rose.

    'Ruddigore'; crimson red.

    'Sweetheart'; blush pink.

    'White Bouquet'; pure white.

    'Satin Cups'; semidouble flowers; 16", 19.

    'Salmon Princess'; frilled Begonia-like flowers; overlaid with orange; 10-12", 92.

    'Single'; close to the wildflower form and beautiful when massed; 12". 5; 101; 168.

C. pulchella, Beautiful Clarkia; double and semidouble blooms; mixed colors; 12-15". 92.

    'Plena' (popular in the 19th century). 18.

C. unguiculata (old style)/*C. elegans*, Rocky Mountain Garland; single wildflower; 2'. 166.

(old style) double Carnation-like flowers; mixed colors. 92; 101; 3. Separate colors are available from 3.

❀ *Clematis* spp. and hybrids

Ranunculaceae
1700-1900   Zones 3-9

Clematis

Type: Perennial Tendril Vine
Height: 8-30'   Bloom: Spring-Fall
Site: Sun/Partial Shade

About 230 species of Clematis (from the Greek *klematis*, "climbing plant") are distributed throughout the Northern Hemisphere, including some beautiful, extraordinarily hardy natives. Most Clematis, except for a few herbaceous types, are tall climbers, twisting their tendril-like leaf stalks around any support. Unlike twining vines, they do not usually do well on single upright supports but require horizontal support, such as latticework, around which they can fasten their tendrils. The fragrant showy flowers, borne profusely either separately or in clusters, vary in shape from urnlike to starlike. These are actually composed of very small flowers surrounded by larger sepals; their colors include white, rose, purple, and shades in between, sometimes striped, as well as a few yellows. Both the handsome foliage — large, toothed, sometimes brilliant in the fall — and the seed heads (in some species the most attractive feature) are ornamental long after the flowers are spent. "*Klem*-a-tis" is the favored pronunciation.

One of the first, if not *the* first, Clematis to be grown in North America was the native *C. virginiana*, American Virgin's-bower. It grows wild in thickets, at the wood's edge, and along streambanks from western Canada and Maine southward, bearing long panicles of small white flowers with prominent stamens and fantastic curled seedpods in the fall, punctuated by purple leaves — quite spectacular.

Eighteenth- and nineteenth-century American gardeners grew wild Clematis until the introduction of hybridized forms. The wild types are similar in that they bear small flowers in profusion, are rapid growers, and, with few exceptions, are suitable for screening with their dense foliage. They also were used for climbing over fences, arbors, porches, and rocky areas. The very popular Sweet Autumn Clematis from Japan, with fragrant sprays of small white flowers in the fall, and Traveler's-joy or Old-man's-beard (for its fluffy seed heads) from Europe, were both used, we are told repeatedly in period literature, for "covering unsightly roofs." Landscape architects of the day considered vines the "draperies" of a house. They were valued not only for climbing on walls and trellises but also for climbing up and over tree stumps, presumably left from clearing one's plot of land. The vigorous wild types were well suited to this purpose.

The Clematis picture changed dramatically in 1858 when the British firm George Jackman and Sons of Woking introduced the first large-flowered hybrid — *Clematis × jackmanii* — a cross between the Ningpo Clematis from China and the Italian Vine-bower from southern Europe and western Asia. The Jackman Clematis, with its large purple flowers, was an instant success and remains so today. It is synonymous with the word *Clema-*

Clematis × jackmanii

tis, vigorous but not so wild as the species, and more manageable for working in small areas. The Jackman was the beginning of the flood of hybrids, many choice heirlooms of which are still available today. More loose and open in habit of growth, shorter, and with fewer masses of foliage than their wild cousins, the hybrids add beauty to any planting with their large, colorful, long-blooming flowers.

My friend Hank, who grows more kinds than he can remember in his Zone 6 garden, plants hybrids to cover the stumps of pine trees he has been clearing away on his two-acre plot — a labor of love extended over thirty years. And, just as the nineteenth-century garden guides advised, Hank's Clematis scrambles over stumps and up trees on chicken wire wrapped around the trees' trunks. They thrive in these conditions, with their feet in the shade and their heads in the sun.

Which Clematis does Hank grow? He pays no attention to their names, but his eighty-five-year-old mother-in-law knows them all, and she says her favorites are the Jackman hybrid and 'Nelly Moser', an English introduction (1897), that is neat in habit with very showy, twice-blooming flowers — pink outside petal edges with a rose-pink center bar. 'Nelly Moser' is virtually carefree and requires no pruning. Whether or not Hank knows the names of his cultivars, his garden overflows with such heirlooms because they give him the desired results: plenty of flowers with a minimum of

Clematis paniculata

trouble. In the case of Clematis, not always the easiest plants to grow, he has met their special requirements with little effort — the way folk gardeners have always met such challenges.

Aside from the various uses of Clematis to screen (wild types) or to climb up trellis supports (hybrids), the latter should be considered for container planting, making them useful in even the smallest garden.

To Grow: Clematis needs to grow in rich, humusy, well-drained light loam on the alkaline side, usually in full sun, though some will take a little shade. The advantage of some of the wild types is that they are especially suited to very dry or moist conditions (see "Collector's Choice"). Dig a hole two to three feet wide and deep, fill it with the prepared soil, and leave it to settle over the winter. In early spring, or whenever the plant is dormant, bury the roots two to three inches in the soil, spreading them out horizontally. If the plant is grafted, it is especially important to bury the union well below the soil so it will establish its own roots. During the first season, remove the flower stems so the plant's energy returns to the work at hand: forming heavy roots.

One way to keep the roots moist in the summer (which is essential) is to plant shallow-rooted annuals such as Petunias at their feet; otherwise, a light mulch will do (a heavy mulch is not recommended because it may promote Clematis wilt). Better yet, place a slab of stone at the base of the plant. A winter mulch of compost or rotted manure will perform the double function of protecting the plant from alternate freezing and thawing, while adding nutrients to the soil. Otherwise, mulch with straw or evergreen boughs, and twice yearly add one handful of balanced garden fertilizer and another of lime around the root area. Plant roots extra deep in containers, burying the

bottom two or three buds for more vigorous development.

A good rule of thumb for pruning is to prune early-flowering types lightly to shape *after* bloom. Severely cut back later-blooming vines to within two feet when the plant is dormant (this type blooms on new growth). Some gardeners leave the old growth as a support for the new growth.

Clematis can be left undisturbed indefinitely. To propagate it, take cuttings from young wood in May or June and root them in a cold frame. Wild types often layer themselves, but they can also be grown from seeds. Freeze the seeds for three weeks, then plant them. Germination takes one to nine months at 70°F. to 75°F. (21°C. to 24°C.). You can also plant the seeds directly in a cold frame in the fall.

Collector's Choice:

Wild Types:

Clematis montana rubens, Anemone Clematis (1900); one of the best E.H. Wilson introductions from China; masses of small pink flowers in varying shades; spring-early summer bloom; 18-24'; Zone 5. 44; 137; 138; 149; 120; 100 (all plants).

C. paniculata, Sweet Autumn Clematis (1864); small white very fragrant flowers in masses; vigorous; evergreen in the South, nearly evergreen elsewhere; late summer bloom; 15' or taller when mature (to 30'). 39(p); 87; 92; 137 (all seeds); 61(p); 153(p).

C. tangutica, Yellow Lantern Clematis, Golden Clematis (1890); yellow lantern-like flowers and silvery pods; late summer bloom; 9'; Zone 5. 86(p); 137(s); 92(s); 34; 114; 169 (all plants).

C. texensis, Red-bell Clematis (before 1924); native; small scarlet urn- or tulip-shaped flowers and fuzzy seedpods; a 5-year-old plant can produce thousands of blooms, each about an inch long; evergreen for southern regions; withstands dry soil; blooms early and late; 6'; Zones 4 and 5 (to Bar Harbor, Maine). 100(p); 87(s).

C. virginiana, American Virgin's-bower (1700-1776); native; small white flowers in masses with fluffy seedpods in the fall; early bloom; withstands wet soil; 18-20'. 108(p); 26(s); 6(s).

C. vitalba, Traveler's-joy (before 1820); greenish white flowers with billowy white fruits; late bloom; 18-20'. 92(s); 108(p); 100(p).

Hybrids:

C. x jackmanii, Jackman Clematis (1858); dark purple velvet flowers; partial shade O.K.; summer bloom; 12'. 167; 169; 133; 61; 33; 153 (all plants).

C. x jackmanii 'Alba' (1878); white flowers. 100(p); 157(p).

'Belle of Woking' (1885); large silvery gray flowers; early bloom; 12'. 45; 31; 100; 114; 160; 134 (all plants).

'Duchess of Edinburgh' (1887); large double white flowers; especially fragrant; early bloom; 9'. 20; 138; 63; 31; 45; 153 (all plants).

'Elsa Späth' (1891); bright blue flowers 8" across; summer bloom; 9'. 45(p); 100(p).

'Lord Neville' (about 1870); dark plum purple striped blooms with wavy edges; blooms almost continuously early to late summer; 8-12'. 100(p).

'Mme. Edouard André' (1892); medium-size red velvet flowers; summer bloom; 8-12'. 163(p); 100(p).

'Mrs. Chomonderlay' (1870); large light blue flowers 8" across; early and late bloom; 8-12'. 69; 100; 138; 164 (all plants).

'Nelly Moser' (1897); pale mauve-pink striped blooms; early and late bloom; 8'. 169; 137; 153; 134; 164; 31 (all plants).

❀ *Convallaria majalis*

Liliaceae
1600-1699   Zones 3-8

Lily-of-the-valley

Convall-lillie, Ephemera, Lily-convally, Liriconfancy, May-lily, Our-Lady's-tears

Type: Hardy Bulb
Height: 8"   Bloom: Late Spring-
                            Early Summer
Site: Partial Shade/Shade

There is either one or three species in this genus, as the three are so much alike that botanists do not agree on the distinctions. They all grow in the Northern Hemisphere, including North America (*Convallaria montana*). Lily-of-the-valley grows from creeping rhizomatous roots and fleshy crowns known as *pips*, which contain the whole flower in embryo. When these are chilled, then exposed to warm temperatures, they grow into the familiar white waxy (and very fragrant) bells that hang down in a graceful line from upright spikes six to eight inches tall. The long green leaves, which also grow from the pip, remain attractive over a long period, making the plant very useful as a groundcover. Variations in the familiar form include pinkish, double, and large-flowered types, as well as variegated-leaf strains.

Lily-of-the-valley has been cultivated since at least 1,000 B.C., making it a true ancient heirloom. Its hardiness and ease of culture, not to mention its fabled fragrance, recommended it to early gardeners who were familiar with the plant from the Old World. Its use as an herb was preserved by the indefatigable Gerard, among others, who reported that "the flores . . . distilled in wine and drunke the quantitie of a spoonful restoreth speech unto those that have the dum palsie and that are falne into the Apoplexie," while other authorities have reported that all parts of the plant are poisonous. This apparently does not extend to the perfume of the flowers, which is extracted and still used to scent various products, including a favorite soap. Essence of Lily-of-the-valley is often used to scent potpourri.

The pinkish type, less well known among gardeners, sparked an interesting controversy beginning in the sixteenth century, when Gerard mentioned having grown both the pink and white forms. He speculated about a red type (like any curious gardener, he would have liked to have grown it in his garden) that was known before 1599 as 'Rubra'. Whether this was indeed red or, as is common in the flower world, a bit of hyperbole, we do not know. Perhaps it was not much different from the pink type with which Gerard was familiar.

Several other gardeners have carried on about the pink form. In the nineteenth century, English writer Shirley Hibberd extolled its virtues, calling it "exquisitely beautiful . . . running hither and thither, mixed with white." In the 1930s, gardener and writer Louise Beebe Wilder stated her opinion, as usual, without beating around the bush: "I do not think it very pretty." Decades later, Henry Beetle Hough recounted the story of how his wife, Betty, dug up the pink type from her childhood home in Uniontown, Pennsylvania, and planted it in the Houghs' new garden in Martha's Vineyard in the 1920s. Neither of them liked the color much, but it was grown, like many plants, for nostalgia's sake. Betty died in 1965, and Henry lived to comment that it continued to bloom in

Convallaria majalis

her memory, as it may still do in his.

Such variations in flowers are a matter of taste. Mrs. Wilder, ever an opinionated gardener, called the double-flowered form "lumpy," while others thought it exquisite, an example of more being better — more flowers, more perfume. Fortunately, the ancient and antique types are still available, and the heirloom gardener is invited to investigate them and form his or her own opinion.

All types of Lily-of-the-valley make a useful groundcover, creating an attractive leafy carpet most of the season, perhaps beneath the shade of an heirloom shrub or two, while the masses of fragrant bells (in whatever form or color) last for almost a month, from about mid-May to mid-June. Planted along a winding path or near an outdoor seat, their scent (which requires no bruising to be released) can be appreciated to the full. Planted in outdoor tubs, they can be enjoyed anywhere you wish, in sun or shade. The cut flowers should be brought into the house without restraint, where they will fill an entire room with their sweetness.

Any of the types are striking when grown outdoors in a strawberry jar. Plant prechilled pips in light, fibrous soil or peat moss, with one pip emerging from each opening. In three to four weeks, after being exposed to temperatures of about 70°F. (21°C.), the flowers will begin to bloom. Discard the pips after blooming or replant them in the ground.

You can force pips indoors during any season by storing them in the refrigerator, then trimming the long roots about halfway back and placing them in a six-inch bowl (ten to twelve pips per bowl) with their tips just showing over the edge of the bowl. Press a mixture

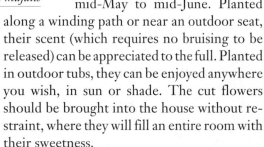

of sand and peat moss around them, fill the bowl with lukewarm water, and place it near light, adding water as necessary. The pips should produce blooms in three to four weeks.

To Grow: Outdoors, plant the roots in the fall about five inches apart in rich, slightly acid, damp but well-drained soil, in partial or full shade. Cover the pips with one inch of soil and leave the planting undisturbed. A yearly application of compost or well-rotted manure (or nothing at all) is all that they need. Propagation is by division after the foliage dies. In growing zones beyond Zone 8, Lily-of-the-valley can be induced to grow in cool microclimates, or it can be forced by prechilling the roots.

Collector's Choice (all sold as plants):

Convallaria majalis, Lily-of-the-valley. 177; 169; 133; 36; 137; 153.

C. majalis 'Flore Pleno' (1770); double white flowers; spreads more slowly than the single-flowered type. 153; 74.

C. majalis 'Rosea' (1830); mauve-pink flowers. 149; 78.

C. majalis 'Variegata' (1870); creamy yellow variegated leaves; needs more sun than green-leaved types. 74.

Cosmos bipinnatus

Asteraceae
1800-1850

Cosmos

Mexican Aster

Type: Annual Flower
Height: 4-6'   Bloom: Summer-Fall
Site: Sun/Partial Shade

Cosmos is a striking annual native to Mexico and Central America. It bears daisy-like flowers, four inches across, with a single row of silky, serrated petals (pink, rosy lilac, deep crimson, or white) overlapping and radiating from a somewhat raised golden center. The flowers grow on tall, branching stems — to ten feet in the wild — with feathery foliage. Cosmos is a short-day plant, which means that it does not begin to bloom until the days get shorter in the fall.

Cosmos was "discovered" in Mexico in 1799, and by 1838 the George Thorburn Seed Company of New York was offering seeds of six-foot 'Late Cosmos' to its customers. More than fifty years later, the late-flowering Cosmos was little changed. In 1891 the Peter Henderson and Company *Manual of Everything for the Garden* offered the same Cosmos, "resembling single Dahlias."

By the early decades of this century, choice cultivars were available: 'Lady Lennox Pink' — "lighting up well at night," we are told — and 'Lady Lennox White'. An 'Early-flowering Mix' (sixty to seventy days) promised earlier blooms, always the subject of discussion in gardening magazines and catalogs, for the long season required to bring Cosmos to flower often meant that it bloomed only a short time before a killing frost.

By 1926 double-flowered types were offered: 'Pink Beauty' ("the center is double with many small petals and a rim of larger outer petals") and 'Extra Early Double Crested' or 'Anemone-flowered', a double crimson type.

In 1930 or thereabouts, a new early strain of Cosmos called 'Sensation' appeared on the market, winning an AAS Gold Medal in 1936. Its introduction radically changed the culture of Cosmos and ensured earlier bloom — fifty-six days after sowing. This strain, or one very similar to it, is still the most popular Cosmos today, considered by connoisseurs to be the choicest type: large (four- to six-inch) single blooms in the classic design, with almost translucent petals; sturdy, somewhat branching (but not rangy) four- to five-foot stems decorated with feathery foliage. Two selections from this strain also have endured: 'Purity', white with a satiny sheen, and 'Radiance', a deep rose with a rich crimson center.

'Sensation' had a huge impact on the cultivation of Cosmos — now considered one of the easiest annuals to grow. Before its introduction, various strategies were recommended to encourage earlier bloom and larger flowers and discourage ranginess, with the inevitable staking that it implied. Gardeners were advised, for instance, to start the plants in the house at the same time as Castor-beans, to sow the seed later in poor soil to dwarf the plants, and to remove some of the buds to encourage fewer and larger flowers. Altogether, 'Sensation' was well named for the gardeners of the day.

Other cultivars have come and gone, but gardeners know what they want in Cosmos —

Cosmos bipinnatus

the simple single-petaled daisy flower with few embellishments. The introduction in the late 1890s of the Yellow Cosmos (*C. sulphureus*) did not diminish the popularity of the taller pink-flowered type — the one that inevitably comes to mind whenever Cosmos is mentioned.

A 1939 Farmer's Bulletin from the U.S. Department of Agriculture advised gardeners to plant Cosmos in broad masses, at the back of the border, against evergreens, or by fences at some distance from the house, "where their special beauty can be appreciated." That is still

sound advice. I like to plant 'Purity' with burgundy Dahlias and mixed China Asters in front of a stockade-style fence that is about six and a half feet tall. There they receive sun for half a day and, protected from the wind, never need staking. Cosmos, mixed with Dahlias and Nicotiana ('Limelight'), are indispensable for fall bouquets. Birds are attracted to the conelike seed heads, which are easy to gather.

To Grow: Plant seeds in warm, well-drained soil, barely covering them, since light helps germination, which takes only three to eight days when soil temperatures reach 70°F. to 85°F. (21°C. to 29°C.). Thin the plants to twelve inches apart. Full sun or partial shade and soil that is not overly rich are the primary requirements. If the plants are protected from strong winds by a fence or shrubbery, staking is not usually required; if it is, use twiggy brush. Self-sown seedlings will bloom earlier, but eventually these will be mostly light pink. It's a good idea to save seeds, especially of the white flowers, since they do not appear to be as vigorous. Keep an eye out for promising sports. I like the variations on the daisy theme, with dark-rimmed centers and noticeably wavy-edged petals, so I carefully keep seeds from these separate to keep this strain alive.

Collector's Choice (all sold as seeds):

Cosmos bipinnatus 'Sensation', Cosmos. 133; 96; 42; 34; 101; 92; 19.
   'Purity'. 6; 92.
   'Radiance'. 133; 6; 101; 87.

Dahlia hybrids

Asteraceae
1850-1900

Dahlia

TYPE: TENDER BULB
HEIGHT: 1-5'   BLOOM: SUMMER-FALL
SITE: SUN

The modern Dahlia has evolved from several species native to the mountains of Central and South America to Colombia, where they grow as perennial shrubs as high as twenty feet, in volcanic soils that provide them with the long season of moisture necessary for their growth (the Aztec name for Dahlia, *acocohxihuitl*, literally means "water pipe"). Dahlias grow from fleshy roots, not true tubers or bulbs, and the plants in their modern form

Dahlia

range from about one foot to five feet and over. They have stiff stems bearing round flowers in varying colors — shades of yellow, red, purple, white, and bicolors — and forms, divided by the American Dahlia Society into twelve groups. Among these are the following types: Cactus **(C),** a profusion of straight or rolled petals, incurved or recurved in varying degrees; Informal Decorative **(ID),** a profusion of generally flat petals, sometimes slightly rolled at their tips, irregularly arranged from the center of the flower head; Formal Decorative **(FD),** many neatly and regularly arranged petals turning back slightly toward the stem; Pompom **(P),** small ball-shaped flower heads with lush petals produced in masses on freely branching stems;

Anemone-flowered **(An),** a single outer row of petals, with a central mat (like a pincushion) of short, tube-shaped petals. Flower sizes vary from less than four inches to more than eight inches (the "dinner plate" type) across. The genus is named for Anders Dahl, a contemporary of Linnaeus, who had hoped to find in the Dahlia a substitute for the potato.

Although introduced late into American gardens, the Dahlia had probably been grown and refined in Mexico by the Aztecs long before it was discovered by the Spanish in 1519. Many centuries passed before it became the focus of breeding, resulting in the flower we recognize today, which bears very little resemblance to the Mexican wildflower. The early hybrids, much to the disappointment of antique plant collectors, have not survived, at least on this side of the Atlantic, where the earliest surviving types can be traced back only to the 1920s. (Early nineteenth-century-type Dahlias at Old Sturbridge Village are modern Dahlias *in the spirit of* older strains.) From what we know, the earliest hybrids were very unattractive and stiff, their colors hard and flat. The more modern hybrids appear to have improved the form for gardeners.

Whatever Dahlias looked like, Americans were wild about them from the beginning because, like Glads, they thrived in the hot summers characteristic of much of North America, providing a succession of bright blooms. Their primary requirements were no more complicated than those of potatoes, which is why they were often paired with them at the end of the vegetable plot. Also, like Glads, they

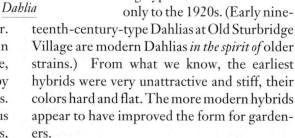

were highly valued as cut flowers.

Joseph Breck, alarmed by this phenomenon, called the Dahlia a "new flower of fancied merit," an opinion that has been proved wrong, thanks in great part to modern breeding. It should be pointed out that, in 1845, Breck's own firm carried, as his catalog proclaimed, "upwards of 200 varieties, including the finest new ones to be obtained in England," selling at two dollars for eight dozen tubers.

The star of the summer and fall flower garden became the focus of my exploration for heirlooms after I'd met several old-time gardeners (interestingly enough, they were all men) who had been growing Dahlias for fifty years or more, often from the same stock, sometimes carefully preserving color strains. The most common types were medium-sized blooms — three to four inches across in the formal decorative class — on medium-tall stems — about three feet tall — and informal decorative types, with larger flowers on taller stems. The oldest strain I found, traced back to the 1920s, came from a gardener, now in his eighties, who had acquired the original tubers when he was seventeen, from the landlady of a boardinghouse that catered to railroad workers.

He had long forgotten the individual names of all these Dahlias and instead referred to them as "The Big Yellow One" or "The Small Red Frilly One." The former was the 1920s strain I dubbed "Old Railroad Yellow," a magnificent primrose yellow informal decorative "dinner plate" Dahlia that I planted in my dooryard garden, where, with no particular attention, it grew to six feet, bearing in late summer nine-inch-wide flowers, the outer petals quite flared back and the inner ones pointing inward. It was fascinating to observe the unfolding of its mass of petals, with each bloom lasting as long as a month. These large-flowered types set the standard for the modern "dinner plates," whose heads are held on sturdy stems that hold up remarkably well even without staking if they are planted in a protected site. Older types simply could not bear the weight of the massive flower heads, and the weak stems needed much propping up.

Making hedges with Dahlias (especially with the smaller flower types) is one of the most satisfying ways to grow them. At the end of the vegetable garden, such a hedge provides an effective and colorful windbreak, thereby encouraging the healthy growth of all the other plants. Planted closer together than usually recommended (about one foot apart), the tubers become jammed together, thus supporting the stiff stems without staking. Gardeners here plant such hedges with hundreds of tubers, sometimes creating long borders that entirely edge their property — a spectacular sight in mid to late summer and through the first light frosts in the fall.

Groups of the same color can be planted among small, immature shrubs, and if their tips are pinched early in the season, the Dahlias themselves will resemble bushy shrubs covered with blooms for most of the summer. Planted in a flower border, the brilliant flowers, particularly the red and bright yellow types, add a dash of color to a plethora of soft pinks and pastels. The taller types must be planted in the back of the border, perhaps against a fence or stone wall for support, where their large flowers show to advantage. The shorter ones can be grouped together by color in containers. These should be well watered and mulched.

To Grow: Dahlias thrive in sun and well-drained soil rich in organic matter, high in phosphorus and potash, and with a steady supply of moisture. Before planting Dahlias, work up and enrich the soil as necessary with decayed manure or compost and a handful of bonemeal for each plant (or a low-nitrogen fertilizer similar to the kind used for potatoes: 8-16-8 or 6-12-12). When the soil is warm, plant the cut tubers, eyes up, in a hole seven to ten inches wide and deep, so that each cut division has one or two eyes and a piece of stem, without which the tuber will not grow. Cover the tubers with two inches of soil. Add more soil to the depression as the plant grows, until the hole is filled in. Space the tubers according to the height of the Dahlias: two to three feet apart for tall types; two feet apart for medium-sized types; fifteen inches apart for short or dwarf types; twelve to fifteen inches apart for hedges. Tall types may need staking, which is best accomplished at planting by placing the stake beside the tuber and driving it into the ground. For bushier plants, pinch off the tip of the main stem as soon as three to four pairs of leaves develop. When the plants are well established, scratch in a balanced fertilizer (5-10-10), watering it in well. Then mulch the plants with two inches of grass clippings or other material that will help conserve moisture during the growing season. More moisture means more blooms.

Cut plentiful bouquets during the summer to keep the plants trimmed. Cut the flowers in the morning and place the stems in two inches of hot water (160°F. or about 70°C.). Leave the flowers in a cool place for four to six hours, then arrange them in fresh water.

To harvest the tubers, wait for several days after a killing frost. (Dahlias will continue to blossom after several light frosts.) Dig them up with a spading fork to avoid puncturing, and place them upside down on slatted trays or boxes, so the dirt falls off and the air circulates around them. When they are dry, shake off the dirt and store them at a temperature of 40°F. to 50°F (4°C. to 10°C.). The greatest source of failure in wintering-over tubers comes from storing them at the wrong temperature. The kind of material you use to store them — sand, peat, or vermiculite — is immaterial. Old-time gardeners store tubers in wooden boxes or bags with no packing material at all, but they know just where they will winter well. Wherever you store them, check them once a month to see how they're doing. They should be plump, not moldy or shriveled up.

To increase your Dahlia supply, you can take innumerable cuttings from the sprouts of the tubers if they are planted indoors early in equal parts of peat moss and vermiculite, barely covered, with bottom temperatures from 65°F. to 70°F. (18°C. to 21°C.). When the shoots are three to four inches high, take cuttings from them by slicing them off from the tuber with a sharp knife and rooting them in vermiculite or sand. Repot them once more and let them grow in containers until all danger of frost has passed. Then plant out the cuttings with the tubers as already described. Although plants from cuttings will not have very large, tuberous roots, they will flower in season with the other Dahlias.

In Zone 10, plant the tubers in late summer for winter bloom.

Collector's Choice:

The following selections and comments come from Arthur Haskins, Dahlia expert and founding member of the Dahlia Society of Nova Scotia. In the Dahlia world, these hybrids are considered "antiques."

Hybrids (all sold as plants):

'Autumn Blaze' (1947); **ID;** a true giant Dahlia, sometimes with blooms more than 12" across; a blend of red and orange; 4'. 25.

'Croydon Masterpiece' (1948); **FD;** another giant Dahlia; bronze color; a top show variety. 25.

'Gerrie Hoek' (1945); **FD;** a personal favorite; a lovely pink Water Lily type; great for cut flowers and basket displays for halls or churches; 4'. **Note:** Water Lily types are almost saucer-shaped, like a true Water Lily, with fewer rows of petals than FDs. 133; 25; 1 30; 85.

'Glorie dan Heemstede' (or 'Glory of Heemstede') (1947); **FD;** a personal favorite; another Water Lily type from Holland; a nice yellow for cutting; one of the top Water Lily types for exhibiting; 4'. 133.

'Kidd's Climax' (1940); **FD;** perhaps the Dahlia that has best stood the test of time; 10" blooms of pink and yellow; despite all the top competition in recent times, it continues to be ranked as one of the best Dahlias in the world; 3-4'. 34; 25; 130; 159.

'Lavender Perfection' (1941); **FD;** about 8" blooms; a beautiful lavender; planted at Old Sturbridge Village to represent an early nineteenth-century type. 133; 25; 34; 160; 171.

'Little Willo' (1935); **P;** dainty white Pompom, still one of the best grown; 15". 25; 85.

'Miss Rose Fletcher' (1948); **C;** a pink Cactus type with 6" blooms; 4'. 25; 130.

'Reedley' (1947); **FD;** a personal favorite; a Water Lily type; orange 5" flowers; good for cut flowers and garden display; 4'. 154; 25; 130.

The following are not on Arthur's list but are historic and choice:

'Betty Anne' (1928); **P;** rose-pink; still a show winner. 66; 154; 25; 130.

'Honey' (1956); **An;** 3-4" flowers with a primrose yellow center and apricot-pink outer petals; great for cutting and bedding; 30". 20; 130.

'Jersey Beauty' (or 'Jersey's Beauty') (1924); **FD;** representative of the type with large (6-10") pink flowers; 5'. 135; 130.

❧ *Dianthus barbatus*

Caryophyllaceae
1750–1800   Zones 4–10

Sweet-William

Bunch Pink, Poet's Pink, Sweet-John

Type: Short-Lived Perennial/Biennial Flower
Height: 1-2'   Bloom: Late Spring
Site: Sun/Partial Shade

Sweet-William is a short-lived perennial or biennial native to Europe and Asia that has been cultivated at least since the early sixteenth century. It is distinguished from other Pinks by its stiff, compact mounds of tightly clustered Phlox-like flowers in brilliant shades of crimson, pink, or white, sometimes banded and edged in contrasting colors, with a dark band around the center of the bloom (referred to as *auricula-eyed*). The petals, single or double, are somewhat toothed or fringed. The jointed stems and glossy leaves lie close to the ground in mats before sending up several flowering stalks the second season. Sweet-William may be naturalized in some areas of North America, growing quite well on its own as a wildflower.

"To praise this flower would be like gilding refined gold," a nineteenth-century writer declared. Single-flowered types were always popular with gardeners, and by the seventeenth century in England, doubles were considered choice. With very little effort, Sweet-William produced bright flowers on stiff stems perfect for bouquets. Some of the older strains were sweetly fragrant like their famous cousins in the Pink family, a characteristic that is lacking in the dwarf annuals today.

Some of the best Sweet-William cultivars

were associated with the efforts of the Scottish Paisley weavers, who took some interest in creating long-stemmed florist flowers. Among these was 'Pink Beauty', which had large trusses of soft pink, clove-scented flowers flushed with salmon on long stems (no longer available). Among the double-flowered types, often referred to as Sweet-Johns, were the "Mule" Pinks, so called because they were sterile (all the flower's reproductive parts having been turned into petals). One of these, perhaps a cross between Sweet-William and Carnations, is the salmon-pink 'Emile Pare', which heirloom gardeners can still grow today (see "Collector's Choice"). If one looks hard enough among the dwarf annual types offered today, several of these old strains, probably from the Victorian era, can still be found. One of these is 'Harlequin', in which each tiny flower opens white and gradually turns red, so that at any time a single cluster shows many different colors, from white and rose to several shades of red. A Dutch friend told me that in the Netherlands Sweet-William is called "Thousand Colors," a reference to this phenomenon.

Because Sweet-William is a short-lived perennial, I didn't expect to find it among the heirloom flowers still growing on our peninsula. I was astonished to find a thriving colony of fragrant, large-flowered, pure white Sweet-William locally that had been growing and self-seeding for more than fifty years. No one could tell me when the colony was first seeded or whether there were colors other than pure white (most likely), but the woman who lived on the farm where they were growing told me

Dianthus barbatus

they were there when she arrived in 1940, growing in what had been her mother-in-law's garden. To establish her own turf, as it were, the woman, then a young bride, had created a garden close to the house, and over the years her mother-in-law's garden had been gradually abandoned. The only remnants were the Sweet-William and one Peony under a clump of trees, cast-offs from the local plant peddler, who couldn't sell them and so gave them to the family that put him up for the night.

To ensure the survival of this extraordinarily hardy Sweet-William, dubbed 'Kathleen's White', I harvested a small number of seeds and raised a group of lusty seedlings, whose seeds in time were passed around to individuals and organizations interested in preserving ornamentals.

The availability of nineteenth-century florist strains in separate and mixed colors suggests a cutting garden just for bouquets in addition to the lavish use of Sweet-William in the flower border for late spring and early summer bloom among Dame's-rocket, Mountain-bluet, and Sweet Cicely. Jefferson grew a crimson type (you can, too) in a circular bed and an oval bed, both adjoining his house at Monticello, among brilliant flowers such as Scarlet Lychnis, Cardinal Flowers, Double Anemones, and Poppies.

To Grow: Sow seeds in a cold frame in late summer for bloom the following year. Cover the seeds with a little soil to encourage germination. This takes seven to fourteen days when the soil temperature is 70°F. (21°C.). Older strains will need no coddling over the winter. Once planted out nine to twelve inches apart in early spring, they may self-sow indefinitely, provided the soil is perfectly drained and moderately rich. If moisture collects around the crowns of the plants in the winter, they will not survive. Mature plants may grow for two or three seasons, but seedlings should always be encouraged. Double-flowered strains can be propagated by "blind shoots," nonflowering stems taken when the plant is in full flower. Root these in a cold frame and plant them out in fall or very early spring, when they will grow best in the cool weather they favor.

Collector's Choice:

Dianthus barbatus, Sweet-William (17th-century type grown by Jefferson); shades of red, pink, and white; bicolors; 2'. 147-8; 18; 168; 3 (all seeds).

'Harlequin'. 87(s); 92(s).

'Holborn's Glory' (by 1926); white with a crimson zone. 3(s).

Old-style Bouquet Strain; pink; 1½'. 5(s).

Old-style Double Ruffle; pink; 1½'. 5(s).

Old-style Double-flowered; mixed colors; 20". 3(s).

'White' (in the spirit of 'Kathleen's White'); extra-large flowers; 20". 3(s). **Note:** The following separate colors and bicolors (auricula-eyed) are available from the same source (3): scarlet crimson; crimson red with white eye; deep salmon; bright scarlet (all 19th-century florist strains).

Hybrid:

'Emile Pare' (1840); double salmon; 1½'. 45(p); 105(p). **Note:** Plants are also available from the Thomas Jefferson Center for Historic Plants (see Sources list, p. 217); no mail order.

Dicentra eximia

Fumariaceae
1850-1900   ZONES 2-9   NATIVE

Fringed Bleeding-heart

Fernleaf Bleeding-heart, Plumy Bleeding-heart, Staggerweed, Turkey-corn, Wild Bleeding-heart

D. formosa

NATIVE

Western Bleeding-heart

D. spectabilis

Bleeding-heart

Lady's-heart, Lady's-locket, Old-fashioned Bleeding-heart, Seal Flower

TYPE: PERENNIAL FLOWER
HEIGHT: 2-3'   BLOOM: SPRING-SUMMER
SITE: SUN/PARTIAL SHADE

Nineteen species of Bleeding-heart are native to North America and Asia, several of which are widely cultivated. Foremost among them is *Dicentra spectabilis* from Japan. This Bleeding-heart, as its Latin epithet suggests, is remarkable. Spreading as wide as it is tall, up to three feet, its arching stems bow to the ground in late spring, laden with dangling racemes of perfectly shaped dark pink, white-tipped hearts of fascinating construction. There are two pairs of flower petals: one outer, forming the heart; the other inner, forming the "drop of blood" as the heart spurs open to reveal the inner stamens. The deeply divided blue-green leaves gradually die back with the rest of the plant, whose growing tips poke through the ground the following spring to begin another extravagant cycle of growth. The white types are elegant, but not as vigorous.

The other two species are native to North America in mountainous areas from New York to Georgia (Fringed Bleeding-heart) and from British Columbia to California (Western Bleeding-heart). These slender plants are valued for their subtle beauty — hearts in racemes dangling over clumps of ferny foliage — and long season of bloom (most of the summer). In the Western

Dicentra spectabilis

Bleeding-heart, the leaves are noticeably grayish, while in both species the hearts are less clearly defined than *D. spectabilis* and rather puffy, coming in shades of mauve, purplish pink, and white. Both types grow rapidly by rhizomatous roots.

One story surrounding the Asian Bleeding-heart is that it was discovered by Robert Fortune in a mandarin's garden on the Isle of Chusan in China around 1848. It seems, however, that it was first introduced to the West in 1810, then "lost" and reintroduced by Fortune. In any case, it was one of the most successful introductions in the gardening world, for by the turn of the century it was already regarded as "old-fashioned" and is still referred to as Old-fashioned Bleeding-heart by many old-time gardeners.

Under optimum conditions, growing in a moist, partially shaded habitat in enriched soil, undisturbed clumps of Bleeding-heart can attain great size — up to thirty feet wide and five feet high (as reported by Stuart and Sutherland).

I have never seen a clump even approaching that size, but I did find one that greatly impressed me with its vigor and air of happiness — that look a plant gets when it is growing just as it likes.

This Bleeding-heart was obviously self-sown, perched on the edge of a deep ravine about thirty feet away from an old abandoned garden, the outlines of which could be just discerned from a row of rhubarb and a languishing Bleeding-heart. The magnificent specimen at the ravine's edge spread in an area about three and a half feet wide and almost three feet tall, literally dripping with pink-scarlet hearts to the ground. The soil was moist and humusy from the fallen leaves of nearby trees. There was filtered shade, but also morning sun, since the scrubby growth and trees around it had not yet completely leafed out. I learned once more from nature itself that many heirloom types, closer to the wild species than more refined and highly bred modern types, occasionally adjust quite well to neglect if they find their preferred habitat. By the time the Bleeding-heart completed its growth cycle, its spot of ground would be covered by the surrounding vegetation, as artful a planting as I would have wished in my own garden, where it is often difficult to achieve such balance.

Both my Fringed and Western Bleeding-hearts came from older gardens, and though I could at first discern little difference between them, the grayish foliage of the latter is special enough to warrant growing both types, especially if the white form of Western Bleeding-heart — with its very distinctive contrast between foliage and flowers — can be found.

Although both types are easy to grow, Western Bleeding-heart is especially recommended where summers are cool and moist. Both are invaluable as a long-season flowering groundcover, since many groundcovers offer foliage only. Either type can be restrained to grow in shade or semishade, among Primroses, Ferns, and Daylilies, or in the sun wherever long-season bloom and foliage is needed at the front of the border as an edging plant.

It's a challenge to find the perfect spot for Bleeding-heart (*Dicentra spectabilis*). Although it is often described as "easy to grow," many gardeners are frustrated by their failure with this plant. In truth, scarcely any plant is always, under all circumstances, easy to grow. The term is relative — easy for you, perhaps, but difficult for someone else. As with any planting, care must be taken to provide the minimum growing requirements, which in this case are moisture and partial shade.

Bleeding-heart makes a fine specimen plant, overplanted with annuals or placed in the corner of a border where its dying foliage is soon covered by other perennials. If you are lucky enough to have a ravine on the premises, try naturalizing Bleeding-heart, as described (though any spot that provides similar conditions will do).

In my garden, Bleeding-heart is glorious mulched in a sea of Forget-me-nots in early summer, combined with pale yellow Tulips (just edged with rose) and my middle-aged Bearded Iris, 'Blue Shimmer'. Tall white Nicotiana fills in nicely for the rest of the summer, right into the fall.

To Grow: Plant any of the Bleeding-hearts in moist, well-drained, humusy soil, in partial shade (the native species take sun well). Space Bleeding-heart (*Dicentra spectabilis*) at least three feet apart and the other types fifteen to eigh-teen inches apart. Bleeding-heart especially thrives where it receives morning sun and afternoon shade. You can sow seeds of any of the Bleeding-hearts in a cold frame in the fall to flower the following season, but propagation is more easily accomplished by simple division of the clumps every three or four years after blooming or when the plants are dormant. *D. spectabilis* can be left undisturbed if it seems happy. I have successfully transplanted it (a chunk from an established clump) in bloom with a good ball of earth around the roots. In Zones 8-10, *D. spectabilis* is short-lived and needs to be grown as an annual. Since white forms of Western Bleeding-heart are hard to come by, keep an eye out for sports.

Collector's Choice:

Dicentra eximia, Fringed Bleeding-heart. 20; 141; 34; 63; 115 (all plants).

'Alba'; white. 45; 111; 74; 149; 164 (all plants).

D. formosa, Western Bleeding-heart. 45; 61; 153; 127 (all plants); 92(s); 125(s).

D. spectabilis, Bleeding-heart; 137(p & s); 167; 169; 153; 136; 34 (all plants).

'Alba'; white. 167; 97; 114; 56; 44; 31 (all plants).

Digitalis purpurea

Scrophulariaceae
1700-1750   ZONES 4-10   NATURALIZED

Purple Foxglove

Bloody-fingers, Common Foxglove, Dead-men's-bells, Fairy's-cape, Fairy's-glove, Fairy's-hat, Fairy's-thimbles, Folk's-glove, Foxglove, Gloves-of-Our-Lady, Virgin's-glove, Witches'-gloves

TYPE: BIENNIAL HERB/FLOWER
HEIGHT: 4-5'   BLOOM: EARLY SUMMER
SITE: SUN/PARTIAL SHADE

Purple Foxglove is one of about nineteen species of *Digitalis* native to Europe and northwest Africa to central Asia. During the first season of growth, it forms a rosette of light green, tapered, somewhat downy leaves that send up, during their second year, tall stalks to five feet bearing large, hanging bell-shaped flowers. The flowers are one and a half to two and a half inches long and come in shades of purple and white, usually speckled with maroon at the throat. The spots attract bees and hummingbirds, thus ensuring the fertilization of the flowers and prolific seed production, which explains in part Foxglove's ability to naturalize as a

Digitalis purpurea

garden escape in North America. A vast literature surrounds the many folk names (only partially listed here), which refer to the glove-shaped flowers (worn by the fox to soften his tread when approaching the chicken pen!). It has also been suggested that the name is derived from the Anglo-Saxon *foxes-gleow*, a musical instrument of arching form hung with bells, like Purple Foxglove in full bloom. The genus name is more straightforward, having been derived from the German word *fingerhut* — literally "finger-hat" or "thimble," a reference to the flower's shape — translated into Latin as *Digitalis*, from *digitus*, which means "finger."

Purple Foxglove is an English wildflower, cultivated in cottage gardens since at least the fifteenth century. It was not grown in American gardens until the eighteenth century. Since

ancient times, Foxglove has been considered beneficial for healing bruises, but it wasn't until the late 1700s that an English doctor, William Withering, described the powerful alkaloid in its leaves — *digitalin* — and proved its medicinal value as a heart stimulant.

Dr. Withering sent Purple Foxglove seeds to a doctor in New Hampshire, who, in 1789, sent seeds to another doctor in Boston, with the advice "to try of its efficacy" and to grow it "as a beautiful flower in the garden," which is how Americans have been growing it, possibly since the early 1740s. Digitalin in pill form is still manufactured and used as a heart stimulant.

The elegant white form 'Alba' was offered in Joseph Breck's 1838 and 1884 seed catalogs, a testimony to its enduring popularity (especially striking among Old Garden Roses and for bouquets). In the late 1800s, the Reverend Henry Wilkes (of Shirley Poppy fame) produced his large-flowered strain, 'Giant Shirley' (named after his village), the result of selection and reselection and breeding among variants of the common wildflower. How I would love to have had a glimpse of his garden of variant Corn Poppies and Purple Foxglove on their way to becoming the flowers of his dreams. In the case of Foxglove, 'Giant Shirley' had large, bell-shaped flowers in the classic design — closely packed on sturdy stems up to five feet high, facing down at a 60-degree angle to the stem — in an extended color range — white, dark rose, purple, maroon, and crimson, all heavily spotted. A luscious 'Apricot' cultivar, produced in England probably in the early 1900s, adds another color to the repertoire of variations on the classic Foxglove theme, one that was altered in the 'Excelsior' hybrids introduced by 1950. In these, the florets, facing outward rather than downward, are borne all around the stem. As for the wide-open Gloxinia forms (*Digitalis purpurea* 'Gloxiniiflora'), they are so different in appearance from the fabled glove-shaped flowers that it is difficult to consider them as belonging to the same group of plants. They may be beautiful in their own right, but to me they don't say "Foxglove."

Foxglove is another of those "easy-to-grow" plants that many gardeners, including myself, have had difficulty establishing. How frustrating to raise healthy seedlings with all the promise of future bloom, only to have them die over the winter. Until I learned the secret of success, I killed many generations of seedlings, generously supplied by my neighbor, who did nothing at all to encourage their springing up around the basement of her house every year.

One spring I found a large population of Purple Foxglove naturalized at the edge of a road on forested Skye Mountain, unpopulated since the early 1940s. At first they weren't apparent among great sheets of white Bunchberry flowers, brushy Raspberries, Goldenrod, and Ferns, but getting down on my hands and knees, I suddenly saw their healthy, downy leaves everywhere — first- and second-year plants. Here, where they were virtually smothered in weeds in unfertilized ground, they thrived, while in my garden, where I had coddled them, I had known nothing but failure.

Later in the summer I returned to see the Foxglove in full bloom: tall stalks with masses of bells — all variants of purple, pink, and white and heavily spotted — towering over brushy plants and weeds, totally at home in gravelly soil in partial shade or full sun on a slight incline. I gathered ripened seeds, sowed them in my cold frame, and the following year planted the healthy clumps in a slightly raised bed in the sun, the soil lightened with gritty sand. Skye Mountain Foxgloves now self-sow in my garden from year to year, though not as prolifically as those I saw growing *au naturel* (in which case there would be no room for anything else in my garden). There are enough, though, to make a good show in early summer among Bellflowers, Oriental Poppies, Mountain-bluet, and Lupines. The tall stalks, especially the white form, are distinctive among low-growing shrubs, to be followed by Regal Lilies. Where Foxglove can be grown in light or full shade (where summers are very hot and drainage is perfect), they are lovely companions for Hostas and Ferns, as well as Bleeding-hearts (any type).

Foxglove is a striking and long-lasting cut flower. If you have the room, try naturalizing Purple Foxglove on a sunny or partially shaded bank where they can self-seed from year to year. Even out of flower, the downy leaves are attractive for much of the season.

To Grow: Purple Foxglove and its variants can be grown in Zones 4-10, except in Florida and along the Gulf Coast. Where early summer is hot, plant Foxglove in partial or full shade and always in well-drained ordinary garden soil on the light side. The primary cause of winter kill is from moisture gathered around the leafy crowns in winter. If you are in doubt about drainage, work in some gritty sand and mound the area where you plant the clumps, about fifteen to eighteen inches apart. Cut down the stalks after they have flowered, unless you want to collect seeds from choice colors. Once established, Foxglove should self-seed. The 'Giant Shirley' strain will need to be reseeded (with purchased seeds) if the range of colors is reduced over the years, a process that can be controlled if you take pains to thin out the more vigorous wild strains (pinks and purples). You can take stem cuttings from the 'Apricot' strain to keep it pure (plant these anytime during the summer in a cold frame).

To grow Foxglove from seeds, sow the seeds in a cold frame in mid- to late spring. Very early the following season, plant out the clumps, which should blossom in the summer.

Collector's Choice:

Digitalis purpurea, Purple Foxglove. 18; 147-8; 6; 177; 143 (all seeds); 36; 116; 133 (all plants).

'Alba'. 18; 92; 15 (all seeds); 45; 20; 149 (all plants).

'Apricot'. 92(s); 15(s).

'Giant Shirley'. 3(s); 6(s); 138(p).

Gladiolus spp.

Iridaceae
1800-1900

Corn-flag

Sword-lily

Gladiolus hybrids

1900-1958

Glad

TYPE: TENDER BULB
HEIGHT: 1-5'   BLOOM: SUMMER
SITE: SUN

More than two hundred species of Corn-flag are distributed over South Africa, Europe, and the Mediterranean area. These grow from round, flat, bulbous roots, or corms, that shrivel and die over the course of one growing season, producing offspring to carry on the growth of the plant. The flowering spikes, rising to about three feet, bear small, bright, funnel-shaped flowers — often deep red or yellow — opening in succession from two-valved spathes, or bracts. The modern hybrids — large ruffled flowers in many colors produced in great numbers on a single stem — are almost unrecognizable as the simple, graceful wildflower. The Corn-flag's long, narrow, swordlike leaves are preserved in the genus name, derived from the Latin *gladius*, meaning "sword."

We tend to think that Glads are a recent phenomenon, and in a sense they are, having been developed since the early decades of this century. But the wild Corn-flag, from which the modern flowers have been developed, was grown in the earliest American gardens, from the seventeenth through the nineteenth centuries. Lady Skipwirth of Virginia, a curious and dedicated eighteenth-century gardener, listed Corn-flag as among those "Flowers for Mrs. Boyd": the Yellow and Tawny Daylily, English Cowslip, and Lily-of-the-valley. She grew *Gladiolus communis*, introduced from Europe in the eighteenth century, with its loose spikes of bright purple flowers curving outward from narrow stems about two and a half feet high.

By the nineteenth or twentieth century, other species were introduced, among them the very hardy *Gladiolus byzantinus* (Hardy Glad) from Turkey. This Glad, growing two to three feet high, has magenta red flowers and is sometimes found naturalized near graveyards. Several important species and types had been introduced by 1900, and these became important in the breeding of the modern Glad. The first ruffled sort appeared in 1911, by which time the race was on. Thousands of cultivars were produced, bred for bigger flowers, more flowers per stem, and an ever-wider range of colors. Glads, like Iris, are accommodating subjects for plant breeding because they readily hybridize. These Glads were prized for their adaptability throughout North America, blooming in Florida during the winter months and in the Northeast, from wintered-over corms, during the summer. Their ease of culture, bright flowers (especially valued for cutting), and instant popularity encouraged the breeding of new cultivars, each one slightly different to the experienced eye, with the result that "new" became (and becomes) "old" and obsolete in a very short time.

Commenting on this development, Mrs. King remarked, "In looking over the Cornell list of 1916 it is surprising to see how few of the named varieties have survived in the average lists of the day." She goes on to mention their names (long vanished from the marketplace): "'Panama', a lovely tone of warm pink . . . . 'Baron Hulot', always conspicuous for its rich violet, 'Alice Tiplady', 'Mary Virginia', 'Maiden Blush', 'Orange Queen', 'Salmon Beauty'. . . the earliness, the grace, and delicate yet glowing colours of this tribe commend it everywhere, and in the South as well as the North they are treasures for gardens."

Like Iris, antique Glads are defined as those introduced by or prior to 1960, and considering the speed with which cultivars appear and disappear from the market, this is a reasonable definition. Among the thousands that over the years have been bred and offered for sale, there are good, bad, and indifferent plants, as well as superior ones. Unfortunately, we can no longer evaluate most of them, since most are no longer available, unlike antique Iris, many of which are still carried — true to type — by specialty nurseries. So how do we

Gladiolus byzantinus

know which are the choice Glad heirlooms?

As Grant Wilson, general editor for the Canadian Gladiolus Society, told me, the society is always evaluating and reevaluating Glads through a comprehensive rating system. A drop in their ratings, he observed, results not so much from the introduction of better varieties, but from the fact that the older varieties have deteriorated. That is, they are no longer the plants they were when they were first introduced, having changed in form or color over many years of propagation.

He also pointed out that many Glad fanciers still consider two cultivars — 'Picardy' and 'Violet Charm', long out of the annual rating — to be the greatest of all time. Both were produced in Canada, where breeding has a long tradition (which is why the society is one of the world's oldest Gladiolus organizations). 'Picardy' was introduced by Dr. Palmer of Vineland, Ontario, in 1931, and 'Violet Charm' was introduced by Milton Jack, the son of Canadian garden writer Annie Jack, in 1953. Another of Jack's introductions, the 1945-46 AAS winner 'Dawn Glow', has survived the fierce Glad competition (see "Collector's Choice," below).

"If 'Picardy' and 'Violet Charm' could be grown today as they were for several years after their introduction," Wilson noted, "they would very probably be in the present top 10 or even right at the top overall. . . . Someone, somewhere may still have 'Picardy', 'Violet Charm', or others which they have grown for forty-five years or so and from which they have planted and multiplied only the best." This is, of course, what heirloom gardening is all about, and one only hopes that these antiques can be preserved for future gardeners to enjoy. If you already grow Glads, you may have an older type you cherish for its dependability and special beauty. If not, ask around the gardeners' network, and you may find a gem — maybe even the fabled 'Picardy', described in a 1945 catalog as having very large shrimp pink flowers and offered for a dollar a dozen (as corms). Otherwise, check out my brief list of survivors to compare with the latest introductions.

It has been observed that great breeders such as Childs, Coblentz, Vilmorin, Van Fleet, and Groff took a despised semitropical plant with insignificant flowers and developed it into a magnificent creation with waxy blossoms as wide as a man's hand. I admire the hybrids, but I am one of those who also looks with favor on the old Corn-flag that charmed Lady Skipwirth, for it possesses a simple grace that is lacking in the stiff, highly elaborated hybrids. The wild types are lovely if left in the ground to multiply and naturalize (where conditions permit). Similar in habit to wild Iris, they form a bright mass of color and swordlike foliage for most of the season.

A perennial question among gardeners is where to plant the modern Glad. The tried-and-true strategy of two end rows in the vegetable garden, perhaps alongside Dahlias, is a straightforward, honest solution and should not be dismissed, for the flowers add color to the garden, make a dramatic border, and are close at hand for cutting (one of the Glad's chief claims to fame).

As Mrs. King maintained, however, "This flower, old yet ever new, is susceptible of the most exquisite treatment in the right hands." So I include her advice for finding the Glad's proper companions in the flower border: "When the gladioli are all in bloom, cut a few spikes, label them, and after rain, when the ground is soft, take these hither and yon

throughout the garden, holding now one and another against a flower which may seem to provide for it a lovely foil." Make a note of this match for next season.

Gertrude Jekyll, with whom Mrs. King carried on a lively correspondence, did not hesitate to include bright Hybrid Glads in her famous color-coordinated borders. In the late summer border, for instance, she included dark red Hollyhocks and Dahlias, Phlox, scarlet and orange Nasturtiums, and scarlet Glads, backed by Golden-glow — a planting that is worth repeating. She also planted wild Glads (*G. x colvillei*), set in tubs, next to the house. Other suggestions include planting eight to ten of the same color in front of hedges, among low-growing shrubs, or in the perennial border to fill in after early-flowering bulbs.

To Grow: Glads thrive in enriched, sandy loam that is on the light side. Work compost, leaf mold, or peat moss into the soil in the fall. For a succession of bloom throughout the summer, plant the corms at intervals from the last frost in spring into early summer (during the month of June). Plant them in full sun, four to six inches apart, and cover them with four to six inches of soil. When the plants are a foot high, start hilling up the soil around their base to about six inches, to support the stems; otherwise, the large-flowered types will probably need staking. Mulch around the plants with a one-inch layer of grass clippings to conserve moisture throughout the season. To encourage prolific flower production, scratch in some 5-10-5 fertilizer (at a rate of one cup per twenty-five-foot row) around the plants when the spikes appear, watering the fertilizer into the soil. After the foliage yellows or after frost, lift out the corms, cutting off the fresh corms close to the old ones, and dry them in the sun for an hour or so before storing them at 40°F. to 50°F.

(4°C. to 10°C.) in an old nylon stocking or onion bag to provide good air circulation. Save the cormels (little corms) and plant them out the following season if you like. They take two seasons to produce flowers. In Zones 8-10, you can leave the corms in the ground, but for better flower production of the hybrid types, follow the preceding directions.

For cut flowers, cut the flowering stems in the early morning when just one or two flowers have begun to open. Be sure to leave at least four or five leaves per stem to feed the corms. Wild Corn Flag is highly desirable for cutting as well.

Collector's Choice (all sold as corms):

Gladiolus byzantinus, Hardy Glad; Zone 5. 137; 162; 170.

'Albus'; white; especially recommended for cutting. 114.

G. carneus; bicolored light pink and crimson; 2'; Zone 7. 108.

G. x *colvillei* 'Albus', Colville Glad; white; 2'; Zone 7. 45.

G. x *gandavensis*, Breeder's Glad; red, streaked yellow; parent of many hybrids; 2½'; Zone 9. 108.

Hybrids (3-5'; medium-sized flowers are about 3½" across; large flowers are about 4½" across; giant flowers are 5½" or larger across):

'Dawn Glow' (1945-46); large, heavily ruffled, bright purple-pink flowers with a white throat. 133; 31; 160; 34; 71.

'Glacier' (1959); large white flowers. 135.

'Green Woodpecker' (1953); medium-sized green flowers with purple markings; early bloom; rated number 4 in the top-rated Glad antiques at the 1990 symposium of the Canadian Gladiolus Society. 171.

'Oscar' (1958); giant dark reddish pink flowers. 96; 114; 171.

'Peter Pears' (1958); large, ruffled apricot-red or dark orange flowers; early bloom. 133; 114; 165; 171.

'Spic and Span' (1946); large salmon-rose flowers. 135; 171.

Hemerocallis fulva

Liliaceae
1600-1699   ZONES 2-10

Orange Daylily

Corn Daylily, Daylily, Fulvous Daylily, Tawny Daylily

❀ H. lilioasphodelus (H. flava)

Lemon Yellow Daylily

Custard Lily, Lemon Daylily, Lemon Lily, Lily Asphodel, Yellow Daylily, Yellow Tuberose

---

TYPE: HARDY BULB
HEIGHT: TO 3'   BLOOM: SUMMER
SITE: SUN/PARTIAL SHADE

About fifteen species of Daylilies from Europe and Asia, especially Japan, belong to the large Lily family, from which come some of our most beautiful garden flowers — Lilies, Tulips, and Hyacinths. Daylilies form clumps of narrow evergreen foliage and spread by tuberous rhizomatous roots, which send up tall, bare stalks — as high as six feet in the wild — bearing lilylike trumpets in branched clusters. Although each flower blooms for only one day, continuous color is ensured by the production of many buds. The Orange or Tawny Daylily is a vigorous species with large flowers about five inches across — orange with darker zones and stripes in shades of red and mahogany — giving the effect of a tawny color, preserved in the Latin epithet *fulva*. The less vigorous Lemon Yellow Daylily is shorter, growing to three feet or less, with smaller flowers and grasslike foliage. It is highly regarded for its more delicate form and lemon yellow, sweetly scented trumpets, about four inches across. Its former Latin name, *Hemerocallis flava*, refers to its yellow flowers, while its current name, *H. lilioasphodelus* (actually an older name) describes its asphodel-like roots and lilylike blooms. The wonderfully descriptive genus name, *Hemerocallis*, is derived from the two Greek words *hemeros*, "day" and *kalos*, "beautiful."

In Asia, where Daylilies have been cultivated for thousands of years, they are regarded as a source of food and medicine. The flowers are picked fresh and fried in batter or dried and used to thicken soups. Preparations from the plant are used to relieve jaundice and dropsy and to reduce fever and pain. In Europe and the New World, the Daylily has always been cultivated for its beauty alone. The Lemon Yellow was a special favorite in English cottage gardens. Both the Orange and Yellow Daylily were brought to the New World during the seventeenth century and widely cultivated across the land. The more vigorous Orange remains a faithful signpost to many heirloom plant collectors, who know that where it grows, an old garden cannot be far away.

Until the late nineteenth century, these two species were the only ones grown in America. By 1860 a double form of the Orange — crowded with petals — was introduced from Japan, where it had been noticed by European

Hemerocallis

travelers since about 1712. In 1865 a variegated leaf form (with white-striped foliage) was introduced. Both of these were known as 'Kwanso' types, presumably after their place of origin. In 1897 a new Orange, 'Maculata', was added to the pool of Daylilies, this one offering later bloom and larger flowers with a deep bronze patch on each petal.

These species liked their new home, where they found growing conditions especially suitable for their cultivation. It was a reciprocal affair: Americans loved Daylilies for their ease of culture, midsummer bloom (at a time when other flowers languish from the heat), and beauty of form.

By the 1920s, America had become the leading center for hybridization, the goal being the creation of ever-new types with larger flowers of diverse forms — wavy, frilled petals, for instance — an expanded color range, and a longer blooming period. The old Orange, naturalized along roadsides across the country, was one of the leading contributors to the breeding process. Although a seed-sterile triploid, its pollen was used to crossbreed with other species. In 1929 the noted hybridizer A.B. Stout attached the cultivar name 'Europa' to it, by which it is sometimes sold today.

By 1970 twelve thousand cultivars had been registered with the American Hemerocallis Society; since then at least eight hundred new types have been added each year, inevitably resulting in the disappearance of older forms. Any that have survived the incredibly tough competition of the marketplace (as is the case with Glads, Iris, and other greatly hybridized types) are especially noteworthy. Among these is 'Hyperion', developed by Franklin B.

Mead around 1925. Many consider this Daylily unsurpassable within its type: a majestic four feet high with large, very fragrant, wide-open, clean-cut canary yellow blooms with a green-flushed throat and prominent golden stamens. Older plantings of this are often mistaken for the daintier Lemon Yellow, pure strains of which are now increasingly rare.

Having been dug up extensively from naturalized stands that take longer to establish than the Orange, the Lemon Yellow is not seen as often as the Orange, either as an escape or in old gardens. I became aware of its precarious condition several years ago when Bernard S. Jackson, curator of the Memorial University Botanical Garden in St. John's, Newfoundland, and the driving force behind the preservation of old ornamentals in Canada, sent me a box of roots of sixteen perennials from his Heritage Garden (where every plant is grown from actual plants found in local gardens planted before 1940). Among these were two carefully labeled bags of *Hemerocallis fulva* and *H. flava*, "120 years plus." Having been delayed in the mail over a week, I did not think either would bloom that season, already well advanced by early June. Nevertheless, I planted the Daylilies in a specially prepared bed and was astonished when the Orange shot up and bloomed on time in early July. I was very curious to see what the blossoms of an Orange Daylily, grown from 120-year-old stock, would look like, so I anxiously peered into a newly opened flower: deep orange flared-back petals with mahogany stripes, exactly like the ones blooming in my sixty-plus-year-old patch. Gorgeous! What I learned is that the Orange or Tawny Daylily, often taken for granted as a weed, is a most beautiful flower.

By contrast, the old Lemon Yellow, assuredly the much sought-after *lilioasphodelus* (from its date of origin in the garden and its remote circumstances), has not yet bloomed after two seasons of growth, though the leaves are thriving. It obviously requires more care than the Orange to put forth its fabled flowers. Fortunately, plant nurseries are beginning to rise to the demand for a return of this exquisite flower, which some Daylily fanciers consider the choicest of all for its purity of color and unmatched fragrance, but it is often difficult to sort out the different plants that masquerade under its name.

The Orange Daylily is very useful to hold soil on steep slopes or to naturalize in sun or partial shade wherever an all-season groundcover is needed. I have found glorious fields of them by garden remnants, thriving without any care at all. I plant it as a no-care border for one of our rustic log cabins. Planted in semi-shade, it never fails to put forth plentiful blooms for over a month during the summer. The decaying foliage provides a permanent mulch and source of nourishment. It should be noted that the older, unimproved species are virtually maintenance-free and very hardy. Any of the Daylilies make handsome border plants. The old Lemon Yellow is lovely planted beside blue Bearded Iris, both of which bloom at the same time. I have seen effective plantings of Lemon Yellow with Ribbon Grass as a garden room divider. Grown as accent plants, the Daylily's leaves are attractive all season long, unlike many other flowers that, when their blooms are spent, "seem to lose ambition and more or less go to pieces," as one astute garden writer has observed.

To Grow: Daylilies grow in almost any soil but thrive in well-drained, fertile soil enriched with leaf mold or compost, in sun or partial shade. Set the tubers with their crowns one inch below the soil's surface, eighteen to twenty-four inches apart. The old Orange and Lemon Yellow can remain undisturbed for years; newer types should be divided and replanted every three to six years, or when they appear to lose their vigor. Propagation is easily accomplished by division of the tubers.

Collector's Choice (hardy to Zone 2; all sold as bulbs or tubers; * indicates fragrant types):

Hemerocallis fulva, Orange Daylily; midseason bloom. 61; 66; 52; 151; 108.

* *H. lilioasphodelus (H. flava)*, Lemon Yellow Daylily; early bloom. 174; 61; 66; 115; 108.

H. middendorffii, Amur Daylily; pale orange flower clusters; early bloom; 1-3'. 61; 174; 44.

* *H. minor*, Grass-leaf Daylily; valuable rock-garden plant with copper-yellow fragrant flowers; dwarf form; early bloom. 108.

Hybrids (hardy to Zone 3; all sold as bulbs or tubers):

'Caballero' (pre-1953); bicolored rose-yellow; early to midseason bloom; may bloom again in the fall; 3'. 37.

'Goldenii' (1929); deep golden orange; 3'. 108.

* 'Hyperion'; very fragrant; midseason bloom. 160; 20; 84; 115; 149; 142.

'Kwanso', 'Kwanso Flore Pleno'; double orange flowers with bluish green foliage; midseason bloom; 40". 37; 149; 45.

'Kwanso Variegated'; less vigorous. 37.

'Maculata'; similar to *H. fulva*, with larger flowers and pronounced red-purple bands; late bloom. 108.

* 'Mikado' (1930s); large golden yellow flowers with mahogany blotch at base of each petal; early bloom, recurrent in fall; 3'. 64.

'Pink Charm' (pre-1953); coral pink with orange throat and pink stamens; midseason bloom; 4'. 133; 142; 169.

'Tangerine' (1877-1920s); the first recorded *Hemerocallis* cross, by British school-teacher George Yeld; semidwarf; dark orange flowers with red buds; early bloom. 149.

'Valiant' (1920s); orange, spider-shaped flowers; midseason bloom. 149.

❀ *Hesperis matronalis*

Brassicaceae

1600-1699   ZONES 4-9   NATURALIZED

Dame's-rocket

Damask-violet, Dame's-violet, Evening-rocket, Garden-rocket, Mother-of-the-evening, Rogue's-gilliflowers, Queen's-gilliflowers

TYPE: SHORT-LIVED PERENNIAL/BIENNIAL
      FLOWER
HEIGHT: 2-3'   BLOOM: SPRING-SUMMER
SITE: SUN/PARTIAL SHADE

Dame's-rocket is a sweetly fragrant member of the Mustard Family, long valued as a garden flower. Native from southern and central Europe to Siberia, it is widely naturalized in North America, especially in damp meadowland. It may grow to three feet or more and has many branched stems bearing toothed leaves (larger near the bottom of the plant) and loose terminal clusters of four-petaled, Phlox-like flowers. The blooms, three-quarters of an inch across, come in purple, dark pink, lilac, and white and have a wonderful clove scent that is evident in the evening air, when they attract moths for pollination. The distinctive cylindrical seed capsules are upright, like long, slender bean pods (similar to those of the other Rocket, *Eruca sativa*, the salad green, to which it is related). The genus name is derived from the Greek *hesperos*, "evening star," an apt reference to the flower's starring role in the night garden.

Although Gerard and other herbalists have recommended using the distilled water from Dame's-rocket flowers to induce sweating, this plant has been mostly appreciated for its beauty and evening perfume. The fabled double-flowered white Dame's-rocket familiar to Gerard, with foot-high spikes of sweet double blooms, was commonly grown in seventeenth-century English cottage gardens and had reached the New World by 1725, when Lady Skipwirth grew it with English Cowslips, Columbine, Sweet-William, Hollyhocks, and Monkshood. The single flowers in mixed colors have been grown in America since the 1600s.

Although the double white was still being offered by Joseph Breck in the mid-nineteenth century, by 1884 double whites and double purples had vanished from commerce on this side of the water. An English friend reports having found a double white recently at a plant sale. It was not in the best condition at the end of the day, but she grabbed it up and took it home at once to plant in her garden. "We would all like to grow it," noted Margery Fish, who once having gotten it from a cottage gardener, could not keep it (it must be reproduced from cuttings). Just in case you should ever find it, follow Gertrude Jekyll's sound advice in such matters: "The massive spikes of double flower necessarily exhaust a good deal of the strength, and the plant remembers that it was originally only a biennial; but at the base of the flowering stem there are always one or two tufts of young green growths; these must be carefully taken off and grown on separately to form flowering plants for the next year" (*A Gardener's Testament*, 1937).

Writers of the past recorded double pink Dame's-rockets, as well as double reds and even a striped form. Like any curious gardener, I would like to grow these types (especially the legendary white, a source of mystery and desire), but I am thankful to have the singles in assorted shades of lilac, purple, a nice dark pink, and pure white, so easy to grow in the border or to naturalize in a spot of damp ground with wild Iris (Blue and Yellow Flag) and Bouncing-bet or in partial shade at the edge of the woods, taking care of itself from year to year, quite happy in the cool, humusy soil. In the more formal plantings of a flower bed proper, I let Dame's-rocket sow where it will among Lupines, Foxglove, Mallows, Bellflowers, Sweet-William, and Clary Sage. It softens and complements the brilliant blooms of Oriental Poppies. I make a point of strolling by the gardens in the evening, so I can enjoy its delicious clove scent.

Frequent cutting for bouquets helps to keep the plants in trim and prolong their blooming. Once they are established, you will have short-lived perennials (two or three years old) growing with one-year-old plants and little seedlings, resulting in almost continuous bloom.

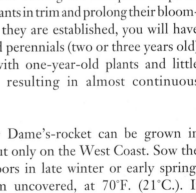

Hesperis matronalis

To Grow: Dame's-rocket can be grown in Zone 9, but only on the West Coast. Sow the seeds indoors in late winter or early spring; leave them uncovered, at 70°F. (21°C.). If planted out early enough, the seedlings may produce flowers the first year. Plants can be started outdoors by sowing seeds in a cold frame and planting out the seedlings early the following spring, fifteen to eighteen inches apart. Once established in moist, well-drained soil, in sun or partial shade, Dame's-rocket should replenish itself by self-sowing. The seedlings should be thinned for optimum blooms. Small plants can be lifted and replanted in early spring, though they will wilt at first. Plantlets at the base of older plants can be separated and grown in a cold frame as cuttings or planted out in the garden. Flowering stalks should be cut back after bloom to prolong the life of each plant. Enough seeds will spill out on the ground to ensure a continuous supply of seedlings. Be sure to keep seeds from your favorite colors separate, since mauve may overtake the planting in time. Resow your area with purchased seeds when plants become rangy or when you want to extend the color range.

Collector's Choice:

Hesperis matronalis, Dame's-rocket. 62(p); 96(s); 6(s); 36(p & s); 120(p).
    'Lilac'. 3(s).
    'White'. 3(s); 6(s); 120(p).

❈ *Hosta* spp.

Liliaceae
1850-1900   Zones 3-8

Hosta

Autumn Lily, Corfu Lily, Fragrant Plantain, Funkia, Japan Day-lily, Lilac Funkia, Old White Day-lily, Plantain Lily, Seersucker Plantain Lily

---

Type: Perennial
Height: 6"-5' Season of Interest:
    Summer-Fall Foliage and Flowers
Site: Sun/Partial Shade/Shade

About forty species of Hostas native to Asia (mostly Japan) are noted for their varied leaves, growing from fairly shallow, fleshy roots from early summer to fall. The size of the plant is often measured not so much by its height as by its spread. Under optimum conditions, for instance, *Hosta sieboldiana* 'Elegans' can grow to six feet across, though more usually it is about thirty inches high and forty-two inches across. Leaf shape, size, texture, and color all vary considerably from very broad (to one foot wide), puckered, ribbed, or glossy to slender and twisted and from shades of pale green and deep greenish blue to gold-edged and variegated white. Leaf colors change with the season and exposure to sun, in most species turning gold in autumn before dying back to the ground over the winter. The flowers, borne in loose clusters, are lily- or funnel-shaped (quite fragrant in the Autumn Lily, *Hosta plantaginea*). In some species, the flowers lie fairly hidden among enormous leaves; in others, they rise well above them in elegant spikes to five feet, in shades of lilac, mauve, purple, and white. Formerly classified as *Funkia*s, the *Hosta* genus is named for N.T. Host, who was a physician to the emperor of Austria.

Hostas became part of America's ornamental plant pool by the mid- to late nineteenth century, due to many introductions from Asia, collected by professionals such as Robert Fortune, working for the Royal Horticultural Society in Britain, and amateurs such as Franz von Siebold, who spent six years in Japan with the Dutch East India Company, and who is credited with introducing a number of important plants to America (via Europe), including the Flowering Crab (*Malus floribunda*), Japanese Dogwood (*Cornus kousa*), Hydrangea (*Hydrangea paniculata*), and Siebold Plantain Lily (*H. sieboldiana*), the Hosta that most frequently comes to mind whenever we hear that name. This species has long, waxy, bluish leaves — ten to fifteen inches long and six to ten inches wide — with fragrant pale lilac flowers that are shorter in stem length than the leaves, which largely hide them from view — a foliage plant par excellence. This still-popular species has been described as a classic by Will Ingwersen, who calls it "one of the most handsome of a popular family of garden plants" (*Classic Garden Plants*, Hamlyn, 1975).

Unfortunately, their ease of culture, as well as their tolerance of shade or sun and neglect, has relegated Hostas to dim passageways, shady corners, and undistinguished borders in bright sun along the driveway, a horticultural cliché that in my opinion is not worth repeating. I have seen too many unhappy Hostas in this situation. They deserve a better fate than to be planted in lozenge beds around trees or in a dank shrubbery hidden from view. The situation is not helped by gardening guides that refer to Hostas as "serviceable plants."

Until several years ago, when my husband and I were guests of Audrey Harkness O'Connor, retired editor of *Cornell Plantations*, I did not even regard Hostas as ornamentals. Who wants "just foliage" for summer gardens when we wait so many months for bright blooms? That opinion, based on ignorance, was altered forever when we saw her Hostas in Pimpernel Gardens at her home in Ithaca, New York. Planted adjacent to the house, they spread out generously, a sea of melting shapes, colors, and heights, yet still distinct in their individuality — green, white, and golden. The sun, filtering through a limbed-

Hosta

up grove of white pines and the spreading branches of a single birch tree, allowed us to view and appreciate the full range of Hostas in a play of light and shadow. At the far edge was one of Mrs. O'Connor's favorites among the smaller types: 'Louisa', a chance seedling from the garden of Frances Williams (whose name is preserved in a popular Hosta cultivar), featuring dainty green leaves edged with white and pure white flared flowers on thirty-inch stalks. To think I had passed up such gorgeous landscaping possibilities — a whole world of interesting forms in foliage and flowers!

Since the late 1960s, hybrids and sports have proliferated at a rapid rate, introduced by hobbyists and professional hybridizers. But for many gardeners, several of the "oldies" are still tops, among them Mrs. O'Connor's favorite large type, Siebold Plantain Lily, and little 'Louisa'.

Hostas are slow-growing, so don't expect to duplicate Audrey O'Connor's mass planting for at least three to five years (she started her collection in 1965 when Hostas were Funkias). Once planted, however, they can be left undisturbed indefinitely, swelling with pride from year to year, which is why they are still found growing on their own in neglected gardens. Mrs. Wilder gave us a poignant description of such a discovery: "My first recollection of it [the Corfu or Old White Day-lily, *Hosta plantaginea*] was in a deserted garden in Delaware persisting in the tangled grass beneath immensely tall high-branched evergreen trees of some sort, a garden that I used to steal into whenever happy chance offered. . . . To smell the old white Day Lily brings back those days

and that enchanted old garden to me. . . .
Doubtless the garden was long ago reclaimed
or is lost beneath the inexorable march of some
development scheme, but for me it will always
live, enchantment, youth, high aspirations, and
all, so long as the frosted white Day Lilies make
their punctual appearance in my garden."

Group Hostas among other shade- or
semishade-loving plants, such as Ferns, Bleeding-heart, and the true Daylily. Plant them as
a cover to fill in after fading Daffodils under the
spreading limbs of an old Lilac tree. I hesitate
to advise planting Hostas around or in front of
shrubberies, as a groundcover, or along walk-
ways. Such plantings *do* have long-term appeal,
but only if executed with flair and imagination.
The main thing is to avoid creating big, fat
clumps with no raison d'être, stuck in a place
where nothing else will grow. Plant no fewer
than three of one kind together; plant several
different types together for diversity of form
and color. Planted on a hillside, Hostas provide
spectacular cover all season long. Use the foliage and flowers in bouquets.

To Grow: Hostas are very hardy and will thrive
even where winters are mild, except in Zones 9
and 10. They grow well in complete or filtered
shade, but prefer several hours of morning sun
a day. Plants should be set out in the fall or
anytime during the growing season up to mid-
September (where winters are severe). They
require well-prepared ground: moist, humusy,
well drained, and enriched with compost. Set
the plants with the juncture of roots and leaves
at ground level and space them according to
their expected full size: allow three feet for
large-leaved types and eight to twelve inches
for the smaller-leaved types. Propagation is by
division from the spring into the fall. Hostas
(those that aren't sterile types) also can be
grown from seeds gathered from the ripened

brown capsules and sown in a cold frame in the
fall. This can be an interesting experiment,
since seedlings are often variable and you may
discover a new type that you like and want to
preserve (as well as name).

Collector's Choice (* indicates especially fragrant types):

Hosta fortunei 'Hyacinthina', Fortune's Plantain Lily; large blue-green leaves; violet flowers; July-August bloom; 2-3'; added to Mrs.
O'Connor's collection in 1971. 29; 169; 88;
142; 20; 78 (all plants).

'Aureo-marginata'; gray-green leaves,
waxy underneath, with a narrow gold edge;
lavender flowers; July-August bloom; 2'. 17;
133; 56; 153; 149; 61 (all plants).

H. lancifolia, Narrow-leaved Plantain Lily;
shiny, slender green leaves (6"); low, dense
clumps; numerous blue-lavender flowers; late
summer-fall bloom; one of three species that
formed the basis for Mrs. O'Connor's collection in 1965. 45; 49; 61; 153; 76; 82 (all plants).

H. plantaginea, August, Autumn, or Corfu
Lily; pale green heart-shaped leaves; large,
fragrant white trumpet-shaped flowers with
pinkish stamens; August-September bloom;
protect over the winter in cold climates until
established; 2'; Zone 4. 119; 82; 115; 49; 165
(all plants).

H. sieboldiana 'Elegans', Siebold Plantain
Lily; large, rounded gray-green leaves; nearly
white flowers; 18-24"; nearly 6' across in Mrs.
O'Connor's garden in a wet season. 169; 88;
115; 138; 17; 76 (all plants).

H. undulata 'Albo Marginata'; large, waxy
leaves with a narrow white edge, more pronounced in the shade; lavender flowers; early
August bloom; 48". 155; 20; 78; 49; 115; 157
(all plants).

H. ventricosa, Blue Plantain Lily; glossy,
dark green heart-shaped leaves; large, showy

purple flowers (plant this with Daylilies); July-August bloom; 3'; another of the originals in Mrs. O'Connor's collection. 115(p & s); 92(s); 125(s); 88; 17; 136 (all plants).

Hybrid:

'Louisa'; narrow green leaves with a white margin; August-September bloom; try in the rock garden; 30". 115(p & s); 49; 63; 45; 29; 17 (all plants).

❀ *Humulus lupulus*

Cannabaceae

1600-1699   ZONES 3-9   NATIVE/
                          NATURALIZED

Hop Vine

Old Cluster Hop

TYPE: PERENNIAL TWINING VINE/HERB
HEIGHT: TO 20'   BLOOM: MIDSUMMER
SITE: SUN

The perennial Hop Vine, one of a few species native to Europe, western Asia, and North America, is a vigorous twining vine with rough stems and almost heart-shaped, finely toothed leaves (similar to grape leaves) that grows back each season to a height of at least twenty feet. The pleasantly bitter hop flavor used to preserve and flavor beer and once used to raise bread is found deep within the papery leaves of the cone-shaped female flowers in the form of powdery, dark yellow-grained fruits. Over the summer, the loose clusters of flowers, first appearing as tight, light green cones, turn gradually to partially open, light

Humulus lupulus

amber-bronze rosettes. This is when they have the greatest flavor. Both native and introduced Hop Vines grow wild in vacant fields and along rivers throughout the United States. The genus name is possibly derived from the Latin *humus*, meaning "ground," an apt description of the vine's sprawling habit when unsupported and its preference for rich, humusy soil.

The European Hop Vine, known as Old Cluster Hop, was introduced to North America by the Massachusetts Company in 1629; by 1648 its commercial production had spread to Virginia. The settlers brought seeds with them to grow the vine for their own use. As garden historian Ann Leighton observed, "Hops would seem to rank somewhere with the domestic cat as an indispensable adjunct to any household . . . its functions are as humble and cosy as those of the cat, and as ancient" (*Early American Gardens*, University of Massachusetts Press, 1986). The colonists must have been relieved to find it growing wild on the banks of Maine rivers — no need to worry about an adequate supply for barm, the name of the mixture used as yeast.

By 1800 hops, used for beer-making, were an important field crop in America, especially in the East. By the 1920s, however, due to an epidemic of downy mildew, their cultivation shifted to the northwestern states, where it remains today.

When the household friend was no longer needed, it lingered on to find a use as an ornamental, providing dense shade for porches and verandas, as at home in California as in the East. When other perennial vines — such as Climbing Roses and Clematis — were introduced to North Ameri-

---

can gardens, the Hop Vine declined in favor, but it is still highly regarded in colder regions, where other perennial vines are unreliable, and as an ornamental — a mass of leaves all season and dense clusters of intriguing flowers from midsummer into the fall.

I found many old Hop Vines in the local area, often grown neatly up a pole by the side of the house for more than seventy years. Kenneth Roberts has an amusing essay about purchasing a "house in the country" and trying to turn it into the proverbial vine-covered cottage, only to have it strangled by a rampant Hop Vine. It is only fair to say that, while the Hop Vine *is* vigorous, its growth can be brought under control.

The oldest Hop Vine I ever saw was prominently featured in Mr. Jackson's Heritage Garden at the Memorial University Botanical Garden in St. John's, Newfoundland. He found the original (from which this vine was grown) climbing up a tree in a garden abandoned more than 116 years ago. It had been brought to Newfoundland by an immigrant from the Isle of Skye who originally settled in Cape Breton. When he moved, he took with him one of his most prized possessions, just as Ann Leighton described. Now the old Hop Vine was trained over a quiggly fence (as described on p. 12) of woven softwood saplings. The vine completely framed a tall stand of Golden-glow (*Rudbeckia laciniata*) in full bloom — a brilliant combination of plant and vine and a clever way to protect both in a windy site.

We became devotees of the Hop Vine when we acquired a piece of root from an old garden and planted it by the doorway of our shop. The second season it shot up, framing the doorway in a "bosky dingle," spreading sideways along the wall, supported by a piece of old nylon parachute line. I was particularly enchanted with the flowers, dry on the vine by late summer in bouquetlike clusters. As an herbalist, I was already planning how I would use them: in dried bouquets, wreaths, perhaps little sleep pillows (the flowers are said to be soporific, supposedly used in pillows by eminent people in need of a good night's rest, such as Abraham Lincoln and King George III) — maybe even to raise bread. The ornamental quality of the vine itself and the ornamental uses of the dried flowers have been greatly underestimated. The British have always prized the dried flowers in floral art.

The Hop Vine grows by twining and needs the support of a pole, trellis, or fence on which to climb and drape itself. As Mr. Jackson proved in his Heritage Garden, it can be a smashing addition to the back of a perennial border if trained along a fence. It was traditionally used to shade porches and verandas, appreciated as a quick-growing vine (six to twelve inches of growth in a single day have been recorded), but it still can be grown to advantage up a tall pole, just as the settlers probably did.

To Grow: Sow the seeds in late spring in well-drained, rich, humusy soil, in a sunny site. Plant the roots at the same time, eighteen inches apart, to grow up a trellis or some support. It will take two seasons for the plants to flower when grown from seed. Propagation is by division of the roots. To keep the vine from spreading on the ground (by the lateral multiplication of its roots), ruthlessly pull up new plants growing alongside the "mother" and keep the grass well mowed around the planting. Make sure the vine has plenty of moisture: mulch or water during a dry spell. Cut the whole plant down to the ground in late fall or clean out the old vine in early spring. You can also leave the old vines for support.

Collector's Choice:

Humulus lupulus, Hop Vine. 110(p); 177(p &

s); 15(s); 121; 137; 114; 31 (all plants).

'Old Early Cluster'; discovered in the late 1800s at Washington State University; produces flowers about two weeks earlier than the species and is very hardy. 151(p).

❦ *Hydrangea paniculata*

'Grandiflora'

Saxifragaceae
1862 Zones 4-9

Peegee Hydrangea

Tree Hydrangea

❦ *H. anomala petiolaris*

Climbing Hydrangea

TYPE: HARDY SHRUB/CLINGING VINE
HEIGHT: 10-75' BLOOM: SUMMER-FALL
SITE: SUN/PARTIAL SHADE/SHADE

The Peegee Hydrangea from Asia is a late-blooming tree-like shrub that can grow to twenty-five feet (usually considerably less, to about twelve feet). It has large, coarsely toothed green leaves and immense (one foot long) white pyramidal flower clusters that turn pink, then bronzy green, with age. Its common name (Peegee) is a welcome abbreviation for the mouthful *paniculata* 'Grandiflora'.

The Climbing Hydrangea, also from Asia, clings to brick or stone by

Hydrangea paniculata

means of aerial rootlets on its main and lateral branches. Its fragrant flowers, which bloom in mid-June, are white and showy — flat clusters six to ten inches wide. Its nearly heart-shaped lustrous leaves and vigorous habit make it a very useful vine for covering walls or ground.

These species are part of the treasures from the Orient introduced to American gardens in the late nineteenth century. They thrive in growing conditions similar to those in their native habitat.

"The Japan Hydrangea [Peegee] bids fair to be the most valuable of the Hydrangeas," one nineteenth-century authority asserted. A down-home type of shrub, whose overuse is the despair of landscaping authorities and the delight of those who grow it, it is still a hallmark of rural and small-town North America, as immune from fashion as the people who grow and admire it: dependable, easygoing, and highly decorative, with large, fluffy, oversize blooms of changing color, always anticipated with fresh joy each summer when new blooms, particularly on shrubs, are most wanted in the garden. Even with age, and entirely dried up on the bush, the Peegee's pinkish flower clusters are eagerly sought for use in winter bouquets.

I found an admirable fifty-year-old specimen in full bloom on a hillside farm, where descendants of the original Scottish settlers from the Isle of Barra treated it almost reverently, like an old family friend. It grew in a bower of shrubbery — among Lilacs, Spirea of several sorts, and Weigela — all purchased as rootstock from the traveling plant peddler's last trip to the area in 1939. Several generations of children had played beneath its branches, and countless bouquets, in summer and winter, had been made from its plentiful flowers.

In early fall, I found a Climbing Hydrangea under quite different circumstances, growing untended for at least the past thirty years up the side of "The Lodge," a large turn-of-the-century structure that is the oldest building on the grounds of Beinn Breagh, the summer estate of Alexander Graham Bell and his family. The Lodge eventually became the summer home of the Bells' famous son-in-law, plant collector David Fairchild, who was responsible for the plantings I found there, all now left to their own devices: a once splendid perennial border and rock garden, various Roses, and the Climbing Hydrangea. Keeping company with its old and twisted branches, plastered against the wall like an aged one-dimensional tree, was the native Virginia Creeper (*Parthenocissus quinquefolia*) in all its autumn splendor, a brilliant mass of scarlet leaves.

The Peegee Hydrangea should be planted where its multitude of extravagant blooms can be easily seen and cut for bouquets. It is a fine specimen shrub, being somewhat on the order of a small tree, and is striking by itself on the side lawn or behind lower-growing shrubs. (You can remove the lower branches to encourage a cascading form, which is especially beautiful if the bush is planted near the top of a stone wall.) The Climbing Hydrangea, one of the most beautiful of all vines, can be used to clothe buildings, climb over doorways, or climb up stone or brick walls — no support needed. It is also useful for covering eyesores (rock piles and the like) and for climbing up tall, open tree trunks, such as elms. Donald Wyman reported seeing one of the finest specimens of Climbing Hydrangea growing up an American Elm in front of the house where the great plant collector Ernest H. Wilson (of Regal Lily fame) once

lived. The tree, Wyman pointed out, was beautiful in its own right, "but with the vine growing up its trunk to the lower branches it was of unusual interest to all who passed under it." This vine is ideal for tree climbing (something I've always read about but not practiced yet), since it tends to grow right up the tree or very slowly around it, not causing any damage (such as constricting translocation in the trunk).

To Grow: Most Hydrangeas do well in moist soil. The Peegee prefers sun or partial shade, while the Climbing Hydrangea can be grown equally well in sun or even shade. If the Peegee is grown in fertile soil, it should be severely pruned in early spring. This will produce large flower heads. Mulch the Peegee in the winter with organic matter (rotted manure or compost) and fertilize it again in the spring with a general fertilizer scratched into the soil around the shrub. It is easily propagated by softwood cuttings in spring or early summer, rooting in two to three weeks when planted in sand and kept moist.

Climbing Hydrangea takes a few seasons to get started, but growth is rapid after that. It grows best on the north or east side of a building, where it is protected from strong sun in early spring. In their early growth, the crowns of the vines should be protected in the winter with a covering of straw or evergreen boughs. The plant is best propagated by layering, though the vines are slow to root.

Collector's Choice (all sold as plants):

H. paniculata 'Grandiflora', Peegee Hydrangea. 167; 169; 36; 120; 112; 97.
Hydrangea anomala petiolaris, Climbing Hydrangea. 134; 160; 138; 118; 20; 293.

❧ *Impatiens balsamina*

Balsaminaceae
1700-1800

Balsam

Bush Balsam, Garden Balsam, Lady's Balsam, Lady's-slipper, Rose Balsam, Touch-me-not

TYPE: TENDER ANNUAL
HEIGHT: 8"-2½'   BLOOM: SUMMER
SITE: SUN/PARTIAL SHADE

Balsam, a native of Asia, is a frost-tender species of the genus *Impatiens*, so called because the fruits are anxious to pop open and spread their seeds at the slightest touch. The species form is branching and busy to two and a half feet, with spurred flowers — white, yellow, or dark red and often spotted — growing close to the stem under overhanging, lance-shaped, sawtooth leaves. Cultivated forms are very double and often dwarf. They come in a variety of shades — scarlet, soft rose-pink, deep violet, and pure white — and are often lightly scented. Lady's-slipper, an old-fashioned name for Balsam, is now used almost exclusively in reference to the wild orchid, Showy Lady's-slipper (*Cypripedium reginae*).

Balsam was introduced to Europe in 1596 and grown in the New World by the seventeenth century, but it was not really well known until the eighteenth and early nineteenth centuries. "Double Balsam" was grown at Shadwell, Jefferson's birthplace, in 1767, and at Monticello in 1812, ordered from Bernard

Impatiens balsamina

M'Mahon, who regarded it as among a group of "valuable and curious sorts of tender annuals." He gave out detailed instructions on how Balsam could be raised in hotbeds (cold frames heated from below by straw-rotted horse manure). Such a bed is demonstrated at Old Sturbridge Village's early nineteenth-century Parsonage kitchen garden, where such tender annuals as Balsam, African and French Marigolds (*Tagetes erecta* and *T. patula*, respectively), *Lavatera*, and Snapdragons are germinated and grown for transplanting into the flower borders by late May.

By the nineteenth century, three cultivated forms of Balsam were widely recognized: Camellia-flowered, in mixed colors and spotted; Rose-flowered, a perfect double; and Carnation-flowered, with stripes. All these came in dwarf forms as well. In my experience, the differences are academic, as all types resemble little Roses. I have listed the various types available today so you can make up your own mind. All are lovely and worth having in the heirloom garden.

In the Victorian-era passion for double flowers (when *didn't* gardeners like the showier type?), Balsams reined supreme, their stiff forms especially suitable for bedding displays. But by the early 1900s, they, along with other old-fashioned flowers, had become passé, though favorites still among those who looked back with nostalgia to "Grandmother's garden" and an idealized past when the world moved at a slower, saner pace.

Despite their ups and downs in popularity, Balsams have been offered continuously to American gardeners since the eighteenth century, in increasingly improved form, so that the showy flowers aren't hidden by overhanging leaves as in the older types (the soft scent is a recent addition, too). Still, one wonders about reports from nineteenth-century writers who tell us of having seen Balsam plants of shrublike proportions growing in the Tuileries Garden of Paris with flowers "as large as a moderate rose." Hyperbole or truth? We will never know.

In the wake of the herb renaissance, which we are still enjoying, the highly ornamental Balsam, we are told, is an herb, so if you should plant it in your herb garden as a colorful foil for greenery, you can tell the curious that the flowers mixed with alum are used to paint fingernails. It is not a use I have ever tried myself. I enjoy the lovely shrubby Balsam at the front of a perennial border to fill in the bare spots left by early-blooming plants such as Sweet-William. The dwarf forms are valued for container planting, moved around wherever colorful long-season bloom is needed. The taller sorts are fine filler among the evergreens of a foundation planting or to fill in among newly planted shrubs. If well grown, Balsams resemble little shrubs themselves, a mass of double Roses (or Camellias, etc.) from early summer to frost. A mass planting of either taller or dwarf forms is a welcome change from the usual Impatiens *(I. wallerana)*. The bouquetlike blossoming stems can be cut for *real* bouquets all season long.

To Grow: In warm regions, Balsams can be seeded directly in the garden, but for earlier bloom elsewhere, start plants indoors four to six weeks before the last frost. Plant seedlings out when the weather has warmed (when you set out tomato plants), allowing ample space (up to eighteen inches for the taller types) for them to develop. An old-time gardening trick is to pinch off the side branches and the first flowers to encourage a profusion of blooms near the top of the plant. When in flower, Balsams should resemble a ready-made bouquet. Balsams endear themselves to me by their accommodation to being moved, even when in full bloom, as long as a ball of soil is attached to the roots. In hot climates, give them a little shade; in cooler areas, plant them in full sun. Always plant them in rich, well-drained soil. Water them well during dry periods.

Collector's Choice (all sold as seeds):

Impatiens balsamina, 'Camellia-flowered Mixed'; lightly scented; 16-28". 101; 92; 87; 168; 137.
'Extra Dwarf'; 8-12". 101; 92.
'Gardenia-flowered'; 14". 160.

Inula helenium

Asteraceae
1600-1776   ZONES 3-8   NATURALIZED

Elecampane

Elf-dock, Elfwort, Helen's Flower, Horseheal, Scabwort, Velvet-dock, Wild-sunflower

TYPE: PERENNIAL HERB/FLOWER
HEIGHT: 4-6'   BLOOM: MIDSUMMER
SITE: SUN

Elecampane originated in the Old World. It is a tall plant, downy in all of its parts, with long, tongue-shaped light green leaves around the base of the stout stem. The flowers, borne at the top of the plant, look like daisies or sunflowers — about three inches across, golden yellow, and thinly rayed. Elecampane is naturalized in North America along roadsides and clearings from Ontario and Nova Scotia south to North Carolina and west to Missouri.

This herb, a staple of the well-run medieval household, has been described by all the usual commentators, from the first-century Roman naturalist Pliny the Elder to the indefatigable Gerard in sixteenth-century England. A fourteenth-century cookbook tells how to make a sweetmeat of its roots (reportedly very bitter no matter how well sugared), whose main use was to treat whooping cough, bronchitis, and asthma. One of Elecampane's common names from the Middle Ages was Horseheal, denoting its use in treating horse complaints, from weak lungs to rough coats.

Elecampane was also highly regarded as an herb in New World gardens. It was planted at George Washington's birthplace in Wakefield, Virginia, where all the "yarbs" known to the colonists were laid out in square and rectangular beds. There, Elecampane grew among the tall herbs, such as Tansy, Monkshood, Clary Sage, Bergamot, and Wormwood — a planting worth repeating today in the herb or flower garden. It also turns up on assorted lists of herbs grown as medicinals in America into the nineteenth century. It would appear that this herb was highly valued for its medicinal properties — one of the most useful being as an antiseptic in surgical dressings. Experiments carried out in Germany in 1885 showed that a preparation of Elecampane root killed bacteria. Before 1914, the United States imported fifty thousand pounds of Elecampane roots annually to use primarily in veterinary products associated with treating horse ailments. With the decline in the use of horses and with the general availability of other medicines,

Inula helenium

Elecampane fell out of favor (though it may still be used in patent medicines) and was not taken up again until the herb renaissance of the 1930s.

Elecampane was my introduction to the world of flowering herbs and to the idea that plants known primarily for their usefulness could be grown solely for their ornamental virtues. In one of my earliest attempts to establish a flower garden on the old farm, Elecampane, along with Chives and Hyssop, was one of the few perennials to survive over the winter. As the summer progressed, I was surprised to find that by midsummer the clump of homely, oversize Elecampane leaves had changed, like the ugly duckling, into a tall, stately plant bearing cheerful sunflowers, so pretty among purple Monkshood. Though we keep horses, I have never been tempted to use the roots for anything other than establishing a garden on the wild side in a damp, sunny spot, where Elecampane does well on its own among mauve-flowered Chives, Blue and Yellow Flag Iris, Purple Loosestrife (noninvasive Morden cultivars), and the double pink Bouncing-bet — a whole season of bloom with virtually no effort, except mowing around the edges. The original plant in my flower garden (now a mixture of herbs and flowers) has not been divided in twenty years. It grows on from year to year with very little attention, faithfully poking its long leaves through the soil in early summer, a reminder of the beauty to come.

To Grow: Elecampane grows best in deep clay loam on the moist side. In lighter soil where summers are hot, grow it in partial shade, which will prolong its bloom period (about two weeks where summers are hot, longer elsewhere). Its natural range suggests that Elecampane accommodates well to various soils and climates. To increase the plant, dig up a piece of root about two inches long with a bud or eye and replant it, watering it well until new growth appears. Elecampane can be left indefinitely unless it shows signs of decreased bloom. Though fairly tall, the stout stems usually do not need staking, another thing in its favor.

Collector's Choice:

Inula helenium, Elecampane. 93; 116; 77; 45 (all plants); 121(p & s); 6(s); 177(s).

Ipomoea purpurea

Convolvulaceae

1600-1699   NATURALIZED

Morning-glory

Bindweed, Blew Bindweed

❀ I. alba

1700-1750

Moonflower

Moonvine, Prickly Ipomoea

I. nil 'Scarlet O'Hara'

Imperial Morning-glory

TYPE: ANNUAL/TENDER PERENNIAL
　　　TWINING VINE
HEIGHT: TO 20' OR MORE　　BLOOM:
　　　　　　　　　　　　SUMMER-FALL
SITE: SUN/PARTIAL SHADE

Ipomoea, from the Greek for "bindweed," is a large genus of more than five hundred species, among which are twining vines such as the prosaic sweet potato and the ornamentals Morning-glory and Moonflower, quick-growing and prized for their lovely trumpet flowers and abundant, attractive foliage.

The Morning-glory, as the name suggests, blooms from dawn to early morning, remaining open longer in cloudy weather and when summer temperatures cool down. The trumpet- or funnel-shaped blooms, up to five inches across and borne profusely on twining stems that grow to ten feet or more, may be blue, purple, pink, scarlet, or any shade thereof, as well as white-throated or striped. An annual from tropical America, it is naturalized in North America.

The Moonflower, also native to tropical America, is a tender perennial, usually grown as an annual. Its large, silky white, clove-scented flowers, six inches across or more, open at dusk or late afternoon and remain open until noon. They are said to bloom by the moon and close by the sun. The moonflower also grows by twining, bearing a great many eight-inch heart-shaped leaves, attractive in their own right.

Morning-glories were planted in the earliest American gardens and are featured in the dwarf form at Colonial Williamsburg. Eighteenth-century gardener Lady Skipwirth grew many colors. By the mid-eighteenth century, the tender perennial climber *Ipomoea tricolor* had been introduced, a somewhat tamer, less vigorous sort (of which the dwarf form is one type) from Mexico, where, we are told, it was used by the Aztecs as a hallucinogen in religious ceremonies. There is no record of this lovely vine being used for the same purposes in American gardens, but it did become important in the breeding of several very popular cultivars, among them the aptly named 'Heavenly Blue', perhaps introduced around the turn of the century (late 1900s), but in any case before 1911. Sky blue, white-throated, and five inches across, it has become synonymous with the term "Morning-glory."

By the nineteenth century, the Imperial or Japanese Morning-glory (*I. nil*) had been introduced from Japan. The ever-popular 'Scarlet O'Hara' — a dark, wine red flower that covers the vine from top to bottom all summer — was derived from it. The pure white 'Pearly Gates', derived from *Ipomoea tricolor*, was introduced by 1940. Both these cultivars have shown marvelous endurance in the form of undiminished popularity since their introduction. 'Scarlet' won an AAS Gold Medal in 1939, 'Pearly' an AAS Silver Medal in 1942.

The Moonflower, with its distinctive night-blooming habit and large scented flowers, has never needed improving. Where winters are frost-free and it can be grown as a perennial, it reaches as high as forty feet in a single season. Even in my

Ipomoea purpurea

Zone 4 garden, it makes a good show along our shop wall or on a trellis by a dooryard garden, where we can enjoy its clove-scented flowers in the late afternoon and evening. If left to their own devices, the Moonflower and the rest of the Morning-glories are valuable as a temporary groundcover.

Given any support — a trellis, fence, arbor, pole, wires, or twine — these beautiful vines take off, "lifting their heads toward the sky as though they were trying to compete with the sun, moon or stars," as a writer once observed. A cliché, (but one that is always welcome) is to plant any of the Morning-glory vines so they twine around the back supports of a rural mailbox. I have seen this neatly done in the most decorous suburbs, where the blue, pink, mauve, or white trumpets are the only bright color in a monotonous sea of green lawns and evergreen shrubs. If planted side by side, the Morning-glory and Moonflower complement each other's bloom cycle, one taking up where the other leaves off, providing continuous bloom, night and day. Where these vines are grown as annuals, they can be planted in tubs or raised baskets in even the smallest city garden.

To Grow: Sow Morning-glory seeds in a sunny spot in the spring when the soil is warm. Where the growing season is short, start the seeds indoors. In either case, nick them with a file and soak them overnight in lukewarm water to speed germination, which should occur in a week at 75°F. to 80°F. (24°C. to 27°C.). Since the roots don't like being disturbed, plant the seeds in peat pots and set them out in holes in the ground after all danger of frost has passed, spacing them about eight to twelve inches apart. The Morning-glory is quite drought-resistant and does not need a rich soil (this will only produce a lot of leaves and few flowers).

In Zones 9 and 10, the Moonflower can be grown as a perennial; elsewhere sow the seeds as for the Morning-glory, spacing the plants nine to twelve inches apart. Moonflowers respond to a weekly feeding of balanced fertilizer (20-20-20) with micronutrients. Use one-half teaspoon per gallon of water at the seedling stage. Plant out the seedlings when all danger of frost has passed and feed them once a month with a Rose fertilizer, which promotes flowering. If the vines are growing too tall for your

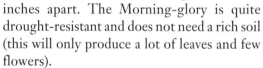

supports or your liking, cut them back and pinch off the tips to slow growth. Be sure to provide sturdy support for either type of vine early in its growth.

Collector's Choice (all sold as seeds):

Ipomoea alba, Moonflower. 6; 34; 126; 137; 15; 87.

I. nil 'Scarlet O'Hara', Imperial Morning-glory. 133; 6; 160; 34; 101; 92.

I. purpurea, Morning-glory; mixed colors (indigo, maroon, and white). 92.

'Crimson Rambler'; crimson flowers with a white throat. 6.

'Kniola's Purple-Black'; velvety purple-black 2" flowers; discovered by a Mr. Kniola on an abandoned Indiana farm, a genuine heirloom type. 6.

I. tricolor 'Heavenly Blue'. 177; 126; 6; 133; 101; 42.

'Pearly Gates'. 133; 6; 160; 101.

✿ *Iris* spp.

Iridaceae
1600-1960   ZONES 3-10

Iris

TYPE: HARDY PERENNIAL BULB/HERB
HEIGHT: 3"-4'   BLOOM: SPRING-EARLY
SUMMER
SITE: SUN/PARTIAL SHADE

Two hundred or more species of Iris grow in the Northern Hemisphere, among them the interesting group of garden flowers with rhizomatous, rather than bulbous, roots treated here. These grow horizontally on or underneath the ground, sending up a succession of grassy or swordlike leaves with flower-bearing stalks of six-petaled, often fragrant blooms. The blooms consist of three upright petals (*standards*), three lower hanging or recurved petals (*falls*), and three strap-shaped divisions or *style branches*. This distinct form is the pattern for the fleur-de-lis, an ancient symbol of French royalty. In bearded types, raised hairs, sometimes brilliantly colored, grow from the base of the falls, luring insects to the heart of the flower, where they inadvertently fertilize it with pollen carried on their bodies. Both the genus and family names are derived from Iris, the Greek goddess of the rainbow, suggestive of the varying colors and shimmering quality of the blooms.

Although several Iris were known in the seventeenth century, the early settlers brought with them or sent for only one, the Yellow Flag or Flower-de-luce (*Iris pseudacorus*), apparently for its well-known medicinal properties and ease of culture. It will grow almost anywhere, even (or especially) in swamps and wetlands. Described as "a sovereign remedy for weak eyes" when properly prepared, it also was used to treat ulcers and make a yellow or black dye. Who could ask for anything more from a plant that is also beautiful: bright yellow flowers in the classic fleur-de-lis design (sans beard) and green swordlike leaves.

During the next two hundred years, until the twentieth century, Americans were content to grow a variety of wild Iris and their superior strains from many parts of the world. The bearded German Iris (*I.* x *germanica*) varied from blue to purple and red, and its variety, 'Florentina', the Florentine Iris (almost white) was fabled as a source for violet-scented orris-root, used as a fixative in making perfumes and potpourri. As a garden plant, the 'Florentina' has always had its admirers: "In spite of the fact that it is not new or in the least expensive," Helen Fox wrote in the 1930s, "its pearly iridescent color and delicate iris-like fragrance make it one of the most desirable irises" (*Gardening with Herbs for Flavor and Fragrance*, Macmillan, 1933).

Another sweet-scented Iris is Sweet Flag (*Iris pallida*), a bearded type with lavender-blue to white flowers, whose silvery, long-lasting foliage is especially appreciated. Nineteenth-century introductions included Japanese Iris (*I. kaempferi*), with large, graceful, almost flat falls, sometimes veined and mottled, with blue, lavender, and orchid-rose flowers, and Siberian Iris, a wetland type daintier than Yellow Flag but tough, with a crisp fleur-de-lis in shades of purple, blue, or white.

Native Iris were introduced from the late eighteenth century through the mid-nineteenth century. Among them are the lovely Crested Iris, growing wild from Maryland to Georgia and Missouri, perhaps the finest of all dwarf Iris. It has a distinct fluted yellow-and-white crest on its pale lilac or blue flowers. Blue Flag, native from eastern Canada to Pennsylvania, and Southern Blue Flag, native to the southeastern United States, are wetland types with variable purple and blue flowers, sometimes splashed with yellow.

Iris × germanica

Whatever their differences, all of the assorted "flags" in grandmother's or great-grandmother's garden were dependable, iron-clad Iris with many, though smallish, blooms during their brief season (early spring to early summer). Hybridization of several species (among them *Iris × germanica* and *I. pallida*) began by the 1820s, and by the turn of the century hundreds of new cultivars poured forth, extending the color range, height, and size of flowers — not surprising, considering the Iris is one of the easiest subjects for cross-pollination. The goal was to produce showier flowers of the bearded type, to which hardiness and ease of culture were sometimes sacrificed. The modern Iris, unlike the wild types, are tetraploid, with two sets of chromosomes, resulting in a doubling of everything. But while the flowers are twice as large as older forms, there are fewer on a stalk. There is no doubt, though, that the appearance of these hybrids dazzled the gardening authorities of the day (early 1900s), one of whom likened their beauty to that of the sea: "Everything about it seems mutable and insubstantial as if it had been made by enchantment and might vanish by the same means" (A. Clutton-Brock, *Studies in Gardening*).

In fact, many of these shimmering beauties have vanished, despite their fine qualities, because of the fierce competition among the thousands offered and because what is new instantly supersedes what is "old." Where are the once celebrated Bearded types with the jaunty names: 'Kum-on' (1955), 'Plum Cute' (1963), and 'Sugar Pie' (1965)? Where is 'Patience' (1955), a shade of magenta that, according to aficionados, has yet to be matched by any other Iris? Where is the Siberian Iris 'Perry's Blue' (1921): "Whenever I see *Iris sibirica* 'Perry's Blue'," Mrs. King wrote in the 1920s, "I bless the name of Perry afresh."

Some of these Iris are known to exist in collectors' gardens, but they are no longer in general circulation. This brings up a point that often vexes fans of antique Iris (and Roses, as well as other groups of plants): the tendency of hybrids or strains to deteriorate over time, as the *inherent variability* in any genetic structure makes itself apparent in characteristics at variance with the distinctive feature of the named cultivar. Now, instead of, say, a brilliant red, you begin to see a shade of pink, blossoms are fewer and smaller, and so on. In other words, the plant in question is no longer true to its name.

With seed strains, the process of keeping an old strain up to standard is called *reselection*. 'Shirley Reselected Poppies', for instance, indicates that the original Shirley Poppy strain, created by Reverend Wilkes from variants among wild Corn Poppies *(Papaver rhoeas)*, deteriorated over time. Perhaps there were fewer desirable flower types apparent in a group of plants grown from Shirley Poppy seeds; perhaps the wild form was becoming dominant. At some point, a nurseryman or seed company took great care in selecting the seed parents to ensure that the original characteristics that defined Shirley Poppies were reintroduced and preserved. The process of reselection is common among vegetable strains as well.

The problem of plant deterioration was suggested by Grant Wilson in his discussion of antique Glads. If the older Glads could be grown in their true form (as they looked when originally introduced), he felt they might compare very well with the newest introductions, but he did not think such specimens were in circulation, so the question was academic.

The situation with antique Iris is, fortunately, quite different. Although many old types have probably deteriorated in form as they have been passed from gardener to gardener, a few commercial collectors guarantee the authenticity of a number of historic Iris. (Unfortunately, 'Perry's Blue', so far as I know, is not among them.) I should point out that not every old Iris (or every old plant of any kind) has garden value, although all have value for the garden historian. One of the points made by those who have preserved all the American Dykes Medal winners since 1927 is that such exhibitions provide the opportunity to see the vast improvement in Iris breeding.

I was introduced to Iris through the far less complex ancient types closer to the wild when we moved to our backland farm and I found a sixty-year-old clump of Yellow Flag languishing by the kitchen door, promising much and delivering little — heaps of swordlike kelly green leaves and, in early summer, small bright yellow flowers on three-foot stems. I moved them twice before I found the perfect spot, or spots. The original population, having swelled under my tutelage to a horsedrawn wagonful of roots, was flung off by pitchfork into various damp, even boggy, areas in the hope of naturalizing them. I have seldom witnessed such a transformation in the plant world. It was as if each established clump, in sun or dappled shade, was saying "Thank you." Now, in early summer, they bloom, without any aid from me, in lovely yellow drifts among the native violet-blue *Iris versicolor* and golden yellow Buttercups, with tiny wild blue Forget-me-nots at their feet.

Any of the Iris species can be naturalized in their favorite habitat — damp or dry ground — and by careful selection among the various hybrids, the Iris blooming season can last three months — April, May, and June, or from early spring through early summer. Plant dwarf or shorter types in rock gardens with Moss Phlox; plant the Bearded types according to size and color, grouped among low-growing plants such as Columbine and Lungwort, combined with Oriental Poppies (a favorite and always welcome combination) and the flowers of early summer: Dame's-rocket, Foxglove, and Lupines. If you begin collecting Iris types, you will want to consider separate beds to accommodate them. Consider planting Iris among Peonies and Roses, as well as Daylilies. The old Lemon Yellow Daylily and *Hemerocallis middendorffii* bloom at the same time as the Bearded types. For cut flowers, cut Iris when the first buds begin to unfold.

To Grow: Bearded Iris grow best in full sun and enriched, well-drained soil in Zones 3-10, except in Florida and along the Gulf Coast. Plant them from July (in the north) to early fall (in the south) by digging a hole, mounding the soil, and placing the rhizomes on top, ten to fifteen inches apart. Cover them so their tops are even with the soil's surface. Fertilize the area around the planting in the spring with a low-nitrogen fertilizer and divide the plants when needed (every four or five years). Nonhybrid older types can be left undisturbed for many years.

To divide the plants, dig up the rhizomes after the flowers fade, shake off the soil, and remove two-thirds of the foliage. Select two small rhizomes growing at an angle from the large one, cut them with a sharp knife, and reset them in the soil six to eight inches apart.

Beardless Iris can be divided in late summer or early fall, but you will probably need a bulldozer to dig up established clumps of some types (such as Yellow Flag and Siberian Iris). Japanese Iris roots work to the surface about every three or four years; divide the clump at this time. Cut back the spent flowering stalks of all types, but let the leaves ripen.

To grow wild types from seed, sow the seeds when ripe or after six weeks of freezing. Germination should occur in two to four weeks in early summer. Shade seedlings during the summer and keep them moist.

Collector's Choice (all sold as plants unless noted; spring-summer bloom; * indicates es-

pecially fragrant types):

Iris cristata, Crested Iris (1850-1900); useful as a groundcover in partial shade; early bloom; 3-4"; Zone 3. 68; 142; 91; 37; 129; 20.
'Alba'; white. 74; 20; 108; 115; 44; 129.
I. x germanica 'Florentina', Florentine Iris (1600-1699); early bloom; 2½'; Zone 4. 75; 116; 106; 36; 49; 177(s).
I. kaempferi, Japanese Iris (1850-1900); likes lime-free soil and partial shade in warmer regions; needs moisture during growth and blooming but drier conditions later; late bloom; 2-4'; Zone 4.
'Asagira' (1930); red-violet standards; blue-violet falls. 53.
'Azure' (1919); vigorous; double violet-blue flowers. 53.
'Goldbound' (1885); double white flowers with yellow veins. 53.
'Kongo-San' (1900); double dark purple flowers; extra-late bloom. 53.
'Korcho' (1920s); white flowers. 53.
'Mahogany' (1893); double dark wine red flowers. 53.
'Rose Cavalier' (1950); white-rimmed violet-red flowers. 53.
I. pallida 'Dalmatica', Sweet Iris, Sweet Flag Iris (18th century); early bloom; wide leaves; 2'; Zone 5. 149.
'Variegata'; cream- and green-striped foliage. 45; 75; 138; 149.
I. pseudacorus, Yellow Flag Iris, Flower-de-luce (1600-1699); sun or partial shade; plant along streams or ponds; late bloom; seedpods attractive; 3-4'; Zone 4. 46; 63; 108; 149; 6(s).
I. sibirica, Siberian Iris (1850-1900); adaptable to soil and site but prefers moist soil and sun; very hardy; late spring-early summer bloom; 2-3'; Zone 3. 46; 59; 99; 6(s); 158(p & s).
'Eric the Red' (by 1946); wine red flowers. 61; 149.

'Helen Astor' (by 1942); rose red flowers. 63.

'White Swirl' (1957); white flowers. 149; 61; 45; 20; 138; 104.

I. versicolor, Blue Flag Iris (1776-1850); for poolside or wetland planting; seedpods attractive; late spring bloom; Zone 3. 68; 106; 120; 117; 26(s).

I. virginica, Southern Blue Flag Iris (1776-1850); similar to *I. versicolor*; Zone 7. 108; 144.

Bearded Iris Hybrids:

TB=Tall Bearded, more than 28" tall, 4-8" flowers

BB=Border Bearded, up to 28" tall, 3-4" flowers

IB=Intermediate Bearded, 15-27" tall, 4-5" flowers

SDB=Standard Dwarf Bearded, 10-14" tall, 3-4" flowers; very free-blooming

MDB=Miniature Dwarf Bearded, up to 10" tall, 2-3" flowers or a little larger

Earliest to bloom are the MDB Iris, followed by the SDBs, then the IBs and TBs for April-June bloom.

'Amigo' (1934); **BB;** pansy coloring; light violet-blue standards; intense purple velvet falls edged with blue. "The form is much wider than most Iris of this time, very pleasing, and it has always been in my garden" (Verna Lauren, Secretary, Canadian Iris Society). 89.

'Black Forest' (1945); **BB;** black as pitch (ebony/blue-black). "This is an oldie I would like to have" (Verna Lauren). 89.

'Blue Denim' (1959); **SDB;** purplish blue with a bluish white beard. 97.

❀'Blue Shimmer' (1942); **TB;** fragrant, large white flowers feathered blue. 89.

'Honorabile' (1840); **MDB;** yellow standard and fall; veined maroon red; historic plant. 83.

'Jungle Shadows' (1960); **BB;** used as the standard for the type; slate gray standards flushed purple; grayish brown-tinged lavender falls. 89.

'Ola Kala' (1943); **TB;** golden yellow. 89.

'Wabash' (1937); **TB;** blue-white standards; blue-violet falls. "I have replaced a few older Iris that have disappeared over the years, but only if I felt strongly about them. 'Wabash' is in this group" (Verna Lauren). 89.

'Zua' (1914); **IB;** icy blue; crepe-paper texture. 83.

Several of these Bearded Iris have won medals in their class over the years. Three of them are among the top ten Iris (in popularity) according to Historic Iris Preservation Society surveys. These are #1, 'Honorabile'; #2, 'Wabash'; and #9, 'Ola Kala'.

❀ *Kalmia latifolia*

Ericaceae

1700-1776   ZONES 4-9   NATIVE

Mountain-laurel

American-laurel, Calico Bush, Ivybush, Spoonwood

TYPE: HARDY SHRUB
HEIGHT: 10'   BLOOM: SPRING-EARLY
                        SUMMER
SITE: SUN/PARTIAL SHADE/SHADE

Mountain-laurel is one of North America's loveliest native shrubs, the only one of six *Kalmia* species to be cultivated in the garden. In its perfectly wild state, it needs no elaboration: showy clusters of fragrant, white cup-shaped flowers flushed pink, six to eight inches across, held above handsome, glossy evergreen leaves. Even in bud, this shrub has great charm. The buds are deep rose, a striking contrast to the pale flowers, and are composed of ten little pouches into which the stamens fit, held under tension until discharged by the opening of the flower, when the pollen is scattered "as though by a catapult," someone once observed. Mountain-laurel grows wild in the hills and mountains from New Brunswick south to Florida, and west to Ohio and Tennessee.

In 1748 when Peter Kalm, a Finnish pupil of Linnaeus, arrived in the New World looking for interesting flora, he found a genus already named in his honor. In 1786 Jefferson had *Kalmia* seeds or plants sent to France, and during the centuries that followed, it was widely cultivated in America, loved for its beauty, ease of culture, and accommodating, uncomplicated nature. "There is no shrub, foreign or native, that will exceed this in splendor," Joseph Breck wrote in his nineteenth-century catalog. Not only was Mountain-laurel garden-worthy, but as the common name Spoonwood suggests, its wood was used to make brush and chisel handles, as well as spoons and pipes.

As far as I can tell, Mountain-laurel has only two faults: the time required to propagate it and its inability to be easily transplanted. To transplant it, you must cut the whole bush down to the ground before moving it, and several more growing seasons are required to get it back in shape. At one time, due to its popularity, millions of plants were dug up from their native habitats and shipped by the carload to nurseries, where they were regrown to size and then sold. This practice has been largely replaced by the development of tissue culture, a propagation technique that is fast and requires very little plant material to produce

Kalmia latifolia

many identical seedlings.

Some friends of mine inherited a planting —at least seventy years old—that continues to delight them every spring with its profuse blooms — a delight increased because they have done virtually nothing to encourage it. "The beauty of the flower," Gertrude Jekyll observed, "was always an unending delight." I can think of no other shrub that is so universally loved by both the experienced gardener and the novice.

When the glorious blooms have faded, Mountain-laurel is striking wherever it grows — as background for a perennial bed, as a specimen planting on the front lawn, by the side of the house, in a mixed shrubbery, or naturalized in a light woodland among Azaleas and Ferns. It can even be used to clothe bare banks or in any place that needs a handsome long-season cover in bush form.

To Grow: Mountain-laurel prefers light, sandy, moist soil on the acid side (pH 4.5 to 6.0). It will grow, even thrive, in shade, but it produces more flowers in sun or light shade. Work peat moss into the soil when planting and mulch with one to two inches of pine needles, well-rotted oak leaves, or shredded bark. Pruning is seldom needed except at planting time or when moving the shrub, at which time the bush will have to be cut back to the ground. Propagation by the usual means is easy but slow. The best method (aside from tissue culture) is to take softwood cuttings, plant them in a peat moss and sand mixture, and overwinter them (protected) in a cold frame. Be patient. It will take several seasons before the cuttings can be planted out as shrubs.

Lathyrus latifolius

Fabaceae
1600-1699   ZONES 3-10   NATURALIZED

Everlasting Pea

Perennial Pea

❧ L. odoratus

Sweet Pea

Lady Pea, Painted Lady Pea

TYPE: ANNUAL FLOWER/PERENNIAL
       TENDRIL VINES
HEIGHT: 6-9'   BLOOM: SPRING-SUMMER
SITE: SUN

Both species of *Lathyrus*, native to southern Europe, are climbing plants whose flowers are characteristic of the pea family to which they belong: a large upper petal (*standard* or *banner*), two side petals (*wings*), and two smaller bottom petals (*keel*), joined to resemble the prow of a ship. There the similarity ends. The perennial Everlasting Pea bears large rosy or white flowers almost in clusters, climbs to nine feet, and grows as an escape from Indiana to New England and south to Missouri and Virginia. The species form has been improved by selection, but it has not been greatly altered.

Lathyrus odoratus

The Sweet Pea is a weedy annual that grows to six feet, with almost insignificant reddish purple flowers. Its culture is notoriously difficult, and its breeding has been raised to an art form. The Sweet Pea's exquisite perfume, preserved in the Latin epithet *odoratus*, sets this species apart from its scentless cousin and is responsible for the flower's almost mystical hold on generations of gardeners. Both vines climb by tendrils that attach themselves to any support.

Both Washington and Jefferson grew Everlasting Pea; Jefferson planted it (apparently the pink-flowered kind) in the oval bed at Monticello in 1801. Its popularity remained constant through the nineteenth and early twentieth centuries, as long as arbors, fences, porches, and verandas needed clothing. Unsupported, it was valued for covering unsightly odd corners or slopes, where it makes a good show from spring through summer with almost-evergreen foliage and faithfully returns each year with little encouragement. When climbing plants fell from fashion, the Everlasting Pea found new homes along roads and at the edges of fields, a neglected garden escape. It is a shame, for this plant has much to offer — not only beautiful flowers over a long season and ease of culture but also adaptability, for if it is used with imagination, the Everlasting Pea can be grown at the back of a perennial border, supported by the stalks of tall perennials such as Elecampane or Globe-thistle. Some of the finest old cultivars are still available: 'White Pearl', with very large pure white flowers on foot-long stems, wonderful for cutting; 'Pink Beauty', with cascading shell pink flowers, perhaps the sort that Jefferson grew. The virtues of the Everlasting Pea have been overlooked for too long.

The story of the Sweet Pea, discovered in Italy in 1695 by an amateur botanist and monk named Dupani, is more complex. Although it was grown very early in American gardens, it was not seriously considered as an ornamental until improved by breeding, mainly in England in the 1800s. Hundreds of cultivars poured forth from individual breeders, who focused first on expanding the color range — shades of pink, purple, blue, crimson, violet, rose, orange, and white, as well as marbled and striped types — and then the size and shape of the bloom. The shape was changed most notably by the introduction of the wavy, ruffle-petaled Spencer strain introduced in 1901.

By the turn of the century, C.C. Morse Farms of San Francisco began breeding Sweet Peas, mostly scentless, that were better adapted to the North American climate, where summers are hot and dry. Burpee was the first to introduce the all-American 'Cupid', pure white and only six inches tall. However much modern cultivars have answered the needs of American gardeners, there is the yearning to experience "The Essential Sweet Pea" — climbing, sweetly fragrant, and rather small-flowered — as generations of earlier gardeners knew and loved it, when the old hedge of Sweet Peas was the sweetest thing in the garden. "Oh, when the blossoms break . . . like heavenly winged angels," wrote Celia Thaxter, "and their pure, cool perfume fills the air, what joy is mine."

If you want to experience this phenomenon, you can still grow the old strains, a few of which are offered in mixes of unnamed cultivars. The sole exception is 'Painted Lady', a truly historic plant, the very first one named (1730): carmine and white bicolor (*Painted Lady* being a generic term to describe such color combinations), intensely fragrant, and climbing in the classic form. It was offered in J.B. Russell's 1827 seed catalog. When cutting the flowers for bouquets, follow Mrs. Wilder's sound advice to pick them "when the dew is still upon them. It is then that they are the sweetest and most refreshing to inhale. . . . If not gathered before 10 o'clock they should be left until evening."

To Grow: The Everlasting Pea will grow in almost any well-drained soil, but it prefers soil on the sweet side. It also prefers sun but tolerates partial shade. Add some horticultural lime or hardwood ashes if your soil is acid. Plant the seeds in the late fall or early spring (fall-sown peas will germinate early the following growing season) and give them some support. The tendrils will cling to almost anything. Try the Everlasting Pea as an all-season groundcover with a support of twiggy branches for a stunning effect in the perennial border. However these plants are used, space them eighteen to twenty-four inches apart. Pick the spent flowers to encourage continued bloom. Propagate the plants by division or by sowing fresh seeds.

To grow the old-fashioned climbing Sweet Pea, begin your campaign the season before you want to grow it and remember that it thrives in rich, well-drained soil, in a cool, sunny spot. Scorching winds and blistering sun will kill it. The classic planting method is to dig a trench one foot wide by two feet deep and fill it to within four inches of the top with 40 percent loam, 40 percent manure or compost, and 20 percent sand. It wouldn't hurt to add a handful of bonemeal or high-phosphate fertilizer such as 0-20-20. Sow the seeds early, by St. Patrick's Day if possible, a few every twelve inches. Press them down into the soil (they need darkness to germinate). Germination takes about fourteen days at 55°F. to 65°F. (13°C. to

18°C.) and is speeded up by soaking the seeds in tepid water for a few hours prior to sowing or by cutting off a small piece of the seed coat on the side opposite the growing point. If such seeds are sown half an inch deep in sand, they will readily absorb water and germinate more rapidly. Keep in mind that red, crimson, and scarlet types bear the hardest seeds, while white, lavender, and mottled types produce softer, light-colored seeds that will decay in the ground unless germinating temperatures are optimum. If the seeds are sown early, the roots will be well established by the time the hot weather hits. In Zones 8-10, sow the seeds in late summer or early fall for early bloom the following season. If you want to get a head start, sow the seeds indoors in peat pots, plant cells, or any container where the roots won't be disturbed when planting the seedlings out.

Outside, when the seedlings are two inches tall, start filling in the trench, making sure there is enough soil around the young stems to give them support. Keep filling in the trench with enriched soil with each two inches of growth until the trench is almost filled to ground level. Leave a slight depression to gather moisture and mulch around the roots to protect them from hot, dry conditions.

Pinch back the plants to the topmost leaves when they reach four inches so they will develop side branches. Pinch back the first set of buds to encourage the development of more blooms on each stem. To make a screen of flowers, set six-foot stakes in the ground six feet apart and stretch and secure netting from end to end. Plant Sweet Peas in a double row, on either side of the fence. Or omit the netting and tie strings to top and bottom wires, one foot apart, and train the plants on them. Tall, twiggy brush also can be used for support, as can chicken wire. For an interesting effect, sow the seeds in a circle and provide support within

(netting wrapped around three stakes, set as for tomatoes in a tepee shape). This will produce a mound of blooms in almost a bush shape. Pick the spent blooms, as for Everlasting Peas, to promote long blooming.

Collector's Choice:

Lathyrus latifolius, Everlasting Pea; mixed colors. 20(p); 133(s); 147-8(s); 155(p & s); 5(s) — rose only.

'Pink Beauty' (before 1924). 31(p).

'White Pearl' (before 1924). 31(p); 92(s).

L. odoratus, Sweet Pea

'Butterfly Hybrids Mixed' (old style); striped and marbled; red, pink, mauve, and chocolate; lightly scented. 92(s)

'Old Spice' (old style); small; intensely fragrant; rose, red, blue, violet, and white. 5; 96; 6; 126; 3; 87; 42 (all seeds); sold as 'Antique Fantasy', 92(s).

'Painted Lady' (historic strain). 92; 18; 3 (all seeds).

❧ *Levisticum officinale*

Apiaceae

1600-1776   ZONES 3-9   NATURALIZED

Lovage

Old English Lovage

TYPE: PERENNIAL HERB
HEIGHT: 5-6'   SEASON OF INTEREST:
                NEARLY EVERGREEN
                LEAVES
SITE: SUN/PARTIAL SHADE

Lovage originated in southern Europe and may grow to six feet in rich, moist soil, though it usually reaches five feet or less. The hollow stem in the center of the plant bears umbels of tiny yellowish flowers in early summer, while the many side branches bear shiny, dark green, deeply divided leaves — like celery on a grand scale — giving the plant a bushy appearance. Lovage has naturalized in the United States from Pennsylvania south to Virginia and west to Missouri and New Mexico. The long, thick taproot seeks moisture and ensures Lovage an acceptable habitat under diverse conditions, provided there is a period of dormancy (freezing temperatures) in winter. Old English Lovage is a common name once used to distinguish this plant from Scotch Lovage (*Levisticum scoticum*), a plant of similar habitat and use. All parts of the plant are strongly aromatic, reminiscent of a strong celery flavor with a dash of Angelica.

Mrs. M. Grieve (*A Modern Herbal*, Dover, 1971) tells us that Lovage was never an official remedy for anything, but it does carry the epithet *officinale*, meaning, roughly, "from the drugstore." Those tireless English herbalists Gerard and Culpeper noted that the roots are good for "all inward diseases" and that the seed warms the stomach and helps digestion. Distilled Lovage water, they claimed, "cleareth the sight and putteth away all spots and freckles," is good for gargles, and helps break fevers.

The New England colonists were familiar with these uses and grew Lovage in their early gardens. Besides its medicinal properties, the aromatic seeds flavor confections, and the young stems and leaves can be eaten raw in salads. Even more important for the early settlers, these could be blanched to prolong their sweetness. At a time when fresh vegetables were hard to come by, Lovage provided an acceptable substitute, and it was easy to grow. Perhaps,

Levisticum officinale

too, the handsome leaves were admired for their own sake.

Lovage was mentioned in Samuel Stearns' *American Herbal* (1801), then, like so many once useful plants, disappeared from view until its many virtues were rediscovered by pioneering American garden historians and herbalists such as Helen Webster, who in the 1930s observed it growing in a restored colonial garden in Marlborough, Massachusetts, the old Deacon Goodale farm, where the plantings showed "how the yarbs [herbs] might have been grown in the eighteenth century. It also reveals how truly beautiful an old yarb patch must have been" (*Herbs*, Ralph T. Hale & Co., 1942). There, Lovage grew in the back of a border along a winding path with Angelica, bordered by Scented Geraniums, Rosemary, and Mignonette. What contemporary gardener would not love to have a similar planting?

We first grew Lovage nearly thirty years ago in our vegetable/herb garden. When we moved, we potted a few roots and gave the container to a friend for safekeeping, thinking no more about it. Our friend gave the potted plant to his mother, who shortly afterward won first prize for it in a local *flower* show. Evidently, the uses of Lovage as an ornamental are as versatile as its uses as an herb. I grow Lovage in almost full sun and moist soil as a background for potted brick red bedding Geraniums; in filtered shade it makes a handsome foil for Cowslips, white Bleeding-heart, and Daylilies. In early spring, as the reddish tips poke through the still-cold ground, I cut them off to flavor an eagerly anticipated spring salad of wild greens, in the best settler tradition.

To Grow: In frost-free climates, Lovage, like most perennials, can be grown as an annual. Elsewhere, plant the roots about one foot apart in rich, moist soil, in full sun or partial shade (partial shade is best in hot summer regions; otherwise the foliage will yellow). Seeds sown indoors at 60°F. to 70°F. (16°C. to 21°C.) take ten to fifteen days to germinate. Seeds also can be sown in a cold frame during the summer and the seedlings planted out the following season. Established clumps can be divided (not a dainty job). Almost any little piece of root will grow into an identical plant as long as it is kept moist, either well watered or mulched. The long roots can be trimmed so they are equal in length to the top part of the plant. To maintain a healthy clump, cut it back when it flowers and make sure the ground is enriched enough to support regrowth later in the season. The second time around, Lovage will be more compact, its leaves remaining green for some time into the fall. The cut foliage and stems make very good mulch.

Collector's Choice:

Levisticum officinale, Lovage. 177(p & s); 5(s); 93(p); 110(p); 133(p & s); 126 (p & s).

❀ *Lilium* spp.

Liliaceae
1600-1900   ZONES 3-10

Lily

TYPE: HARDY BULB
HEIGHT: 1-7'   BLOOM: SPRING-FALL
SITE: SUN/PARTIAL SHADE

More than eighty species of Lilies are native to Asia, Europe, and North America. Some of them have been very important in breeding the hybrids with which most gardeners are familiar (the Asiatic and Oriental hybrids, for instance).

Lilies grow from underground bulbs made up of fleshy scales that lack the papery protective layer associated with Tulips and Daffodils. The showy, often fragrant blooms, whatever their form — trumpet, bowl, bell, or recurved (like a Turk's cap or turban) — or their position — out-facing, down-facing, or up-facing — grow on tough, wiry stems and have six petals and six prominent stamens surrounding a long pistil. To sort out the multiplicity of Lilies, complicated by hybridization, the Royal Horticultural Society has organized them into nine divisions based on flower forms and species derivation. These are discussed under "Collector's Choice" on p.113.

The first Lily grown by the Plymouth settlers in the 1630s was "the fair white lily," or Madonna Lily (*Lilium candidum*), a cottage garden favorite for centuries and probably the oldest garden plant in the world. It could have been grown for nostalgic reasons or, more probably, for its ancient use in the preparation of an ointment ("stamped with honey"). This Lily's natural characteristics have rarely been combined with such perfection by the breeder's art: the stem rises from a rosette of green leaves close to the ground and bears at its top five to twenty intensely fragrant (like Honeysuckle) pure white trumpets, "within which shyneth the likenesse of gold," a reference to the flower's golden-tipped anthers.

Other Lilies, easier to cultivate than the sometimes temperamental Madonna Lily, were soon introduced to American gardens, among them the Martagon or Turk's-cap Lily (*Lilium martagon*) from Europe, with pendulous purplish pink flowers, and the lovely native Canada or Meadow Lily, with drooping, funnel-shaped yellow or red flowers, common in wet meadows and bogs from southeastern Canada to Georgia. The latter was one of the first native plants to be exported to Europe.

By the eighteenth century, Jefferson was growing the ancient "Fiery Lily" *(Lilium chalcedonicum)* from Greece, described as one of the most thrilling reds in the garden. Jefferson, who seems to have had a penchant for bright red flowers, planted beds of these Lilies at Monticello.

Plant exploration reached a zenith of activity in the nineteenth century, reflected in the growing number of Lilies at the gardener's disposal, among them several fine native species later important in breeding programs: the Panther or Leopard Lily *(Lilium pardalinum)* from California, vigorous and variable, with down-facing Turk's-cap blossoms, crimson toward the petal's tips and brown-spotted and light-colored toward the center; and the American Turk's-cap Lily *(L. superbum)*, common in moist and acid soils

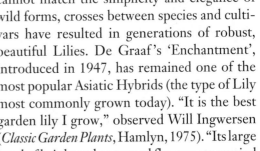

Lilium

from eastern Massachusetts to northwestern Florida and Alabama. The New World was obviously rich in Lilies.

Several introductions from Asia became very popular: the Tiger Lily *(Lilium lancifolium)*, with strongly recurved pinkish orange flowers heavily spotted black and distinctive black bulblets that grow in the axils of the plant's glossy green leaves (by which means it has naturalized as a garden escape when it was no longer wanted), favored for its dependable beauty and resistance to drought and just about anything else, except as a carrier of a virus (to which it is immune) to other Lilies; the gorgeous Goldband Lily *(L. auratum)*, a striking

fall-flowering type with large, fragrant trumpet flowers — ivory with broad yellow bands down the center of each petal and purple blotches on its inner surface; and the Regal Lily *(L. regale)*, discovered in China by E.H. Wilson and first grown at the Arnold Arboretum in 1908. Growing to six feet, each stem of the Regal Lily bears as many as twenty large, fragrant trumpet flowers — white on the inside and rose-purple on the reverse. It is a strong competitor to the Madonna Lily in magnificence and is easier to grow.

Although natural and intended hybrids existed well before the twentieth century, it was not until the 1920s that breeders pursued hybridization in earnest, in an attempt to produce more vigorous, disease-resistant, and easily grown types in a wider range of colors. Jan de Graaf, a great-great-grandson of Cornelis de Graaf, who began hybridizing Lilies in 1790, founded Oregon Bulb Farms in 1934. He was instrumental in taming the wild Lily and devising methods for the mass production of bulbs, making Lilies both attractive and affordable to the ordinary gardener, who no longer had to rely on expensive, sometimes diseased imported bulbs.

While it is probably true that the hybrids cannot match the simplicity and elegance of wild forms, crosses between species and cultivars have resulted in generations of robust, beautiful Lilies. De Graaf's 'Enchantment', introduced in 1947, has remained one of the most popular Asiatic Hybrids (the type of Lily most commonly grown today). "It is the best garden lily I grow," observed Will Ingwersen *(Classic Garden Plants,* Hamlyn, 1975). "Its large head of bright red upturned flowers are carried on sturdy two-foot stems."

I first became aware of Lily mania from my neighbor's daughter, Anne, who grew 'Enchantment' and other hybrids in the unpromising clay sod of northern New Brunswick. Having grown up on a farm barren of all ornamentation, she must have been drawn to the sensuous beauty and brightness of the modern hybrids that de Graaf's work enabled her to enjoy. Her letters were filled with news of her Lily gardens and often with Lily bulblets as well, which she urged me to raise up to maturity. Although she knew she might not live to see them, she had planted wild Lilies in the hope of naturalizing them in a stand of hardwoods, and with a gardener's optimism she wrote, "If they grow or not I'm hoping to try again . . . this spring." She died a few weeks later at age thirty-two, as beautiful as any of the Lilies she loved.

Aside from naturalizing wild Lilies, all types are shown to advantage among shrubs — evergreens such as Mountain-laurel and Rhododendrons or deciduous shrubs such as Mock Orange, Hydrangeas, and Azaleas. Classic combinations include the Regal or Madonna Lily with Roses (especially the Cabbage Rose); Lilies paired with Climbing Roses; and Lilies mulched with low-growing plants such as Violas, Petunias, Columbine, and Forget-me-nots — a fulfillment of the old adage that "Lilies should grow with their feet in the shade and their heads in the sun."

Lilies are often most striking when planted in groups of one kind and one color to form a colony: Tiger Lilies, for instance, by a doorway; Regal or Madonna Lilies by a stone or brick wall; Canada Lilies along a streambank or at the edge of a woodland; Leopard Lilies rising among Maidenhair Ferns in filtered shade. Madonna, Regal, and Tiger Lilies adapt well to the conditions of a herbaceous border, as do any of the hybrids grown in groups among Lupines, Hostas, and Bellflowers.

To Grow: Lily culture is not difficult if you follow a few basic principles. The first and most important one is that Lilies require perfect drainage. My friend Anne grew hers in raised beds or on a natural slope, adding sharp sand and leaf mold to improve the soil's tilth and discourage excess moisture. John Moe, an experienced Lily grower on the West Coast (Washington State), adds peat to his sandy loam to retain moisture. Any soil that grows good potatoes, de Graaf claimed, will grow good Lilies (meaning that the soil should be friable to at least a foot).

Lilies will do well when planted in partial shade in warmer regions (afternoon shade is best), as long as they receive at least five to six hours of sun each day. Full sun in the north is recommended, or plants will be forever looking for it instead of producing flowers.

Plant Lilies in the fall or spring as soon as you receive them, because, lacking a protective papery coat, the bulbs will soon dry out. Set them nine to eighteen inches apart, depending on their height, and cover them with four to six inches of soil (one to two inches for the Madonna Lily). A little bonemeal in the planting hole is O.K., but no other fertilizer should be applied at this time. For lavish display, plant three to five bulbs per square foot.

When the shoots poke up out of the ground, spread fertilizer around the plants and water it in well. Advice varies as to which kind is best. John Moe uses 9-9-9 formulated for Roses and says "that works just fine for me." Lilies need this annual boost to produce many large flowers throughout their season of bloom. Let the leaves wither naturally, as for Daffodils, to help feed nutrients to the bulb. Remove spent blooms.

A mulch, with either plants or other material, is necessary to keep the soil moist around the Lilies. Use whatever you have at hand, such as wood chips, rotted sawdust, or even rotted manure. When the ground freezes, a mulch of coarse litter or evergreen boughs will protect the plants over the winter.

Do Lilies need staking? That depends on their site (if it's very windy, yes) and type. Most Lilies are sturdy if they are growing in self-supporting clumps. Otherwise, stake them with a circle of bamboo sticks held in place with string, or use individual stakes and tie a loop around the plant's stem in several places before looping and tying it around the stake (so the Lily won't choke to death).

In Zones 9 and 10 where winters are mild (above 40°F., or 5°C.), dig up Lilies and refrigerate them for eight weeks to simulate winter rest — unless the plant nursery's instructions indicate otherwise.

Lilies can be left undisturbed for years, but if they lose their vigor, divide them. New plants are easily propagated from roots or stem bulblets. Replant them in a special bed, and don't expect bloom for two or three years.

A cutting garden may be a good idea if you want lots of bouquets, because cutting Lily stems is injurious to the plant's vigor (leave more than one-third of the stem when you cut for flowers). And please don't remove the anthers as florists often do for cosmetic reasons. "Much of the beauty of the flower," wrote the eminent Lily authority George Slate, "is in the richly colored, delicately poised anthers."

The Lily divisions that concern us here are the following:

Division 1 (June bloom) — Asiatic Hybrids; 1-6'; usually with upright flowers; easy to grow.

Division 2 (June bloom) — Turk's-cap Hy-brids, 3-4'; prefer neutral or acid soil and light shade.

Division 4 (late June or early July bloom) — American Hybrids, mostly derived from West Coast species; these include the Bellingham Hybrids; 4-8'; good cut flowers.

Division 6 (July or midsummer bloom) — Trumpet/Aurelian Hybrids from Asiatic species; 2-6'; very fragrant; trumpet or starburst form; sun or partial shade; hummingbirds love them.

Division 7 (August or late bloom) — Oriental Hybrids; 2-6'; fragrant, very showy, orchid-like blooms; partial shade in the afternoon and slightly acid soil; disease-resistant; in warmer regions, plant these deeper than usual; in colder regions, mulch for winter protection.

Division 9 — Wild types such as *Lilium candidum*, *L. auratum*, and *L. regale*.

Collector's Choice (all sold as bulbs unless noted; ※ indicates fragrant types):

Division 9:

※*Lilium auratum*, Goldband Lily (1776-1850); fall bloom; 4-6'; Zone 4. 160; 138; 21; 92(s).

L. canadense, Canada or Meadow Lily (1600-1699); prefers partial shade and leaf mold or humusy soil; July bloom; native. 150.

※*L. candidum*, Madonna Lily (by 1630); prefers dry soil; plant in fall so it can establish its basal leaves; also decorative; June bloom; 3-4'. 50; 162; 20; 138; 133.

'Cascade'; stockier, more disease-resistant strain; the work of George Slate and Oregon Bulb Farms; usual heady fragrance. 150.

L. lancifolium (*L. tigrinum*), Tiger Lily (1800-1850); cultivated longer than any other Lily except the Madonna Lily; plant deep (7-9"); will grow in almost any lime-free soil; full sun best; August bloom; tolerates both dry and damp soil. 133; 138; 175.

'Splendens' (1870); larger-flowered than the species type; nodding, rich salmon red flowers with darkly spotted reflexed petals; awarded the Lily Cup for best spike of blooms at the Fifth International Lily Conference in London, 1989. 50; 175.

L. pardalinum, Leopard or Panther Lily (1850-1900); easy to grow in the Pacific Northwest and northern California, its native habitat; July bloom; 4'; John Moe's favorite among the species. 150; 7.

❀*L. regale*, Regal Lily (1908); July bloom; protect shoots from late frosts in the spring; 5'. 45; 137; 50; 150; 170.

❀*L. speciosum* 'Rubrum', Rubrum Lily (1850-1900); fragrant, pendant recurved white and crimson blooms; fall bloom; 5'; Zone 4. 135; 79; 157; 20.

L. superbum, Turk's-cap or Swamp Lily (1776-1850); magnificent native; 40 or more flowers per stem; likes moist loam; July bloom; 6'; Zone 5. 138; 21; 114; 45.

Hybrids:

❀'Black Beauty' (1958); **Division 7;** outstanding; this Lily has won so many North American Lily Society popularity polls that it was moved to the Lily Hall of Fame; very dark red recurved flowers with a green star in the center, outlined in white, and white-edged petals; 50 or more flowers per stem; indestructible and vigorous; 5-9'; John Moe selection. 45; 150; 88.

'Citronella' (1958); **Division 1;** down-facing golden flowers covered with small black dots; as many as 30 flowers per stem; July bloom; 4-5'; John Moe selection. 88; 150; 178; 45; 20; 138.

'Enchantment' (1947); **Division 1;** up-facing nasturtium red flowers; 2-3'; for Anne. 170;

50; 64; 150; 20; 138.

❀'Moonlight' (1958); **Division 6;** chartreuse-yellow; 3-5'; John Moe selection (he describes the fragrance as "Exquisite, ambrosia"). 20; 150.

'Mrs. R.O. Backhouse' (pronounced "Backus") (1921); **Division 2;** best known of the Martagon Hybrids, bred by Mrs. Back-house, now rare; yellow Turk's-cap flowers flushed magenta-rose with slight spotting; 6'; John Moe selection. 138; 150.

'Shuksan' (1924); **Division 4;** the most famous Bellingham Hybrid; yellow flowers tipped with red and spotted black; needs perfect drainage and moist conditions during active growth; don't water when in flower; protect from winter rains (if there is no snow cover) by placing a flowerpot or tub over the plant; 4'. 150.

❀'White Henryi' (1945); **Division 6;** a magnificent Lily bred by Leslie Woodriff ('Black Beauty') with sunburst-type blooms — white with a pale orange throat and cinnamon-colored flecks in the center; hardy and disease-resistant; consistent winner in NALS popularity polls; 4-5'; John Moe selection. 45; 150.

❀ *Lobularia maritima*

Brassicaceae
1776-1850   ZONES 9–10

Sweet-alyssum

Snowdrift, Sweet-Alison

TYPE: PERENNIAL/HARDY ANNUALFLOWER
HEIGHT: 3-12"   BLOOM: LATE SPRING-
FALL
SITE: SUN/PARTIAL SHADE

Sweet-alyssum (formerly classified as *Alyssum*

maritimum) is a perennial of Mediterranean origin, usually grown as an annual. Its honey-scented, tiny white flowers bloom in elongating racemes on stems with small, narrow light green curved leaves over an extended period — all year where conditions permit — creating masses of mounded bloom spreading in a mat wider than the height of the plant (one foot in the species form). As the flowers fade, they leave behind a series of round pods, each containing one seed.

Introduced into late eighteenth-century American gardens, this profusely blooming little plant of easy and accommodating culture soon became very popular — indispensable for the front of the border and especially favored in the nineteenth century for massing with the annual Edging Lobelia (*Lobelia erinus*), a combination first introduced into the gardening world in 1862 at Kew Gardens and one that is still going strong today.

In the 1930s, Mrs. Wilder recommended planting Sweet-alyssum to edge broad walks and soften the rawness of the ever-popular Scarlet Sage (*Salvia splendens*). The colored type she mentioned, 'Violet Queen' (a washed-out lilac) was, apparently, the only colored form available until the 1950s, when two more were introduced: 'Royal Carpet' (1953), a dwarf form with deep purple flowers with a white eye, and 'Rosie O'Day' (1961), a dwarf form with light pink flowers. Both are still popular, and both have been All-American Medal winners. We tend to think they've been around forever. The favored white dwarf form is 'Carpet of Snow', introduced prior to 1926. Also introduced at that time was the now rare 'Little

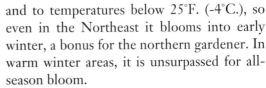

Lobularia maritima

Dorrit', a bushy dwarf form especially suited to pot culture.

Of all the types, nothing beats white Sweet-alyssum for fragrance — "drifts of sweetness," it has been called, like new-mown hay. It can be tucked into small pockets here and there between rocks (as it probably grows in its native habitat) or planted to spill out over the border and along walks, to fill in over spring-flowering bulbs, or to cascade from window boxes or planters of any type. The most beautiful and sprawling Sweet-alyssum I ever saw was a self-sown white type in a Zone 4 city garden, frothing over the side of an old dark brown bathtub, blooming away in late November. Sweet-alyssum is among those annuals resistant to frost and to temperatures below 25°F. (-4°C.), so even in the Northeast it blooms into early winter, a bonus for the northern gardener. In warm winter areas, it is unsurpassed for all-season bloom.

Turn-of-the-century literature mentions double flowers and even variegated leaves — "a variety much used for borders has paler and white-edged leaves" (Asa Gray, *Gray's School & Field Botany*, Ivison, Blakeman & Co., 1887) — both long since vanished from cultivation. But the unimproved Sweet-alyssum is bounty enough for any heirloom gardener.

To Grow: Sow the seeds indoors four to six weeks before the last frost. Leave them uncovered to promote germination in seven to fifteen days at 60°F. to 70°F. (16°C. to 21°C.). (Sow thinly, since the germination rate is usually very high.) As early as possible, plant the seedlings outside four to eight inches apart, depending on the type. Or sow the seeds outside two to three weeks before the last frost. Just scatter them on the ground; later thin the seedlings to the required distance. Sweet-alyssum thrives in sun but tolerates light shade. It prefers well-drained soil on the light side. If you shear the plants halfway back four weeks after blooming, their season will be extended and the spreading mat will not become too rangy. This is especially important to remember where summers are hot and the plants may bloom themselves out unless cut back. Plants can be moved in small clumps anytime during the season to fill in empty spots in the garden. Be sure to cut them back and water them well. To ensure a continuous supply of flowers on fresh mats of foliage, make a second sowing in early June. These plants are especially suited for winter bloom indoors if they are cut back and potted in early fall, or for very early bloom the following spring when planted back outside (see directions for wintering-over annuals on p. 20).

In Zones 9 and 10, Sweet-alyssum blooms year-round and grows as a woody shrublet, which may need to be replaced periodically with fresh plants.

Collector's Choice (all sold as seeds):

Lobularia maritima, Sweet-alyssum; close to species form; fragrant; 1'. 166; 5; 18; 6.

'Carpet of Snow'; dwarf type; to 5"; spreading wide to 12". 87; 133; 101; 92; 168.

❀ *Lonicera* spp.

Caprifoliaceae
1600-1900   ZONES 3-10

Honeysuckle

TYPE: HARDY SHRUB/TWINING VINE
HEIGHT: 5-50'   BLOOM: SPRING-FALL
SITE: SUN/PARTIAL SHADE/SHADE

Although several other plants are sometimes referred to as "honeysuckle," the term most aptly applies to the *Lonicera* species (named for a German doctor, Lonicer) and in particular to the Scarlet or Coral Honeysuckle *(L. sempervirens)*, a beautiful native vine that grows from Connecticut to Florida and Texas. The genus is large — more than 150 species — and includes hardy, vigorous vines and shrubs, several of which are highly regarded for their profuse, usually fragrant blooms beginning in the spring and sometimes lasting all season. The showy trumpet- or funnel-shaped flowers vary from scarlet to yellow or white, grow in pairs or whorled at the ends of branches, and in some species are followed by decorative fruits. The handsome leaves may be evergreen into the fall (longer in the South) or bronze.

"Honeysuckles," wrote Alfred Hottes, "twine through our memories of delicate fragrances. They typify to our mind the cooling influence of shade during the hot days of summer" (*A Little Book of Climbing Plants*, A.T. De La Mare Co., 1933). This is especially descriptive of the Scarlet Honeysuckle, which was grown by Washington and Jefferson, both of whom would have valued a cool bower in their hot summer climates, just as gardeners do today. Although other *Lonicera* vines were introduced later, the Scarlet Honeysuckle remained one of the most popular, particularly loved for its ease of culture; abundant, nearly evergreen, heart-shaped leaves; and continuous flow of lovely tubular flowers — bright scarlet on the outside, soft yellow on the inside — blooming their hearts out from June through August.

Occasionally, a plant "from away" found conditions in the New World so favorable that it made itself at home, growing where it liked across the land (the Kudzu vine is a cautionary tale). This was the fate of Hall's Honeysuckle (*Lonicera japonica* 'Halliana'), introduced by George Rogers Hall of Rhode Island, who practiced medicine in China in the late 1840s and is credited with the greatest number of nineteenth-century introductions from the Orient. His Honeysuckle is widely naturalized in the Middle Atlantic states and elsewhere, but its commonness should not obscure the fact that it is "one of the aristocrats of the garden," according to the discerning Henry Mitchell. Its white trumpets, mellowing with age to buff yellow (its Chinese name means "gold and silver flowers"), delicate fragrance, and bronze leaves in the fall certainly merit this well-earned reputation.

Lonicera sempervirens

In the nineteenth century, Hall's Honeysuckle was virtually synonymous with the vine-covered veranda or porch, as its foliage rapidly makes a dense cover. The Honeysuckle's ability to draw nourishment from the sun to grow abundant leaves that forbid the sun's entry is one of nature's most wonderful designs. My husband remembers when he and the neighborhood kids would gather by his porch to suck the sugary nectar from deep within the flowers of Dr. Hall's Honeysuckle vine.

Several fine species of *Lonicera* shrubs, not to be outdone by the virtues of the hardy, vigorous vines, were introduced during the eighteenth and nineteenth centuries. Foremost among them is the Tatarian Honeysuckle or Bush Honeysuckle (*L. tatarica*) first grown by English gardener and writer Philip Miller in 1752, from seeds obtained from Siberia. It is probably the easiest shrub in the world to grow (it grows on dumps, my local wildflower guide reports), but it is no less desirable for the most discriminating shrub authorities. It is "one of the best of all hardy ornamental woody shrubs," Donald Wyman noted, with no further recommendation being required.

I found three bushes of Tatarian Honeysuckle (white, pink, and dark red) growing in a well-kept vintage 1920s shrubbery, among Hawthorns, Spireas, Hydrangeas, and Roses — all soon to be sacrificed to one of the "Big Ds" in our area (a deck — on which no one ever sat, as far as I could tell). I vividly recall the Honeysuckles at their height of bloom: profuse funnel-shaped flowers literally covered with foraging bees, eager to fill up on an early source of nectar during the shrubs' brief blooming period (about two weeks). I found more specimens in a nearby abandoned garden. Although their flowers were spent and they had not been pruned for at least twenty years, they were still handsome, an effective background (I imagined) for the ruined garden in their midst (Daffodils, Bleeding-heart, and Peonies). A nineteenth-century judgment still rings true today: "Old and common, it still takes the front rank among ornamental shrubs . . . were we to have but one, we would probably choose the honeysuckle."

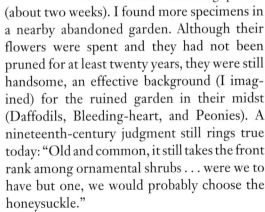

Plant the shrub types in a mixed border, where their brief bloom will be superseded by later-flowering Roses, Hydrangeas, and Viburnums; as a screen (a single specimen will attain nine feet or more); or as a focal point for a flower garden, where their green leaves will help show off perennials such as white Lilies. The twining vines need the support of a trellis, arbor, fence, or wires. Hall's Honeysuckle, left to its own devices, will cover steep slopes or banks or wherever it is needed as a dense groundcover.

To Grow: Honeysuckles of all types grow well in open, sunny spots, but all will tolerate partial shade (Hall's Honeysuckle grows well in shade). Make generous planting holes, mound the soil, drape the roots over it, fill in the hole, tamp down the soil, and water well. A seasonal dressing with well-rotted manure or compost is sufficient. For shrubs, prune out the oldest branches to let in light and renew vigor. With the early-blooming Tatarian, it's better to prune after the fruit is shed. Hardwood cuttings root readily at any time. Plant vines three feet apart to cover banks or six to eight feet apart to romp over fences, arbors, and porches. The vines readily root where they touch the ground. In early spring, prune out old and hardwood branches.

Collector's Choice (all sold as plants):

Lonicera x *heckrottii*, Everblooming Honeysuckle (before 1895); of uncertain origin; carmine buds; fragrant rose-pink trumpets with soft yellow inside; a vinelike shrub; scent released in the evening; well suited to the smaller garden; June bloom until frost; fairly resistant to the honeysuckle aphid; to 5'; Zone 4. 133; 97; 153; 20; 163; 120.

L. japonica 'Halliana', Hall's Honeysuckle (before 1860); twining vine; white to buff trum-

pets; evergreen or bronze leaves; black berries; 12-15'; Zone 4. 97; 31; 114; 138; 34.

L. sempervirens, Scarlet Honeysuckle (1600-1699); native twining vine; scarlet-orange trumpets; red berries; mid-June to August bloom; fairly resistant to the honeysuckle aphid; to 50'; Zone 3. 104; 139; 21; 105; 142.

L. tatarica, Tatarian Honeysuckle (1752); pink-white flowers; red berries; spring bloom; resistant to the honeysuckle aphid; 9'; Zone 3. 31; 114; 30; 21.

'Arnold's Red' (1945); originated at Arnold Arboretum; dark red; very resistant to the honeysuckle aphid. 167; 86; 27; 160; 34; 114.

Lupinus polyphyllus

Fabaceae
1827-1900   ZONES 3-9   NATIVE

Wild Lupine

Purple Lupine, Washington Lupine

Russell Hybrids

1937   ZONES 4-9

Garden Lupine

TYPE: HARDY PERENNIAL FLOWER
HEIGHT: 5'   BLOOM: SUMMER
SITE: SUN/PARTIAL SHADE

Wild Lupine is one of ninety species native to western North America (California and British Columbia), but it is widely naturalized along roadsides from Prince Edward Island and Nova Scotia south to New England. The tall, stout five-foot stalks, with the last two feet densely packed with pealike flowers — shades of bluish purple, red to pink, and white — grow from a rosette of deeply divided leaves, shaped like the palm of a hand, and from a long taproot. Some species are said to be poisonous to cattle, perhaps the source of the genus name, from the Latin *lupus*, meaning "wolf" or "destroyer of the land" — not a pretty description for such an attractive wildflower. In the hybrid form, the color range includes yellow, red, orange, and bicolors, and the plants are shorter, stockier, and more short-lived.

The Wild Lupine was discovered in British Columbia in 1825 and offered soon thereafter to the American gardening public in J.B. Russell's 1833 seed catalog, where it was described as "new and rare." It soon became a popular garden plant, highly valued for its relative ease of culture and showy spikes of flowers in early summer. The color range, from selection and crossing of wild strains, included white, rose, purple, and bicolors.

Several other species of Western Lupines were added to the plant pool in the nineteenth century. Among these were the Tree Lupine (*Lupinus arboreus*), a tall, shrubby plant growing to five feet, with many small spikes of pealike flowers that are often yellow but also white and mauve. In

Lupinus polyphyllus

Britain, hybridization to broaden the Lupine's color range probably began by crossing *L. polyphyllus* with *L. arboreus*, culminating in the work of George Russell of York, who by crossing and recrossing desirable color strains over a period of ten to fifteen years, finally began to achieve his goal. His Lupines were greatly admired by all who saw them and were the occasion for lavish words of praise by the Royal Horticultural Society when the flowers were exhibited in 1937, winning the coveted Gold Medal.

"My first impression was indescribable," wrote D. W. Simmons, one of the judges. "Never before have I seen such marvellous colouring, or been thrilled by such exotic blendings . . . self-colours in rich pink, orange-yellow, strawberry-red; bi-colors of royal purple and gold, apricot and sky blue, rose-pink, and amethysts, and dozens of intermediate shades and combinations on hundreds of massive spikes."

And what became of the native wildflower, once so popular in American gardens? I gained an insight into its history throughout the Northeast, where it is commonly seen along roadsides, on banks, and in fields in early summer. I had always assumed these were garden "escapes," but I observed locally that they are often planted deliberately. On a visit to the Alexander Graham Bell Estate to find remnant plantings of old ornamentals, I had the opportunity to discuss Lupines with Dr. Graham "Sandy" Fairchild of Hollyhock dollies fame, and a highly respected medical entomologist. He and his sister confirmed the truth of what had appeared to be an apocryphal story regarding how their famous father, David Fairchild, had planted Wild Lupines along the roadsides, thus introducing them to the area. Sandy described in detail how his father heeled the seeds into the soil (making a depression in the soil by digging in one's heel, then using the whole foot to cover the seed over with soil after it is planted). Mrs. Fairchild also tossed seeds out the car window. They planted not only *Lupinus polyphyllus* but other Western species as well, none of which has survived. But in early July, the roadside areas are spectacular for the great drifts of Wild Lupines in various shades — bluish purple, pink, bicolored, and white.

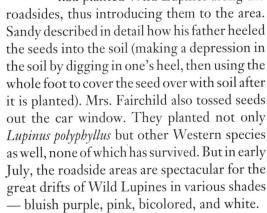

I had always wondered why the hybrids seem to "run out," or revert to the wild bluish purple color. Sandy Fairchild explained that the hybrids are not as hardy as the wild species; the various strains that produce the incredible color range eventually die out, leaving the field clear for the more vigorous wild type, which is predominantly bluish purple. He also explained why the wild species thrive on roadsides and barren banks (unlike the hybrids, which require richer soil). They prefer disturbed areas where nothing else will grow, so once they find a habitat to their liking, they take it over, much to the delight of those who enjoy seeing the great spikes of bloom, usually from a passing car. Because of their vigorous growth in these circumstances, many people assume that Wild Lupines are very easy to grow and thus are frustrated by their failure when the seeds they plant — as Dr. Fairchild did, simply by heeling them in — fail to germinate. Choice of the Wild Lupine's preferred habitat — barren slopes — is the secret to its success.

If you are content to let them reign supreme, naturalize a colony of Wild Lupines where you know they would like to grow. The seed stalks and the foliage have a long season of interest. And who needs to be told the value of the Russell Lupines in the garden? Their gorgeous stalks rise above early summer flowers. On either side of the pergola at the Bell Estate, Lupines still bloom among the old Lemon Yellow Daylilies and white Siberian Iris, in borders that have long been neglected. In my own garden, in sun or partial shade, Russell Lupines grow with Oriental Poppies, Sweet Cicely, Dame's-rocket, and Mountain-bluet. The distinctive tall clumps of leaves are attractive all season long, and the long flower spikes make excellent cut flowers.

To Grow: Wild and Garden or Hybrid Lu-
pines thrive where summers are cool and moist: New England, the Canadian Maritime Provinces, and the Pacific Northwest in Zones 8 and 9. Hybrid Lupines are hardy from Zone 4, but they are short-lived relative to the Wild Lupine. The Wild Lupine, though hardier, is more specific in its growth requirements: dry, light soil and full sun. For best success with the seeds, freeze them for two days, soak them in hot water overnight, and plant them outside, where germination should occur in fourteen to twenty-one days at 55°F. (13°C.). An easier way to establish Wild Lupines by seed is to nick the seeds with a file, then heel them into the soil in the fall. Germination should occur the following spring. They also can be grown by digging up the basal rosettes from an established population when the plants are dormant in very early spring. These should bloom in the first season after transplanting. An established population growing in a favored habitat can be left undisturbed indefinitely.

Plant roots of the Russell Hybrids about eighteen inches apart in well-drained, neutral or slightly acid soil, in sun or light shade. Scratch in bonemeal around the clumps in early spring to ensure the production of many flower spikes. Cut back the spikes after blooming for a second, sparser bloom in the fall. You can propagate these Lupines by seed (as for Wild Lupines), but to retain the most highly prized strains, take four- to six-inch stem cuttings in early spring, making sure a bit of the crown (top of the root structure) is attached. These should flower the following season. Clumps should be divided every three or four years in the fall, when the plant is dormant. The taproot is very long, but it can be trimmed before replanting if the top growth is cut back in equal proportion. If you plant these Lupines in an exposed, windy location, staking may be required.

Collector's Choice:

Lupinus polyphyllus, Wild Lupine; mixed shades. 120; 62; 68 (all plants); 87(s).

'Russell Hybrids Mixed'; pink, salmon, yellow, red, blue, white, and bicolors. 133(p & s); 167(p); 206(s); 111; 79; 138 (all plants).

The following choice cultivars are offered in the spirit of the original Russell Hybrids:

'Chandelier'; yellow shades. 164(p); 3(s).
'Chatelaine'; pink bicolor. 164(p); 3(s).
'My Castle'; red shades. 164(p); 3(s).
'Noble Maiden'; pure white. 164(p); 3(s).
'The Governor'; marine blue bicolor. 45(p); 164(p); 3(s).
'The Pages'; carmine red shades. 164(p); 3(s).

Lychnis chalcedonica

Caryophyllaceae
1600-1699   ZONES 3-10   NATURALIZED

Jerusalem-cross

London-pride, Maltese-cross, Red Champion, Scarlet-lightning, Scarlet Lychnis

L. coronaria

ZONES 3-10   NATURALIZED

Rose Campion

Constantinople, Dusty-miller, Flower-of-Bristol, Flower-of-Bristow, Lampflower, Mullein-pink, Nonesuch

TYPE: PERENNIAL/BIENNIAL FLOWER
HEIGHT: 2-3'   BLOOM: SUMMER
SITE: SUN/PARTIAL SHADE

Although both are members of the Pink Family, Jerusalem-cross and Rose Campion are quite different in appearance, at least to the untrained eye. Jerusalem-cross, a perennial native to northern Russia, bears brilliant scarlet or orange-red, one and a half inch flowers—distinctly cross-shaped and very similar in form to the Maltese cross, once a knightly emblem. The plant grows to two feet on stout, erect stems with coarse, clasping green leaves. The biennial Rose Campion bears magenta or fuchsia (purplish red) flowers along branched stems with narrow, spear-shaped leaves. Both the stems and leaves are noticeably covered with a whitish wool that gives them a gray appearance. The one-inch flowers are flat — five broad, slightly overlapping petals, similar in form to those of Phlox — and are borne singly rather than in clusters. Rose Campion is native to southern Europe and, like Jerusalem-cross, is naturalized locally in North America. The genus name is derived from the Greek *lychnos*, "lamp," a reference to the brilliance of the flowers.

Jerusalem-cross was common in English gardens by the late sixteenth century. Contrary to the folklore that surrounds it, and which its name suggests, Jerusalem-cross does not grow in the Holy Land and was probably not introduced by returning Crusaders, who were often given credit for plant introductions in lieu of any other evidence. By 1629 a double red or scarlet form was known, as well as white and blush singles. By 1772 a double white form was grown. Virtually nonexistent by the 1920s, it may still grow somewhere. Both it and the double red are high on many heirloom plant collectors' wish lists.

Rose Campion was known as a garden plant by the mid-fourteenth century in Europe. By 1597 the white type also was being grown, but rarely. By 1614 the double magenta

---

Campion was introduced, and by 1615 the double white, which by the eighteenth century had almost displaced the singles. Today gardeners are offered the single white or magenta, as well as 'Oculata', a rare type with a purplish red eye, perhaps known since the seventeenth century.

Both Jerusalem-cross and Rose Campion were favorite flowers in early American gardens. Jefferson grew Jerusalem-cross at Monticello, where it was planted in the oval bed in 1807. Rose Campion bloomed in 1767 at Shadwell, his birthplace.

By the end of the nineteenth century, these plants were regarded as "old-fashioned" types, fondly remembered by Alice Morse Earle in her chapter on New England "Front Dooryards" in *Old-Time Gardens* (Macmillan, 1901). She recalled the sorts of flowers one would find in these simple yet pleasing plantings: "ample glowing London Pride" *(Lychnis chalcedonica)* grew among Daylilies, "Flag" Iris, and Canterbury-bells. She described these enclosures, hard-won from the forest, as emblems of the woman's world in earlier days — narrow and monotonous. Yet it was a world easily satisfied by small pleasures, as reflected in those carefully cultivated gardens, pleasant to the home and "no mean things."

Though called "London Pride" in Joseph Breck's catalog, I had never heard Jerusalem-cross referred to by that name until an old-time gardener repeated the name when she gave me a clump of *L. chalcedonica* from her garden, along with some of her cherished beauty, Rose Campion, which she had kept going for fifty years. I soon discovered so many other "Lon-

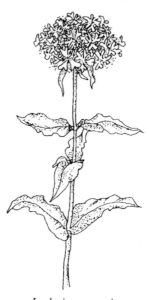

Lychnis coronaria

don Prides" that I concluded it is a generic term for many older favorites.

I have found folk gardeners to be less intimidated by Jerusalem-cross's brilliant color than are contemporary gardeners, who are often afraid of offending sensibilities by planting it near the varicolored flowers of early summer and midsummer. But it blends surprisingly well with soft pink Musk Mallow *(Malva moschata)*, Lupines of all sorts, Siberian Iris, Bellflowers, Foxglove, the lilac-white plumes of Clary Sage, and the yellow daisy-flowered Golden-Marguerite. One is often advised to banish Jerusalem-cross to the safety of low-growing evergreens, where its glowing color will be reduced or neutralized. Consider that Gertrude Jekyll, the mistress of color in the garden, grouped it among orange Daylilies, Dahlias, Marigolds, and Nasturtiums.

The magenta-fuchsia flowers of Rose Campion also blend well with the flowers of early summer and midsummer, the only caution being not to plant it next to its bright red cousin. Its distinctive gray foliage beautifully offsets the brilliant flowers and remains ornamental all season, providing a dramatic contrast to almost any flower in the vicinity. The white-flowered form, with its pristine blooms, is welcome throughout the border, planted in generous drifts among the dark pinks, blues, and purples of Bellflowers, Lupines, and, later, Monkshood. Both Jerusalem-cross and Rose Campion (or its white form) are excellent cut flowers.

To Grow: Jerusalem-cross and Rose Campion can be grown in Zones 3-10 except in Florida and along the Gulf Coast. Seeds can be sown indoors in midwinter and planted out in the spring after all danger of frost has passed. Jerusalem-cross may bloom the first year but won't produce many dense clusters until the following year. Seeds of either also may be sown in a cold frame and the seedlings planted out the following spring, twelve to fifteen inches apart. Jerusalem-cross prefers rich, moist soil and full sun, although it will grow in partial shade in warmer growing regions. In the Northeast or in colder areas, it is especially important to make sure that the soil is moist but well drained. The established clumps do not need dividing for many years.

Rose Campion (or its white form) needs full sun and a light, perfectly well-drained soil. If left to its own devices, it will self-sow with abandon, since it is a short-lived perennial or biennial that must seed prolifically to ensure its survival. In the garden, it's best to control this inclination by cutting down the stalks after flowering, leaving one or two to self-seed. Keep the white and magenta types separate, or the latter will overrun the former.

Collector's Choice:

Lychnis chalcedonica, Jerusalem-cross; perennial. 15(s); 45(p); 6(s); 153(p); 26(s); 62(p); 18(s).

'Alba'; white. 111(p); 92(s); 108(p).

L. coronaria, Rose Campion; biennial or short-lived perennial. 18; 147-8; 5 (all seeds); 49(p); 87(s); 120; 63; 16 (all plants).

'Alba'; white. 111(p); 93(s); 120(p); 15(s).

'Oculata'. 45(p).

Lythrum spp.

Lythraceae
1776-1850   ZONES 3-9   NATIVE/NATURALIZED

Purple Loosestrife

Fine-leaved Willow-herb, Milk Willow-herb, Purple European Willow-herb, Red-Sally, Spiked Loosestrife, Winged Lythrum

TYPE: PERENNIAL FLOWER
HEIGHT: 2-6'   BLOOM: SUMMER
SITE: SUN

Two species of Loosestrife, *Lythrum salicaria* and *L. virgatum*, were introduced from Eurasia; another, *L. alatum*, is native from Ontario west to British Columbia and south to Georgia and Texas. All prefer a moist habitat and produce showy spikes of pink-purple flowers during the summer.

Winged Loosestrife *(L. alatum)* grows to three to four feet and is distinguished from the other species by its wide-angled, or "winged," stem. *L. salicaria*, which grows two to six feet, is the most rampant species and is naturalized over wide areas of North America, growing especially well in wet meadows and ditches. It is distinguished from *L. virgatum* by its downy leaves. Despite these differences, the Purple Loosestrifes are very similar in appearance and difficult to tell apart. The genus name, *Lythrum*, comes from a Greek word meaning "blood," a reference to the brightly colored flower stalks preserved in the common name Red-Sally. The hybrid types of interest here were developed in Canada by the late 1930s, the product of crosses between the native Purple Loosestrife and the less rampant *L. virgatum*.

Alien species of Purple Loosestrife were introduced early into American gardens, appreciated for their dramatic and vigorous wands of brilliant flowers (that never need staking) during the heat of summer. As with many native species, the native Winged Loosestrife was not brought into the garden until later, but by the nineteenth century it, too, was a popular garden flower. All three Purple Loosestrifes were among the most cultivated ornamentals in nineteenth-century America.

Gradually, cultivars — improvements in color and habit — were introduced. Various shades of red, rose, purple, magenta, and pink were combined with a bushier habit for longer bloom on less aggressive plants, some reportedly sterile (not producing seeds, which is the way *L. salicaria* spreads at such an alarming rate, producing *1.2 million* seeds per square meter in an established stand). Early 1900s cultivars were 'Rose Queen' (*L. virgatum*), 'Superbum' (*L. salicaria*), 'Dropmore Purple', 'Perry's Variety', and 'Lady Sackville'.

In 1934 a bud sport of *L. virgatum* appeared in the trial gardens of the Canadian Government Experimental Farm in Morden, Manitoba. Reaching four feet and bearing many spikes of pure pink flowers, it was introduced to the gardening world in 1937 as 'Morden Pink'. Later crosses were made between 'Morden Pink' and the native Winged Loosestrife, producing two more very popular cultivars — 'Morden Gleam' (1953) and 'Morden Rose' (1954) — both with long-lasting rosy red flowers and a pleasing habit of growth. The Morden cultivars reportedly are all sterile, a claim being checked out by scientists at the University of Minnesota, where the

Lythrum

planting of all forms of Purple Loosestrife is banned. They want to find out if they, as well as other sterile types such as 'Dropmore Purple', have the ability to hybridize with the rampant *L. salicaria* or otherwise mutate into seed-producing forms.

Many gardeners who have had long experience growing the sterile types report that they have not increased significantly over the years. Locally, I have found three plantings established forty or fifty years ago from Morden cultivars that have not ventured far from their original sites, though in all three instances, the plants were growing on their own, untended. In the most spectacular find, the rosy pink wands of a Morden Loosestrife were combined in perfect harmony with *Achillea ptarmica* 'The Pearl', both blooming here in midsummer. I took cuttings from both and soon established them in my own garden among Bergamot, Phlox, and Daylilies. I agree wholeheartedly with Elizabeth Lawrence, who observed that Purple Loosestrife "comes as near any plant I know to filling the requirements for a perfect perennial." Once it is planted, it only improves with age and is immune to both disease and drought. In addition, the flowering season can be extended by cutting the spikes of spent blooms. Mrs. Wilder suggested planting Purple Loosestrife by a pool of water, "where we may have the added beauty of wind-stirred reflections," to which I would add other moisture-loving plants such as Yellow and Blue Flag Iris, Hostas, and Bouncing-bet. Purple Loosestrife also makes fine cut flowers.

To Grow: Plant the roots in ordinary garden soil, preferably moist, in early spring in cold

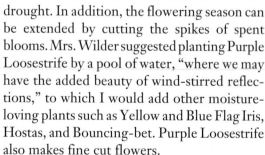

climates and in fall in warmer regions, whenever the plant is dormant. Cover the growth buds, or eyes, with two inches of soil. You can induce bushiness in Loosestrifes with a tendency to bear single stalks by pinching off the stems, just below the top leaves, when the plants are about a foot high. To ensure a good snow cover in windy areas, do not cut the plant back all the way after blooming; leave some "arms" to catch the snow, a useful technique to use with any perennial. The surest way to propagate the Morden cultivars is with stem cuttings taken from shoots at the base of the plant. These easily root in water or any fine medium. Winter-over established plants in a cold frame and plant them out the following spring, fifteen to eighteen inches apart. These Loosestrifes will thrive in full sun but tolerate light shade, especially in warmer climates. They reportedly cannot be grown in Florida and along the Gulf Coast.

Collector's Choice:

Lythrum hybrids (all sold as plants):
'Morden Gleam'; carmine; red-purple fall foliage; 4'. 180; 109; 31; 20; 44; 45.
'Morden Pink'; rose-pink; about 3'. 44; 115; 167; 20; 147; 133.
'Morden Rose'; rose; 3'. 45; 111; 142.

Mahonia aquifolium

Berberidaceae
1822   Zones 5-8
Native

Oregon Holly-grape

Blue Barberry, Holly Barberry, Holly-grape, Holly Mahonia, Mountain-grape, Oregon-grape

TYPE: PERENNIAL SHRUB
HEIGHT: 3-6' BLOOM: SPRING
SITE: LIGHT SHADE

Oregon Holly-grape, native to the northwestern United States and British Columbia, is one of more than one hundred species of evergreen shrubs that also grows in Asia and Central America. It possesses every characteristic a gardener could want in a shrub: medium-short height; spikes of bright yellow flowers in the spring, followed by light blue, then black berries in thick clusters during the summer; glossy hollylike, nearly evergreen leaves changing to bronzy purple in the fall — a plant for all seasons. It is one of the floral treasures brought back from the early nineteenth-century Lewis and Clark Expedition to the Northwest. The genus name is a tribute to Bernard M'Mahon, a Philadelphia nurseryman.

A book about American heirloom plants would be incomplete without acknowledging the efforts of M'Mahon, one of the earliest nurserymen to recognize the horticultural value of native flora. His catalogs, the first of which was published in 1806, regularly offered a wide range of plants — no fewer than one thousand in each issue — including the finest plants from abroad and the most garden-worthy from North America. M'Mahon is closely associated with the Lewis and Clark Expedition, which is said to have been planned at his house. He was the first to ask President Jefferson for some of the collected seeds so that he could raise the plants himself and then distribute them to American gardeners.

Mahonia aquifolium

Jefferson reportedly gave M'Mahon *all* the seeds that had been given to him from the expedition, apparently recognizing their significance for future gardeners. (How fortunate to have had a gardening president!) Thus, M'Mahon was the first one to cultivate the Oregon Holly-grape, which is now the most widely grown of the Western species, popular in the East as well as the West. It is easily grown, and it thrives even under seemingly adverse conditions.

The virtues of the Oregon Holly-grape were well recognized abroad, especially in England, where it received a series of Royal Horticultural Society awards in 1957, 1959, 1962, and 1969 and is regarded as a classic plant, one of Will Ingwersen's choices. Ingwersen referred to its unelaborated wild form as "this magnificent garden shrub." From its earliest introduction in America, it has been praised as "one of the finest low evergreen shrubs we have."

Oregon Holly-grape is favored for foundation plantings because of its moderate height (it won't block windows), distinctive evergreen leaves (like Christmas Holly), and long season of interest, with its beautiful flowers, clusters of grapelike fruits, and, later, handsome colored foliage. It is the perfect choice for shaded or semishaded spots or for massing with Rhododendrons and Azaleas in light, open woodlands. If kept pruned, it can also be used to cover banks or areas where it is difficult to establish a groundcover. There are dwarf strains available for this purpose as well.

To Grow: Oregon Holly-grape grows in almost any type of soil, even dry and sandy; it prefers light shade and protection from the wind to keep its foliage glossy and healthy. Prune it back in early spring to prevent legginess and maintain a fairly short stature (to three feet). A little bonemeal at planting time (in the hole, mixed with the soil) and a dressing of rotted manure will help keep the shrub in good health. Propagation is by suckers, layering, or softwood cuttings taken in the summer and rooted in a cold frame. The foliage and flowers should be considered for use in fresh bouquets.

Collector's Choice:

   Mahonia aquifolium, Oregon Holly-grape. 7; 45; 39; 134; 120; 138 (all plants).

Malva alcea fastigiata

Malvaceae
1850-1900   Zones 4-10   Naturalized

Hollyhock Mallow

Garden Mallow

❁ *M. moschata*

1600-1776   Zones 3-10   Naturalized

Musk Mallow

Type: Perennial Flower/Herb
Height: 2-4'   Bloom: Summer
Site: Sun/Partial Shade

Both the Hollyhock Mallow and the Musk Mallow are native to Europe and quite similar in appearance. The Musk Mallow grows to about two feet; its soft green leaves, which exude a musky fragrance when rubbed or brushed, are finely divided into three to seven lobed segments. The five-petaled, wavy-edged flowers, similar in design to those of the Hollyhock, are in shades of light pink or white and are almost transparent, with a hint of veining.

The flowers grow mostly at the top of the plant in clusters, with the buds jammed into the axils of the leaves (a Mallow Family trait), which accounts for its tremendous flower and fruit production. The fruits are greenish disks packed with little black seeds that must be separated to be planted, just like the larger Hollyhock seeds. Musk Mallow is naturalized along roadsides and in old fields all over the northeastern United States and eastern Canada, extending south to Tennessee and Delaware.

The leaves of the Hollyhock Mallow are not so finely divided, and the plant is taller with showier flowers — rosy pink with more noticeable veining. The more upright stems of the variety *fastigiata* (which means 'upright') are bristly, whereas the Musk Mallow's stems are smooth. The less hardy Hollyhock Mallow is naturalized over a smaller area than its cousin, mainly in the eastern United States. Like the Musk Mallow, it produces plentiful blooms and fruits over a long period in the summer.

The Musk Mallow was grown in colonial gardens, probably for its ease of culture and lovely flowers, fondly remembered from the Old Country, where it grew wild in abundance. Perhaps it was also valued as an herb. "Whosoever takes a spoonful of Mallows," proclaimed the first-century Roman naturalist Pliny the Elder, "will from that day be cured of all diseases that come to him." For centuries species in the Mallow Family have been used to soothe inflammations and a variety of complaints. All parts of the Musk and Hollyhock Mallows contain a mucilaginous sap suggestive of soothing. The genus name, *Malva*, comes from the Greek *malakos*, meaning "softening."

Malva alcea fastigiata

Unlike other useful plants that were abandoned once they were no longer valued for their healing properties, the Musk Mallow was a favorite ornamental throughout the eighteenth and nineteenth centuries. The elegant white form, 'Alba', and the Hollyhock Mallow also were appreciated in the flower border for their beautiful and plentiful shimmering blooms and accommodating habit.

The Musk Mallow is invariably found in older or abandoned gardens in Maritime Canada and the northeastern United States, a garden escape growing among old Lilacs and Rhubarb. It is cherished locally, and, according to legend, is one of the plants the Scottish Highlanders brought with them to the New World, ranking with the Scottish Bluebell (*Campanula rapunculoides*) for Old Country nostalgia. There is a subtle variety in the pink shades of the flowers, and enthusiasts are always on the lookout for superior colors (usually darker pink), collecting seeds and passing them around in the best heirloom gardening tradition.

I discovered Musk Mallow as a field weed on our farm, and in the tradition of countless folk gardeners before me, I dug it up to plant in my herb and flower garden, where I value it for its long season of bloom, beautiful and plentiful flowers, and ease of culture. It is one of the few perennials that really *does* bloom a second time, as advertised, if cut back after the first flowering. In fact, it is so accommodating that new blooms open from the base of the plant even before the old flower stalks have been cut. The Musk Mallow's soft pink or glistening white flowers complement every other garden plant, toning down, for instance, the hard red of the Jerusalem-cross, a combination I learned about from an old-time local gardener. This partnership works wonders for both plants.

I found a fine specimen of the Hollyhock Mallow growing in a tiny garden literally at the edge of the North Atlantic in a fishing village, braving stiff winds, its stems unbowed. The plant, covered with rosy blooms, had been grown from seeds brought to the site by a young bride more than forty years before. The seeds had been taken from plants originally raised by her mother many years earlier. It was evidently a family favorite, passed down from generation to generation.

Both Mallows bloom most of the summer, first among Foxglove, Dame's-rocket, and Sweet-William, and then among Wild-bergamot, Annual Clary Sage, Nicotiana, Feverfew, and, in light shade, Monkshood.

To Grow: Both species of Mallow are easily grown from seeds sown in well-drained garden soil. Seedlings should be thinned to about one foot apart. If you sow the seeds in summer, the plants will bloom the following season. If you sow them in spring, when the soil has warmed, they will bloom by late summer and self-seed thereafter for a fresh supply, if needed. Where summers are very hot, plant Mallows in partial shade and cut them back after blooming for a second round. Plants also can be propagated by division or stem cuttings in spring or summer. Neither species grows well in Florida or along the Gulf Coast.

Collector's Choice:

Malva alcea fastigiata, Hollyhock Mallow. 6(s); 137(s); 20(p); 87(s); 164(p); 109(p).

M. moschata, Musk Mallow. 177(s); 120(p); 164(p); 87(s); 121(p); 5(s).

'Alba'; white. 15(s); 61(p); 26(s); 149; 133; 45 (all plants).

Malva sylvestris

Malvaceae

1800-1850   ZONES 4-9   NATURALIZED

Wild Mallow

Billy-buttons, Blue Mallow, Cheese, Cheese Mallow, Chinese-hollyhock, Common Mallow, Flibberty-gibbet, French Mallow, High Mallow, Pancake Plant, Rags-and-tatters

---

TYPE: ANNUAL/BIENNIAL/SHORT-LIVED PERENNIAL HERB/FLOWER
HEIGHT: 3-6'   BLOOM: SPRING-FALL
SITE: SUN/PARTIAL SHADE

Wild Mallow, native to Eurasia, usually grows to five feet from a long taproot. The strong, round stems bear large, very lobed leaves whose axils produce five-petaled mauve flowers in profusion. Each petal is delicately veined with purple. When the flowers fall, round cheeselike fruits are quickly formed — hence the many country names associated with this plant, which grows wild along roadsides throughout the northeastern and north-central United States. The Latin epithet *sylvestris* means "wild" (literally, "of the forest"), to distinguish it from the Garden Mallow.

A common weed of the English countryside, the Wild Mallow, like other Mallows, is associated with healing powers because of its mucilaginous flowers and leaves, which are also rich in vitamins. The leaves have been a source of food, especially in times of famine, for millennia in the Middle East. The leaves also are used, like okra, to thicken soups, while the juice of the Wild Mallow's leaves is said to soothe bee and wasp stings.

There is not a shred of evidence to support

the idea that the Wild Mallow was used as an herb in the New World, but it is considered an early nineteenth-century plant and was grown by Jefferson at Monticello. He was, it seems, fond of or curious about Mallows in general, for he grew other flowers in the family, including Hollyhocks, the Marsh Mallow (*Alcea officinalis*), and *Lavatera*, besides the Wild Mallow, which he called "French Mallow" because of its mauve flowers (the flower's French name means "mauve").

Elizabeth Lawrence recounted her adventures with *Malva sylvestris* and the cultivar 'Zebrina', describing how she finally learned their identity through correspondence with country gardeners via the market bulletins she made famous: "A little striped mallow that I had been trying to name for some time was in bloom, so I sent a flower and asked whether it was Chinese Hollyhock. It was. It is a biennial but reseeds itself indefinitely. I am always coming on it in old gardens, but no commercial seed companies seem to list it, despite its attractive pink blossoms with lavender stripes and its resistance to heat and drought" (from *American Garden Writing*, ed. Bonnie Marranca, PAJ Publications, 1988). She eventually found the cultivar 'Zebrina' for sale under the name *Malva alcea* rather than *M. sylvestris*.

Years after she wrote of her adventures with the Mallows, I discovered them both. The origins of 'Zebrina' are unknown, so it is not surprising that it should be listed under both *M. alcea* and *M. sylvestris*. Mallows readily cross-pollinate, so it could be a sport of either. Although it shares an upright habit with *M. alcea*, it is a biennial or hardy annual like the Wild Mallow (*M. sylvestris*). Unlike the wild species, it holds its showier flowers above the leaves rather than underneath them.

What is really surprising, considering Elizabeth Lawrence's observation that these Mallows can withstand heat and drought in southern gardens, is that in my northern garden, they really take off as the summer wanes and the temperature begins to drop. 'Zebrina' is an especially beautiful plant, not at all what I had expected from the advertised "striped Hollyhock." It begins to blossom when less than a foot high in early summer, literally covered all along its short stem with shimmering light pink to cream rounded petals that have darker veins radiating out from the center of the bloom, giving the effect of little upturned bells. Later, at about two and a half feet, the side branches also are packed with buds, like so many tightly rolled pink party favors, all crowded in the axils of broad ivy-shaped leaves. By fall, the little Mallow, at three feet, is still valiantly pouring forth its buds, flowers, and fruits (our resident rooster really enjoys these), seemingly impervious to freezing nighttime temperatures and surviving hard frosts into November. I photographed it once still blooming under a light blanket of snow. Like other hardy plants, its flowers seem to take on a more intense color under cold conditions.

Malva sylvestris mauritiana is a variant Mallow type. Taller than the usual form (growing to six feet), it has spectacular flowers — rosy mauve, loosely doubled, and deeply veined. It was introduced to American gardeners with great fanfare in 1987 as "new," but it was commonly grown long before that, for it is listed in Liberty Hyde Bailey's authoritative 1942 *Gardener's Handbook* (Macmillan).

All these Mallows look best when massed against a stone wall, a fence, or a building, especially against weathered or white boards, where the beautiful blooms show themselves to advantage. The shorter 'Zebrina' is stunning when planted in groups in a mixed flower border, where they always elicit favorable comment. Jefferson's Mallow (*Malva sylvestris*) can be planted in a sunny wild garden where it can sow as it likes from year to year.

To Grow: Wild Mallow and 'Zebrina' can be grown from seeds sown outside in spring when the soil has warmed (when you plant beans). They like light, not overly rich soil (which produces many leaves and fewer flowers). The seedlings should be thinned to one foot apart.

Drora's Jerusalem Mallow Pie

The large leaves of the Wild Mallow or its variant mauritiana *can be used to make this delicious quiche.*

DOUGH
Makes enough for two pies, both thinly covered.

1 cup yogurt
¾ cup margarine
3 cups flour
Salt to taste

Mix all the ingredients together, and roll out the dough as for a pie.

FILLING

1 cup cooked wild mallow leaves
5 ounces cheese cut in small pieces (two or three kinds, one salted)
4 eggs
½ cup flour
2 to 3 tablespoons powdered mushroom soup mix
Garlic powder and black pepper to taste

Mix all the ingredients together. Spread the filling on the bottom crust. Cover the filling with another thin layer of dough. Bake about 40 minutes at 350°F.

Once established, the plants should self-seed. In warmer regions, where the plants are almost evergreen, they may be perennials or short-lived perennials, always leaving progeny behind from season to season. The more compact 'Zebrina' can be cut back in the fall and potted to grow and bloom profusely in a cool greenhouse, then cut back and replanted in the spring. Since 'Zebrina' may revert to type or cross-pollinate with Wild Mallow, it is best propagated from stem cuttings or plantlets that grow at its base. Never plant these two Mallows near each other if you want to keep the strain pure.

Malva sylvestris mauritiana needs a longer growing season than the other two Mallows. Except in southern gardens, it should be grown from seeds started indoors in late winter or early spring. Seeds germinate in fifteen to twenty-one days at 70°F. (21°C.). Plants need full sun, light soil, and some protection from the wind (otherwise they may need staking). The other two Mallows can grow well in filtered shade.

Collector's Choice:

Malva sylvestris, Wild Mallow. 147-8(s); 177(s); 121(p).
M. sylvestris mauritiana. 92(s); 87(s).
M. sylvestris 'Zebrina', Zebrina Mallow. 15(s); 22(s).

Mertensia virginica

Boraginaceae
1700-1776   ZONES 3-8   NATIVE

Virginia-bluebells

Blue Funnel Flower, Mountain-cowslip, Roanoke-bells, Virginia-cowslip

TYPE: PERENNIAL FLOWER
HEIGHT: 2'   BLOOM: SPRING
SITE: PARTIAL SHADE

Virginia-bluebells, one of our most beautiful wildflowers, have long been cultivated as garden plants. They are native to Virginia, but also grow in moist woodlands and along streams from New York south to Tennessee and Alabama and west to Kansas, which suggests that they adapt well to different climatic conditions. They are among the earliest flowers to break through the ground in early spring, rising to about two feet and bearing trumpetlike blooms — pink in bud and light blue in flower — that are most attractive to bees (like Lungwort, *Pulmonaria officinalis*, to which it is related by family). The smooth oval leaves are strongly veined, emerging first as pink shoots and then turning silvery green. After the flowers have bloomed, the whole plant gradually dies back to earth.

Mertensia virginica

The early settlers compared Virginia-bluebells to the Lungwort they remembered from cottage gardens — a cure-all for lung ailments. By the eighteenth century, Virginia-bluebells were grown as ornamentals, as in the gardens of Lady Skipwirth of Virginia. She called them the "blue funnel flower" and probably got them from the wild to plant among her Monkshood, Florentine Iris, Cowslips, and Sweet-William. She and her husband, Sir Peyton, left detailed records of their gardening activities, which were discovered in 1946 when their estate was being auctioned. These were sometimes written on the backs of old bills and scraps of paper, in the tradition of gardeners since time immemorial (or at least since the invention of the alphabet and paper). Pieced together, they give us a good idea of what was grown in eighteenth-century American gardens and the sorts of native plants — like Virginia-bluebells — that were considered choice. These records also tell us that while nursery stock could be ordered from commercial sources (some came from William Prince Nurseries on Long Island — a source for Washington and Jefferson as well), many other plants came from various other sources, including neighbors and the wild: "Shrubs to be got where I can," Lady Skipwirth noted. "Bulbous roots to get when in my power." Only a determined and curious gardener like Lady Skipwirth (with the means at her disposal) could have assembled the wide variety of plants grown at Prestwould, the family estate.

I first saw Virginia-bluebells growing in a sprawling garden on a remote hillside farm among bright yellow Leopard's-bane — a striking combination. I should add that these were planted in full sun, in contradiction to the usual advice to plant Virginia-bluebells in partial shade. Probably like most plants that require such conditions as a rule, Virginia-bluebells will grow well in a sunny spot the farther north they are planted, provided soil conditions are suitable. Since they are dormant by late spring or early summer, consider grouping them among other plants that will fill in after them — Wild Bleeding-heart, Maidenhair Fern, Bergamot, and Nicotiana, all of which grow well in light shade or in sun in the North. Hostas of different sorts also work well.

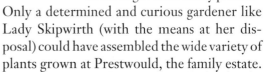

To Grow: Where springs are warm, plant Virginia-bluebells in partial shade; elsewhere full sun is O.K. if the soil is moderately moist, cool, and humusy. Plant the roots one foot deep and about six inches apart. The plant increases rapidly under optimum conditions and can be divided anytime after blooming. Replant young roots (not old black ones) or collect seeds and sow them in a cold frame anytime during the summer (preferably when the seeds are fresh) to produce blooming plants the third year.

Collector's Choice:

Mertensia virginica, Virginia-bluebells. 35(p & s); 26(s); 108; 20; 142 (all plants).

❧ Monarda didyma

Lamiaceae
1700-1776   ZONES 4-10   NATIVE

Bee-balm

Bergamot, Fragrant-balm, Oswego-tea, Red Bee-balm, Red-bergamot, Red-mint, Scarlet-bergamot, Sweet-bergamot

❧ M. fistulosa
Wild-bergamot

Blue Monarda, Purple-bergamot

❧ M. punctata
Horsemint

Dotted Monarda

TYPE: PERENNIAL FLOWER/HERB
HEIGHT: 2-5'   BLOOM: SUMMER-FALL
SITE: SUN/PARTIAL SHADE/SHADE

The native Bergamots grow by vigorous stolons or runners that develop a dense mat of basal foliage — tapering, toothed, and aromatic. Bee-balm can grow to six feet, though cultivars and hybrids are shorter (three to four feet). It favors moist woodlands and bottomlands from New England to Georgia and Tennessee. The whorled flowers sit atop square stems — typical of the Mint Family, to which Bergamots belong. They are borne in clusters, sometimes two-tiered, from red-tinged bracts. The scarlet petals are long and tubular, giving the flower head a ragged or fringed appearance. Hummingbirds, rather than bees (as the common name would suggest), visit the blooms to sip the sweet nectar with their long beaks.

Wild-bergamot grows in a quite different habitat — in the dry soil of abandoned fields and mountainous areas from New England south. Its flowers, growing from lilac-tinged bracts, are pale lilac in color. The petals are shorter than those of Bee-balm, thus allowing fertilization by visiting bees and large moths.

Both species have a sweet, citrusy aroma (evident when weeding or even just walking in their vicinity) similar to that of bergamot oil, which is actually extracted from the tropical tree *Citrus aurantium.* The genus is named for Nicholas Monardes, a Spanish physician and sixteenth-century author of *Joyful News of the New Founde World*, wherein the useful properties of such native herbs as the Bergamots are described.

The herbal uses of both Bergamots were well known to the Indians, from whom the early settlers learned to use the leaves to make a soothing tea, flavor meat dishes, relieve bronchial congestion, and dry up pimples, as well as in a pomade to oil the hair.

Bee-balm has earned a permanent place in American history because of its widespread use as Oswego tea by American patriots during their struggles with the British over import duties on Chinese teas. Oswego tea was first associated with the Oswego Indians, who lived by the shores of Lake Ontario, where Bee-balm was gathered for tea and other purposes. By 1656 the British were enjoying Wild-bergamot as an herb and garden flower, and after 1744, when Bartram sent seeds of Bee-balm to Peter Collinson, it, too, was cultivated and enjoyed as an American exotic.

By the nineteenth century, a number of other species were introduced to American gardeners. Two of these were Dotted Monarda or Horsemint (*Monarda punctata*), with

Monarda didyma

whorls of yellow, purple-spotted flowers and showy white or lilac bracts, and Red and White Monarda (*M. russeliana*), named for Dr. Russell, who aided the English botanist Thomas Nutall in his 1819 explorations in Arkansas. Both these Bergamots prefer the same habitat as the Wild-bergamot (dry, sandy soil), though both are less hardy. Hybrids and cultivars, mostly from *M. didyma* and *M. fistulosa*, followed; the most popular and enduring one was 'Cambridge Scarlet', developed in the early 1900s.

My experience many years ago with the Bergamots is a cautionary tale for the novice who admires a plant in bloom and wants it without ever considering its proper Latin name. I thought I was raising up the bright scarlet Bee-balm, from seeds listed simply as "Bergamot" under the heading "Herbs" in a seed catalog. In fact, the flower that eventually bloomed was the pale lavender Wild-bergamot, a fine plant, too, and one I learned to value in the garden, but not what I had had in mind. One need not be a botanist to order plants and seeds, but a good working knowledge of botanical nomenclature is helpful.

The Bergamots are valued in the garden for their fresh flowers — flamboyant in the case of Bee-balm — in midsummer, when their long-lasting blooms bring new life to any planting. All species can be naturalized in their favored habitats. Bee-balm does best along streams and ponds and in light woodland settings, with Hostas and Maidenhair Ferns, or in the shade of a perennial border. In filtered shade, the glorious scarlet flowers are brighter and longer-lasting than in sun. The other species that favor dry, sunny growing conditions can be naturalized with such natives as Butterfly Weed and Black-eyed-Susans or grown in a more formal flower border. All the Bergamots are surprisingly adaptable as long as their basic requirements are met. I like to use them as easy-care plantings wherever possible.

One summer a young guest was given the task of pulling the petals off the bright flower heads of Bee-balm to scatter over a large bowl of colorful lettuces. She really enjoyed the job, which was new to her, but the next day we were puzzled when she asked whether it was "O.K. to eat a whole big bowl of petals," nodding toward our twelve-inch wooden bowl. After the guests left and we'd tidied up the little cabin — bordered generously with Bee-balm — we understood the significance of her question: she had plucked and eaten every petal (apparently none the worse for it), but there would be no more hummingbirds that season to entertain guests.

To Grow: Bergamots can be grown to Zone 10, except in Florida and along the Gulf Coast. Plant the roots one and a half to two feet apart and one inch deep. Bee-balm will grow in full sun if the soil is moist, but its flowers are not as brilliant or as long-lasting as in dappled shade. Rich soil is best. Clumps should be divided every three or four years because the center loses vigor and becomes hard. Use side shoots with their roots to establish new plantings, discarding the hard center mat. Seeds can be sown indoors in January for bloom the first season. Germination takes one to two weeks at 70°F. (21°C.). Or sow seeds in a cold frame during the summer and plant out the seedlings the following spring. Save the seeds of favorite strains or sports, or carefully propagate them by division.

Wild-bergamot and Horsemint can be grown in light shade where summers are hot; elsewhere they prefer full sun and light, even poor soil for best blooming. They bloom earlier than Bee-balm, so if you cut their stalks back after flowering, a new mound of fresh leaves will be of interest the rest of the season.

Collector's Choice:

Monarda didyma 'Cambridge Scarlet', Bee-balm. 121; 133; 137; 77; 169; 155 (all plants).

M. fistulosa, Wild-bergamot. 73(p & s); 15(s); 36(p); 108(p); 35(s); 164(p).

M. punctata, Horsemint; thyme-scented; Zone 6. 6(s); 15(s); 108; 68; 142; 155 (all plants).

Myosotis spp.

Boraginaceae
1776-1900   Zones 3-10   Naturalized

Forget-me-not

Garden Forget-me-not, Scorpion Grass, True Forget-me-not, Woodland Forget-me-not

Type: Annual/Biennial/Short-lived
        Perennial Flower
Height: 4"-2'   Bloom: Spring-Summer
Site: Sun/Partial Shade/Shade

Forget-me-nots, members of the Borage Family, are widely distributed throughout the temperate zones. Both native and introduced types (from Europe and Asia) grow across North America, mainly in damp or wet areas. The plants are easily recognized by their small sky blue or bright blue five-petaled flowers, usually with a bright yellow center, growing on erect and trailing stems with angled, lance-shaped downy leaves. A profusion of flowers is borne in false racemes or rolled-up spikes that uncoil over the course of the season as the flowers open, leaving behind seedpods along the length of the stem that spill out over the ground to ensure a new generation of plants. The genus name, *Myosotis*, from the Greek *mys*, "mouse," and *otis*, "ear," refers to the plant's leaves.

The Forget-me-not of romance and legend is the perennial bright blue True Forget-me-not *(Myosotis scorpioides/M. palustris)* from Europe and Asia, so named, the story goes, because a knight who drowned while fetching the pretty flowers for his lover called out, "Forget me not!" Ever since it has been a symbol of loving remembrance. Less well known (and far less romantic) is the legend that Henry Bolingbroke, banished from England by his cousin King Richard II, adopted the flower as a badge of revenge, an association based on the curled-up flower spikes' supposed resemblance to a scorpion. This characteristic led to the belief among ancient herbalists that the Forget-me-not was an antidote for venomous bites. The scorpion association is preserved in the Latin epithet *scorpioides*, while the romantic legend is preserved in the plant's common name.

Although known since antiquity and introduced to American gardeners by the eighteenth century or earlier, Forget-me-nots were not widely grown until the nineteenth century. Like other plants that were introduced relatively late but that enjoyed great popularity, Forget-me-nots are considered old-fashioned in the best sense — "the heart's darlings of the garden," one early twentieth-century writer observed.

There are two types of Forget-me-nots for heirloom gardeners to consider: the short-lived perennial True Forget-me-not of romance and legend and the Garden or Woodland Forget-me-not *(Myosotis sylvatica)*. The latter is an annual or biennial that has been the source of most of the cultivars that remain popular today and is most commonly found around old homesites and graveyards, growing as a garden escape. The advantage of the perennial type is that it has flowers all season long, not just in the spring. The advantage of the annual/biennial is that, except for pulling out excessive growth, virtually no attention is required after its initial establishment. In fact, one tends to forget the bright blue perennial, and after several seasons it may disappear unless care is taken to replenish the planting by division or reseeding. This habit of growth is always a sure test of the gardener's observance.

I like both types: the perennial for its everblooming nature and the annual/biennial for its froth of bloom, which is inextricably associated with the flowers of spring — foamy clouds of blue, rose, or white (natural variations) that look particularly at home among Daffodils, Bleeding-heart, Columbine, Sweet Cicely, and Cowslips. The perennial provides bright blue mats of color in shady and damp spots, often so difficult to embellish with flowers. There it can grow with Bee-balm and Monkshood, as well as the stunning Japanese Primrose. Both types of Forget-me-not can be cut for bouquets, especially little nosegays (tussie-mussies).

To Grow: Sow seeds of either type indoors six to eight weeks before the last frost. Keep them at 55°F. to 60°F. (13°C. to 16°C.) and cover them well, since they need darkness to germinate. This should occur in five to twelve days. Plant out the seedlings nine to twelve inches apart, keeping in mind that they may spread in an area as wide as their height. The annual/biennial may bloom the first season, self-seeding thereafter. Don't worry about ruthlessly thinning it out after its bloom has passed; enough seeds will be left to sprout plenty of new plants. Untended, this Forget-me-not will form mats that can smother other plants or take up needed room. Choice cultivars may need to be reseeded or watched closely to keep the strains pure.

Alternatively, you can sow seeds of either type outdoors in a cold frame or directly in the ground anytime over the summer for bloom the following spring (or winter where conditions permit). The perennial type needs dividing every three or four years or reseeding if necessary. Both types of Forget-me-nots will grow in sun or shade as long as the soil is moist; wild forms will grow in very wet conditions.

Myosotis sylvatica

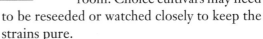

Collector's Choice:

Myosotis scorpioides/M. palustris, True Forget-me-not; perennial; bright blue with yellow, pink, or white eye; 1½'. 18(s); 111; 74; 117; 149 (all plants).

M. sylvatica, Garden Forget-me-not; annual/biennial; sky blue; 1-2'. 109(p); 6(s; sold as 'Tall Blue').

'Blue Bird' (by 1934); large bright blue flowers; 1'. 133; 126; 92 (all seeds).

'King Henry' (old strain; close to wild form). 5(s).

'Rose'; pale rose; 16". 6(s); 168(s).

'Royal Blue' (by 1928); early, free-flowering type; deep blue; 12". 92(s); 168(s).

'Victoria' (by 1928); large flowers; sky blue or mixed; dwarf form; good for pot culture. 137(s); 138(p); 62(p).

❧ *Myrrhis odorata*

Apiaceae
1600-1776   ZONES 3-10

Sweet Cicely

British Myrrh, Giant-chervil, Shepherd's-needle, Sweet-bracken, Sweet-chervil, Sweet-fern, Sweets

Myrrhis odorata

TYPE: PERENNIAL HERB/FLOWER
HEIGHT: 2-3'   BLOOM: SPRING
SITE: PARTIAL SHADE/SHADE

Sweet Cicely's Latin name *(Myrrhis odorata)* comes from the Greek word for perfume, a reference to this plant's sweetly fragrant flowers, leaves, and seeds (similar to anise or licorice). A native of Europe, it has naturalized in Great Britain along riverbanks and in wet, shady areas. In spring the stalks rise to three feet from ferny mounds of soft green leaves with whitish flecks, bearing saucer-sized umbels of sweet white florets. The roots are thick (about two inches around) and grow down about a foot into the ground, making it difficult to dig up a plant once it's established. Sweet Cicely spreads its long, flat, oily seeds generously, however, ensuring new seedlings every year.

This plant has been cultivated at least since the sixth century for culinary and medicinal purposes. All its parts — leaves, seeds, and roots — can be eaten. The pressed oil was once of great value for scenting and polishing oak floors and furniture; the stalks and leaves are said to yield a beautiful green dye. Medicinally, Sweet Cicely was used to treat coughs, flatulence, consumption, and other complaints.

Sweet Cicely was cultivated in the earliest American gardens, probably by the Plymouth settlers — a hardy, unpretentious lot, who would hardly have had the time or the need to scent their furniture. Most likely Sweet Cicely was regarded as very useful because all its parts were edible and it was easy to grow. In lieu of other fresh vegetables, a salad of boiled roots dressed with oil and vinegar would have been quite acceptable. And it was said to be "very good for old people that are dull and without courage; it rejoiceth and comforteth the heart and increaseth their lust and strength" — altogether a most useful settler herb.

Once it was no longer needed, Sweet Cicely disappeared from the American garden scene. "It had a certain vogue in the sixteenth and seventeenth centuries," observed American herbalist Helen Fox, "but now is rarely cultivated in gardens" (*Gardening with Herbs for Flavor and Fragrance*, Macmillan, 1933). The herb renaissance that Mrs. Fox pioneered helped to bring this lovely plant back in fashion among herb gardeners and, increasingly, among all discerning gardeners partial to beautiful and hardy perennials.

Sweet Cicely has a most pleasing habit, whether in leaf, bloom, or seed. It is essential in the early spring border — its graceful umbels rising from the ferny mound of leaves, growing among old-time favorites such as Bleeding-heart (*Dicentra eximia*), Cowslips, and early Iris. The long, shiny black seeds that quickly follow the flowers make a spectacular backdrop for later-blooming plants such as Mountain-bluet and Poppies. After it is cut back, the leaves quickly return as an attractive evergreen mound until the snow flies.

To Grow: Sweet Cicely is usually grown in shade or partial shade but it can be grown in sun if the soil is moist and the roots are well covered and shaded by nearby plants such as Forget-me-nots. The soil, in any case, should be enriched and humusy. The plants are most easily propagated by self-sown seedlings that turn up in the vicinity of the mother plant in early spring. At this stage, they are easy to pull up and replant where you want them. If you are lulled by the beauty of the plant covered with its distinctive seedpods, you can expect a little forest of seedlings the following season. The fresh seeds fall to the ground and germinate after freezing during the winter. To grow Sweet Cicely from seed, freeze the seeds for one to three months before sowing them outside in early spring. Thin the seedlings to about one foot apart.

Collector's Choice:

Myrrhis odorata, Sweet Cicely. 93(p); 133(s); 77(p); 87(s); 36(p); 49(p).

❀ *Narcissus* spp.

Amaryllidaceae
1600-1950   Zones 3-8

Daffodil

Daffadowndilly, Jonquil

Type: Hardy Bulb
Height: 6-18"   Bloom: Spring
Site: Sun/Partial Shade

There are about twenty-six species of *Narcissus* native to Asia, the Mediterranean region, and Europe, where they have been highly regarded for centuries, if not millennia, for their beauty. For instance, the "lily among thorns," from the Old Testament's Song of Songs, alludes to the dainty bunches of *N. tazetta* that grow wild in the fertile valleys of the Holy Land among the spent stalks of wild thorns.

Daffodils grow from underground bulbs that send up strong stems with strap- or rushlike foliage in early spring, sometimes breaking through snow or frozen ground in colder regions. The beautiful six-petaled flowers, fragrant in varying degrees, are usually white, yellow, or a combination of both and are composed of a *perianth* (the petals) and a *corona* (the central cup or trumpet). This structure has been of great interest to breeders, who have created hundreds, probably thousands, of variants since the early nineteenth century, when botanical knowledge was greatly expanded. In nature, Daffodils also cross-pollinate readily, giving rise to natural hybrids.

Although Jonquil is frequently used as a generic term to describe *Narcissus*, this word actually refers to only one species, *N. jonquilla*, an especially fragrant type with rushlike foliage. Daffodil, however, correctly refers to all the many species, hybrids, and cultivars.

The colonists in New England and the Dutch settlers grew Daffodils (Daffadowndillies) as early as the 1600s — "trumpets, poets, doubles, and multiplex" types. Since these have no medicinal value worth noting (though the poisonous bulbs have been used in the preparation of ointments), they were obviously grown for the same reasons they are today. "No other flower in the world," Rockwell and Grayson noted, "is quite so universally and definitely associated with any one season, or so completely embodies in its characteristics the atmosphere and essence of a season. Nature has made the daffodil the perfect symbol of that time of year . . . that not all the hybridizers in the world have been able to change" (*The Complete Book of Bulbs*, J.B. Lippincott, 1977). Daffodils bloom brightly and bravely in the face of stiff winds and cold temperatures, heralds of the new growing season ahead. How that must have cheered the early settlers!

Old Daffodils of various types still mark the remnant gardens of abandoned homesteads throughout North America, proof of their tremendous vigor. Finding and collecting them, thus saving them from extinction, is one of the most pleasurable pursuits of the heirloom gardener. And where they bloom, other treasures may not be far away.

When we moved to the old farm in 1970, I noticed a Daffodil I'd never seen before: a small, very late-blooming type (often a sign of

Narcissus

an old type) with white double flowers, faintly tinged with yellow centers, growing on tall stalks (to eighteen inches) with long, narrow leaves. Just a few of these in a vase fill our farm kitchen with their sweet, though not cloying, fragrance after the hundreds of Daffodils naturalized along our lane have spent their beauty. Locally, this type is known as the "French Lily" or "White Lily," rather common in old gardens but not commercially available.

Another old type that now grows in my garden (a gift from a neighboring farm) is the very early golden yellow "Double English Daffodil," described by Parkinson as "Pseudonarcissus Anglicus flore pleno," with very doubled trumpets. When it first bloomed, it had the appearance of a "Ragged Robin" type, with both double corona and perianth, often described as "sloppy." This is the Telemoneus Plenus or Van Sion also described by Parkinson in 1629. It is common here in older gardens. It could be that the blooms have actually been transformed in my garden, reacting to soil or climatic conditions. A.E. Bowles, an authority on the genus and its variants, observed in Reynolds and Tampion's book *Double Flowers* (Van Nostrand Reinhold, 1983) that "the origin of the common double daffodil is as much a mystery as that of domestic animals," so I no longer worry about its identity but enjoy its hardiness, very early bloom, and extraordinary vigor, flowering in drifts among the multicolored little pink and blue bells of my old Lungwort (*Pulmonaria officinalis*) beneath the dappled shade of an old Lilac tree. A favorite later in the season is Old Pheasant's-eye, strongly perfumed with flared-back white petals and a flat, disk-shaped cup rimmed in

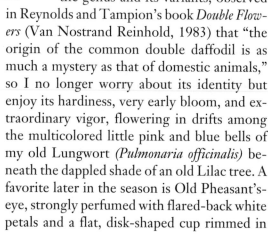

red with a large green eye. This was an early nineteenth-century introduction and a variant form of the older Poet (*Narcissus poeticus*) that was grown in America between 1700 and 1776. In my opinion, there has never been an improvement in the form of my Old Pheasant's-eye, but connoisseurs might disagree.

Modern Daffodil forms, now regarded as old-fashioned classics, also can be found in local gardens, doing very well on their own. One day in late spring my husband and I were exploring the remnants of an old garden recently demolished by one of the island's "3 Ds" (in this case a 'dozer; the other two being the deck and the satellite dish). We were startled by a great expanse of bright yellow carpeting the ground beneath a stand of poplars. All around were piles of brush from a recent logging operation, but the poplars, of no commercial value, had been left untouched. The bright yellow came from a large population of the splendid 'King Alfred' Daffodil, a feature of North American gardens since it was bred by English clergyman John Kendall and introduced to the gardening world in 1899, the eve of the modern era. 'King' has been described as the "single greatest advance ever made in the progress of daffodils." It is certainly one of the best loved, with its clean lines and large, bold yellow trumpets — the essence of Daffodil for many gardeners.

The uses of Daffodils in the landscape are varied, but foremost among them, if you have the space, is to plant them generously beneath old fruit trees (plum, cherry, or apple) or any deciduous tree or shrub (Lilac or Mock Orange), where they will receive sufficient sun before the trees leaf out and sufficient shade later in the season to allow the foliage and bulbs to ripen without drying out. The diminutive types, such as Angel's-tears (*Narcissus triandrus*), are well suited to rock gardens or pot culture (as is almost any Daffodil) for the terrace or patio. Choice cultivars such as 'Mrs. R.O. Backhouse', the first pink Daffodil (it's really a light apricot) is seen best in a flower bed among a cloud of blue Forget-me-nots and Virginia-bluebells (*Mertensia virginica*). Annuals such as Poppies, Marigolds, Balsam, and Nicotiana fill in nicely when the Daffodils' blooms are spent. By planting early, midseason, and late-blooming types, you can have eight weeks or more of bloom.

To naturalize Daffodils, use this simple method: Throw a handful of bulbs in the area where you want them to grow, then plant them where they fall by plunging in your trowel to its handle; planting the bulb, growing tip up, at the bottom of the opened slit of earth; and covering the slit well with your foot. Dust the area with bonemeal once a season and remove spent flower stalks (not everyone thinks this is necessary, but I do it). Gardeners are usually advised to plant one of a kind — one hundred to each drift — but I prefer a mixed planting (I have the deservedly famous collection known as "The Works") where the bloom period is extended by a range of beauties, from early-flowering singles to later, very fragrant doubles and multiple-flower types. Such a planting provides great scope for bouquets, which brings me to the cutting bed.

After you become familiar with the possibilities within the range of heirloom Daffodils (far more than I have listed), you will know which ones you like best for cutting. Dig these up after they have flowered (see the directions in Part I, p. 22), either setting aside the bulbs to dry and replanting them in the fall in a specially prepared cutting garden with plants arranged in rows for easy access, or replanting the bulbs at once with a good ball of dirt still around their roots. In either case, mulch the area with several inches of material (not grass) so the ground will retain moisture all summer. Plant extra-early and extra-late varieties to prolong the "golden and glorious" Daffodil season indoors. When cutting stems for bouquets, choose flowers that are well budded out and just barely opened. After cutting, plunge the long stems into deep, *cold* water for several hours before making your arrangement.

To Grow: Daffodils grow best in well-drained clay or sandy loam with a pH of 6.0 to 7.0. In Zones 3-5, plant the bulbs in September or early October; in Zones 6-7, in October or early November; and in Zones 8-10*, in November or December. Daffodils planted during the optimum period have the best chance of developing roots in the fall and plentiful flowers the following spring.

The rule of thumb for planting depth is two to three times the height of the bulb; large bulbs need five to six inches of soil on top of them, while smaller species types need only three inches. Put a teaspoon of bonemeal in the bottom of each hole, cover it with a little loamy soil or sand, and plant the bulb on top, firming it in place and covering it with the required amount of soil. Allow five large bulbs, or seven to ten smaller ones, per square foot.

Daffodils, especially the wild kinds, are perfectly designed to supply their own nutrients through their decaying leaves, which in turn feed the underground bulb. The secret of success, in my experience, is not to interfere in this process, which takes up to six weeks, after which the leaves may be cut back or removed. Dust the plants with bonemeal annually; a good time is after flowering, while the leaves still mark the spot. Dig up and replant bulbs

only when they lose their vigor, apparent in reduced blooms. The small bulbs that develop around the larger ones can be replanted; it will take a few years before they reach the blooming stage.

Division 1: Trumpet Narcissus. The most popular type, with one flower per stem and the trumpet as long or longer than the perianth ('King Alfred').

Division 2: Large-cupped Narcissus. One flower per stem, with the cup or trumpet more than one-third but less than the total length of the perianth ('Mrs. R.O. Backhouse').

Division 3: Small-cupped Narcissus. One flower per stem, with the cup not more than one-third the length of the perianth, ('Barrett Browning').

Division 4: Double Narcissus. All with more than one layer of petals ('Cheerfulness').

Division 5: Triandus Narcissus. Hybrids or cultivars derived from *Narcissus triandus.* Characterized by slender foliage and one to six flowers (often fragrant) per stem, with the petals turned back and slightly twisted ('Thalia').

Division 6: Cyclamineus Narcissus. Hybrid descendants of *Narcissus cyclamineus,* so called because the petals curve back away from the cup as in the Cyclamen flower.

Division 8: Tazetta Narcissus or Poetaz Narcissus, descended from *Narcissus tazetta.* One of the most widely distributed and oldest known forms of Narcissus, characterized by clusters of many small white flowers per stem with prominent golden crowns or cups; usually quite fragrant and tender ('Silver Chimes').

Division 9: Poeticus Narcissus, also called Poet's Narcissus or Old Pheasant's-eye, derived from *Narcissus poeticus.* Usually one flower per stem; pure white petals with a small, almost flat, red-rimmed and red-eyed cup ('Actaea').

*Most of the daffodils discussed here are hardy to Zone 8 and require freezing temperatures to break their dormancy. Tender types are listed under "Collector's Choice"; these do not require freezing temperatures to bloom.

Division 10: All known cultivated forms of wild *Narcissus* and natural hybrids. Highly regarded for their unique, delicate forms and ease of culture.

Collector's Choice (all sold as bulbs; ❀ indicates especially fragrant types):

Division 10 (Wild Types):

Narcissus bulbocodium 'Conspicuous', Hoop-petticoat Daffodil (1776-1850); dainty golden yellow, almost funnel-shaped flowers, said to resemble an old-fashioned hoop petticoat; Zones 6-9. This species, said to be overcollected from the wild, is reported to be nursery-grown, as offered by the following sources. 145; 20; 162; 50; 170.

❀*N. jonquilla*, Single Jonquil, Early Louisiana, Sweeties (1700-1776); two or three deep yellow flowers per stem; late bloom; 10-12" (or shorter); Zones 6-9. Favorite Daffodil of Celia Anne Jones: "The aroma is heavenly. Here in Louisiana at least one blooms before anything else." 124; 162; 51; 38; 170; 12.

❀*N. × odorus*, Single Campernelle (1776-1850); golden yellow, bell-shaped corona with rounded petals; midseason bloom; 12"; Zones 6-9. 146; 162; 170.

❀*N. × odorus plenus*, Double Campernelle; same as previous entry but double. 146; 162.

N. triandus albus, Angel's-tears, Silver-bells; midseason bloom; two to five bell-shaped cream flowers per stem; good for rock gardens and containers; likes some shade and rich soil; 6"; Zones 4-9. This species, said to be overcollected from the wild, is reported to be nursery-grown as offered by the following sources. 145; 138; 20; 51; 170.

Other Types:

❀'Actaea' (1927); **Division 9;** supposed to be the largest Poet flower ever raised; yellow eye; red-rimmed cup; midseason bloom; 16". 96; 145; 138; 20.

❀'Apricot Distinction' (1942); **Division 3;** apricot perianth; red-orange cup; prefers light shade. Meg Yerger, daffodil collector and poet breeder, said, "I would hate to be without this in my Maryland garden." 162.

'Barrett Browning' (1945); **Division 3;** circular white perianth with large, slightly frilled orange cup; early bloom; 18". 170; 50; 150; 162; 52; 146.

❀'Beersheba' (1923); **Division 1;** pure white perianth and trumpet; midseason bloom; 14". "Still to me the most beautiful of all white trumpets" (Elizabeth Lawrence). 146; 52; 162; 50.

❀'Canatrice' (pre-1936); **Division 1;** star-shaped ivory perianth and ivory trumpet; one of the great whites hybridized by Guy Wilson in the 1930s; 16". "Elegant" according to Meg Yerger. 170; 146; 133.

'Carlton' (1927); **Division 2;** giant, frilled golden yellow cup with soft yellow perianth; early bloom; 18". 146; 52; 162; 170.

❀'Cheerfulness' (1923); **Division 4;** double white flowers in clusters with creamy yellow centers; late bloom; a sport of 'Elvira', another *N. tazetta* hybrid, from which later came 'Yellow Cheerfulness'; both now classics; 15". 137; 145; 20; 52; 162.

'Fortune' (1923); **Division 2;** large bright orange cup with bright yellow perianth; midsummer bloom; 17". 63; 162; 50.

'King Alfred' (1899); **Division 1;** so well known it hardly needs description; early bloom; 18". It has been called "the most loved Daffodil of all time." 138; 20; 52; 133; 137; 170.

❀'Limerick' (before 1938); **Division 3;** white perianth; red cup; midseason to late bloom; another Meg Yerger favorite; 15". 146.

'Little Witch' (1929); **Division 6;** yellow

perianth with yellow trumpet; midseason bloom; 8". 146.

'Mary Copeland' (1914); **Division 4;** double white flowers with small tufts of orange between petals; midseason to late bloom; 16". 133; 162; 50.

❀'Mega' (1950); **Division 9;** large Poet; white perianth; small, flat yellow corona rimmed in red with a small green eye; late bloom; now rare; 20". "A tall Poet with a large beautiful flower, a good parent for hybridizing" (Meg Yerger, who has a large collection of Poets). 146; 170.

❀*N. poeticus recurvus*, Old Pheasant's-eye (early 19th century); **Division 9;** green eye and flat, red-rimmed cup; white flared-back petals; late bloom; like all poets, grows well in damp conditions; 18-20". 146; 52; 170.

'Mrs. R.O. Backhouse', Pink Daffodil (1923); **Division 2;** named for the famous English breeder; the first pink daffodil; white perianth with shell pink or apricot trumpet; midseason bloom; 15". 133; 162; 50.

❀'Silver Chimes' (1916); **Division 8;** a fairly hardy tazetta with silver-white petals and a pale yellow cup; blooms in clusters; late bloom; 12"; Zones 6-10. 145; 138; 52; 162; 133.

❀'Thalia' (1916); **Division 5;** several pendant white blooms (two or more), with the petals reflexed "like the wings of an angel"; late bloom; 16". 146; 137; 138; 20; 50.

'W.P. Wilmer' (1884); **Division 1;** a tiny version of the large trumpet form in sulfur-white; early to midseason bloom; pot culture or rock garden. 146; 52; 51; 50; 162.

Note: Gardeners in Zones 9 and 10 can grow hardy varieties by prechilling the bulbs for eight to ten weeks at 40°F. to 45°F. (4°C. to 7°C.) before planting in December.

❀ *Nicotiana alata*

Solanaceae
1850-1900   ZONES 3-10

Nicotiana

Flowering Tobacco, Jasmine Tobacco, Winged Tobacco

TYPE: HARDY ANNUAL/SHORT-LIVED
    PERENNIAL
HEIGHT: 1½-4'   BLOOM: SUMMER-FALL
SITE: SUN/PARTIAL SHADE

Nicotiana alata, native to tropical South America, is one of several species of ornamental Tobaccos of the Nightshade Family. It is a branching plant, growing to four feet, with long, soft green felty leaves mainly clustered at its base and five-petaled, long-tubed flowers growing in graceful sprays all along its stems. These flowers open wide in the evening and release a sweet, jasmine-like scent. They close by noon the following day, drooping their heads as if from exhaustion. The species flower is creamy white tinged with green on the outside of the petals and pure white inside. The genus takes its name from the Frenchman Nicot, who in 1560 obtained *Nicotiana tabacum* (smoking tobacco) from a Belgian merchant and presented it to the queen of France.

Ornamental Tobaccos were among the tender annuals and short-lived perennials whose discovery in the tropics and Mexico during the nineteenth century caused a sensation in American gardening circles. The Breck catalog carried *Nicotiana longiflora*, Long-flowered Tobacco or Star-petunia. Nicotiana flowers do resemble those of Petunias (both belong to the Nightshade Family): rounded petals somewhat pointed at the tip, the flowers releasing their scent in the evening. But Nicotiana blooms close up by noon, having spent all their energy on the debauchery of the night before. This habit was considered very unfortunate, and by 1916 hybrids, the result of crossing *N. alata* with other species, resulted in shorter, virtually unscented, day-blooming plants with a wider range of colors. By the 1930s, 'Crimson King', a velvety crimson red and only fifteen inches tall, was introduced (a fine plant, still available), and by the late 1940s or 1950s, 'Sensation' hybrids in mixed colors and two white cultivars — 'Daylight' and 'Snowstorm' — were available to American gardeners.

Nicotiana alata

Louise Beebe Wilder observed that the old "dumb white nicotine," celebrated in Edna St. Vincent Millay's poem, ("which wakes and utters her fragrance/In a garden sleeping"), "makes a poor figure by day, and we are apt to feel that it takes up a good deal of room. But with the coming of the night the long creamy tubes freshen and expand and give forth their rich perfume and we are then glad we have so much of it. . . . There are varieties with rose and crimson blossoms but they are not as sweet as the old white kind."

I discovered the old white after having grown all the latest hybrids. I liked their bright colors, ease of culture, accommodation to heat and cold, and long blooming season (from early summer to late fall). I was tantalized by a whiff of sweet scent in the evening air. I wanted more of that, and I was not satisfied until I grew *N. alata* in its unimproved form. Contrary to my expectation of an old-fashioned (in the passé sense), gawky plant whose only redeeming feature was its celebrated perfume, I found that it makes a great splash in the garden, lighting up shady places in the rear of the border (stately among Monkshood and Bee-balm), equally striking in the sun (featured among annuals such as Poppies), and useful in covering up holes left by early-flowering perennials (Bleeding-heart and Oriental Poppies) or spring bulbs. Cut back in the fall and potted up, it makes a decorative windowsill plant — a mound of tapering velvet leaves and rising (to fifteen inches) stalks of bloom by midwinter.

I still favor a few older strains, such as the incomparable non-hybrid, thirty-inch 'Lime Green'. Its exquisite color has never been rivaled, as its chartreuse blooms complement every other color in the garden and are beautiful in fall bouquets with scarlet Dahlias and white Cosmos. I plant 'Crimson King' in containers for reliable all-season color in the sun or shade. I plant the old white in large tubs (at least three plants per tub) or mass them near doorways, along paths, and beside the porch, where we can enjoy their fragrance and beauty. In my experience, the flowers open by midafternoon, well before evening. I suspect that flower opening has a lot to do with climatic conditions, day length, and whether any shade is provided. And when the flowers do open, Nicotiana shows off another of its many attributes — as a great plant for attracting hummingbirds.

To Grow: In warm winter regions, if you sow the seeds outdoors, Nicotiana will grow as a short-lived perennial. Elsewhere, sow the seeds indoors four to eight weeks before the last frost, sprinkling them with a little sand for even distribution. (There is no need to cover them, since light speeds germination.) This should occur in five to twenty days at 70°F. to 85°F. (21°C. to 29°C.). The seedlings resemble Petunias at first but soon develop their characteristic long, tapering leaves. Plant the seedlings out after all danger of frost has passed. Put them in fertile, well-drained, light soil, nine to twelve inches apart, in full sun or partial shade. In many regions, even in my Zone 4 garden, Nicotiana will self-seed for many years. It may be wintered over and propagated by stem cuttings (see "Wintering Annuals," p. 20).

Collector's Choice (all sold as seeds):

Nicotiana alata, Nicotiana. 87; 5; 6; 101; 19; 18; 92; 147-8.
    'Crimson King' (by 1930s). 101.
    'Lime Green' (before 1950). 6; 92.

❀ *Paeonia* spp.

Ranunculaceae
1600-1950   Zones 2-9

Peony

Piony

Type: Perennial Flower
Height: 1½-4'
Bloom: Spring-Early
        Summer
Site: Sun/Partial Shade

Paeonia lactiflora

Peonies are very hardy shrublike perennials native to Europe and Asia, where they have long been cultivated. By 1086 A.D., for instance, the Chinese were growing superior strains of *Paeonia lactiflora*, from which has come the most popular type grown today. Its large double blooms are synonymous with the word "Peony."

Peonies grow from fleshy rhizomatous roots whose crowns sprout red buds in early spring after a period of dormancy, usually brought on by freezing temperatures. The plants are unusually long-lived, with fifty-year-old specimens being common. The often fragrant flowers grow out of round, tightly wrapped buds on sturdy stems. The stems vary in height from the dainty, very early-blooming Fern-leaved Peony (*Paeonia tenuifolia*) — one and a half feet tall with three-inch single or double crimson or white flowers; to the old-fashioned Grandma's or Memorial Day Peony (*P. officinalis*) — two to three feet tall; with five-inch double crimson or white blooms; to the later-blooming Asiatic hybrids, mostly developed from *P. lactiflora* — up to four feet tall and varying in flower form from elegant single-petaled types with numerous golden stamens to enormous fully double globular blooms as wide as ten inches across. The Fern-leaved Peony dies back after flowering, but the other types retain their glossy foliage all season.

The genus name is derived from the Greek *paeon*, a word associated with healing. In the well-regulated medieval household, the European *Paeonia officinalis* was a sovereign remedy for a variety of complaints and a food item, too. The Alewife in *Piers Plowman* declares, "I have pepper and peony seed and a pound of garlic . . . for fasting days." The root was used as a cure for palsy and, according to Gerard and Culpeper, as an antidote, in some form, for "nightmares" and "melancholie." This was the so-called "Female Peionie" (*P. mascula* was known as the "Male Peionie") — single-petaled and crimson, commonly grown in England by the sixteenth century, when Gerard also knew the "double red with flowers like the great double rose of Provence." The latter was the form grown in early American gardens (whether for use or pleasure is not recorded).

The Chinese Peony (*Paeonia lactiflora*), whose roots were used as a source of food in China as early as 536 A.D., was introduced to American gardeners by the early nineteenth century, when it was greatly valued for its enormous blooms. By 1820, breeding of Peonies began in Europe using *P. officinalis* and *P. lactiflora*, resulting in popular strains that are still with us today. Foremost among these is the classic 'Festiva Maxima' (1851), regarded as the greatest of white Peonies: large, fragrant white blooms flecked with crimson, vigorous and early blooming, three to four feet high, and always loaded with flowers, their centers hidden in a mass of petals. In 1866, Joseph Breck offered one hundred Peonies, "all desirable," including the newest cultivars from Europe and the indestructible, ever-popular *P. officinalis* 'Rubra Plena', a household friend since earliest settler days.

Peonies, like Roses, epitomize the heirloom quality inherent in certain plants that seem to embody cherished family ties and associations. I have discovered many venerable clumps, lovingly planted by young brides more than fifty years ago from a few pieces of roots carefully brought from the home farm. Peonies, also like Roses, often endure neglect, living on long after the people who planted them, surviving among weeds, even in light woods (unblooming), a mute testimony to former human activity. One reason for Peonies' longevity is that they have no natural enemies. They are cherished for their beauty of form, color — pink, rose, crimson, and white — and fragrance.

In older gardens, Peonies are often found growing in grand spreading clumps by themselves in a bed cut into the grass. After the flowers bloom in late spring and early summer (the late-blooming types), the foliage is still attractive. Another device is to plant them near early-flowering bulbs as an all-season cover. Borders of Peonies planted as a hedge along driveways or to define garden "rooms" also provide gorgeous blooms and handsome all-season foliage. The shorter, less vigorous types can be combined with Bleeding-heart (*Dicentra eximia* or *D. formosa*), early-flowering perennials such as Dame's-rocket and Lupines, and later-blooming Daylilies. Bleeding-heart will carry on with flowers all season, a low-growing groundcover among the handsome Peony shrubs. The Fern-leaved Peony, a mass of small blooms in very early spring, is a perfect rock garden plant. By carefully choosing from among the surprising forms of heirloom types (many bred in the United States), you can extend the Peony's period of bloom over six weeks, from early spring to early summer.

Generous bouquets of Peonies are certainly part of the pleasure of growing these plants. If cut when some of the flower buds are just beginning to open, bouquets will keep a week in water. Never cut more than two-thirds of the buds from a four-year-old plant, or more than 10 percent from a younger one, and leave two or three leaves on each stem to nourish the plant in the ground.

To Grow: Plant the roots with three to five buds in the fall, in rich, slightly acid, well-drained soil well supplemented with organic matter. Choose a sunny spot (slightly shaded in warmer regions) protected from high winds —

near an established shrubbery, for instance. Dig a hole about two feet wide and one and a half feet deep and throw in a couple handfuls of bonemeal mixed with soil; fill in the hole with a compost-soil mixture. The tops of the buds should be no more than two inches below the soil's surface. Too deep planting is the most common cause of unblooming peonies, an unfortunate state of affairs. Remember that patience is required, for Peonies do not attain perfection for three to five years. In heavy clay and in warmer growing regions, plant the buds only one inch deep. Shallow planting actually encourages flower production. Space the plants three feet apart, and for the first winter mulch the area when the ground freezes with a blanket of straw or evergreen boughs. Once the plants are established, no winter protection is required. Peonies do best in cold climates but can be grown in the West Coast areas of Zone 9, where nights are cool. In that area, withhold water in the early fall, from September through mid-October, and cut the plant to the ground. This will induce dormancy, which is needed for another season of bloom.

Heavy-headed types probably will need some support, such as circular rings set around each plant before it begins to grow. Divide the plant if you wish (you don't have to) in the fall, cutting large, fleshy roots into smaller pieces with three eyes each.

If you're familiar with only the commonly grown large double-flowered type, explore this rich world of heirloom Peonies, classified below according to flower form:

S=Single, with one row of five or more petals and showy golden stamens.
SD=Semidouble, with more than one row of petals and stamens still apparent.
D=Double, with stamens entirely hidden in petals.

J=Japanese, with two or more rows of petals, usually flattish, and feathery petaloid stamens (staminodes).

Collector's Choice (all sold as plants; ❀ indicates especially fragrant types):

❀*Paeonia officinalis* 'Alba Plena' (1600-1800); double white; early bloom; 2-3'. 45; 61; 149.
   ❀'Rosa Superba'; double pink. 61; 149.
   ❀'Rubra Plena', Grandma's Peony; double crimson. 45; 61; 149.
   ❀*P. tenuifolia* 'Flora Plena', Fern-leaved Peony, Adonis Peony (1776-1800); small, erect double flowers with ferny foliage; very early bloom; 1½'. This is supposed to be one of the plants the settlers took westward from the East. 58; 60; 66; 79; 80.

Hybrids:

❀'Chestine Gowdy' (1913); **D;** silvery pink with a creamy collar of petals; late bloom; 2-4'. 70; 60.
   ❀'Duchesse de Nemours' (1856); **D;** white with a yellow center just apparent; midseason bloom; 2-4'. 169; 60; 133; 45; 160; 80.
   'Elsa Sass' (1930); **D;** creamy white; late bloom; 2-4'. 60; 149; 80; 70.
   'Felix Crouse' (1881); **D;** deep rosy red; late bloom; 2-4'. 174; 33; 20; 66; 164; 45.
   ❀'Festiva Maxima' (1851); **D;** white-flecked crimson; especially fine cut flower; early bloom; 3-4'. 20; 31; 164; 84; 149; 97.
   'Firelight' (1950); **S;** rosy pink with red stigmas; early bloom; 2-4'. 60; 54.
   'Gypsy Rose' (1939); **J;** rosy pink with mass of curled staminodes; midseason bloom; 2-4'. 60; 80.
   'Harriet Olney' (1920); **S;** rose; midseason bloom; 3'. 60; 70.
   ❀'Martha Bulloch' (1907); **D;** large pink and ivory flowers (8-10"); midseason bloom; 4'. 31; 149; 60; 70.

'Mikado' (1893); **J;** crimson red with yellow staminodes; late bloom; 2-4'. 60.

'Miss America' (1936); **SD;** large, white bowl-shaped blooms; early bloom; recommended for warmer regions; 2-4'. 60; 20; 57; 119; 80.

'Nippon Beauty' (1927); **J;** deep red; late bloom; 2-4'. 60; 61; 149; 70.

'Rosedale' (1936); **SD;** dark red; roselike in form; early bloom; 2-3'. 45; 137; 149; 80; 70.

☀'Walter Faxon' (1904); **D;** bright pink; midseason bloom; 2-4'. 34; 80; 70.

Papaver spp.

Papaveraceae
1600-1930   ZONES 3-9

Poppy

TYPE: HARDY ANNUAL/PERENNIAL FLOWER
HEIGHT: 1½-4'   BLOOM: SPRING-FALL
SITE: SUN

About fifty species of Poppies, annuals and perennials, are native to Europe; a few also are native to western North America. The types discussed here share silky, crinkled single or double flowers with four or five petals — from two inches wide in the annual Corn Poppy *(Papaver rhoeas)* to as big as twelve inches wide in the perennial Oriental Poppy *(P. orientale)* — in colors ranging from brilliant vermilion to pastels, sometimes delicately bordered white or blotched black, with showy black stamens and anthers in the center of the bloom. Leaves vary from

Papaver orientale

deeply lobed, almost ferny in the Oriental Poppy to grayish, jagged (like lettuce), and clasping in the annual Lettuce Poppy *(P. somniferum).* Two subspecies of this Poppy have been cultivated since time immemorial as a source of medicine and food.

The garden form — Peony Poppy — is grown for its beautiful double flowers and distinctive seed heads, which are often used in indoor arrangements. An ancient symbol of fertility, a single plump Peony Poppy pod can hold as many as thirty-two thousand seeds (Linnaeus is supposed to have counted them).

The Lettuce or Opium Poppy was the first type to be grown in America, perhaps for medicinal and culinary purposes, but soon ornamental types, valued for their diverse forms — fringed, delicately veined and splotched, and peony-flowered (very double) — and colors — white, red, purple, and pink — were favored for late spring and summer bloom. They cause a sensation when massed, as there are usually a wide variety of flowers and seed heads in any planting. The various colors and forms readily crossbreed, creating new designs. Collecting and swapping seeds of these crosses was a regular feature of old-time gardening and is still practiced in some areas. I have found old peony-flowered strains kept alive by an eighty-year-old gardener who called them "Champagne Poppies" — very elegant on three-foot stems with bluish green pinked and clasping leaves and fully double flower heads of numerous translucent peach-pink petals, lightly veined a darker pink. As with many naturally occurring double-flowered forms that have been selected and cultivated for many years, there is always some variation in form — some flowers with fewer petals, some with a grayish blotch. This gardener rogues out the undesirable types to keep his strain pure.

Jefferson grew both the single white Poppy *(Papaver somniferum)*, which he called the "Larger Poppy," and the Corn Poppy *(P. rhoeas)*, which he referred to as the "Lesser Poppy." This is the humble weed of European grain fields, grown for centuries as a medicinal and ornamental plant. In England, where the red petals were gathered from the fields to use in the preparation of a syrup (to soothe various ailments), the children employed to gather them in vast amounts were advised to wear small muslin bags suspended from their necks so both hands would be free to pick the petals.

Double garden forms were known as early as 1629, and by the eighteenth century there were many variants, one of which was described by Philip Miller, curator of the Chelsea Physic Garden, as "very double firy flowers, which are beautifully edged with white." It wasn't until the 1880s that the Reverend Wilkes, continuing the same process of selection and breeding, produced a similar type from a wild sport — one flower in a mass of wild Corn Poppies, the margins of its petals lined with white — the descendants of which bear the name Shirley Poppies in honor of the village where Wilkes lived. He worked diligently and methodically to achieve his results. Every growing season he selected seedlings that showed marked variation, carefully collecting their seeds and sowing them again. Eventually, he created a well-defined strain characterized by an infinite range of colors from crimson and orange-scarlet through tints of rose and salmon pink. These silky-petaled, waved flowers were edged with white and still had all the airy grace of the wild type — an achievement that remains a lasting tribute to his breeding skills.

Although the single form was reported to be Wilkes's favorite type, many gardeners prefer the doubles out of sheer greed — the blooms last longer, as do most double types in general. Both the Peony and Corn Poppy types are hardy annuals, surviving into the fall and self-seeding from year to year.

The flamboyant Oriental Poppy, a long-lasting perennial, was introduced around 1744 from Armenia. The extraordinary size of the flowers — at least six inches across and often bigger — and their incredible color made them an immediate success with gardeners. As Mrs. Wilder complained, however, after the first thrill had subsided, its very brilliance became the reason for its fall from grace, as if "a scarlet flower was only less terrible than a scarlet sin." Added to this, its vigorous, sprawling habit of growth and early bloom tended to cause an undeniable hole in even the best-planned border. Gertrude Jekyll offered a solution that has been standard advice for decades: overplant with Baby's-breath *(Gypsophila paniculata)*. In fact, Baby's-breath is not so easy to establish for all gardeners, and other devices must be sought.

In my own gardens, I have a running battle with my husband, who adores the sinful scarlet flowers — the more the merrier. No matter how they flop, smothering everything in their midst in a three-foot-wide circle, and how they propagate, we must have them all. In defense, I have resorted to ruthlessly pulling out extras in the spring (not to worry, they come right back from their roots), ringing them with slender stakes, and against them planting lower-growing bushy perennials such as Mountain-bluet, whose silvery gray leaves are decorative all season. Then the gorgeous Oriental Poppies complement the flowers of early summer — blue Lupines, Iris, and Foxglove. With a few seedlings of the Hollyhock Mallow growing in their vicinity, and Nicotiana on hand as well, I know I can carry on without shame for the rest of the summer.

My favorite Oriental Poppy is a self-seeded soft salmon pink one that never spreads and grows conveniently under the low branches of an old plum tree along our lane, blooming just after the Daffodils are finished for the season. I have found surviving Oriental Poppies doing very well on their own in abandoned gardens after more than thirty years, blooming in spring shade. From these observations I have concluded that naturalizing them, if you have the room, may be the ultimate answer to their tendency to sprawl.

Superior strains, some of the best developed by the English nurseryman Amos Perry (of 'Perry's Blue' Siberian Iris fame), are still available, all developed in the early 1900s. "Earth tones!" my husband complains, but they are undeniably beautiful and far easier to accommodate to planting schemes. The best are 'Mrs. Perry', a handsome apricot pink, and 'Queen Alexandra', a lovely pink, which gave rise to 'Silver Queen', the first white, no longer available. 'Mrs. Perry', though, threw up some chance white-flowering seedlings in the garden of one of Mr. Perry's customers. He went to see them and eventually brought the new variety to market as 'Perry's White' (1914), a satiny white Oriental Poppy with a conspicuous eye or blotch, a favorite since it was introduced. All of these are hybrids arising from initial crosses with *Papaver bracteatum* and introduced sometime in the nineteenth century. The true species form of the Oriental Poppy is the only one to come true from seed — an unmistakable, unregenerate, brilliant vermilion. "Its immense flame-colored blossoms . . . will astonish the novice," nineteenth-century Canadian writer Annie Jack observed. And, she could have added, it will thrill even the most hardened gardener.

Annual Poppies are elegant additions to any planting, either of perennials or annuals, and two sowings, early and later, will ensure a long season of bloom. Corn Poppies, especially the form known as 'Lady Bird' (derived from *Papaver commutatum*, introduced in the nineteenth century), are dramatic if planted in a large group bordered by single white Petunias. Annual Poppies are especially beautiful in summer bouquets. One is advised to singe their stems to prolong their bloom indoors, but this has never worked for me. The ephemeral flowers last well in bouquets if picked when the drooping buds are just beginning to look up but before they have opened at all. Peony Poppy seed heads, on their long stems, are used to great effect in winter bouquets.

To Grow: While annual Poppies are easy to grow, their growth requirements are quite specific. The three most common reasons for failure are as follows:

1. Too deep planting of the seeds. Sow seeds sparingly with a small amount of sand, then lightly press them on top of the soil with a board (they need light to germinate).
2. Too late planting. The seeds must be sown outdoors, since Poppies don't transplant well, and they need cool temperatures to germinate. The best plants are produced from seeds sown in late fall, which germinate the following spring; in Zones 8-10, such a sowing produces blooms by late winter or very early spring. For almost continuous bloom from late spring to fall, you can sow twice — once in the fall and once in early spring — to establish a cycle of early- and late-blooming plants.
3. Too close planting. Poppies should be thinned way back in their early growth, to nine to twelve inches apart. This will encour-

age vigorous, healthy plants with large, beautiful flowers. The soil should be well drained and moderately enriched, and the site should be sunny, preferably protected from the wind, though the thin, wiry stems are tougher than they look.

Oriental Poppies, if grown from seeds in moderately enriched, well-drained soil, need full sun and a 55°F. (13°C.) soil temperature to germinate in about ten to fifteen days. Young plants should be set out when dormant, at least fifteen to eighteen inches apart, with the top of the roots three inches below the soil's surface. I have never found them difficult to divide and replant in late fall (they can be left undisturbed for years), but a bit of root is inevitably left behind. Mature plants die back after blooming in early summer, but fresh leaves, and even a few flowers, reappear by fall. Oriental Poppies are perennial to Zone 9 where nights are cool. Elsewhere, they can be grown as annuals, from plants rather than seeds, in a cool, protected spot.

Collector's Choice:

Papaver commutatum 'Lady Bird' (1876); vigorous, showier type of Corn Poppy; bright red with black blotch; 20". 92(s); 172(s).
P. orientale. Oriental Poppy (18th century, around 1744); late spring bloom; 3'. 5(s); 18(s).
'Beauty of Livermore'; close to species form. 109(p); 6(s); 126(s); 133; 116; 88 (all plants).
'Mrs. Perry' (before 1914); apricot pink. 61(p); 33(p).
'Perry's White' (1914); white with maroon blotches. 45; 61; 149 (all plants).
'Princess Victoria Louise' (by 1930s); salmon pink. 109; 133; 116; 164 (all plants).
'Queen Alexandra' (before 1912); soft rose. 52(p); 115(p).

P. rhoeas, African-rose, Corn Poppy, Corn Rose, Flanders Field Poppy, Redweed (1700-1776); 3'. 5; 9; 177; 143; 24; 87 (all seeds).
'Single Shirley' (late 19th century); 18-24". 6(s); 101(s); 92(s; offered as 'Rev. Wilkes Mixed', semidoubles and singles).
'Double Shirley'. 101; 42; 137; 3 (all seeds); 92(s; offered as 'Shirley Reselected Double Mixed').
P. somniferum 'Peony Poppy' (1600-1699); to 4'. 92; 147-8; 3 (all seeds); 18(s; offered as *Papaver paeoniflorum*).

Parthenocissus quinquefolia

Vitaceae
1600-1699   ZONES 3-10   NATIVE

Virginia Creeper

American-ivy, Five-leaved-ivy, Woodbine

TYPE: HIGH-CLIMBING PERENNIAL
TENDRIL/CLINGING VINE
SEASON OF INTEREST: ALL-SEASON
FOLIAGE
SITE: SUN/PARTIAL SHADE

The Virginia Creeper is one of about fifteen species native to North America and the West Indies. It grows wild from Quebec west to Minnesota and south to Florida, Texas, and Mexico in woods and on rocks. Rapid-growing, of loose, open habit, it is highly valued for its ability to grow in damp or dry conditions and to cling to walls by means of tendrils, like the grapevine and Clematis. The much-admired foliage — long and coarsely toothed with five leaflets — turns a brilliant scarlet in early fall when few other leaves have colored.

The bluish black berries are handsome, too — a contrast to the foliage and especially attractive to birds. When the leaves eventually fall, they reveal a delicate tracery of woody stems.

The ornamental value of this easily grown native vine must have been apparent to early American gardeners, who could not help noticing its brilliant autumn foliage and loosely branching habit, for which it became prized for covering arbors, the side shoots gracefully drooping downward. The bark is reported to have a medicinal use, but if the settlers used the vine for this purpose, they have left no record of it. The Virginia Creeper maintained its popularity throughout the nineteenth century, when it was described as "the most ornamental plant of its genus." Joseph Breck was lavish in his praise, pointing out that it could be found growing on the best houses on Beacon Street in Boston. Elsewhere, its uses were more humble, but highly regarded nevertheless, when, for instance, it was planted on railroad embankments to help prevent erosion. Discerning gardeners such as Mrs. Wilder valued the Virginia Creeper for clinging to trees "up which it clambers, twining free here and there, and in the autumn making the tree appear as if on fire." And, as she pointed out, the scarlet leaves can be added to indoor bouquets for a dramatic effect.

I found the Virginia Creeper in two quite different circumstances: the first was growing up the side of a tumbling-down farmstead built in the 1870s by descendants of settlers from the Isle of Skye; the second was growing up the side of the elegant Lodge, built around the same time, on the Bell Estate. Both vines had been growing untended for decades and were none the worse for it, as far as I could tell. David Fairchild had planted the Virginia Creeper at the Lodge as a climbing companion for the Climbing Hydrangea, and they made a handsome pair — one a mass of green leaves, the other brilliant red — almost side by side against the wooden wall soaring to the top of the roof. Evidently, the Virginia Creeper has always had a wide appeal, at home in the country as well as in the city, on all types of buildings, and in a variety of situations.

It should be pointed out that Fairchild, despite his fame and fortune as a plant collector and author, never forgot that he was a country boy who, until the age of eighteen, lived where streets were made of dirt and mud holes a matter of course. His taste in flora was shaped by his travels to exotic places, but he valued native plants, too, as reflected in the surviving plantings at the Lodge,

Parthenocissus quinquefolia

particularly in the high-climbing Virginia Creeper, a lasting tribute to this American who worked all his life to enlarge our collective pool of useful and ornamental plants. "Fragrant and charming . . . vines and trees," he noted, "enrich our lives with a beauty far more lasting than casual visits to any museum of art" (*The World Grows Round My Door*, Scribner's, 1947).

Although the species form is a splendid plant, Engelmann's-ivy (*Parthenocissus quinquefolia* 'Engelmannii'), introduced in the late nineteenth century, is denser in habit, with smaller, leathery leaves. A more refined type, it also makes a good groundcover and screen, as well as a climber on stone walls or trellises. The wild form, used to cover steep banks, makes a foot-high carpet. Boston-ivy or Japanese Creeper (*P. tricuspidata*), introduced from Japan in 1862, is considered by some to be the best for clinging to stonework, which it does by means of small, rootlike holdfasts. It is very well suited to city conditions, immune to dirt and pollution, with overlapping leaves like shingles that also turn with the season. "In sheer splendor," a New Jersey Experiment Station Bulletin proclaimed (circa 1900), "there is no climbing plant that equals the Japanese Ivy when it assumes its October garb . . . it seems as if the artist had dipped the giant brush in a harmonious mixture of crimson and gold and touched the walls as an earnest of Infinite purpose and perfection."

To Grow: All of these vines are rapid growers, attaining six to ten feet during their first season and much more thereafter, growing as high as sixty feet. They tolerate dry or wet conditions, sun or partial shade. For best growth, plant them in moist but well-drained, loamy soil. Set the plants three to four feet apart near the wall, arbor, or support you want them to climb. Prune them early in the spring to restrain unwanted growth, redirect growth, or induce side branching for use as a groundcover. Propagate by spring cuttings or from self-rooted layered stems.

Collector's Choice (all sold as plants):

Parthenocissus quinquefolia, Virginia Creeper. 58; 123; 97; 114; 167; 161.
  'Engelmannii'. 169; 167; 58; 123; 97; 114.
  P. tricuspidata, Boston-ivy, Japanese Creeper. 45; 31; 97; 79; 160; 163.

❧*Pelargonium* spp.

Geraniaceae
1760-1948

Scented Geranium

Storksbill

TYPE: TENDER SHRUBBY PERENNIAL HERB/FLOWER
HEIGHT: TRAILING, TO 5'
BLOOM: SUMMER
SEASON OF INTEREST: ALL-SEASON FOLIAGE
SITE: SUN

Scented Geraniums belong to the large and interesting *Pelargonium* genus of about 280 species, mostly native to South Africa, which also includes the familiar Garden Geranium (*P. x hortorum*), the Ivy Geranium (*P. peltatum*), and the Martha Washington Geranium (*P. x domesticum*). These tender perennials should not be confused with the hardy perennials from Europe of the genus *Geranium* that are commonly known as Cranesbill. All of these plants belong to the same family and share distinctive fruits shaped like a bird's beak, as preserved in their common names.

Scented Geraniums are extraordinarily varied in leaf form and habit, ranging from low, bushy trailing types to medium-sized shrubs. The leaves, gray to deep green and usually velvety in texture, are curled and crimped, deeply lobed, large or small, undulating, variegated, and even fringed. Fragrance (the plants' main claim to fame) matches leaf form in diversity: light to heavy rose, mint, lemon, musk, fruit, pine, and pungent, as well as combinations of these. In areas where they enjoy the same climate as in their native habitat (hot, dry summers with cool evenings and frost-free winters), they may attain their maximum size — four to five feet. Elsewhere they are grown as annuals in the summer and as houseplants in the winter.

Fragrant oils, distilled from their leaves, have been used to scent perfumes, soaps, and cosmetics, often as a cheap substitute for the more expensive attar of roses. Scented Geraniums have been grown in England since the reign of Charles I, when they were used as a strewing and potpourri herb by cottagers and gentry alike. Although they are useful as a flavoring, in much the same way as vanilla, for cakes and puddings, it seems unlikely that the early settlers regarded them as a household necessity. The earliest record of any *Pelargonium* in America is 1760, when John Bartram received seeds from abroad. By 1791 Jefferson was growing potted Geraniums in the White House (the familiar Garden Geranium), but after the 1840s, all types marched westward with the pioneers, one of a group of treasured plants that was gradually introduced across the land.

In time, the scented types were regarded as passé, of interest only to those who liked to have a pot or two around the kitchen to flavor jellies, add to potpourri, or slip into nosegays. Of greater interest were the brightly flowered bedding Geraniums that filled Victorian flower beds with solid blocks of dazzling color — scarlet, red, bright pink, and white. But the wheel of horticultural fashion keeps going around, and today's gardeners are beginning once more to appreciate the more subdued beauty of Scented Geraniums, with their infinite variety and appealing fragrances. Scented Geraniums can be grown all winter indoors on

Pelargonium

the windowsill, then planted out to enhance any garden, especially an herb garden. Where conditions permit, they can be grown as perennial shrubs of varied habit — upright, stocky, and branching or low and trailing — often with beautiful flowers.

Perhaps the best way to show off a group of choice cultivars is in containers set in a sunny spot, "standing on the terrace or porch where we drink tea or after-dinner coffee to give off their pleasant perfume as we walk past them and our clothes and hands touch their leaves" (Helen Fox, *Gardening with Herbs for Flavor and Fragrance*, Macmillan, 1933). "Dampness is said to bring out their scent," Fox observed, "so they are placed along the margins of our garden pool as in Spain, where the fragrance in flowers or leaves is as much valued as their form or color."

To Grow: Indoors, pot Scented Geraniums in humusy soil, slightly on the heavy side to retain moisture (three parts loam to one part sand plus a little peat moss) and somewhat acid. Place the pots where conditions are cool and sunny. They thrive in 70°F. (21°C.) daytime and 55°F. to 65°F. (13°C. to 18°C.) nighttime temperatures. Turn the pot occasionally for even growth and water it thoroughly when the soil is dry below the surface. All Geraniums are remarkably drought-resistant and can do with very little water. Fertilize the soil about every three weeks with a dilute solution of indoor plant food.

Outdoors, space plants one foot or more apart, depending on the type, in humusy, friable soil, prepared to a depth of ten to twelve inches. Prune the plants regularly to maintain their shape, cutting out woody and weak branches. Frequent cutting of branches for use is probably all that is needed, especially for plants grown in containers. For potting Geraniums outdoors, use the same soil mix as for indoors. Depending on the size of the container and the site, these will need more frequent watering than in the garden proper. Both indoors and out, Geraniums appreciate good air circulation to discourage disease, so don't crowd them.

When you pot outdoor plants before frost, prune back the roots and top in equal proportions, or take midsummer stem cuttings from tender, not woody, tips of branches, sliced cleanly with a sharp knife just below a node or joint (short joints make the best plants). I have increased plants of my hand-me-down Rose Geranium by rooting a branch in soil, but more care should be taken to ensure success. The goal of every gardener is to grow bushy plants of whatever type. To encourage this, pinch back the growing tips when the plant is four to five feet tall, repeating the process until you achieve the desired shape. Move the plant to a larger container (only one size larger) when it has entirely filled its pot and has lost its vigor. Up to a point, Scented Geraniums like to be pot-bound.

Collector's Choice (all sold all plants):

Though scented Geraniums are famed for their fragrance, the beauty of their flowers should not be overlooked, as represented in this collection of heirloom types.

Pelargonium capitatum 'Attar of Roses', Rose-scented Geranium (1923); descended from the species form introduced into English gardens circa 1690; rose scent; rosy pink flowers in dense clusters; useful wherever a strong musky rose scent is wanted; to 3'. 16; 177; 116; 36; 49.

P. x *citrosum* 'Prince of Orange', Orange Geranium (before 1850); orange scent; large form with broad leaves and lavender-pink flowers feathered red. 16; 116; 36.

P. crispum 'French Lace' (1948), Lemon Geranium; lemon scent; bushy, with white-margined leaves; also known as 'Prince Rupert Variegated'; to 3'. 16; 116; 36.

P. denticulatum 'Filicifolium', Fern-leaf Geranium (1879); pungent scent; shrubby and branched with finely cut feathery leaves; purple-veined pink flowers. 16; 177; 116; 93.

P. fulgidum 'Scarlet Unique' (before 1855); mild scent; large, brilliant scarlet flowers feathered deep purple; deeply cut grayish green leaves; very tall, to 5'. 16; 43; 93.

P. graveolens 'Lady Plymouth', Rose Geranium (1852); strong rose scent; green leaves blotched creamy white; rosy pink flowers; low-growing shrub; useful wherever strong rose scent is desired. 16; 116; 49; 93.

P. logeei 'Old Spice' (now classic; hybrid from Ernest Logee, 1948); nutmeg/old spice scent; grayish, deeply lobed ruffled leaves with whitish flowers veined pink; fine basket plant. 16; 43; 93.

P. quercifolium 'Pretty Polly', Oak-leaved Geranium (1850); almond scent; deeply lobed heart-shaped leaves blotched brown or purple; rarely flowers; short and shrubby. 45; 16; 177; 93.

'Skeleton's Unique' (1861); pungent; vigorous habit; branching, with dense light pink flower clusters and waxy leaves; prostrate when potted; fine for baskets. 16; 43; 93.

P. tomentosum 'Joy Lucille', Herb-scented Geranium (Ernest Logee, 1940s); peppermint scent; tall habit with large leaves and small carmine-pink flowers; to 3'. 16; 43; 93.

❀ *Petunia* x *hybrida*

Solanaceae
1850-1900

Petunia

TYPE: TENDER PERENNIAL/ANNUAL
HEIGHT: 6"-1½'   BLOOM: SUMMER-FALL
SITE: SUN/PARTIAL SHADE

The parents of the modern Petunia are two wild, short-lived perennials of the Nightshade Family discovered in South America by a French botanist named Petun, for whom the genus is named. *Petunia axillaris* was discovered in Brazil in 1923. Its small, white funnel- or trumpet-shaped fragrant flowers are about two inches across. *P. violacea*, discovered in Argentina in 1830, grows to ten inches, has violet to rose flowers one and a half inches across, and is naturalized locally in the warmer regions of the United States. The hybrid forms, commonly grown as annuals, bear little resemblance to the originals and are generally sold as single or double Multifloras, with two- to three-inch-wide flowers, or single and double Grandifloras, with five-inch-wide frilled, fringed, veined, striped, or starred flowers in many shades, including red, blue, yellow, and everything in between.

Although a relative newcomer to American gardens, Petunias were enormously popular by the mid-nineteenth century, valued for their accommodating habit (they can be grown in the varying soil and climatic conditions that exist across North America), and for giving

Petunia

themselves over so completely to flowering nonstop from early summer to well into the fall (and beyond in warmer regions). By the mid-1840s, deeply fringed and semidouble flowers were described, and, not long after, double bicolored types were introduced from France, causing a sensation with their carnation-like, vigorous, long-lasting blooms. These types were (and are) expensive to reproduce because they are female-sterile (the flowers have anthers but not pistils); pollen must be laboriously collected from the blossoms and fertilized with emasculated single flowers. While initially popular as something out of the ordinary, double-flowered forms were not considered as useful as the single varieties, especially the smaller-flowered Multiflora types, with their long season of hundreds of flowers from a few plants that could be grown in the flower border, window boxes, hanging baskets, and containers of all kinds. Mrs. Wilder, an American Gertrude Jekyll when it comes to refined gardening taste, recommended planting the small single-flowered 'Rosy Morn' — rosy carmine trumpets with a creamy yellow throat — with the gentian blue *Salvia patens*.

Not everyone celebrated the phenomenal rise of the Petunia. It has always had its detractors, who consider it common and vulgar. European visitors to America in the 1860s, for instance, deplored the widespread planting of Petunias, referring to them as "worthless and weedy with no shading in color, no luring perfume."

One wonders what these visitors to America actually saw, for the 1865 Breck catalog gloried in the ever-new and colorful strains from this "worthless weed": white, rose, or light purple, beautifully veined, striped or shaded crimson or purple, with dark throats.

As for scent, Mrs. Wilder, our unfailing guide in such matters, observed that "the deep purple single kinds enrich the borders with both colour and fragrance, but the old single white is best for sweetness, particularly after sunset," when the scent is a "refined and delicious perfume."

Since the early introductions, hundreds of cultivars have appeared and disappeared with great frequency. Mrs. Wilder's 'Rosy Morn' held out for decades because of its unusually beautiful color (for which there is no modern substitute). It was probably introduced well before the 1930s because it was offered in a 1930 catalog as a "Reselected Strain." It was last seen around 1945. 'Black Prince' (a pendulous or balcony type, deep velvety mahogany with a black throat, unlike any contemporary Petunia among the hundreds now offered) also disappeared after 1945. Still available is the heavily veined *superbissima* type introduced by Mrs. Theodosia Burr around 1800, known as 'Giants of California'. The original type was reported to have been up to seven inches wide, had a wide-open throat, and came in various pastel colors.

As for the small-flowered, open-pollinated Petunias that Mrs. Wilder preferred — the purple velvet and sweet white forms close to the wild type — they are almost impossible to find, as are the pendulous, small-flowered balcony types. The question is, are they worth finding and growing with so many improved types on the market, particularly the F_1 hybrids developed in the mid-1950s? The seeds from these F_1 hybrids are obtained by cross-pollinating two inbred hybrids whose characteristics — large flowers and vigorous growth — are not usually passed on to the second generation of seedlings. Old-style open-pollinated Petunias, (often referred to as OP Petunias), were established from hybrid strains, inbred and standardized. They retain the same general characteristics as the variety, except for small variations in color and form.

I don't condemn this development out of hand as some critics have done ("just mutant blobs"), for I recognize it as an achievement in plant breeding. For many years, I bought these expensive seeds and raised generations of seedlings, wintering-over choice types by making cuttings in the early spring. Then, on impulse, I bought a packet of very cheap (by Petunia standards) seeds, advertised as balcony types. That summer, when the flowers from the plants I'd raised opened their trumpets, I discovered something I'd never seen before and that I now recognize as "The Essential Petunia": that unassuming but delightfully graceful little flower with waved petals, sweetly scented in the evening, ranging in color from deep purple velvet to pure white, as well as shades in between, variously striped and starred. The flowers of even one plant may differ among themselves, but all have the same classic design. I was so enchanted with my discovery that I kept close watch on the opening blossoms, to see anew a flower that was basically unknown to me before. I soon began to grow all the OP Petunias I could find, either balcony types for container planting or dwarf bedding types such as 'Snowball', introduced in the early 1900s. Surviving strains of the fabled 'Giants of California', a modest four inches across, brought me beautifully striped, veined, and blotched Petunias in a style, like blowsy Old Roses, seldom seen in the newer types.

The old strains are becoming increasingly hard to find. When I asked J.L. Hudson's, a repository of many hard-to-find seeds, why it had discontinued selling the wild purple type *(Petunia violacea)*, I was told that it is almost impossible to find commercial seed growers for OP Petunias because the demand does not justify growing them on a wide scale. Perhaps the increased awareness of the heirloom value of OP Petunias — their irreplaceable charm, ease of culture, and value in the garden — will initiate small-scale seed production so that future generations can discover "The Essential Petunia." Maybe an enterprising breeder will, like the Reverend Wilkes, recreate 'Rosy Morn' and 'Black Prince', introducing them as "New!" in the best seed catalog tradition. You can create your own heirloom types by back-breeding — that is, collecting and sowing seeds of successive generations of F_1 Petunias to produce the simple single type. You also may create interesting forms of OP Petunias by cross-pollinating until you achieve a 'Rosy Morn' or 'Black Prince' yourself.

The uses of Petunias in the garden hardly need elaboration. Containers of all types can be planted with Petunias, including hanging baskets for the balcony strains. The dwarf bedding type can be used to edge or define a bed of annuals or perennials — a foil for annual Poppies (especially the old red Corn Poppies) — or to fill in the front of the border to complement soft, furry Lamb's-ears spilling over the rocks of a raised bed.

To Grow: Eight to ten weeks before the last frost, sow the tiny Petunia seeds, mixed with a small amount of fine sand, on top of a pulverized soil-vermiculite mix and gently firm them down. Don't cover the seeds, as they need light to germinate. Germination should occur in seven days if the soil temperature is kept at 80°F. (21°C.). I set an old heating pad wrapped in a plastic bag (over a heating pad cover) under the seeding tray for bottom heat; this works as well as a heating cable. After germination and moving the seedlings to light, try to maintain a soil temperature of 60°F. (16°C.). When the little plants have three or four sets of leaves, transplant them to individual pots or plant cells two and a half to three inches wide. Harden them off in a cold frame (buds develop best at 55°F., or 13°C.), then plant out the seedlings, spaced eight to twelve inches apart, when all danger of frost has passed, pinching back the tips of the plants to encourage stockiness. The soil should be rich and well drained, and the site should receive at least half a day of sun. Remove spent flowers to encourage constant bloom (cut for fresh bouquets when flowers are almost open). Save the seeds of desirable types and/or winter-over and propagate the plants by stem cuttings (see the directions under "Wintering Annuals," p. 20).

Collector's Choice (all sold as seeds; all OP):

Petunia x *hybrida*, Petunia (old style); single-flowered bedding type; cream, red, silver-blue, rosy pink, salmon, and bicolors; 12-14". 87; 168; 172; 173.

'Balcony Petunia' (old style); single-flowered pendulous form; white, rose, red-starred, and carmine. 6.

'Blue Bedder' (old style); medium blue; 12-14". 6.

'Celestial Rose' (old style); deep rose; small white throat; almost a stand-in for 'Rosy Morn'; 12-14". 171.

'Fire Chief' (AAS Gold Medal, 1950); brilliant scarlet red; 12-14". 171.

'Giants of California' (late 19th century); dwarf florist strain; heavily ruffled and veined; flowers 4" wide; reported to be the largest Petunia flower; for pot culture. 171.

'Snowball' (1903-1914); pure white dwarf; 6-8". 6; 171.

Phalaris arundinacea picta

Poaceae
1850-1900   ZONES 3-9

Ribbon Grass

Dodder, French Grass, Gardener's-garters, Lady's-garters, Lady's-laces, Lady's-ribands

TYPE: PERENNIAL GRASS
HEIGHT: 1½-3'   SEASON OF INTEREST:
                 ALL-SEASON FOLIAGE
SITE: SUN/PARTIAL SHADE

Ribbon Grass is a cultivated form of Canary Grass that has been grown in Europe for centuries. The plants form tight mats of growth by means of spreading underground stolons, while the flowering stems (which grow to three feet) bear colorless panicles of flowers typical of grasses. Interest is centered almost wholly on the plant's attractive leaves—green with white or cream stripes — which are about six and a half inches long and three-quarters of an inch wide.

Phalaris arundinacea

This ornamental grass belongs in the category of truly antique plants. Judging from its many folk names, it has been around a long time. The French called it "Aiguillette d'Armes," because the striped leaves were said to resemble the pennants used by knights at war. Gerard knew it as "Ladies' Laces," yet another variant of the names associated with the Virgin's dress. Commenting on this phenomenon, folklorist Hilderic Friend remarked,

"Having adjusted her hose, the Virgin stoops to tie her laces; for the plant Dodder, whilst it is associated by some with the Evil One, is by others dedicated to Mary, and called Lady's Laces" (*Flowers and Flower Lore*, George Allyn & Co., 1883).

Despite its long history in the garden, Ribbon Grass was not widely grown in America until the Victorian era, when grasses in general were called upon to make a grand statement in the garden. Other types, such as the Giant Reed (*Arundo donax*), as well as huge clumps of *Miscanthus*, Plume Grass, and Pampas Grass, were better suited for this purpose than the old cottage garden favorite. An unsophisticated and undemanding plant, easily tamed by repeated mowing, Ribbon Grass was more suited to humble, easy-care gardens from Maine to Alabama, where it was used to light up shady corners behind the house, appreciated by those who paid less attention to style than to what grew easily.

Some of the best and longest-lasting plantings I have seen were in small, unpretentious rural gardens. In one it was used to edge a thick bed of Lemon Yellow Daylilies in full sun by the front porch. In the other it was used as a divider in a partially shaded garden bordered by a 1920s-vintage shrubbery. In these cases, Ribbon Grass gave a sense of form, like a little wall, continually refreshed by mowing and never (miraculously enough) overstepping its assigned role. Sometimes a creative planting brings out a new dimension of the plant, as in a shrubbery where it is left to flower — its long leaves distinctive against the greenery, the foliage turning from variegated to ivory to cream by winter.

Margery Fish had the right idea about Ribbon Grass: "The handsome striped grass that we know as Gardener's Garters spreads . . . but it does it in an . . . honest, straightforward way, and one deals with it firmly by planting it in an old bucket, without a bottom, and enjoys it without worry" (*Cottage Garden Flowers*, Collingridge, 1961). Elsewhere she describes planting it in a large drainpipe sunk in the ground and as an accent plant wherever needed. The leaves should not be forgotten for fresh bouquets, especially striking with the purple-flowered stalks of Monkshood.

To Grow: Ribbon Grass is grown from roots in ordinary soil (not too rich), in sun or in varying degrees of shade. Space plants six to twelve inches apart to establish them as a groundcover. You need only three plants for accent or bucket planting, as described. Mow them back several times during the summer to control their spread if they are used as an edging, at the front of a border, or as a divider. Propagation is by division, which can be done almost anytime during the season.

Collector's Choice:

Phalaris arundinacea picta. 68; 99; 44; 111; 149; 164 (all plants).

Phaseolus coccineus

Fabaceae
1700-1825

Scarlet Runner Bean

Fire Bean, Scarlet Flowering Bean

P. c. 'Albus'

White Runner Bean

White Dutch Runner Bean

TYPE: ANNUAL TWINING VINE
HEIGHT: 6'-8'   BLOOM: SUMMER
SITE: SUN

The Scarlet and White Runner Beans are one of four groups of garden beans native to tropical America. These two beans, referred to as pole beans, grow by twining themselves around any support, climbing to eight feet. They bear bright scarlet or pure white flowers that mature over the summer to form four- to twelve-inch pods filled with large, edible black beans mottled purplish pink (Scarlet Runner) or pure white beans (White Runner).

One of nature's greatest gifts must be a plant that can be enjoyed both as a delicious food and as a beautiful ornament. The Scarlet Runner Bean was the first to be introduced to American gardens, sometime before 1750, followed by the White Runner Bean before 1825. How they must have been valued for their ease of culture, decorative flowers, and very useful beans, harvested over the whole summer to use at their different stages of development in a variety of ways. Before frost the long pods, almost dry on the vine, could be picked and shelled, the beans stored for winter use and for replanting the following season. As a quick-growing screen to divide the vegetable garden, shade the porch, or cover an arbor, these vines had many garden and landscape uses. Both vines are planted at Old Sturbridge Village to climb the rustic little arbor in the children's garden at the Fenno House. It is clear that by the early nineteenth century, the Scarlet Runner Bean, at least, was highly regarded as an ornamental, for it is listed under flowers in the D. & C. Landreth Company of Philadelphia catalog.

One hundred years later, Runner Beans were still in vogue with even the most discerning gardeners. Gertrude Jekyll reminded her readers in the early 1900s that "where the space devoted to flowers requires a screen from the vegetable ground, it may be well to remember that a hedge of Scarlet Runner Beans, trained in the usual way, is beautiful as well as useful." It may not be what she had in mind, but many gardeners today train them up chicken wire in the vegetable garden, often on the pea fence, where they can be easily harvested yet still contribute to the overall beauty of the planting.

The White Runner Bean is seldom grown now, and commercial sources are hard to find. But since bean seeds are the most widely collected heirloom seeds, because of their size and individual beauty, it is likely that gardeners may find old strains through seed exchanges (see the resources section in Part III). Perhaps the type known as 'Painted Lady', once classified as *Phaseolus multiflorus*, which has large flowers with white wings and salmon standards, is being kept alive somewhere. In my experience, the white-flowered beans are a little harder to grow in cold climates and not as vigorous as the scarlet-flowered type under these conditions, but they are still worth growing as a twining vine. I trained both types up baling twine to frame our shop windows — several vines of each type on either side, meeting in the middle — and, in the fall, we reaped a generous bounty

Phaseolus coccineus

of large-podded beans for winter soups and baking.

You can run either type of bean up a pole, as the name *pole bean* suggests, or let them twine around strings or wires trained over fences, gates, arbors, trellises, porches, or doorways. You can make a simple trellis by setting two fence posts in the ground, then running a wire along the top and bottom between them. Loop strings, baling twine, any stout string, or wire up and down between the top and bottom wires to form a trellis.

To Grow: Both Runner Beans require heat and moisture to make them happy, but moisture without heat will cause an early death. The White Runner Bean especially requires heat. Sow the beans outside when the soil is warm (when you plant other garden beans or corn). Plant five or six seeds one and a half to two inches deep in a little hill (this provides drainage). Make sure they are no more than three inches away from the support they are meant to climb. Space the hills six inches apart. If the soil is moderately rich, no further fertilization will be needed. Sow the seeds successively for a week to prolong bloom.

Collector's Choice (all sold as seeds):

Phaseolus coccineus, Scarlet Runner Bean. 147-8; 133; 160; 101; 95; 171; 87.

P. c. 'Albus', White Runner Bean. 171; 19.

❀ *Philadelphus coronarius*

Saxifragaceae
1600-1699   ZONES 3-8

Mock Orange

Orange-blossom, Sweet Mock Orange,
Syringa, White-pipe

TYPE: HARDY SHRUB
HEIGHT: TO 9'   BLOOM: EARLY TO
                               LATE SUMMER
SITE: SUN

More than forty species of Mock Orange are native to the Northern Hemisphere, nearly half of them to North America, though the type most often found growing on old homesteads (*Philadelphus coronarius*) is from the rocky hills of southern Austria and Italy. The most widely cultivated Mock Orange types vary in their height and form from low and moundlike to leggy and upright, some with great arching branches. The four-petaled white flowers — single or double — are loosely formed and slightly cupped with prominent golden stamens. They grow in racemes to the tips of each stem, so that a bush in full flower is covered with blossoms. The Mock Orange's claim to fame rests on its beautiful flowers and their fabled fragrance (sweetly orange-scented), though a few types, such as the native Lewis Mock Orange (*P. lewisii*), have no scent at all. The genus name is derived from Ptolemy Philadelphus, who ruled Egypt around 280 B.C. The epithet *coronarius*, meaning "used for garlands," sug-

Philadelphus coronarius

gests that the supple flower-covered branches were used to make coronets in ancient times. At one time Syringa, the genus name for Lilacs, was the common name for what is now known as Mock Orange.

Mock Orange bushes were cultivated in England at least by 1560. Gerard, who seems to have grown anything worth growing at all, had many in his garden. It is not surprising that it was one of the earliest shrubs grown in the colonists' gardens, rivaling Lilacs in popularity. Both are easy to grow and accommodating to a wide range of soils and growing conditions; Mock Orange is even tolerant of drought. Both shrubs also have a long history of use: White-pipe, a common name formerly used to distinguish the Mock Orange from the Lilac (Blue-pipe), refers to the shrub's wood, once used to make pipe stems. The dried blossoms and the young, scented shoots are reported to have been used to make tea, while the leaves, supposedly cucumbery in flavor, may have been used as a food in Elizabethan times.

The subsequent history of the Mock Orange also closely parallels that of the Lilac, both of which were taken up as the subjects of intense hybridization by the brilliant French nurseryman and breeder Victor Lemoine. But unlike the heirloom cultivars of Lilacs now available in modest numbers (compared to the hundreds that are known to have been created), there is a paucity of antique Mock Oranges, now the stuff of legend.

Alfred Hottes, the noted shrub authority writing in the 1950s, extolled the virtues of Lemoine hybrids, the products of an initial cross between the old Mock Orange of Gerard's garden *(Philadelphus coronarius)* — indestructible, beautifully flowered, and fragrant—with the frost-tender native Littleleaf Mock Orange *(P. microphyllus)* of exquisite fragrance (pineapple-scented) and indifferent blooms: "For beauty of arching shrubs loaded with bloom such varieties as 'Avalanche', 'Bouquet Blanc', 'Glacier', 'Candelabra', and 'Manteau d'Her- mine' should be chosen. . . . Those with a purple or rose center . . . include 'Étoile Rose', 'Fantasie', Oeil d'Pourpre', and 'Sirène'. Other desirable Lemoine hybrids, noted for their fragrance, beauty of form, and flowers, include 'Belle Étoile', 'Boule d'Argent', 'Erectus', 'Fleur de Neige', 'Girandole', 'Innocence', and 'Mont Blanc'."

Of all of these, the only ones still generally available are 'Bouquet Blanc' (1894), a single-flowered, rather late-blooming type of moundlike habit with arching sprays in ready-made bouquets, and 'Belle Étoile' (1925), another single-flowered, late-blooming type with a purple blotch in the center of each blossom. According to some connoiseurs, the latter is the best of all Mock Oranges — "its chalice-shaped flowers of purest white having a refreshing pineapple scent" (Roy Genders, *The Cottage Garden and the Old-Fashioned Flowers*, Pelham Books, 1984).

One of the most popular of the French hybrids today is the double-flowered Virginal Mock Orange *(Philadelphus x virginalis)*, which originated in the Lemoine nurseries, probably from a cross between *P. x lemoinei*, Lemoine Mock Orange, and *P. x nivalis* 'Plena', developed before 1910. The cultivars originating from this cross, of which 'Bouquet Blanc' is one, are characterized by intensely fragrant flowers — single, semidouble, and double — on bushes of varying heights and habits, all less hardy than the old-fashioned, unadorned White-pipe of ancient times. American breeders have worked hard to correct this deficiency (most noticeable in the famous 'Virginal', with very fragrant double flowers). One of the first American cultivars was 'Minnesota Snowflake'. Just as the older French cultivar names reflect the genteel world from which they came, the American types reflect their origin and preoccupation with the American landscape. 'Minnesota Snowflake', created by Guy D. Bush and introduced in 1935, bears very double, almost gardenia-like blossoms. These sweetly fragrant flowers, one and a half inches across and three to seven blooms per cluster, cover the bush from head to toe in early June. This cultivar is hardy to -35°F. (-37°C.) and is a good choice for colder climates, as is the Lewis Mock Orange, native to Alberta, Idaho, Montana, Washington, and Oregon, most likely named after the Lewis and Clark Expedition. While the flowers of the Lewis Mock Orange are unscented, they bloom in dense racemes for a good part of the summer.

Alfred Hottes was right when he remarked that such a lovely flowering shrub as the Mock Orange should not bear a name inferring that it mocks anything. And, as Mrs. King observed, "There is no other such bush of white flowers . . . every bud a pearl; and from all this lovely whiteness a fragrance thrillingly sweet."

Plant your Mock Orange where you can enjoy its wonderful fragrance. We dug up the old one we found on our farm and moved it close to one of our guest log cabins, where its arching sprays curve over the shower curtain of our outdoor shower stall, giving guests an especially fragrant bathing experience. If this is not part of your landscaping scene, consider a border of Mock Orange with Roses. The latter will cover the leggy stems of the former. The general upright habit of Mock Orange makes it a good screen or green barrier wherever it is needed. The individual lawn specimen is striking when the bush is in bloom, and the foliage is attractive most of the season. The Mock Orange can be planted at the back of a flower border as a focal point or among other shrubs that bloom at various times during the season, from Lilacs in the spring to Peegee Hydrangea in late summer and fall.

To Grow: The old Mock Orange, increasingly difficult to find from commercial sources, is the hardiest and most tolerant of soil conditions. All types thrive in enriched, well-drained soil and a sunny site. Mulch in the winter with organic matter and fertilize in the spring with a balanced fertilizer or with rotted manure or compost mixed with wood ashes — this is to counteract the acid nature of compost and manure, since the Mock Orange prefers a little sweetness in the soil. To keep bushes blossoming freely, prune out old wood right after flowering (they flower on wood of the previous season) and remove dead wood as the bush ages. Propagate by digging up suckers (in very early spring when the plant is dormant or in the fall), or take softwood cuttings during the spring or summer. These usually root readily when planted in fine soil.

Collector's Choice (all sold as plants):

Philadelphus coronarius, Mock Orange. 114.
P. x *lemoinei* 'Belle Étoile' (1925); 6'; Zone 5. 138.
P. x *virginalis,* Virginal Mock Orange; 9'; Zone 5. 133; 112; 45; 97; 114; 134.
    'Bouquet Blanc' (1894); moundlike habit; flowers well distributed over whole plant; 6'; Zone 5. 163.
    'Minnesota Snowflake' (1935); somewhat leggy, so plant behind lower-growing shrubs or plants; 8'; Zone 3. 167; 20; 123; 160; 138; 27.
    'Virginal' (1905); vigorous, but lacking in

branches at its base, so overplant with Roses; best for cut sprays of flowers; 9'; Zone 5. 138.
    P. lewisii, Lewis Mock Orange (1823); 6'; Zone 4. 127; 86; 7.

❧ *Phlox* spp.

Polemoniaceae
1776-1900   ZONES 2-8

Phlox

TYPE: ANNUAL/PERENNIAL FLOWER
HEIGHT: 4"-4'   BLOOM: SPRING-FALL
SITE: SUN

Annual and perennial Phlox are among our most valued and beautiful garden flowers, all derived from native species that grow from New York to Texas. Their habits vary considerably, from mat-forming in the very hardy perennial Moss Phlox *(Phlox subulata)*, densely moundlike in the annual Drummond Phlox *(P. drummondii)*, to upright and almost shrubby in the perennial Border Phlox *(P. paniculata, P. carolina)*. Phlox flowers are wheel-like — with narrow, notched petals in Moss Phlox and broad to at least one inch across in the other types — and grow in clusters up and down the stem or in great pyramidal heads that reach six to ten inches in Border Phlox. They come in varying shades of rose, scarlet, lilac, pink, and white, often with contrasting eyes, and are sweetly scented. The genus name is derived from the Greek word for "flame" and aptly describes the vivid scarlet and magenta of the wild types, preserved in the common name Flame Flower.
    Our native Phlox did not become popular in American gardens until the mid-nineteenth century, after they had spent some time in

Europe becoming prettified by breeding and selection, although they were grown earlier. The familiar spring-blooming Moss Phlox was exported to Europe by 1745, when John Bartram sent seeds to Peter Collinson in England. The latter remarked, "It is wonderful to see the fertility of your country in Phlox." It was grown on this side of the water sometime between 1776 and 1850, gaining in popularity with the rise of planting schemes that involved combining spring-flowering bulbs such as Tulips and Daffodils, as well as early-blooming Iris, with low-growing mats of color, for which Moss Phlox was well suited. It also fit in well with the increasing interest in rock gardens, where it flows over and between the rocks, creating a lovely effect when in bloom, while the evergreen needlelike leaves remain a foil for later-blooming plants. It became so popular by the late nineteenth and early twentieth centuries that it was regarded then as old-fashioned. Mrs. Jack could write, without a trace of irony, that it belonged to that group of "dear old-fashioned flowers of English gardens, to which we look back with tender longing." Some of the superior strains, developed by the early twentieth century, are still available, among them 'Blue Hills', with pale lavender-blue flowers; 'Brilliant', a distinctive carmine red, bright without being flashy; 'Apple Blossom', blush pink with dark pink eyes; and 'May Snow' ('Maischnee'), a pure sheet of white. For a change, try planting these in a dry wall — one that is laid up without cement, with earth between the cracks, and slanted slightly backward so that rain will drain into the little crevices to nourish the plant's roots.

Phlox subulata

Annual Phlox was discovered in Texas by Thomas Drummond, a British naturalist, on his second exploration of North America during the 1820s and early 1830s. He suffered great hardships on his journey through Texas and elsewhere and never returned home, but the seeds of the beautiful wildflower Texas-pride — in varying shades of scarlet, rose, purple, and buff — were sent back home, where the flowers became very popular, favored for carpet bedding — a specialized form of planting popular in the Victorian era for which one needs bright-flowered plants, usually tender annuals. These are grouped for mass display, literally covering the ground in a carpet of bloom, as in the dwarf forms. By 1860 a wide range of colors was available, creating quite a show when massed — a sea of crimson, purple, rose, and lilac. "The Annual Phlox alone has produced distinct varieties enough to furnish a garden, with almost every shade of color," wrote William Robinson in *The English Flower Garden* (1883) — high praise for a Texas weed whose great popularity stemmed primarily from its use in a style of gardening (carpet bedding and its variants) that Robinson and Gertrude Jekyll so deplored. Still, the variety of forms — dwarf, large-flowered, fringed, eyed, compact, and bushlike — and their beautiful clear colors must have been irresistible to such a keen gardener.

By the 1870s, the native Drummond Phlox had at last conquered its own country, well established across the land and into Canada. In *The Canadian Fruit, Flower, and Kitchen Gardener* of 1872, author D.W. Beadle describes it in glowing terms as "one of the loveliest flow-

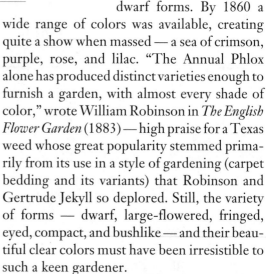

ers in the garden," and so it is today. Though the range of types available to the nineteenth-century gardener (seven in all) are not in circulation today, we have the two basic types: 'Grandiflora', growing to eighteen inches, with flattened flower clusters in mixed colors of pink, lilac blue, salmon, crimson, and scarlet (among them the magnificent 'Brilliant', introduced by 1901, with dense heads of white blending to rose, choice for cutting, as are all the 'Grandiflora' types); dwarf or 'Nana Compacta' types, growing to eight inches, with large flowers in the usual range of rich colors, useful in rock gardens, window boxes, containers of all types, or at the front of the flower border, a brilliant splash of color that lasts until fall.

The sweetly scented "queen of garden flowers," Border Phlox, was the last Phlox to return home — between 1850 and 1900 — though it had been the first to be introduced to England, in 1730. By the time it was being grown in American gardens, the straggly magenta wildflower had been greatly improved by the efforts of Victor Lemoine and others. Few

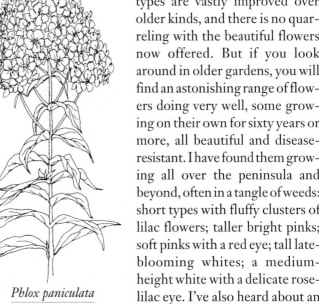

Phlox paniculata

of these heirloom strains have survived commercially (though many still grow in older gardens), but a notable exception is 'Miss Lingard', a slender plant with blooms — white with pale pink centers — all along its stems and thick, glossy leaves, a hybrid form from *Phlox carolina*. 'Miss Lingard' appeared on the scene by the early 1900s, the creation of a British amateur named, not surprisingly, Mr. Lingard.

Elizabeth Lawrence favored white-flowering Phlox in her legendary gardens (in Raleigh and Charlotte, North Carolina) because she found they best withstood the summer heat. Neither of the whites from this group (*Phlox paniculata*) that Elizabeth grew — 'Mrs. Jenkins' and the sparkling white 'Mary Louise' — is available today. Another favorite, the choice old strain 'Graf Zeppelin' — large white flower heads with a cherry-colored eye — is still around for us to enjoy. 'Miss Lingard' also remains popular for its bloom in early summer or late spring, before the other types have flowered.

We are told that modern Phlox types are vastly improved over older kinds, and there is no quarreling with the beautiful flowers now offered. But if you look around in older gardens, you will find an astonishing range of flowers doing very well, some growing on their own for sixty years or more, all beautiful and disease-resistant. I have found them growing all over the peninsula and beyond, often in a tangle of weeds: short types with fluffy clusters of lilac flowers; taller bright pinks; soft pinks with a red eye; tall late-blooming whites; a medium-height white with a delicate rose-lilac eye. I've also heard about an "old red" planted in the 1920s or earlier, but it has vanished.

One of the drawbacks of growing Border Phlox is the dread of powdery mildew. Gardeners are advised to give the plants plenty of air circulation and regular division. This is sound advice, but the older types I saw were crowded and often growing against a building — and yet they were all vigorous. The ones I have included under "Collector's Choice," below, have survived in a tough marketplace for thirty years or more and have proved their value to the gardener, so they may be as tough as the older strains.

Border Phlox is the backbone of a sound perennial border, for it carries on with blooms over a long season when many other perennials are past their prime. The glory of the colors and the size of the clusters make this plant indispensable. A mixed planting could include Glads, Dahlias, Marigolds, China Asters, and Black-eyed-Susans or Golden-glow (*Rudbeckia laciniata* 'Hortensia') — a gorgeous way to conclude the flowering season.

To Grow: Annual Phlox likes hot summers and grows best in full sun or very light shade. Sow the seeds outside in ordinary well-drained soil after the danger of frost has passed. Or plant the seeds indoors six weeks before the last frost if you want earlier bloom. Space the seedlings six inches apart. When the plants have bloomed themselves out, cut them back two inches from the ground, and they will rebloom.

Moss Phlox prefers well-drained sandy soil and full sun. It is quite drought-resistant. Space the plants eight to twelve inches apart and shear them back after blooming to refresh the foliage and encourage repeat bloom in the fall. Propagate by division as needed. If grass grows up between the roots, carefully lift out the whole plant in early spring by shoving a trowel under it (without disturbing the roots) and pulling out the grass. Then carefully reset the plant.

Border Phlox requires deep, rich, moist soil and full sun (dry, windy conditions spell disaster). Space the plants eighteen inches apart and divide them at least every four or five years. Thin out old shoots every spring, as well as half the new shoots on newly purchased plants, to encourage stronger blooming. Be sure to remove spent flower heads before they set seeds. The "running out" about which gardeners often complain is due to the overpopulation of the wild strain of vigorous magenta flowers that crowd out the superior strains, thus reducing the planting to one undesirable color. Border Phlox is splendid for cut flowers.

Collector's Choice:

Phlox carolina 'Miss Lingard'. 109; 61; 153; 142; 20; 104 (all plants).

P. drummondii, Drummond Phlox (old-style 'Grandiflora' type). 18; 147-8; 133; 3; 5 (all seeds).

'Brilliant'. 92(s); 3(s).

'Roseo alba-oculata' (old style). 3(s).

P. drummondii (old-style dwarf or Nana Compacta type). 133; 96; 92; 168; 5 (all seeds).

P. paniculata, Border Phlox; 2-4'.

'Dresden China'; a popular Symons-Jeune strain, bred for disease resistance; shell pink with deeper pink eye; 48". 66; 111; 20; 142; 169 (all plants).

'Graf Zeppelin'. 79(p).

'Leo Schlageter'; red. 45; 61; 153 (all plants).

'Mia Ruys'; white; increasingly rare; 20". 61(p); 149(p).

'Progress'; lavender with blue-purple eye; especially scented; 30". 133; 160; 138; 149; 108 (all plants).

'Sir John Falstaff'; salmon pink; 30". 45(p); 149(p).

'White Admiral'; huge white clusters; 36". 34; 138; 63; 45; 149 (all plants).

P. subulata, Awl-shaped Phlox; Ground Phlox; Moss Phlox; Moss Pink.

'Apple Blossom'. 115(p); 149(p).

'Blue Hills'. 45; 153; 129; 138 (all plants).

'Brilliant'. 45; 111; 153 (all plants).

'May Snow' ('Maischnee'). 74(p); 169(p).

✿ *Primula veris* (*P. officinalis*)

Primulaceae
1776-1850   ZONES 4–8

Cowslip

Fairy-cups, Herb Peter, Key Flower, Key-of-heaven, Mayflower, Palsywort, Password

P. japonica

1870-1900   ZONES 5–8

Japanese Primrose

Candelabra Primrose

TYPE: PERENNIAL FLOWER/HERB
HEIGHT: 1-2½'   BLOOM: SPRING-EARLY
                    SUMMER
SITE: SUN/PARTIAL SHADE

The large *Primula* genus of more than four hundred species, native to the North Temperate Zone, includes many garden types of exquisite beauty, but none lovelier than the humble Cowslip (*P. veris*) of damp English meadows. An unpretentious and appealing plant, it grows from crinkled basal leaves to no more than one foot (usually less), and bears one-half-inch bright yellow, sweetly scented flowers that seem to be held at the end of a pale green tube (an inflated calyx that is longer than the flower). At the base of each petal is an orange dot, said to be responsible for the flower's fabled fragrance "of balmy breath."

Primula veris

The buds stand erect in umbels, but when the flowers open, they hang down like a bunch of golden keys, then become erect again after fertilization so their seeds are not lost.

The Japanese Primrose grows to two and a half feet, also from a basal clump of leaves — in this case, long and tapering. Its flowers bloom in circular tiers as the stem elongates over a period of three weeks, at the end of which the candelabra is wholly lit with several tiers of showy purplish pink flowers about one inch across, some of which have darker eyes. The genus name, *Primula*, is a contraction from the Italian *fiore de primavera*, "flower of spring", a fitting reference to the Cowslip's early bloom.

Since ancient times, cowslips have been used by the bushel to make wine, conserves, tea, and ointments to cure everything from insomnia and palsy to freckles. Considering this tradition, as well as the plant's ease of culture, it is surprising that it does not seem to have been planted generally in America until the eighteenth century. Earlier references to "cowslips" may have alluded to several plants known by this name, including the yellow Marsh-marigold (*Caltha palustris*) of swamps and brooks, whose young leaves were eaten as greens. By the eighteenth century, though, the familiar wildflower of the English countryside was a familiar ingredient in American cookery. Old recipes refer to "gathering 7 pecks of cowslips" to make wine, said to be a very pleasant cure-all similar in flavor to a rich muscatel made from muscat grapes or raisins.

By the early nineteenth century, the Cowslip had been hybridized with its cousin the English Primrose (*Primula vulgaris*), resulting

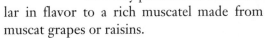

in choice types known as Polyanthus, which were grown by Jefferson at Monticello. Gradually, Polyanthus became synonymous with laced types in which each flower lobe, usually very dark red, is outlined with a narrow band of yellow or white (gold or silver), regularly dividing up the whole flower into ten portions. When these passed from favor, other types were developed in various colors and forms, both single and double, but the original Cowslip remained a favorite in country gardens for its undemanding ways and cheerful, nodding clusters of bright yellow flowers in early to mid-spring. Though rare now, the double form known as "hose-in-hose" (one flower appearing as if slipped inside another) was so common in Gerard's time that "it needeth no description." The reddish orange type, not quite as hardy as the familiar yellow, and used in the earliest Primrose crosses, also is hard to find.

The Japanese Primrose was discovered by Robert Fortune on his fourth and last trip to Japan in 1860. It was only one of several candelabra types discovered in the late nineteenth century in various parts of Asia. All of these were especially valued for their hardiness, showiness, and ability to grow in wet conditions — near streams and pools and even in bogs, where they make a grand show of bloom in late spring and early summer. Gardeners are sometimes advised to grow them in great drifts, which is just how I saw them at Audrey O'Connor's gardens, where they were naturalized in an area of open woodland — growing beneath and among slender hardwood trees, rising above a carpet of green growth in a dramatic and striking mass of tiered blooms in shades of pink and rose.

In my own garden, these lovely Primroses grow very well in unadulterated soggy ground (shaded to boot) near plantings of Siberian Iris. Ferns, Hostas, Bergamot, and Bouncing-bet keep the damp garden in continuous bloom well into the fall.

Cowslips belong in dappled shade in moist, not soggy, ground, blooming among Wild Bleeding-heart and Johnny-jump-ups at the base of a Lilac bush or old apple tree. They show themselves to advantage in a rock garden, where their relative height and conspicuous flowers are distinctive among lower ground-hugging plants such as Moss Phlox. I grow enough in my herb garden (where Cowslips are right at home) to pick as many flowers as I want to add to salads, to decorate cakes (when crystallized, without their long calyx, like rose petals), or for an occasional modest batch of Cowslip wine.

To Grow: Japanese Primroses require moisture and do not take kindly to very exposed, hot, sunny, and windy conditions. So if spring is very hot in your area, plant them in a shaded, protected spot. They can be grown quite well to Zone 4, though they are only reliably hardy to Zone 5.

Sow Japanese Primrose or Cowslip seeds in early spring (prechill Cowslip seeds for several weeks) in a cold frame, or sow them outside in the fall to germinate early the following growing season. Do not cover the seeds, as they require light to germinate (from two to ten weeks at 65°F./18°C.). When planting out the seedlings — six to twelve inches apart for Cowslips; one foot apart for Japanese Primroses — be sure the soil (for Cowslips in particular) is well prepared: deep, humusy, somewhat acid, and moist. Cowslips should be divided every year just after blooming to maintain prolific flowers. Japanese Primroses can be grown quite well in somewhat acid, dampish, heavy soil. In mild winter climates where they may grow as biennials, it's best to sow seeds every year (fresh seeds germinate readily) to ensure a continuous supply of flowering plants. Japanese Primroses, like Cowslips, are easily propagated by division, either after blooming or in the fall. They can be grown indoors in a cool but sunny window. Pinch back the first flush of buds for a bushier plant.

Collector's Choice:

Primula japonica, Japanese Primrose. 125(s); 115(s); 39(p); 92(s); 149(p); 108(p).

P. x *polyantha* 'Gold-laced' (18th and 19th centuries); a very old strain that was almost lost but was rescued and rebred; grow like Cowslips; 6-9". 92(s); 20(p); 13(p).

P. veris, Cowslip. 18(s); 45(p); 6(s); 177(p & s); 13; 105; 120 (all plants).

Cowslip Wine

1 gallon cowslip flower heads
2½ pounds white sugar
Juice of 2 lemons
1 tablespoon baker's yeast (or wine yeast for white wine)
1 teaspoon malt extract or 1 vitamin B tablet (nutrient)

Put the flower heads in a crock or clean plastic bucket and cover with 1 gallon boiling water. Stir often to keep the flowers submerged. After 2 to 3 days, strain off the flower juice, squeezing the flowers dry. Discard the flowers. Add the sugar, lemon juice, yeast, and nutrient to the flower juice. Cover and ferment the mixture. Siphon it into a gallon jug once the foam has died down. Fit the jug with an airlock or stuff the opening with cotton. When all bubbling has ceased and the wine has cleared, *carefully* siphon it into bottles. The wine is potable right away but much better if aged for a few months.

Pulmonaria spp.

Boraginaceae
1600-1960   ZONES 3-8

Lungwort

Adam-and-Eve, Bethlehem-sage, Bloody-butcher, Blue-cowslip, Blue Lungwort, Boys-and-girls, Children-of-Israel, Christmas-cowslip, Cowslip Lungwort, Hundreds-and-thousands, Jacob-and-Rachel, Jerusalem-cowslip, Jerusalem-sage, Joseph-and-Mary, Mary-and-Martha, Mary's-milk-drops, Spotted-comfrey, Spotted-cowslip, Spotted-dog, Spotted-Mary, Spotted-Virgin

---

TYPE: PERENNIAL FLOWER/HERB
HEIGHT: 6"-1½' BLOOM: EARLY SPRING;
SEASON OF INTEREST: ALL-SEASON
FOLIAGE
SITE: SUN/PARTIAL SHADE/SHADE

Despite their biblical names, all the Lungworts are native to Europe. They grow by creeping rhizomatous roots that spread in moist, cool soil, establishing large colonies unless checked. All are characterized by clusters of nodding trumpet-shaped flowers, usually changing from pink to blue as they mature, with heart-shaped, rather downy leaves that in some types are "as rough as a calf's tongue." Blue or Cowslip Lungwort (*Pulmonaria angustifolia*), growing to six to twelve inches, has narrow, unspotted leaves and bright blue flowers. The common Lungwort (*P. officinalis*), growing to one foot, has rough, spotted leaves and pink and violet-blue flowers. Christmas-cowslip (*P. montana/ P. rubra*), growing to one foot, has lightly spotted leaves and coral red flowers. Bethlehem-sage *(P. saccharata)* is the tallest type, growing to eighteen inches, and has heavily spotted, almost silver leaves and pink and violet-blue flowers. The genus name is based on the shape of the leaves, thought to resemble lungs, and their supposed curative powers. "Cowslip" refers to the early-blooming nature of all the Lungworts, which begin to flower with the first hint of spring, even breaking through semifrozen ground in the North. In warmer regions, the aptly named Christmas-cowslip blooms by Christmas. The flowers of all types are well designed to receive hungry bees in search of an early source of nectar or pollen.

According to ancient tradition, Lungwort exemplifies the "Doctrine of Signatures" whereby a plant advertises its uses. Thus, splotched or lung-shaped leaves suggested an antidote for lung or bronchial ailments. All *Pulmonaria* species do contain a mucilaginous substance suggestive of healing properties, and it may be for this reason that the common Lungwort was grown in early American gardens. In this connection, Audrey O'Connor

Pulmonaria saccharata

passed along one of her favorite stories about a Belgian nun who lived among the Sioux at the time of an outbreak of tuberculosis. She is credited with having sent to Europe for seeds of *P. saccharata*, thereby saving so many lives that the Sioux named the plant "Sweet Ann" in her memory.

When Lungwort had outlived its usefulness as a healing plant, it found a welcome place in the flower garden, valued for its ease of culture, early bloom, and attractive, long-lasting foliage. Various types were introduced from the seventeenth through the nineteenth centuries, the last one being the Christmas-cowslip. The one most often found in older

gardens is the easy-to-grow but increasingly rare common Lungwort *(P. officinalis)*. Today one looks in vain between *Perilla* and *Pyrethrum* for this cottage garden favorite.

I inherited a large mat of common Lungwort when we moved to the old farm. Every spring the flowers bring us joy as a herald of the new growing season, never failing to show their deep pink buds through last season's decayed vegetation, even as the winds still blow hard from the north and temperatures remain low. Gradually the little flowers open — first pink, then violet-blue, then white, a family habit preserved in the many two-part folk names, such as Soldiers-and-sailors. Barely discernible in the budding plants, the small, pointed light green leaves grow in importance during the blooming period, to be covered eventually with lighter spots — little moons of varying size that, descending in a rush toward the tips of the foliage, seem to have dropped from heaven.

In full bloom on a warm spring day, these splendid plants are a shimmering mass of violet-blue, their small trumpets nodding in the breeze, calling forth our resident honeybees, which come by the dozens, methodically visiting each opened flower and then returning to the hive with the first harvest of the season. We aren't the only ones to appreciate the common Lungwort. All Lungworts are said to be variable in the coloration of their flowers and the spotting of their leaves. They hybridize readily in nature and under the breeder's hand, but in my many years of growing Lungworts, I have never found any sports. Fortunately, superior strains are available for the heirloom gardener (though not as many as one would wish). These strains have been grown for at least the past thirty years and include the ever-popular 'Mrs. Moon', a well-named cultivar of *Pulmonaria saccharata* with heavily spotted, almost silver foliage. "I have never found out who Mrs. Moon was or where she lived," wrote Margery Fish. Nor have I.

I have found Lungworts to be an effective edging plant for my herb garden — a thick, attractive, and impenetrable barrier to weeds and grass, kept in check by annual mowing (I use a sickle). These plants aren't called Hundreds-and-thousands for nothing! Lungworts also accompany a host of Daffodils in their season of bloom and cover up for them when their foliage withers. They serve as an effective groundcover beneath the dappled shade of trees or shrubs, where their spotted leaves have the best color. If the plant is cut down to the ground after it blooms, its leaves return quickly, refreshed and soft, lasting until the snow flies.

To Grow: While Lungworts grow easily from a piece of root, they do not tolerate dry, windy conditions, so be sure to protect young plants and water them well until they are established. You can plant them in full sun as long as the soil is moist, but the leaves look best in partial shade. Propagation is easily accomplished by division in the fall.

Collector's Choice (all sold as plants):

Pulmonaria angustifolia 'Azurea', Blue Lungwort (*P. angustifolia* was introduced between 1700 and 1776). 61; 115; 149; 133; 45; 164.

P. montana/P. rubra, Christmas-cowslip (early 20th century). 149.

P. officinalis, Lungwort (1600-1699). 93.

'Sissinghurst White' (before 1960); pearly bells. 149.

P. saccharata 'Mrs. Moon' (before 1960; the species form was introduced between 1863 and 1900). 78; 149; 115; 74; 164; 45.

❦ *Rhododendron* spp.

Ericaceae
1731-1930   ZONES 3-9

Azalea

Rhododendron

TYPE: PERENNIAL SHRUB
HEIGHT: 2½-33'   BLOOM: EARLY SPRING-
                              SUMMER
SITE: SUN/PARTIAL SHADE/SHADE

Rhododendrons (from the Greek for "rose tree") are the aristocrats of the plant world, considered by some to be the most gorgeous of all flowering plants in the North Temperate Zone (they appear to grow everywhere except Africa and South America). Azaleas are included in this enormous genus of more than eight hundred species with thousands of named cultivars. Some types are as short as two and a half to three feet, such as the slender, diminutive Rhodora (*Rhododendron canadense*), while others, such as the grand Rosebay Rhododendron (*R. maximum*), are as tall as trees.

The differences between Rhododendrons and Azaleas are as follows: the former generally have long, leathery evergreen leaves and bear their bell-shaped flowers in clusters, with each bloom containing ten or more prominent stamens; the latter are usually deciduous (lose their leaves in the fall) and have funnel-shaped or tubular flowers with five prominent stamens. Colors of both range from delicate pastels — blush, mauve, and lilac — to brilliant orange, scarlet, and crimson. Many of the blooms are noticeably scented. Although most of the popular hybrids today are of Oriental origin (from China, the Himalayas, Japan, and Korea), quite a few choice species are native, growing in the mountains and forests of the Appalachians. Among the native species are the Flame Azalea (*Rhododendron calendulaceum*), with large brilliant yellow, orange, or scarlet flowers and flared-back petals, and the Catawba Rhododendron (*R. catawbiense*), whose white form is regarded as one of the best garden-type Rhododendrons.

One can imagine the astonishment and delight of the early plant explorers when they discovered the first wild Rhododendron in the New World to bring back to enthusiastic Europeans, eager to grow American "exotics." Reverend John Banister, an Oxford-trained naturalist of the seventeenth century, is credited with discovering the beautiful Swamp Azalea (*Rhododendron viscosum*) — fragrant, white tubular blossoms — found in wet soils and swamps from Maine to South Carolina. During the eighteenth century, the French government sent André Michaux to search for likely ornamentals. In 1796, after several years of exploring, he discovered the Catawba Rhododendron, growing in Kentucky and Tennessee, at the westernmost point of settlement. This species became very important in the breeding of Rhododendrons after it was introduced in England in 1809 and crossed with other species. These hybrid forms are probably the most popular types grown today.

Although Europeans were excited about the plants brought back from the wilds of America, gardeners on this side of the Atlantic were generally slow to acknowledge their native wealth, at least in the form of Rhododendrons. It is true that Jefferson grew the treelike

Rhododendron calendulaceum

Rosebay Rhododendron, but it was his French friends who demanded seeds of the elegant False Honeysuckle or Rhodora to grace their gardens. The Rhodora was described by Joseph Breck as "magnificent in appearance with flowers of a fine purple." Another nurseryman observed, "Choice but not very often grown."

"The most entrancing pictures may be made in gardens," Mrs. Wilder commented, "by means of the free use of these lovely shrubs . . . massed against evergreens, where their vibrant colors are thrown into relief, or clustered in thickets in light woods or difficult corners." Gertrude Jekyll gave her readers the same advice — to use Rhododendrons and Azaleas for background plantings, taking advantage of their strong foliage to enhance Lilies (she favored the elegant Goldband Lily), white Foxglove, and white Columbine planted in groups, the ground beneath them carpeted with Daffodils and Lily-of-the-valley.

A few chance seedlings along our lane introduced me to the garden possibilities of the wild Rhodora, which I later saw as a focal point of spring bloom in a striking rock garden planting: colorful splashes of rose-purple rising among bright yellow Cowslips, cascading Moss Phlox in matching rose, and foamy drifts of bright blue Forget-me-nots. When I returned later in the season after the Rhodora blooms were spent, I noted how its handsome evergreen foliage (mostly evident after the flowers have unfurled) was still a striking asset to the garden as an all-season background for later-blooming plants.

Tall types of Rhododendrons and Azaleas

can be naturalized on slopes or planted in the filtered shade of oaks or pines and other evergreens. In the shrubbery they are often paired with Mountain-laurel, another fine native. As for the proverbial "difficult corner," they can provide a long season of interest there with their burst of spring or summer bloom and glossy evergreen foliage (light red or bronze in some types by fall), but it is important to protect such plantings from driving winds or blistering sun, their worst enemies.

Native species provide the gardener with beautiful shrubs for some difficult places aside from corners. The Rhodora, for instance, will grow in heavy soil, even at the edge of bogs, while the Rosebay Rhododendron will grow very well in shade, where it makes a fine screen. The Swamp Azalea, as the name suggests, tolerates damp conditions that would be the death of fancy hybrids. The early Catawba hybrids, developed by the first few decades of this century, are ironclad (superhardy), with large, beautiful flower clusters in a variety of colors — some with frilled petals, all with handsome foliage. These heirloom types continue to be grown in spite of the many newer introductions because they have proved their worth. 'Roseum Elegans', with huge clusters of fuchsia-purple flowers, is nearly indestructible and very hardy.

To Grow: Rhododendrons and Azaleas have shallow roots and require humusy, well-drained, evenly moist soil with a pH of 4.5 to 5.2 (blueberry soil) and a generous amount of peat moss or ground bark to retain the moisture. If necessary, build up the bed to ensure good drainage. Plant out rootstock in early spring or early autumn. Plant it slightly deeper than it was grown in the nursery, and leave a shallow depression around the stem after tamping down the soil. Fill the depression with a mulch of leaves, pine needles, rotted sawdust, or compost, built up as much as six to eight inches over the season. Add new mulch every fall, and if drought or wind is a problem, be sure to water the plants frequently. You can apply an acid-forming balanced fertilizer sparingly in the spring. In the North, Rhododendrons and Azaleas can be grown in full sun if protected from the wind, but elsewhere filtered shade is best. Some species may be easily propagated by tip cuttings taken in the summer or by layering. If plants become leggy, cut them back hard (to one foot) to induce bushiness. Otherwise, pruning is unnecessary, other than to remove dead or damaged branches.

To plant from seed (nonhybrid types), sow the seeds as soon as they are ripe in a cold frame or a cool greenhouse on top of a damp mixture of loam, sand, and leaf mold or peat moss. Shade them from bright light. Germination takes two to four weeks. Transplant the seedlings four inches apart in sandy soil. Water them well and allow them to grow one year before transplanting them to a nursery bed.

Collector's Choice:

Rhododendron calendulaceum, Flame Azalea (1800); large yellow, orange, or scarlet flowers; the most showy native species; unlike fancier hybrids, holds flowers well in full sun for nearly two weeks; early June bloom; 9-15' (usually shorter); Zone 4. 112(s); 40; 118; 99; 139; 23 (all plants).

R. canadense, False Honeysuckle, Rhodora (1756); slender, rose-purple, two-lipped bells; small leaves; low, branching habit; mid-May bloom; very hardy and soil-tolerant; grows well in sun; 2½-3'; Zone 3. 91; 112; 123; 99; 40 (all plants).

'Album'; very elegant white form. 91(p).

R. carolinianum, Carolina Rhododendron (1815); very pretty rosy pink to white flowers;

mid-May bloom; very hardy, 6'; Zone 4. 112(s); 99(p); 62(p).

R. catawbiense, Catawba Rhododendron (1809).

'Album'; perhaps of hybrid origin, with huge flower clusters of pure white with gold-patched throat; late June bloom after other types have faded; very hardy; low, dense habit to 6'; Zone 4. 112(s); 48; 103; 40; 123; 28 (all plants).

Catawba Hybrids (late 19th century):

'Everestianum'; rose-lilac with frilled petals and beautiful dark green foliage; mid-May to early June; Zone 5. 123(p); 103(p).

'Mrs. Charles S. Sargent'; deep rose with yellow-green markings; an old Catawba hybrid favorite; Zone 5. 103(p).

'President Lincoln' (also listed as 'Abraham Lincoln'); rose with reddish markings, fading to pink; May bloom; very hardy for hybrid; Zone 5. 123(p); 103(p).

'Purpureum Elegans'; purple-violet with orange-brown markings; Zone 5. 103(p).

'Roseum Elegans'; the easiest Catawba hybrid to grow; withstands neglect; huge clusters of fuchsia-purple flowers with greenish markings; May-June bloom; Zone 5. 45; 97; 114; 27; 48; 134 (all plants).

R. maximum, Rosebay Rhododendron (1736); rose to purple-pink flowers; a large and vigorous shrub growing to 36' in optimum conditions but usually less (15-20'); dark evergreen leaves 5-10" long; the hardiest of evergreen Rhododendrons; late June bloom; Zone 4 with winter shade. 112(s); 118(p); 139(p).

R. roseum/R. prinophyllum, Rose-shell Azalea (1790); deep pink, very fragrant flowers; late May bloom; 9'; Zone 4. 118; 91; 99; 40 (all plants).

R. vaseyi, Pink-shell Azalea (1891); light pink to rose flowers and light red foliage in the fall;

mid-May bloom; 5-9'; Zone 4. 112(p & s); 99; 40; 122; 142; 132 (all plants).

R. viscosum, Swamp Azalea (1731); blush pink tubular flowers; very fragrant; bronze foliage in the fall; grows well in partial shade; early July bloom, the last of the group to flower; excellent for naturalizing in lightly wooded area; 6-9' or taller; Zone 4. 112; 102; 40; 99; 132; 91 (all plants).

❀ *Ribes aureum*

Saxifragaceae

1830-1850   ZONES 2-9   NATIVE

Golden Currant

Buffalo Currant, Missouri Currant, Slender Golden Currant

❀ *R. odoratum*

Clove Currant

Buffalo Currant, Missouri Currant

❀ *R. sanguineum*

ZONES 6-10

Winter Currant

Redflower Currant

TYPE: PERENNIAL SHRUB
HEIGHT: 6-9'   BLOOM: SPRING
SITE: SUN/PARTIAL SHADE

Several species of *Ribes* native to North America are desirable ornamentals. The very hardy Golden Currant grows from Washington State east to Montana and south to California, bearing a profusion of bright yellow, spice-scented, trumpet-shaped flowers tinged with red in racemes of five to fifteen blossoms on arching stems growing to six feet. Clusters of yellow-orange to red-black berries form by midsummer, followed by burnished purplish gold foliage in the fall, thus extending the shrub's season of interest. The Clove Currant, growing from South Dakota and Minnesota south to Texas and Arizona, is quite similar in appearance, except that the flowers grow in smaller racemes at five to ten blossoms and are larger and more heavily scented, while the fruit is purple-black (fully black when ripe). Its handsome lobed, almost heart-shaped foliage also colors attractively in the fall. Since both types of shrubs are variable, it is sometimes difficult to tell them apart.* One sure way to distinguish them is to examine a flower from each shrub: the Clove Currant flower has a longer calyx tube. The Golden Currant is preferred where growing conditions are drier, while the Clove Currant does better in

Ribes aureum

wet springs and humid summer weather. The Golden Currant's fruit can be used for preserves, but its quality is variable. The large-fruited 'Crandall' cultivar from the Clove Currant has been around for decades and is the type from which most Clove Currant stock is grown, making it highly desirable for landscape and kitchen use.

The Winter Currant grows from northern California to British Columbia and is hardy to -5°F. (-21°C.). An erect shrub growing to nine feet or more in its wild form, it has attractive lobed evergreen foliage and dense racemes of

The New Britton & Brown Illustrated Flora (1952), considers these two species to be synonymous.

clove-scented pink to carmine red flowers beginning in April, followed by inedible, but attractive, bluish black berries with a waxy or grayish bloom.

All of the Currants are associated with western exploration from 1790 to 1879, when plant collectors accompanied expeditions into an unknown and unmapped wilderness. The Golden and Clove Currants were fruits of the 1803 Lewis and Clark Expedition, while the Winter Currant was discovered by Archibald Menzie, a British physician with the Royal Navy, in the late 1700s.

The Golden and Clove Currants were grown in America by 1812. Jefferson, who commissioned the Lewis and Clark Expedition, grew both shrubs at Monticello. When he died in 1826, his granddaughter sent a box of plants to her sister in Boston as a remembrance of their grandfather; among them was the Golden Currant, with its "beautiful yellow flowers."

These shrubs, smothered in golden bloom by mid-May, remained very popular into the late nineteenth and early twentieth centuries, when they could be found gracing doorways, verandas, or shrubberies of modest gardens across America, highly regarded for their numerous flowers, ease of culture, and (not least of all) powerful aroma, "perfuming the whole region in their neighborhood," according to Breck's catalog. With their graceful, rather spreading habit (especially in the Clove Currant), they could be planted to good effect as an accent plant where needed, underplanted with spring bulbs, or placed in front of larger trees. Flowering Currants became synonymous with the American garden style — informal and homey.

With the outbreak of the white pine blister rust disease in the early 1900s (from white pine seedlings imported from Europe, infected with a fungus carried by the European Black Currant, *Ribes nigrum*), all Currants, including natives and ornamentals, were looked upon as a threat to the large white-pine industry, and throughout the country thousands of plants were uprooted and destroyed. With the decline of the white-pine industry in many states and the development of rust-resistant pine trees, Currants of all types have lost their pariah status and can now be grown in most states. (Consult your local Department of Agriculture office.)

The Golden and Clove Currants are enjoying a revival of interest as quintessential cottage garden plants — beautiful, useful, and well suited to contemporary ideas about low maintenance — as well as edible landscapes that are attractive to birds, bees, and butterflies. Both shrubs withstand city conditions well and can be used as informal hedges or lower-story windbreaks.

The more frost-tender Winter Currant enjoyed relative popularity in the nineteenth century, when double-flowered forms such as the Double Crimson Currant were offered. The handsome Winter Currant, "with dangling racemes of rich deep red," became a popular garden subject in Britain in the early nineteenth century after David Douglas (of fir tree fame) rediscovered it in 1822. "Though entering England as an alien," one writer observed of the phenomenon, "it has since found its way there into the gardens of every rank, while here in America, its native country, it is still scarcely known and seldom grown."

In the late 1930s, Mrs. Wilder urged her readers to consider the Winter Currant, "a very old shrub in gardens, so old that in the superabundance of new introductions it is often overlooked. . . . At present it is known and loved in cottage gardens but ignored elsewhere." She advised grouping several shrubs together and carpeting the ground beneath them with early Daffodils and other spring-flowering bulbs. A hybrid cross between the Winter Currant and the Clove Currant, known as the Gordon Currant, also was recommended, created by Donald Beaton of Hertfordshire around 1837 and named after his employer, William Gordon. A robust shrub of free-flowering habit with beautiful pinkish orange blooms, it is about as frost-tender as the Winter Currant, although Mrs. Wilder claimed it could be grown in colder localities. The question is academic today, however, since this lovely shrub is not available to American gardeners through mail-order sources. It is worth hunting for in specialty nurseries, though.

To Grow: All of the flowering Currants will grow in sun or partial shade and in any soil, even dry, though they thrive in well-drained loam with a pH of 6.0 to 8.0. In very hot, humid weather, the Clove and Golden Currants can lose their leaves, so provide them with partial shade under these conditions. Space all Currants five to six feet apart, since they can spread almost as wide as their height. The wild form of the Winter Currant is more upright, so it requires a little less space. All of the shrub types benefit from a thick, yearly mulch of organic material — compost covered by a layer of old sawdust, for instance — and a yearly pruning of unwanted suckers and old woody stems from the base of the plants when they're dormant. After flowering, extra growth can be pruned out as desired to maintain the plant's shape. Propagation is by suckers or softwood or hardwood cuttings taken in the spring or summer.

To grow from seed, sow the seeds in the fall and lightly cover them with a mulch of straw. Or sow them in the spring after stratifying (prechilling in a moistened medium) seeds for three months at 40°F. (4°C.).

Standard advice for all *Ribes* species is to plant them one thousand feet from stands of white pine.

Collector's Choice:

Ribes aureum, Golden Currant; Zone 3. 95(p & s); 123; 151; 167; 86; 7 (all plants).

'Idaho Buffalo'; superior fruit flavor; useful for preserving; very hardy; Zone 2. 151(p).

R. odoratum, Clove Currant; 'Crandall' type or from 'Crandall' stock; all with large flowers and superior fruit; Zone 3. 98; 45; 79; 131; 151; 149a (all plants).

'Aureum'; very hardy, Zone 2. 169(p).

R. sanguineum, Winter Currant; Zone 6. 120(p); 127(p); 125(s); 131(p).

'King Edward VII' (pre-1904); choice cultivar with bright red flowers and more spreading habit than wild type; 6'. 120(p); 122(p).

Currant Jam

4 cups dead-ripe berries mixed with just-ripe berries, all without stems
¼ cup grape juice
3 cups sugar

Cook the berries and grape juice in a covered, wide-mouth stainless steel pot (1- to 2-gallon size). When the berries are simmering, stir in the sugar. Bring the mixture to a boil and simmer, uncovered, for 10 minutes, or until it thickens and just begins to cling to the bottom of the pot. Pour the jam into sterilized jars and seal. (Adapted from my book *The Old-Fashioned Fruit Garden*, Nimbus Publishing, 1989.)

❀ *Rosa* spp. and groups

Rosaceae
1600-1901   ZONES 3-10

Roses

TYPE: HARDY/TENDER SHRUB/VINE/
    HERB/FLOWER
HEIGHT: 3-12'   BLOOM: SPRING/
    SUMMER/FALL
SITE: SUN/PARTIAL SHADE

Look into the face of a wild Rose, and you will find the face of the "Queen of Flowers" in its most simple yet beautiful form: five green sepals, five petals (shades of rose, yellow, or white) loosely arranged around numerous golden stamens, and, in the center, a cluster of pistils. Not all wild roses are single-petaled. Some are semidouble or double. All have varying degrees of fragrance or none at all. All grow on canes of differing lengths and thorniness, with their foliage divided into three to nine leaflets, and after flowering all bear distinctive plump, rosy, urn-shaped fruits (hips) — in some species considered as ornamental as the flowers.

Old Garden Roses (OGRs) are variously defined as those varieties or types introduced to American gardens before 1867 (the advent of the Hybrid Tea Rose) or 1900 (the natural beginning of the modern era). OGRs can be divided into two groups: one group consists of hardy, often blowsy shrublike plants, relaxed in flower and habit, intensely fragrant, cultivated in Europe and Asia Minor since Classical times, and, for the most part, blooming only once a season — the Alba, Cabbage (Centifolia), Damask, Moss, and French (Gallica) Roses, as well as various cultivated wild kinds; and the other group includes tender, more refined (in both form and scent) types from China, introduced to Europe after 1790 — the China and Tea Roses. The most significant characteristic of these lightly tea-scented types is that they bloom nonstop all season long.

The exact lineage of all of these Roses is impossible to discern, as they have been cultivated for thousands of years. Some of them may be the result of the Rose's natural tendency to cross-pollinate from one species to another, creating a new rose, while others are probably the result of early attempts at hybridization. OGRs are not wild Roses, but wild Roses can be OGRs.

The early settlers regarded the Rose as a basic necessity of life in the New World, primarily to cure a thousand ailments and flavor food. Roses were planted just outside the kitchen door, among Lilies, Hollyhocks, Peonies, Pinks, Calendula, Iris, Poppies, and other useful plants, within easy reach to harvest when needed. The wild Roses of the countryside were pressed into service, too, so great was the need for Rose blossoms and their fruits. The best Roses for household use were the Old World types: the Apothecary Rose *(Rosa gallica officinalis)*, the Cabbage Rose, the Wild Brier or Dog

Rosa 'Old Blush' (China)

Rose *(R. canina)*, and a semidouble form of the Damask Rose *(R. damascena* 'Trigintapetala')*.

As Roses took their place in the pleasure garden, more types were added, favored for their ease of culture, fragrance, hardiness, and exquisite beauty. Most of them bloomed only once a season, but what a glorious display they put on, with hundreds, even thousands, of blooms smothering a single bush or vine.

Important things happened in the Rose world in the early nineteenth century, when several important crosses were made between the hardy Old World once-blooming Roses and the tender everblooming Chinas. John Champneys, a rice planter from South Carolina, crossed an old Musk Rose *(Rosa moschata)* with a pink China Rose, from which came a new race called Noisettes, everblooming but tender. Then in 1819 an Autumn Damask, the only repeat-blooming European Rose, was accidentally crossed with a China Rose on the Isle of Bourbon (now Réunion in the Indian Ocean), creating the Bourbon Rose, the first hardy repeat bloomer.

These developments inevitably led to the decline in popularity of the older Roses. The emphasis was on repeat-blooming types with ever-bigger flowers, most of them fragrant. The acme of success in this line was the creation of the Hybrid Perpetual, the glory of Victorian gardens. It was the product of complicated crossings of Damasks, Chinas, and Bourbons, and it promised better winter hardiness and recurrent blooming, though it did not always deliver "perpetually." Profuse bloom in June was followed by moderate bloom in the fall, with occasional bloom in between. Hybrid Perpetuals, with their large, fragrant flowers, were hugely popular, and, by the end of the nineteenth century, three thousand cultivars were being offered to gardeners. These were really the first of the modern Roses, actually a bridge between old and new. They eventually declined in popularity when they were superseded by hardy, more everblooming types.

The first Hybrid Tea Rose, introduced in

1867 (a complicated cross combining the virtues of Chinas with the vigor and hardiness of Hybrid Perpetuals), marked the beginning of a relentless stylistic movement toward developing everblooming, long-budded, strong-stemmed tailored Roses (to which fragrance was often sacrificed), setting the standard by which all later Roses were judged. Hybrid Teas and their descendants — Polyanthas, Floribundas, Grandifloras, and the Ramblers and Climbers bred from them — offered gardeners nonstop bloom, relative hardiness, and crisp, neat flowers in an astonishing range of bright colors —

Rosa 'Louise Odier' (Bourbon)

the sort lacking in the mainly pastel shades of Old Roses and wild Roses.

So why would anyone want to grow OGRs? Enthusiasts may vary in their answers, but among them will be found the following:

1. OGRs grow well, even thrive, with a minimum of attention (with very little or no pruning, for instance).
2. OGRs lend themselves readily to the kind of informal, low-maintenance gardening that is popular today.
3. OGRs are, by and large, resistant to disease. Being less highly bred and closer to wild types, they are better able to withstand the stresses that encourage disease and insect infestation.
4. OGRs *smell* like Roses — an immensely satisfying sweet perfume associated with the fragrance of the Damask and usually absent in modern Roses.
5. OGRs are cherished in a way that modern Roses never can be because they have distinct, often quirky personalities that do not result from anonymous crossings.

OGRs also help to remind us of the simple beauty inherent in the classic wild form. In 1990, Lily Shohan, a guiding light in the OGR revival, related how she won a national trophy at an American Rose Society show with a bouquet of twenty-three OGR varieties — at least fifty blooms ("How to Win a Trophy," *Heritage Roses*, vol.15, no. 3, 1990). Later at the show, several people came up to ask her about the little white flowers with the intoxicating fragrance that she had picked from the wild to use as a dainty filler in her prize-winning bouquet. What were they? They were the clustered, newly opened faces of the humble white Multiflora Rose, once widely grown as a "living fence" and now regarded as a weed: five petals loosely arranged around prominent golden stamens — the "Queen of Flowers" unadorned.

"All Roses are beautiful, but not all are fashionable at any given time," Richard Thomson wrote in *Old Roses for Modern Gardens* (Von Nostrand Reinhold, 1959). We are most fortunate to be living in an era when there are more OGRs available than there have been for many decades, when both old and new Roses are in fashion together.

Most OGRs are best grown as shrubs. When they have bloomed in late spring or summer, other shrubs can take up the slack. Types with long canes (six feet or more) can be trained to grow against walls or along fences (these should be slatted for air circulation). If the side branches are pegged in an arched position to a fence or any horizontal support, they will be encouraged to bloom all along their length. Long canes also can be tied back to stout posts and grown as pillars. Heirloom perennial flowers such as Foxglove, Holly-hocks, and Lilies provide complementary upright forms in a mixed border. Low-growing Sweet-alyssum and Lamb's-ears spilling over the front edge of a bed will gracefully mark a collection of OGRs, perhaps grown on a sunny bank. The brightly decorative fall fruits and the bronzy red foliage of some types, especially the Rugosas, should be considered for their long season of interest. Nothing is lovelier in the late fall and winter garden than a light carpet of snow on rosy fruit-laden bushes. Think beforehand about where you want your Roses so you won't have to move them (not impossible, but not the most pleasant job, as I know from experience).

Rosa 'Alfred de Dalmas' (Moss)

To Grow: Although OGRs survive neglect, they thrive on attention. They prefer a heavy, well-drained soil and at least six hours of direct sun a day. They do best in the morning sun in the North so that they can avoid having moisture linger on their leaves from morning dew. (This condition encourages fungal diseases.) The absence or presence of wind is a factor in determining hardiness, so choose a location where some shelter is available but the air circulates freely. It's not a good idea, for instance, to plant Roses directly against a boarded fence. Again, this condition encourages disease and other problems.

I learned to plant Roses from a guest who showed me his simple procedure when I was planting out my first Rose ('Therese Bugnet', Hybrid Rugosa, 1950) many years ago: Always keep Rose roots submerged in water before planting (at least several hours, even several days). Dig a hole about two feet deep and eighteen inches wide. To one measure of bone-meal, add four measures of rotted manure or compost. Mix this well, sprinkle it in the hole, and cover it with a mound of friable soil. Drape the rose roots over the soil, water the hole, and fill it with friable dirt, tamping down the soil to anchor the Rose in place and fill in any air pockets around the roots. Spread a shovelful of organic fertilizer — manure or compost — around the plant, being careful not to let it touch the main stem. Cover this with two to three inches of organic mulch (whatever you can lay your hands on: old sawdust, wood chips, grass clippings). This helps retain moisture during dry spells (so you won't have to water) and discourages weeds. The organic material breaks down over the season, adding its nutrients to the soil around the Rose. Renew the mulch every season in early spring.

Roses should be planted three to five feet apart, or eighteen to twenty-four inches apart to make a hedge. Climbers should be planted twelve to fifteen inches away from the surface on which they will climb.

Little pruning is necessary other than cutting out dead or broken branches or suckers (*pull* these out) when the plant is dormant. If the shrub becomes too portly, cut it back by a third *after* blooming (otherwise you will sacrifice a lot of flowers). Most OGRs will survive without winter protection, but if you are growing some at the limit of their suggested hardiness, the standard procedure for minimal protection is to heap about ten inches of soil (*not* drawn from nearby plants) around the crown of the plant to protect the roots from heaving during alternate thawing and freezing. This, rather than cold temperatures, is the usual cause of winter kill. A well-planted Rose in a favored position — a sunny spot sheltered from the wind — will survive better where winters are harsh (particularly with a snow cover) than one planted farther south in unfavorable conditions.

Most OGRs are easy to propagate from cuttings. Follow the procedures described on p. 21. (Note: Gardeners in Zones 3-5 should avoid buying grafted Roses, which might die back over the winter to an undesirable rootstock.) To sow seeds, refrigerate them for fourteen weeks. Chip them, then soak them overnight. Seeds require twenty-one to thirty days for germination at 65°F. to 70°F. (18°C. to 21°C.).

Rosa 'Rosa Mundi' (Gallica)

Collector's Choice:

One of the tortures of the damned must be making up a short list of OGRs, as there are so many wonderful ones to choose from. The following are proven performers in a variety of growing conditions and serve as a reliable introduction to the subject. Most OGRs are heavily scented, so only those *without* scent are especially noted. Except for repeat bloomers, OGRs begin blooming by late spring (*Rosa hugonis*) or early summer (Centifolia, Damask, Eglantine, and Gallica).

Wild Roses:

Rosa eglanteria, Eglantine Rose, Sweetbrier Rose (early colonial); especially valued for its apple-scented foliage; small, single-petaled, unscented rosy pink flowers; often used as an informal hedge if clipped once in early spring; orange-scarlet hips; very thorny and hardy; 10-14'; Zones 3-4. 6(s); 11; 120; 113; 4 (all plants).

R. hugonis, Father Hugo's Rose (1899); valued for its striking yellow single-petaled flowers; unscented; a blaze of color in early spring; can be trained up walls or over arches or grown as a shrub with drooping branches and dainty foliage; 6-8'; Zone 4. 45; 153; 176; 163; 14; 120 (all plants).

R. moschata nastarana, Persian Musk Rose (1879); described as a variation or geographical variety of the Musk Rose or a very early cross of the Musk and China Roses; loose, semidouble pure white flowers in clusters; 3-6'; a slender bush, able to withstand drought in the Midwest but probably needs winter protection to grow in Zone 6. 176; 11; 113; 4 (all plants).

R. rubrifolia (R. glauca), Redleaf Rose (1814); a most delightful wild type valued for its plum-green foliage, deepening to purplish red in the fall, with bright red fruits; medium-pink single blossoms on arching stems in early June; good hedge; comes true from seed; Zone 2. Lily Shohan's choice: "The foliage is so fine in arrangements, a good contrast in the garden, and super hardy." 6(s); 92(s); 45; 176; 11; 20 (all plants).

Albas: Cottage Rose (early colonial); very hardy, disease-resistant types requiring little pruning and tolerating shade; Zone 3.

'Felicite Parmentier' (1834); very double light pink flowers; good for hedges; performs well in hot, dry climates; 4'. 176; 11; 90; 14; 113 (all plants).

'Koenigin von Daenemark' (1826); very double bright pink flowers with rich fragrance; great for potpourri; 4-5'. Lily's choice: ". . . is always good." 176; 11; 138; 20; 90 (all plants).

'Semi-Plena'; *R. x alba semi-plena* (before 1867); semidouble white flowers, loosely arranged; bright scarlet hips; 6'. 176; 90; 113 (all plants).

Bourbons: China-Old Rose hybrids; valued for their repeat bloom and relative hardiness to Zone 5.

'Louise Odier' (1851); opulent, very double, dark pink cupped blossoms; good for hedges; hardier than most Bourbons; 5' or more. 176; 11; 20; 113 (all plants).

'Madame Isaac Pereire' (1881); similar to 'Louise Odier', but can be used as a climber; 6'. Choice of Jeanette Dutton from San Diego, who reports that this Rose is disease-resistant and survives both drought and lack of sun in her Zone 10 garden. 176; 11; 113; 2 (all plants).

Centifolia: Cabbage Rose, Rose of a Hundred Petals (early colonial); valued for its full blossoms; "cabbage" refers to the shape of the flower and not its size, for, as someone once quipped, it could as well have been called the "Brussels Sprouts Rose"; very double medium-pink flowers; good for hedges; very hardy; 6'; Zone 3. Invaluable for potpourri, rose-petal sandwiches, and the like: "A bland uncomplicated naive sweetness which is a pure joy" (Richard Thomson). 176; 90; 113 (all plants).

'Robert le Diable' (1850); valued for its ability to perform well in hot weather and for its gorgeous dark color (unusual in OGRs); scarlet-pink to deep purple, as well as compact form; 3'. 90(p); 176(p).

China: Common Monthly, Old Pink Daily, Old Pink Monthly, Parson's Pink China (1752); valued for its continuous bloom, characteristic tea scent, and semidouble medium-pink flowers in clusters; 3-5'; survives to Zone 6 with protection.

'Louis Philippe' (1834); medium-sized double, deep purplish red flowers on a bushy plant growing only to 2'; try in containers. *Antique Rose Emporium; Heritage Rose Gardens* (addresses under Additional Sources in Part III, p. 219).

'Old Blush'. As described above. 176; 11; 113; 4; 2 (all plants).

Tea (1850-1900): One of the parents of the Hybrid Tea Rose, with the characteristic tea scent and repeat bloom; evergreen foliage; Zone 7.

'Duchesse de Brabant' (1857); double pearly pink cupped flowers; 3-5'. Commonly found in old California gardens, where it thrives in humid and warm conditions, but Lily Shohan reports that a friend has been growing 'Duchess' in a sheltered spot for fifteen years in her Zone 6 garden, a perfect example of stretching suggested zone limits by careful choice of site. 11; 2; 10 (all plants).

Damask: Summer Damask (early colonial); valued for its fragrance, hardiness, and fall fruits; Zone 4.

'Celsiana' (before 1750); double light pink flowers and gray-green foliage; heady fragrance; great for potpourri; 4-5'. Lily's choice: "Please include 'Celsiana', which has to be the finest of the lot and an excellent garden plant." One has to see the warm pink crinkled petals to appreciate 'Celsiana's special beauty. 176; 11; 20; 90; 113 (all plants).

Gallicas: French Rose, Apothecary Rose; *Rosa gallica officinalis*) (early colonial); semidouble dark pink flowers; large red hips; very useful for potpourri, since the petals increase in fragrance when dried; suckers profusely; very hardy; 4'; Zone 3. 176; 11; 90; 113; 4; 2 (all plants).

'Duchesse de Montebello' (before 1838); very double light pink flowers; 4'. Lily's choice: ". . . not typical, but is a free bloomer and excellent for cutting as well as in the garden." 176; 90; 113 (all plants).

'Rosa Mundi'; *Rosa gallica versicolor* (early colonial); a sport of the French Rose and the earliest known striped type; large, wide-open, semidouble deep pink and white flowers with golden stamens; good for hedges; very hardy; 4'. 176; 11; 20; 90; 113; 4 (all plants).

'Tuscany Superb' (before 1848); very double crimson-purple flowers; valued for its deep color, a nice contrast to the light pink types; very hardy; 4'. 176; 11; 2 (all plants).

Hybrid Perpetual (1840): First repeat-blooming Rose; valued for its disease resistance and fragrance; Zone 5.

'Baronne Prevost' (1842); medium-pink, many-petaled flowers (large and open with a silvery reverse); blooms nonstop for many gardeners; 4-5'. Lily's choice: ". . . an excellent variety." 176; 11; 90; 14; 2 (all plants).

'Frau Karl Druschki' (1901); still regarded as one of the finest white Roses, though too much like a Hybrid Tea Rose for some OGR enthusiasts; very double white blossoms with blush center; unscented; 4-6'. 176; 11; 45; 164; 113; 10 (all plants).

'Reine des Violettes' (1860); smoky red-purple flowers; glossy leaves; 6-8'. Lily's choice; 176; 11; 138; 113; 4; 2 (all plants).

Moss (1696): Perhaps a sport of the Cabbage Rose; "Moss" refers to the fuzziness around the plant's sepals, calyx, and stem, which gives it a mossy appearance and is responsible for the flower's resiny scent; the globular flowers, very pretty in bud, are highly valued for flower arrangements; very hardy; Zone 3.

'Alfred de Dalmas', Mousseline Rose; repeat bloom, with semidouble blush pink-white flowers; suitable for a low hedge or even a container; a dainty 2-3'. Lily's choice: ". . . a good repeater." 176; 11; 90; 2; 113 (all plants).

'Mme. de la Roche-Lambert' (1851); repeat bloom, with double dark red flowers, an especially nice change from the pinks; very hardy; 4'. 176; 11; 90 (all plants).

Noisette: This type results from crossing the old Musk Rose and the Pink China Rose; valued for its repeat bloom and flowers in clusters; frost-tender; Zone 8.

'Mme. Alfred Cariere' (1879); semidouble blush pink-white flowers; a climber or shrub that is hardier than most Noisettes; 12-20'. 176(p); 11(p).

Rugosa Hybrids: Derived from *Rosa rugosa* (1845); very tough and hardy; introduced from Japan as salt spray-resistant, but in truth Rugosas and their offspring are resistant to everything you can throw at them: wind, drought, poor drainage, thin soil. This type has everything you could want in a Rose: fragrance, repeat bloom, brilliant fall foliage, and hips. Zone 2.

'Blanc Double de Coubert' (1892); semidouble white flowers; especially beautiful orange hips; fine hedge or shrub; 6'. 176; 11; 138; 167; 169 (all plants).

'Roseraie de l'Hay' (1900); double violet-red flowers; fine hedge or shrub; 6'. 176; 11; 90 (all plants).

❧ Modern Roses

Rosaceae
1881–1950   ZONES 3–10

TYPE: SHRUB/CLIMBER/RAMBLER
HEIGHT: 2-20'   BLOOM: SPRING-FALL
SITE: SUN/PARTIAL SHADE

Our adopted Granny, a close family friend, is in her eighties now. She farmed the old-fashioned way on a backcountry farm in Massachusetts in the 1940s and 1950s. The work was arduous. On an average day, for instance, she lugged seventeen pails of water to the house, summer and winter, in a dress. "I had never seen a woman wear pants, and I didn't have any I could use even if I had thought of wearing them," she says. During all the years of her labors on the old farm, her flowers, vines, and shrubs were a source of comfort and joy, and she became quite knowledgeable about them, remembering today the names of every choice cultivar.

When it comes to Roses, Granny does not hesitate to declare herself in favor of the old ones. "I'm an old-fashioned person and I want old-fashioned Roses!" she says. These, by the standard definition, are modern Roses — Hybrid Teas, Polyanthas, Floribundas, Climbers, and Ramblers — introduced from the turn of the century on.

Time has proved the value of Granny's favorites — the middle-aged Roses that form a bridge between the really ancient ones, such as the Albas, Centifolias, and Damasks, and the most modern types. Granny's Roses are of

Rosa 'Crimson Glory'
(Hybrid Tea)

mixed parentage — some, like the Ramblers, close to the wild types from which they were derived; some everblooming and others blooming intermittently or only once a season; many with light to moderate or almost heavy fragrance. What they all have in common is that they have survived in a tough marketplace where, since the introduction of the first Hybrid Tea Rose, thousands of Roses have appeared and disappeared. Commenting on this phenomenon, Richard Thomson noted that "it took originality and beauty for a rose to survive among the hordes of repeat-blooming varieties," introduced since the turn of the century in ever-increasing numbers as the principles of hybridization were better understood and put into practice.

Middle-aged Roses offer, besides originality and beauty, all the qualities most valued by heirloom gardeners: reliability, ease of culture, hardiness, and fragrance. Plant these Roses the same as Old Garden Roses* and follow these rules of thumb: prune everblooming types when dormant; prune once-flowering types after blooming; space Climbers and Ramblers about seven feet apart and all other types about one and a half to two feet apart.

Collector's Choice:

'Betty Prior' (1935), **Floribunda**. Granny's choice. This type is the product of a 1924 cross between Hybrid Teas and Polyanthas, combining the best qualities of both: clusters of

---

* If they are grafted, make sure the bud union, where the Rose is grafted to its rootstock, is one to two inches below the soil's surface.

medium-sized, lightly fragrant flowers on long stems, hardy and everblooming. 'Betty Prior' has bright pink single-petaled flowers on bushy shrubs growing to four to five feet. They are quite spectacular when massed in a hedge. Prune them back to four to five feet in early spring, keeping only the strongest canes. Zone 5. 45; 33; 11; 138; 23; 164 (all plants).

'Blaze' (1932), **Large-Flowered Climber**. Granny's choice. No Rose is a true climber like a vine, but, if offered support, those types with long, supple canes can be trained to climb. The Climbers grow from six to fifteen feet and bear large flowers (two to six inches across) in loose clusters. They may bloom intermittently or all season and are effective as Pillar Roses (tied to a post for full vertical bloom). 'Blaze' has semidouble bright scarlet flowers, two to three inches across. It grows to eight to fifteen feet, blooms all summer, and has a slight fragrance. Zone 5. 133; 66; 31; 160; 163 (all plants).

'Buff Beauty' (1939), **Hybrid Musk**. Jeanette Dutton's choice. Jeanette described 'Buff Beauty', which is especially vigorous, as a survivor in her Zone 10 San Diego garden, where her Roses must survive drought and partial shade (the latter may explain their drought resistance). 'Buff' is almost everblooming, with two- to three-inch-wide double gold-cream flowers that are beautiful in bud (apricot-yellow) and have a strong musk fragrance. Growing five to seven feet high, it makes a good pillar of bloom. It is also handsome as a shrub, with its wrinkled, leathery leaves and drooping branches. Zone 5 with protection. 176; 11; 113; 2 (all plants).

'Cecile Brunner' (1881), **Polyantha**. This type, first introduced in 1875 and the result of crossing dwarf forms of the China Rose and Japanese Rose (*Rosa multiflora*), is a forerunner of the Floribunda. Also called the Mignon or Sweetheart Rose, it bears small clusters of exquisite double pink flowers, yellow at their base, with a moderate fragrance. Its three-foot-high shrubs make it one of the taller Polyanthas. Zone 5. 45; 153; 16; 176; 138 (all plants).

'Crimson Glory' (1935), **Hybrid Tea**. Granny's choice. This is considered one of the finest red Hybrid Teas ever introduced. It has large, double crimson velvet flowers with a clovelike scent ("That's a matter of opinion," according to Granny) and grows to a tidy two and a half to four feet. Prune it back in early spring in the same way as you would Floribundas. Zone 5. 66; 33; 11; 164 (all plants).

'Dr. W. Van Fleet' (1910), **Large-Flowered Climber**. Granny's choice. This plant's fragrant, fully double pink blooms, fading to flesh white, are two to three inches wide and grow on vines fifteen to twenty feet high. It flowers once in the spring, but what a display it puts on! This was Granny's favorite Rose, the only one she took a slip from when she left the farm. Zone 5. 11(p); 113(p).

'Frau Dagmar Hartopp' (1914), **Hybrid Rugosa.** This plant produces single-petaled medium-pink flowers that have a satiny texture and a clear color, along with large, outstanding fruit. It grows to four feet. Lily Shohan notes that it "has a lot of class and it blooms well, too." 176; 11; 2; 4 (all plants).

'New Dawn' (1930), **Large-Flowered Climber.** This magnificent Rose, a mutant branch of 'Van Fleet', superseded both its parent and 'Dorothy Perkins' because it offers clusters of large, double blush pink flowers two

Rose Bouquets

One of the rewards of growing Roses, both OGRs and more modern types, is creating lavish bouquets. Each type lends its special beauty to an arrangement. The OGRs look best in bouquets by themselves because of their more open, relaxed forms. For all types, cut flowers in various stages of opening, even buds, to add interest. Hybrid Tea blooms are usually cut when the outer petals begin to unfurl and Floribundas when a few blooms in each cluster begin to open. Most Roses are best cut in the late afternoon. Remove the foliage from the base of the stems, but retain as much as possible. Place the stems in cold water overnight. You can even refrigerate Roses if you need to for extended periods. Recondition them by recutting the stems and placing them in fresh cold water. Bouquets should last about a week.

Rose Hip Jam

For every 1 pound ripe hips (gather just after your first hard frost), add 1 cup water. Simmer the hips and water until the hips are soft. Put the mixture through a food mill, straining out the seeds and fibers. Add an equal amount of sugar (by weight) to the strained liquid. Boil the mixture for about 30 minutes, or until the jam sets. Pour the jam into sterilized jars and seal.

to three inches across. Everblooming with no disease problem, it also has nice long stems for cutting and a lovely fragrance. It has been unsurpassed since its introduction. Zone 5. 45; 176; 20; 23; 14; 10 (all plants).

'Paul's Scarlet Climber' (1916), **Large-Flowered Climber**. Granny's choice. This is one of the most popular of all climbing plants, though it blooms only once in the spring. Growing to ten to fifteen feet, it puts forth profuse semidouble scarlet blooms in large clusters. Granny grew it alongside 'Van Fleet' by the side wall of the farmhouse, where they both climbed to the roof, nourished, she swears, only by an occasional handful of rusty nails. She maintains that if you grow these climbers on rusty junk, they will receive all the minerals they need to thrive. Train 'Paul's Scarlet' on a split-rail or white picket fence for a gorgeous display. Zone 5. 34; 14; 164; 31 (all plants).

'The Fairy' (1941), **Polyantha**. This Polyantha is especially hardy and bears globular, light pink double flowers that bloom daintily and profusely all summer. Growing only two to three feet tall, it is widely used as a low hedge and for container planting. Zone 5. 2; 164; 90; 23; 20; 11 (all plants).

'Therese Bugnet' (1950), **Hybrid Rugosa**. 'Therese' belongs to the catchall category of shrub or dooryard Roses — types that survive with little or no attention. This is an exceptional Hybrid Rugosa, growing to four to six feet, with almost everblooming fragrant clusters of three- to five-inch lilac-pink flowers and foliage that slowly turns bronze in the fall. Developed in Canada by George Bugnet, it is very hardy and adapts well to poor growing conditions. Zone 3. 169; 86; 14; 167; 163; 35 (all plants).

Rudbeckia hirta

Asteraceae
1700-1776   Zones 3-9   Native

Black-eyed-Susan

R. laciniata 'Hortensia'

1800-1850   Zones 3-10   Native

Golden-glow

TYPE: ANNUAL/BIENNIAL/PERENNIAL
    FLOWER
HEIGHT: 2-8'   BLOOM: SUMMER-FALL
SITE: SUN

There are twenty-five species of *Rudbeckia*, all native to North America. The Black-eyed-Susan (an annual, biennial, or short-lived perennial, depending on its growing conditions) grows to about two feet on stiff stems with toothed, rather hairy basal leaves. The large flowers are perfect daisies with many golden petals, sometimes darker at their base, radiating from a brownish purple raised disk. Originating in the Midwest, the Black-eyed-Susan is now naturalized in dry fields and along roadsides from southern Canada throughout the United States to northern Mexico. It is one of North America's most popular wildflowers.

Rudbeckia hirta

Golden-glow is a long-lived, hardy perennial, double-flowered form of the Green-headed Coneflower (*Rudbeckia laciniata*), a tall plant (to twelve feet) with jagged leaves and long, drooping-petaled flowers around a dark raised cone. It grows in moist ground and thickets south from Manitoba to Quebec. Golden-glow is dainty by comparison — a mere eight feet (usually less) — with jagged leaves, double golden yellow flowers three and a half inches across, and a mass of petals, curved inward toward the center of the bloom and hiding the cone. It is often found growing as an escape around old farms and homesteads.

"I often reflect what a numerous train of yellow flowers with which your continent abounds," Peter Collinson wrote to John Bartram in the 1730s. He was referring to our bright yellow Sunflowers and Coneflowers, welcomed in European gardens long before Americans accepted them as garden subjects. "Here," complained M'Mahon in the early 1800s, "we cultivate many foreign trifles, and neglect the profusion of beauties so bountifully bestowed upon us by the hand of nature."

The Green-headed Coneflower, though not grown in America until the late eighteenth century, was in every English cottage garden during the seventeenth century, having been introduced by plant collector John Tradescant, who was given roots of the wildflowers by French settlers in Quebec. In the manner of gardeners everywhere, he passed along some roots to fellow gardener John Parkinson, who knew it as *Doronicum americanum*. It wasn't given its present name until 1740, when Linnaeus dedicated the genus to two Swedish physicians, the Rudbecks (father and son), who founded the great botanical garden at Uppsala University.

M'Mahon could take some comfort in the fact that the double-flowered Coneflower known as Golden-glow was offered to American gardeners by the early nineteenth century (it is advertised in G. Thorburn & Son's 1828 seed catalog), and before 1850 it was as common in American gardens as the Coneflower had been in cottage gardens a century or more before. Annie Jack described Golden-glow at the end of the nineteenth century as "the darling of the ladies who are partial to yellow. It has spread itself like an epidemic over country towns and byways, and is sturdy and faithful when flowers are wanted for hardiness and careless culture. If cut off when the first flowers are over, a new crop will come from the base, dwarf but pleasing because so colorful." Though rarely offered now (it is becoming more available with the interest in heirlooms), it is still found in older gardens. If left on its own, it will naturalize in the right spot — an open, sunny site with loamy soil — which is where I found a grand show of healthy golden blooms in late summer on an old up-and-down farm (so called locally for its rough terrain), a fitting floral emblem of the pioneers' sturdy and faithful descendants who had farmed this difficult land.

Plant Golden-glow by an old wooden shed, where the bright blooms will be shown to advantage, combined perhaps with the Sweet Autumn Clematis; or by the front or back door, as it so often was in the past, protected there from the wind; or around a rural mailbox. Does it need staking? Not according to old-timers: "I just let it take care of itself." That's sound advice if you can manage it. At the Heritage Garden in St. John's, Newfoundland, I saw it grown at the back of a perennial border against a quiggly fence, framed by the bronze flowers of the Hop Vine, a stunning combination.

The Black-eyed-Susan was grown in American gardens as early as the 1700s, the first *Rudbeckia* to be so honored. Its natural beauty and long blooming season (from at least midsummer to fall) could not be overlooked. It has always been a favorite flower, often dug up from the wild before seeds and plants were readily available. It was not entirely displaced in the public's affection even by the introduction of the more flamboyant (some would say vulgar) Gloriosa Daisy, with its huge yellow pointed petals painted with brown and red. This variation on the Black-eyed-Susan was developed in the 1930s by treatment with the drug colchicine, a process that doubles the number of chromosomes a plant carries, resulting in stronger stems and larger flowers with richer colors. Now also regarded as old-fashioned (though it was not introduced until 1957 by the Burpee Seed Company), the Gloriosa Daisy is often variable in my experience. I was given seeds saved by an old-time gardener, and, after they self-seeded in my garden for a couple of years, I noticed flowers in the subtler form — the Black-eyed-Susan with its simple, clean-cut beauty and appealing charm. It blends nicely with Southernwood and Lamb's-ears in the flower border. Naturalized on a dry, sunny bank with Butterfly Weed and Wild-bergamot, it helps to create a little bit of meadow. The Black-eyed-Susan also can be used to good effect when planted in tubs or containers for the patio or any open, sunny area. It is a terrific cut flower, so be sure to have plants near at hand.

To Grow: Both *Rudbeckia* species tolerate heat, especially Golden-glow, which can be grown as far south as Zone 10. Both can be raised from seeds sown in a cold frame during the spring or summer and lightly covered with soil. The seedlings should be planted out the next spring after all danger of frost has passed: two feet apart for Black-eyed-Susans and three feet apart for Golden-glow. The former needs full sun and light, sharply drained soil (overrich soil produces weak plants with fewer blooms); the latter requires rich, loamy ground. Black-eyed-Susans should be cut back after blooming to prolong their life (two or three years in favorable circumstances). They should self-seed once they are established. Golden-glow is easily propagated by division in early spring every three years or as needed. It may need staking in exposed situations.

Collector's Choice:

Rudbeckia hirta, Black-eyed-Susan. 95(p & s); 114(p); 143(s); 108(p); 35(p & s); 161(s).

R. laciniata 'Hortensia', Golden-glow. 120(p); 45(p); 18(s).

❁ *Salvia officinalis*

Lamiaceae
1600-1699   Zones 3-9

Garden Sage

Sage

S. sclarea

Clary

Clary Sage, Muskatel Sage

S. viridis (S. horminum)
1700-1776

Annual Clary Sage

Annual Bluebeard, Joseph Sage, Painted Sage, Purple-top, Red-top

Salvia sclarea

TYPE: ANNUAL/BIENNIAL/PERENNIAL
    HERB/FLOWER
HEIGHT: 1½-3'   BLOOM: EARLY SUMMER-
        MIDSUMMER
SEASON OF INTEREST: ALL-SEASON
        FOLIAGE
SITE: SUN

More than 750 species of Sage are widely distributed throughout the world. Three of these are of special interest to the heirloom gardener for their antiquity and use in the garden. All of them are native to southern Europe and the Mediterranean region and favor dry, stony ground. The familiar culinary Garden Sage is a perennial subshrub with woody stems; apple green to grayish green pebbly, pungent-flavored leaves; and stalks bearing white or purplish flowers in long terminal spikes, bringing the height of the plant to two and a half feet or more in favorable conditions. Clary, a biennial, establishes large rosettes of distinctive leaves — nine inches long, scalloped, nearly heart-shaped, and covered with silky down — in the first season. In the second year, it sends up tall plumes of small white, lilac, or pale blue two-lipped flowers growing to three feet from pinkish rose bracts. The whole plant exudes a strong, musky aroma. Annual Clary Sage, unscented, is slender in form, growing to about one and a half feet and bearing long racemes of showy top leaves veined purple or red, with very small, insignificant flowers farther down the stem. The genus name is based on the Latin *salvo*, literally, "I save", a reference to the healing virtues associated with the species.

Both Garden Sage and Clary were among

the earliest plants grown in the New World, valued for their medicinal properties. Garden Sage, an apothecary herb from ancient times, was primarily associated with longevity, strength, healing, and fortifying, a shield against the declining faculties of old age (especially memory loss). Its ancient use to flavor such rich meats as pork is a reflection of the widespread belief in its powers to aid digestion.

Clary is also a "head herb," particularly linked to soothing sore eyes (Clary from "clear-eye") with its mucilaginous seeds. The leaves were used with Elder blow (flowers) in wine to copy the flavor of muscatel, hence the common name Muscatel Sage. The distilled oil — pleasantly grape-scented — was (and still is) used as a fixative in perfumes. And, with less to choose from in the vegetable line, people in the past often ate the leaves and flowers of commonly grown herbs such as Clary. Parkinson described a tasty dish of Clary fritters, made by dipping the substantial leaves in batter, "made of the yolkes of egges, flower, and a little milke, and then fryed with butter until they be crispe, serve for a dish of meate accepted with manie, unpleasant to none." The Annual Clary Sage, often referred to as Purple-top, was credited with the same eye-healing properties as its biennial cousin.

With such a wealth of virtues to their credit, it is not surprising that all three were planted in the Wachovia Tract Medical Garden in 1760. Thomas Jefferson, ever an independent gardener, planted Annual Clary Sage as an ornamental at Monticello. By 1835 the London firm of Flanagan & Nuttings was advertising "Red Top" and "Purple Top" to sow in flower borders, but it was not until one hundred years later that herb pioneers such as Helen Fox and Rosetta Clarkson were telling American gardeners how various Sages and other herbs could be used as ornamentals.

Tender variants of the common Garden Sage — Tricolor or Party-colored Sage and Purple-leaved Sage — have been known at least since the seventeenth century in England, but whether or not they were grown in American gardens is not known. Although they are of interest to the antique plant collector, both are frost-tender (marginally hardy in Zone 7) and not as easy to grow as the ever-reliable Garden Sage. This plant has been much undervalued as an ornamental, probably because gardeners know it only as a cooking herb whose apple green leaves are harvested from annual plants. If left as a perennial, Garden Sage develops into a subshrub with fewer leaves for cooking, and these must be harvested early in the growing season, before the flowering stem develops. I value Garden Sage in my flower border as a dependable source of early color, with its distinctive flowering plumes in early summer. The all-season grayish green leaves are pretty, poking here and there through soft yellow blooms of the Lemon Yellow Daylily and Golden-Marguerite. Kept in fresh trim by annual clipping, it can be used as a low hedge, the foliage a restful point of interest among more colorful flowering plants. There are always enough leaves to flavor cottage cheese and pork and chicken dishes, as well as to make a cup or two of tea (to stimulate and fortify the brain).

Clary is a plant I do not like to be without, and every spring I search the ground to find the familiar large, unmistakable rosette of leaves. These biennials self-seed from year to year, and if they turn up where you don't want them, they can be replanted in their early growth. Even when they wilt after being moved, they will come back to furnish the midsummer garden with decorative stalks of bloom attracting the attention of visitors, including hummingbirds. In my herb garden, Clary enjoys the company of Musk Mallow (*Malva moschata*), Wild-bergamot, and nearby Roses.

The Annual Clary Sage is a most interesting plant that deserves more attention for its colorful, long-lasting, brightly veined leaves — stunning when grown in colonies in full sun, as they do at Monticello among Calendula and Corn Poppies. I first saw it growing in its native habitat as part of a winter carpet of bright-blooming annuals, and it wasn't until I returned home that I realized it was the same plant grown by Jefferson. If I had a stone wall, I would establish a colony at one corner where the stems, upright and trailing, would create a wide mat of color well into the fall.

To Grow: Salvias are drought-resistant and sun-loving. Garden Sage can be raised by seeds, planted one to two months before the last frost, to germinate in twenty-one days at 60°F. (16°C.). A week or so before the last frost, plant out the seedlings twenty inches apart in light, even poor, sharply drained soil (all Sages perish from standing water). To keep it going as a flowering shrub, cut it back with clippers in the spring as soon as it has sprouted new leaves (so you will know which part of the plant is dead and which part you want to encourage). I have kept some plants going for many years simply by breaking apart the old plants and severely cutting them back to encourage fresh growth.

Both Clary and Annual Clary Sage can be started from seed sown in midwinter and planted out, like Sage, in a sunny spot with well-drained soil on the light side — twelve inches apart for Clary Sage, six inches apart for Annual Sage. Clary Sage is likely to self-seed; Annual Clary Sage may self-seed in most areas (in my Zone 4 garden, second-year plants have returned, though unprotected over the winter, growing up from last year's crown).

The variegated Sages can be grown as perennials in Zones 7-10. Elsewhere, grow them as annuals and take stem cuttings in midsummer. Carry over the plants indoors, then plant them out as for Garden Sage. Their leaves can be used for flavoring in the same way as Garden Sage.

Collector's Choice:

Salvia officinalis, Garden Sage. 93; 114; 137; 177; 95; 121 (all plants and seeds).

'Purpurascens'/'Purpurea'; Zones 8-10 (possibly Zone 7 in a protected spot). 110; 93; 49; 121; 149; 177 (all plants).

'Tricolor'; as hardy as 'Purpurascens'; variable pink, white, and green. 107; 93; 16; 138; 164; 99 (all plants).

S. sclarea, Clary. 93(p); 177(p & s); 5(s); 116(p); 155(p); 15(s).

S. viridis (*S. horminum*), Annual Clary Sage. 93(p); 126(s); 177(s); 77(p); 15(s).

How to Use Sages

Annual Clary Sage stems can be cut all summer for fresh and dried bouquets. For the latter, pick the stems when the color is brightest, tie them in small bundles, and hang them in a cool, dry, dark room until they are completely dry.

The leaves of Garden Sage can be used fresh or dried. To dry: Pull the young, apple green leaves off the stalks and scatter them loosely on a cookie sheet. Dry them in a just-warm oven (at the lowest setting or after baking), stirring occasionally, until crisp. Do not cook them (you should not smell a strong aroma). Remove any stems and place the leaves, as whole as possible (to preserve the flavor), in a jar. Store the jar in a dark cupboard. Crumble the leaves to use.

✿ *Sambucus canadensis*

Caprifoliaceae
1700-1776   ZONES 3-10   NATIVE

Elderberry

American Elder, Sweet Elderberry

TYPE: HARDY SHRUB/HERB
HEIGHT: 12'   BLOOM: EARLY SUMMER
SITE: SUN

About twenty species of *Sambucus* are widely distributed in temperate and subtropical regions. The American native Elderberry grows wild from Nova Scotia to Florida and Texas, obviously a highly adaptable species. The shrub grows to twelve feet on pithy stems with spreading branches (to eight feet) bearing long, narrow leaves and showy, flat, sweetly scented umbels (six to ten inches across) of tiny white florets that become purplish black berries by late summer and fall. The berries hang down in great clusters — a picture of fall ripeness that is very inviting to local birds.

Sambucus canadensis

Since many of the uses ascribed to the European Elder (*Sambucus nigra*) were well known to the settlers, it is likely that they made similar use of the native species they found growing abundantly at the edge of woodlands in moist soils. There is a use for every part of the shrub, literally from its head (flowers and fruit) to its toes (roots), with plenty of uses in between for stems, wood, and even bark. Preparations could be made to soothe gout, dropsy, and dog bites; the juice was used as a hair dye (whether or not it washes out in the rain is unknown); and the distilled water from its flowers was used as a general skin conditioner — a complete pharmacopoeia in one bush. The settlers, who learned to tap maple trees from the Indians, also learned that the Elderberry's hollow stems could be made into little taps to catch maple sap or into whistles to entertain children.

During the eighteenth and nineteenth centuries, when more attention was given to growing ornamentals, the American Elderberry was pressed into double-duty service. Almost every homestead, and a good many town gardens, included a few of these attractive shrubs to fill the blooming gap left by Lilacs. Where space permitted, it could be paired with Mock Orange and the Rosebay Rhododendron, both of which bloom at the same time as the Elderberry. Neither its blossoms (Elder blow) nor its plentiful berries would go to waste. They were turned into tea, jelly, pie, juice, and wine. Nineteenth-century gardeners were advised to make an infusion of the bruised leaves to expel insects from vines. Able to grow in almost any soil, especially damp areas, Elderberries are incredibly adaptable.

Every garden with enough space should include at least one of these handsome native shrubs. When in high bloom, the Elderberry is the embodiment of early summer's long, sweet days; when in fruit, it signals the end of the growing season and imminent frost. Plant it near Daylilies and great drifts of Siberian or Japanese Iris in shimmering colors, perhaps near a stream or pond, where its spreading limbs will make quite a show loaded with creamy white umbels. Massed on a sunny bank where

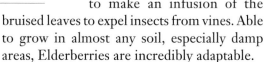

little else will grow, the flowers and berries will provide a long season of interest.

"The elder is a valuable shrub as well as a beautiful one," wrote Elizabeth Lawrence. "If you stand beside it on Midsummer's Eve, with your feet in a clump of wild thyme, you will see 'great experiences . . . from the thyme upon the height/And from the elder-blossom white. . . . In puffs of balm the night-air blows/The perfume which the day foregoes" (*Through the Garden Gate*, UNC Press, 1900).

To Grow: Elderberries thrive in fertile, loamy soil but will grow under most conditions, from moist to dry. Full sun on a rocky hillside, bank, or slope will provide good drainage, as well as some protection from early frost, since cold air flows downward. Space plants about six feet apart with eight to ten feet between rows for mass planting. Mulch the area around the bush when it is first planted. Once it is established, maintain the soil's fertility with an annual mulch of organic matter and a handful of high-phosphate fertilizer. Remove suckers as they appear and replant them as desired. To keep the plants shapely, cut out the oldest wood each spring. To rejuvenate an old bush, cut it off near the ground, and new growth will spring up quickly. Sow fresh seeds in the fall.

Collector's Choice:

Sambucus canadensis, Elderberry. 36; 106; 114; 66; 121 (all plants).

Note: Elizabeth Lawrence's favorite cultivar, 'Maxima', with flower clusters a foot across, is no longer commonly available but worth looking for.

❧ *Saponaria officinalis*

Caryophyllaceae
1700-1776   ZONES 3-8   NATURALIZED

Bouncing-bet

Bride's-bouquet, Bruisewort, Crow-soap, Fuller's Herb, Goodbye-summer, Lady-at-the-gate, Latherwort, Old-maid's-pink, Sally-at-the-gate, Soapwort, Wild-sweet-William

TYPE: PERENNIAL FLOWER/HERB
HEIGHT: 2-3' BLOOM: SUMMER-FALL
SITE: SUN/PARTIAL SHADE

Saponaria officinalis

Bouncing-bet, native to Europe and Asia, is a member of the vast Pink Family. Its shaggy or ragged-petaled pink or whitish flowers grow from a long, cylindrical calyx in loose terminal clusters on thick-jointed, sprawling stems with shiny, lance-shaped leaves. Growing to about three feet, Bouncing-bet is naturalized in large colonies, by means of underground stolons, along roadsides, railroad banks, and ditches; in waste places; and on abandoned farmsites. It blooms during the summer and fall. The flowers release their clovelike scent into the evening air to attract their pollinator, the hawkmoth.

The Latin epithet *officinalis* indicates the plant's long history of use, while its many folk names reflect the affection and interest with which it has been regarded by generations of ordinary gardeners. "Bouncing-bet" is an apt description of the way it moves about by way of its creeping roots.

Used since Roman times as a detergent (all parts of Bouncing-bet contain saponin, a substance that makes lather) and in the fulling process to toughen wool, it was brought to America, or seeds were sent for, in the early eighteenth century, perhaps for the same uses. Especially valued for its mild action in cleaning delicate fabrics, it is also soothing to the skin, which is why it may have been used to treat poison ivy (a condition the settlers learned about soon enough). Double-flowered forms were cottage garden favorites in England beginning in the seventeenth century and soon became a favorite ornamental in America, popular all across the country, from north to south, east to west, adapting to most soils and climates. Their intense fragrance on summer evenings has been described as "fulsomely sweet."

I was given a few roots of a double-flowered Bouncing-bet from a turn-of-the-century planting at the house of a sea captain, who sailed his schooner about the Maritimes, selling, trading, and buying whatever surplus the people had, even ashes from the stove. My neighbor, who now lives in the captain's rather grand house by the water's edge, called his plant "London Pride." I didn't know then that a half dozen plants in this area travel by that name.

As the roots sprouted leaves, I recognized that the new addition to my garden was a member of the Pink Family, closely resembling Sweet-William in its early growth. One evening my husband (the wildflower expert) and I were having a friendly disagreement as to the identity of the mystery plant, when, on a hunch, I went outside with my flashlight, plucked a few leaves, and rubbed them together. Voilà! A green lather. I knew at once my heirloom was *Saponaria officinalis*. Later, when it bloomed, I saw that it was the highly desirable double form, 'Flore Pleno' or 'Rosea Plena'. Regarded locally as a weed, it blooms by midsummer as a garden escape in damp spots and ditches, where it found a congenial home after it was no longer wanted in the garden. Lady-at-the-gate and Sally-at-the-gate are descriptive names for the way this plant was edged out of the garden proper. I did find it still carefully tended in several older gardens, though, where it bloomed among old Phlox and Rugosa Roses, the combined scents creating a heady sweetness.

Do *not* plant Bouncing-bet in a confined bed unless you are prepared to thin it annually (and it may be worth your while to do so). You may prefer to let it have its head where it can form a wide mat of light pink, perhaps at the end of a shrub border, in a damp spot with wild Iris and Bee-balm, or plunked on the lawn as a specimen planting and mowed around with care. This is the old-fashioned way to deal with plants that establish themselves comfortably in large clumps, and it is very effective.

To Grow: Although Bouncing-bet grows in a wide range of soils, it is happiest in moist ground and full sun (or light shade in warmer regions, though its color won't be as bright under these conditions). Plant the roots eight to twelve inches apart in early spring or fall. Cut the plants back after blooming and divide them as necessary, depending on the circumstances. To grow Bouncing-bet from seed, sow them directly outside or in a cold frame, covering them well with soil. Germination takes about ten days when seeds are sown outside in mid-spring.

Collector's Choice:

Saponaria officinalis, Bouncing-bet. 5(s); 72(p); 177(s); 62(p); 155(p); 15(s).
'Rosea Plena'. 45; 149; 164; 105 (all plants).

Stachys byzantina

Lamiaceae
1776-1850   Zones 3-10

Lamb's-ears

Lamb's-lugs, Lamb's-tongues, Woolly
Betony, Woolly Stachys, Woundwort

S. grandiflora (S. macrantha)

Great-flowered Betony

The-King-in-splendour

❀ *S. officinalis*

Betony

Wild-hop, Wood Betony, Woundwort

TYPE: PERENNIAL HERB/FLOWER
HEIGHT: 1-3'   BLOOM: EARLY SUMMER-
                        MIDSUMMER
SEASON OF INTEREST: ALL-SEASON FOLIAGE
SITE: SUN/PARTIAL SHADE

The Woundworts, to which group all three of these plants belong, are native to Europe and Asia, growing from a basal rosette of leaves and bearing spikes of bloom from early summer (Lamb's-ears) to midsummer (Great-flowered Betony and Betony). In Lamb's-ears, the leaves are tapered to four inches and quite downy, giving them a silvery cast. The flower spike also is woolly, growing on twelve- to eighteen-inch stems and topped by a densely packed plumed head of very small pinkish purple flow-

Stachys byzantina

ers. The Great-flowered Betony, as the name suggests, bears showy rosy purple flowers in one-inch-wide whorls on stiff eighteen-inch stems growing from a cluster of nearly heart-shaped scalloped leaves. Betony is a rangier, less compact plant growing to three feet. Its spikes of reddish purple flowers, also in whorls, grow on stems emanating from rosettes of tapered, aromatic, heavily veined, nearly heart-shaped leaves about five inches long. Dioscorides named the genus from the Greek word for "spike."

The Woundworts, especially Betony, an official herb of the pharmacopoeia, have a long and ancient history associated with healing virtues. From medieval times, if not well before, there does not seem to be anything that Betony did not cure, soothe, or charm. An old Italian proverb, "Sell your coat and buy Betony," aptly describes the value once placed on this musky, mint-scented herb. It was especially noted for alleviating, if not curing, all maladies of the head. When not used in this capacity, the dried herb above the root could be used for tea, as a tobacco substitute, and for a yellow dye. Although it may not have been grown in the earliest settlers' gardens, it appears twice in the plant lists of Christian Gottlieb Reuter, the surveyor for the Moravian community in North Carolina. Betony was grown in 1761 and 1764, according to his records, in the medical garden that served the community. As a panacea, effective against both devils and despair, Betony would have been in great demand.

Great-flowered Betony, though a Woundwort, has left no herbal account of itself worth mentioning, but it was favored in English cottage gardens as a showy plant of easy

---

culture. It is seldom mentioned now as a subject for either the flower border or the herb garden. What a shame, since it has a great deal to offer and makes a splendid cut flower as well. Margery Fish regarded Great-flowered Betony as a long-standing friend, "just as I do bits of furniture that have been in the family for a very long time. . . . It is a good furnishing plant with its thick comfortable evergreen leaves and stiff spikes of rosy-purple. Its old name of The King in Splendour is a good one as it has a sumptuous regal look when at the height of its beauty" (*Cottage Garden Flowers*, Collingridge, 1961).

Lamb's-ears, with its soft, furry leaves, must have been handy to grow in a large patch by the kitchen door, to use as a Band-Aid when needed. Although I've never used it for this purpose, I'd feel lost without its handsome silvery foliage in the flower border, the rock garden, or wherever it's needed, cheerful even in the hottest weather (the down on its leaves protects the plant from wilting), the leaves glistening and shedding water in the rain. The ground-hugging mats retain their lovely form well into the winter where they are not completely covered with snow.

I should add that for many years I failed with this plant until a friend gave me a piece from one he'd received from an old-time gardener. I have no idea if my Lamb's-ears is a tough old strain, but it's worth mentioning my experience because other gardeners, suffering from a similar failure with any number of other plants, may find a hardier or easier-to-grow strain still surviving in an old garden. This is one reason, among others, to preserve heirloom ornamentals.

All the Woundworts make an attractive groundcover, especially Lamb's-ears, if the flowering spikes are not allowed to bloom. If you want to use these for dried bouquets (as I do), cut them down as they bloom, and the foliage will carry on. The silvery foliage contrasts well with most bright flowers, especially red and pink Poppies. The leaves spill over rocks, enjoying the heat and creating wide mats that defy weeds and act as a mulch for nearby plants. Great-flowered Betony, grown in groups, would be a good choice for the middle to front of the border, where the showy spikes of bloom show to their best advantage among dainty clouds of Feverfew. The taller stalks of Betony belong toward the back of the border, a dramatic contrast to the lilac-white plumes of Clary Sage. The Woundworts have a place in both the herb and the flower garden — if you can tell where one begins and the other ends.

To Grow: Woundworts can be grown to Zone 10, except in Florida and along the Gulf Coast. Great-flowered Betony is the hardiest, while Lamb's-ears best survives hot temperatures. Plant all types twelve to eighteen inches apart. Lamb's-ears requires dry, well-drained soil and full sun where summers are hot and humid; otherwise its thick rosette of leaves may rot. Betony and Great-flowered Betony can be planted in well-drained garden soil, in sun or light shade (where summers are hot). Propagate any of these by division in early spring, or when the plants are dormant, every two or three years or as needed.

To grow Woundworts from seed, sow the seeds in early spring, or when the soil temperature reaches about 70°F. (21°C.). Cover them lightly with soil. The plants will flower the following season.

Collector's Choice:

Stachys byzantina, Lamb's-ears; Zone 4. 18(s); 96(s); 177(p & s); 109(p); 121(p & s); 36 (p & s).

S. grandiflora (*S. macrantha*), Great-flowered

Betony; Zone 3. 18(s); 45(p); 92(s); 120(p).

S. officinalis, Betony; Zone 4. 6(s); 177(p & s); 36; 49; 116 (all plants).

❀ *Syringa vulgaris*

Oleaceae

1600-1776   ZONES 2-9   NATURALIZED

Lilac

Blue-pipe, Laylock, Lylack

TYPE: HARDY SHRUB
HEIGHT: TO 20'   BLOOM: SPRING-
                  EARLY SUMMER
SITE: SUN/PARTIAL SHADE

The common Lilac is native to the mountainous regions of southeastern Europe and was introduced to the West around 1550 from Turkey. Left to its own devices, as it often is around old homestead sites, it may grow to tree size, with substantial woody stems and spreading branches that bear long, showy, fragrant panicles of lilac or white flowers in mid-May. In cultivation, bushes can reach fifteen feet (shorter in some types). Blue-pipe refers to the once common practice of using the wood to make pipe stems. Lilac is derived from the Persian word *lilak*, meaning "bluish."

No one really knows when the common Lilac was first planted in the soil of the New World, but it is generally believed to have arrived during the colonial period, one hundred years before Washington and Jefferson

Syringa vulgaris

planted them. Jefferson, an indefatigable gardener and recorder, wrote in his garden book of planting Lilacs in 1767 at Shadwell, his birthplace. In the same years, he noted them among the trees and shrubs already growing at Monticello. Washington, also an enthusiastic gardener, wrote in his diary on February 10, 1786, that "the buds of the lylock were much swelled and ready to unfold."

European travelers in the New World just after the Revolution were much taken with dooryard gardens "full of laylocks," observing that the road from Marlborough, Massachusetts, to Boston seemed a continual garden. (So much for the myth of America's lack of a gardening tradition!) While it's true that Americans seldom created grand gardens in the European style, the dooryard garden had its charms even for sophisticated travelers from abroad.

This phenomenon became a quintessentially American symbol, one with which ordinary people could readily identify, as in the famous line from Walt Whitman's poem marking the death of Lincoln: "When lilacs last in the dooryard bloom'd" — an unforgettable image of American spring across the land.

By the early decades of this century, several other species were introduced from Asia, and lovely hybrids, most of them of *Syringa vulgaris* parentage, became available to North Americans, but still the common Lilac did not (and does not) lose its popularity, even among the most discerning gardeners. In her book *Lilacs in My Garden* (Macmillan, 1933), the wealthy American socialite and horticulturalist Alice Harding described the species as "the lavender plumed bush which, with its white variation . . . is used to make the tempting and rapturous hedges throughout the countryside. . . . It is the lilac which in distinction to all others comes to most people's minds when the word lilac is heard."

Mrs. Harding spent considerable time in Europe inspecting and encouraging the creation of ever-new Lilacs. The plant wizard, nurseryman, and breeder Victor Lemoine named two *S. vulgaris* cultivars in her honor: 'Mrs. Edward Harding', a red no longer considered superior, and 'Souvenir D'Alice Harding', a very double white much sought by collectors today (see "Collector's Choice," next page).

While many of the Lemoine cultivars reached America during the early decades of this century, distribution was slow, and only a small number ever became commercially available. Walter Oakes, secretary of the International Lilac Society, wrote, "No one now living knows what the lost cultivars actually looked like. Some of the rarest have been located and interest in them has been revived through the efforts of our members."

Even so, there are quite a few Lemoine and other heirloom cultivars available today, more than there have been in decades. But among such riches, how does one choose?

Recently, a couple from Ohio came to stay at our farm and told us the sad story of how they had planted four choice Lilacs, including the only primrose yellow type, and waited four years for them to bloom. They all produced the familiar lilac flowers of the common form. What had gone wrong?

Charles D. Holetich, who has worked with Lilacs for thirty-two years at the Royal Botanical Gardens in Hamilton, Ontario (where he is in charge of the world's largest Lilac collection), assured me that our friends probably lost their Lilacs because they had been poorly planted, under conditions where hardly any ornamental plant would survive or flourish. Lilacs, he pointed out, are suitably hardy plants from Edmonton to Montreal in the north and from Denver to Philadelphia in the south. Evidently, our friends had bought grafted Lilacs from an uninformed nursery, and they had all died back to the rootstock, *Syringa vulgaris*, after a hard winter. If they had been deeply and well planted, as Mr. Holetich noted, they should have survived. (Grafted shrubs should always be planted four to six inches deeper than they were in the nursery, but it's better to buy shrubs advertised as "own root.") Mr. Holetich also stressed that, even if you live in a growing zone where Lilacs are not normally grown, you can succeed with them by carefully choosing cultivars that do well in higher (mountainous) elevations in the South or in wind-protected (sheltered) areas in the North. This must be so, for a friend who recently moved to Santa Fe, New Mexico, at the edge of the High Desert, extols the glories of purple Lilacs blooming in hedges against whitewashed adobe walls in early spring.

To produce blooms, Lilacs need a period of rest, or dormancy, which can be brought on by either successive nighttime temperatures below 40°F. (4°C.) or several months of drought. Magnificent Lilacs grow in older gardens of the Sacramento Valley in California, where summers are very hot and dry. (Check below for cultivars that do well under difficult growing conditions.) This group is usually referred to as French Hybrids, the result of crossing *Syringa vulgaris* cultivars, thereby producing a wider range of flower color and size of bloom, as well as extending the bloom period. (As for fragrance, even experts admit that the old common Lilac is probably the most fragrant.) Not all the French Hybrids are, in fact, French.

Two of the top heirlooms on my list are 'President Lincoln', bred by John Dunbar, superintendent of parks in Rochester, New York, from 1891 to 1926, and 'Andenken An Ludwig Spath', bred in Germany.

To Grow: There are two things to remember: lilacs need five hours of sun a day and well-drained soil. They prefer a slightly alkaline soil but grow perfectly well in acidic soil. A pH of 6.0 to 8.0 is O.K.

If the planting site is at all soggy, mound the soil and drape the roots over it so that surface water will drain away from the plants. Dig a generous hole to accommodate the roots and plant them about the same depth as they were in the nursery, or according to planting directions supplied by the nursery. Water them well and give the plant a good shake — before and after watering — to eliminate any air pockets in the loose soil. Trim back the terminal buds lightly, even though they may look fat and promising. Don't expect much the first year (or even the second or third with most types). Lilacs take patience.

Authorities usually advise deadheading (trimming off spent blooms), but this is often impractical, especially with a bush of treelike proportions. *Do* pick plenty of bouquets when your beauty finally comes of age — a painless way to deadhead and moderately thin the bush. To prolong cut flowers, trim away some of the lower bark and dip the stems in near boiling water, leaving them in the water to cool before arranging.

Pruning just to keep in shape should be done after the blooming period. There are two ways to rejuvenate old Lilacs in late winter. The more drastic is to cut the whole bush to within six inches of the ground. A demure shrub will grow up the first season, but don't expect any bloom. Radical pruning should be attempted only if some vigorous new shoots or plants are coming up from the base of the shrub; otherwise this method is risky. The second method is the three-year plan: the first season cut out one-third of the largest of the old stems and thin the small shoots; the second year cut out another third; the third year remove the last third. That way the shrub will be gradually reduced in height without sacrificing all the bloom. Lilac experts tell me that this is the preferred plan, though I have seen the other method work.

Alternatively, you can leave your treelike Lilac the way it is, as we do. It not only makes a fine windbreak but gives us a good excuse to create a shade garden of Cowslips, Bee-balm, and Hostas of all kinds beneath its aging limbs.

Collector's Choice (all sold as plants):

The cultivars I have selected all have desirable characteristics of one sort or another, all are beautiful, and all have performed well, often under trying conditions in a variety of habitats. I am indebted to Roger Vick's ad hoc International Lilac Society (ILS) committee for historical data (see "Listing the Loveliest Lilacs," *Kinnikinnick*, vol. 6, no. 3).

All Lilacs are scented to a degree. The ❀ symbol denotes those rated as having the strongest scent. The numbers 1, 2, 3, and 4 represent places where cultivars have performed extremely well:

1. Royal Botanical Gardens, Hamilton, Ontario, Canada.

2. Arnold Arboretum, Boston, Massachusetts.

3. Leona Valley, Southern California (observed by an ILS member).

4. Nebraska (observed by an ILS member).

Syringa vulgaris, Lilac; Zone 2. 31; 169; 151; 30; 134.

    ❋'Alba'. 114; 163; 41.

Hybrids:

(3,4) 'Ami Schott' (1933, Lemoine); double cobalt blue flowers; long bloom; heat-resistant; Zone 3. 81.

(1,3) ❋'Andenken An Ludwig Spath'/'Ludwig Spath' (1883); single purple-red flowers; profuse blooms in midseason; Zone 2. 45; 138; 169.

(2,3) ❋'Katherine Havemeyer' (1922, Lemoine); large, double pink flowers in early midseason; Zone 3. 31; 32; 81; 134; 169; 45.

(2,3) ❋'Lucie Baltet' (pre-1888); single shell-pink flowers; a low- and slow-growing type; Zone 3. 45; 32; 122; 134.

(1,2,3) ❋'Michel Buchner' (1885, Lemoine); double lilac flowers; a heavy bloomer in midseason; Zone 2. 160; 134.

(2,3) 'Miss Ellen Willmott' (1903, Lemoine); double white flowers; very large trusses; Zone 2. 81; 163; 138; 160; 32; 31.

(1,3) 'Mrs. W.E. Marshall' (1924); single dark purple flowers; outstanding foliage; Zone 2. 45; 81.

(1,2,3) ❋'Paul Thirion' (1915, Lemoine); double magenta flowers with silver reverse; a fine cut flower; Zone 3. 45; 112; 32; 163.

(1,2,3,4) 'President Lincoln' (1916); single blue flowers in large clusters; Zone 2. 122; 167; 81; 138; 169; 34.

(1,2,3) 'Primrose' (1949); single yellow flowers fading to creamy white; very unusual; Zone 2. 81; 138; 79; 137; 114; 32.

(1,2,3) 'Sensation' (1938); a bicolor with deep purple flowers edged with white; Zone 2. 45; 32; 79; 138; 81.

(3,4) 'Souvenir D'Alice Harding' (1938, Lemoine); very double white flowers; Zone 3. 112.

Tagetes patula

Asteraceae
1776-1850

French Marigold

Rose-of-the-Indies

❋ T. tenuifolia

Signet Marigold

TYPE: TENDER ANNUAL FLOWER
HEIGHT: 6-10"   BLOOM: SUMMER-FALL
SITE: SUN

In the wilds of Mexico and Guatemala, where it was discovered in the 1570s, the French Marigold is a bushy annual growing to one and a half feet. Feathery scented leaves and single-petaled rays—yellow, orange, or reddish brown —emanated from a domed center or crest. It was called the French Marigold because it was introduced to England (as the Rose-of-the-Indies) by Huguenot refugees. Signet Marigolds, native to Mexico and Central America, grow to two feet and bear intensely scented (citrusy) ferny leaves and tiny, single-petaled yellow flowers. Both Marigolds are scented, but the Signets are the ones whose fragrance is considered desirable.

    Garden historians differ in their dating of Marigolds (either French or African, *Tagetes erecta*) in American gardens, some claiming the early settler period (1600-1699) and others taking a more cautious approach (by the early nineteenth century for French types). Ann Leighton recorded that by 1793 Lady Skipwirth's husband had ordered striped French Marigolds. By 1808 Jefferson had heard of "the two kinds of Marigolds you gave us," and by 1812 he had sown the French kind in his own garden. There is little doubt that both the French and African Marigolds were established in America by the early nineteenth century at the latest, for in 1806 M'Mahon was offering choice cultivars of double-flowered types, as well as quilled African Marigolds. By the 1860s, the Signet Marigold in its dwarf form (*pumila*), had become very popular, especially prized for carpet bedding. Although each flower was small — bright yellow with brown markings — they bloomed in a great mass. In 1866 *The Magazine of Horticulture* described the Signet types as "elegant . . . when fully grown, the plant will measure two feet in diameter, forming a beautiful compact bush, completely covered with flowers, and continuing in bloom until hard frost sets in."

Tagetes patula

Some people have claimed that the Marigolds of the turn of the century were virtually indistinguishable from today's. Such an idea would have been anathema to David Burpee, who took over his father's company, established in 1876. With slumping sales of the Sweet Pea, he turned his attention to improving the Marigold, boasting in later years that he took a scrawny flower of limited color range and smelly foliage and turned it into a garden Cinderella. There is no doubt that Burpee has been at the forefront of Marigold development. In 1939 it introduced the Red and Gold Hybrid Marigold, the first hybrid flower from seed to be offered for commercial sale in the United States. Of the twenty-nine AAS medals awarded for Marigold introductions from 1933 to 1950, fourteen of them were for Burpee introductions, with names such as 'Crown of Gold', 'Early Sunshine', 'Golden Bedder', 'Golden Glow', 'Limelight', 'Real Gold', and 'Naughty Marietta'. The goal in Marigold breeding was to develop disease- and weather-resistant early-flowering types with more densely packed flower heads (of either the French or African type or hybrid crosses between the two) in variations on the basic gold and mahogany color themes. White Marigolds were not achieved until the 1970s.

The only cultivar from the pre-1950 period available today is 'Naughty Marietta', a single-petaled French Marigold introduced by Burpee in 1947, winning an AAS Honorable Mention as well as an Award of Merit from the Royal Horticultural Society. 'Naughty' grows to ten inches and bears flowers of singular charm: bright golden petals with a distinct mahogany cross in the center of each bloom. Recently, dwarf types have been introduced, but the flower type itself, so simple and satisfying in design among the increasingly densely packed colored balls of either French or African Marigolds or their hybrids, has not been improved.

'Naughty', however, did not appear out of the blue. As I learned from Jeanette Lowe, secretary of the Marigold Society of America and retired flower breeder at the W. Atlee Burpee Company, it was probably developed from crossing and reselection, using previous bicolors such as 'Iron Cross' and 'Legion of Honor'. I knew about 'Iron Cross' from my Dutch friend, Brother Gilbert, who remembered it well from his childhood in Holland in the 1930s, where it was known as 'Erekruise'.

'Legion of Honor', also known as 'Little Brownie', was very popular in the early 1900s, appearing regularly in every Burpee catalog into the 1930s, until displaced by 'Naughty', which was more uniform in height and habit and bore larger flowers than the earlier introductions. Brother Gilbert carefully saves seeds of 'Naughty', which he has been growing for the past twenty years. He also saves seeds from sports — some mahogany-edged, slightly ruffled, all yellow, or striped — if he considers them choice. He plants his French Marigolds in masses — bright patches at the front of his generous perennial border — or in tubs placed by doorways, sometimes paired with white Sweet-alyssum. At Old Sturbridge Village, 'Naughty' is planted in the recreated Towne House garden as the most representative of early nineteenth-century French Marigold types.

Signet Marigolds have been least affected by Marigold development as envisioned by David Burpee. The dwarf types available today are probably very similar to those enjoyed by gardeners in the late nineteenth and early twentieth centuries, their distinctly citrus-scented leaves regarded as anything but "smelly" by connoisseurs. Roy Genders considers the foliage of the Signets "more refreshingly aromatic than any other plant, the lemon verbena-like perfume remaining on the fingers for an hour or more after pressing the leaves" (*The Cottage Garden, and the Old-Fashioned Flowers*, Pelham Books, 1984). In recent years, these flowers have been rediscovered as herbs, because the scented foliage and flowers can be used in potpourri, in pressed flower creations, even to flavor hot dessert sauces made with wine. (I've never tried it, but it sounds interesting.) The little flowers can be candied for cake decorations, too.

Signets are very useful for their colorful mounds of flowers from just a few plants blooming well into the fall — surprisingly frost-resistant (more so than other Marigolds, in my experience). If planted in tubs, they can be placed in protected areas, near buildings or taller plantings, to prolong flowering into early winter, or the containers can be moved indoors to a sunny spot. Plant Signets in rock gardens — so beautiful spilling over rocks, lighting up the garden — among evergreens in foundation plantings, or at the front of any flower border. Both cultivars listed below have been around a long time — 'Golden Gem' at least since the 1930s.

To Grow: In Zones 9 and 10, sow Marigold seeds outside almost anytime. Elsewhere, either sow seeds outside when the soil has warmed or start plants inside four to six weeks before the last frost. Space seedlings six to twelve inches apart when planted out. Signets are slow to germinate, but be patient; they're well worth the wait. You can easily remove the spent blooms of these tiny flowers by running your fingers up and down the sides of the clusters. Then you can draw your own conclusions about their scent.

Collector's Choice (all sold as seeds):

Tagetes patula 'Naughty Marietta', French Marigold. 133; 96; 42; 101; 92.

T. tenuifolia 'Golden Gem', Signet Marigold; 6". 133; 92.

'Lemon Gem'; 9". 133; 126; 177; 92.

❀ *Tropaeolum majus*

Tropaeolaceae
1700-1776

Nasturtium

Bitter-indian, Indian-cress, Indian
Nasturtium, Lark's-heel, Spanish-cress,
Yellow-larkspur

T. minus

Dwarf Nasturtium

TYPE: TENDER ANNUAL FLOWER/HERB/
    TWINING VINE
HEIGHT: 8"-12'   BLOOM: SUMMER
SITE: SUN

Garden Nasturtiums are largely
derived from two species of
Tropaeolum, both native to South
America. *T. majus* is a vigorous
climbing plant with twisting,
rather than twining, leaf stalks
and out-facing bright yellow, red,
or orange spurred flowers two
and a half inches across. The
nearly circular green leaves grow
on succulent stems to ten feet or
more. *T. minus* is a low, scram-
bling plant with smaller, bright
yellow spurred flowers — about
one and a half inches across, also out-facing —
spotted orange near the center. It has shield-
shaped, rather than circular, green leaves, which
led to the genus name, meaning "trophy."
Nasturtium flowers, stems, and leaves are spice-
scented and similar in flavor to Watercress or

Tropaeolum majus

Cress, as indicated in their common names.

Spanish explorers introduced the low-
growing *T. minus* to Europe in the fifteenth
century. By the sixteenth century, Gerard was
sharing seeds with Parkinson, who described
the flowers as "the prettiest of a score in the
garden." By 1665 Nasturtiums were so well
known that few European gardens were without them. The more vigorous climbing Nasturtium was introduced to Europe in the late
1600s, although Buckner Hollingsworth, in
her entertaining and well-researched account
of garden flowers, suggested that Parkinson
was growing it by 1629, based on his description of the plant from which he picked flowers
for "his delicate Tussiemussie" as having "very
long trayling branches . . . if you will have it
abide close thereunto, you must tye it, or else
it will lye upon the ground" (*Flower Chronicles*,
Rutgers University Press, 1958).

There is also some discrepancy about when Nasturtiums
were introduced to New World
gardens. Both *T. majus* and *T.
minus* are planted at eighteenth-
century Colonial Williamsburg, and we know from the
records of the Moravian community in North Carolina that
both types, listed as "Spanische
Kresse" and "Capper," with
round leaves like those of the
Marsh Mallow, were planted in
the medical gardens in 1759,
1761, and 1764.

By 1806 M'Mahon carried
both types. He especially recommended the
climbing vine "on account of the beauty of its
large and numerous orange-colored flowers,
and their use in garnishing dishes." These
remarks underscore the use of Nasturtiums as
a food plant as well as an ornamental. But by

the 1850s, utility had given way to aesthetics as Americans began to regard these colorful and easily grown plants solely for their beauty, especially after the introduction of interesting cultivars. These were the result of crossing the two species and adding other colors into the mix from newly discovered types (dark ruby red, for instance), resulting in the 'Tom Thumb' cultivars very popular for carpet bedding. "It is said that a good bed, 6' x 20' will yield about 1,000 flowers each day," a gardening manual declared.

By the early 1870s, an ivy-leaved type with variegated foliage (cream and green) was introduced, followed in 1884 by the very choice 'Empress of India' with crimson-scarlet flowers. Hailed as a "grand novelty" and "the most important annual in recent introduction," it is still enjoyed today for its freely produced flowers and distinctive umbrella-like foliage, attractive even when the plant is not in bloom.

In 1928 California nurseryman J.C. Bolgier discovered what he called the 'Golden Gleam' Nasturtium in a small garden — very fragrant, double and semidouble golden trumpetlike flowers — and by 1932 ten tons of seeds could not meet the demand for them among gardeners. By 1930 'Golden Gleam Hybrids' were on the market in a mixture of colors. The flowers were described in glowing terms as two and three-quarters to three inches across, sweet-scented, and in the "best brilliant colors . . . some . . . never before seen in Nasturtiums— soft primrose . . . pearly lemon." While 'Golden Gleam Hybrids' are still on the market, it is increasingly difficult to find the original golden flower offered alone or the once popular 'Scarlet Gleam' (see "Collector's Choice").

The variegated-foliage Nasturtium and 'Empress of India' are fine subjects for containers, where their distinctive beauty is highlighted. If you have a cool greenhouse, they will bloom into the winter months, and although they are not cascading types, they will overflow their containers with attractive foliage and beautiful flowers. The dwarf 'Tom Thumb' and 'Gem' types make a bright edging for a long walk, perhaps to cover the dying foliage of spring-flowering bulbs. The tall, climbing Nasturtium vine, once so popular in English cottage gardens, is returning to American-style cottage gardens, where it is valued for its trailing habit over fences and arbors (especially a white arbor). Its flowers may be used, as they were in early American gardens, as a tasty, peppery herb.

When choosing heirloom-type Nasturtiums, remember that the old-fashioned ones can be climbing, semitrailing ('Gleam Hybrids'), or compact dwarf types. In all of these, the flowers are out-facing, rather than up-facing, as in the more modern type, but they are held above the foliage.

To Grow: The old adage "Be nasty to Nasturtiums" means don't overfeed them, or you'll get more leaves than flowers. (Don't worry, though, because even mounds of foliage are an effective and attractive groundcover.) The culture of Nasturtiums is easy (a good plant for the children's garden) as long as you supply the heat they need to germinate — a minimum of 65°F. (18°C.) — and the cool temperatures they need for continuous bloom. In frost-free and warm growing regions, plant the seeds outside in early fall for winter bloom; elsewhere plant the seeds outside when the soil has warmed up in the spring. Drop several seeds every six inches for dwarf types and every twelve inches for climbing types. Cover them well with soil. Some protection from the hot sun will prolong their bloom. Nasturtiums don't transplant well, so be sure you plant them where you want them. Double-flowered types can be propagated by stem cuttings taken during the summer and wintered-over indoors. All types of Nasturtiums can be wintered-over and cut back to rebloom the following season (See "Wintering Annuals," p. 20). Seeds of all types are large and invite collecting. Nasturtiums may self-seed, as some do every year even in my Zone 4 garden. As Parkinson noted, the climbing type will need tying to whatever support they're offered.

Collector's Choice (* indicates especially fragrant types):

Tropaeolum majus, Nasturtium; single flowers; mixed colors; 6-10'. 160; 5; 126; 168 (all seeds).

Hybrids (all sold as seeds):

'Alaska Hybrids'; single flowers; mixed colors; variegated foliage; dwarf type; 8". 101; 92.
*'Double Gleam Hybrids'; semidouble and double flowers; mixed colors; semitrailing; 12". 133; 92; 168.
'Empress of India'; single scarlet flowers; dwarf type; 8". 126; 101; 92.
*'Golden Gleam'; semidouble golden flowers; very fragrant; semitrailing; 12". 87.
*'Scarlet Gleam'; fragrant, double, fiery red flowers; semitrailing; 12". 168.
T. minus, Dwarf Nasturtium; single flowers, mixed colors, 6-9". 177 (s).
'Tom Thumb Mixed'; 5(s).

❀ *Viburnum trilobum*

Caprifoliaceae
1700-1776   ZONES 2-8   NATIVE

Highbush Cranberry

American Cranberry Bush, Crampbark, Cranberry Tree, Cranberry Viburnum, Grouseberry, Mountain Viburnum, Squawbush, Summerberry

TYPE: HARDY SHRUB
HEIGHT: 12'   BLOOM: LATE SPRING
SITE: SUN/PARTIAL SHADE

The native Highbush Cranberry, one of about 225 species widely distributed throughout the Northern Hemisphere, grows primarily in the North Country (southern Canada and the northern United States), but it is very adaptable to soil and climate. It bears fragrant white flowers in flat-topped cymes (the lace-cap type) composed of tiny inner fertile florets surrounded by larger, showy sterile florets. The flowers, about four inches across, bloom in late spring. In the fall, the fertile florets produce translucent red berries in heavy clusters and the plant's three-lobed leaves turn a brilliant red, extending the bush's season of interest.

There are many varieties of Viburnums. The first type to be grown in New World gardens was the Guelder-rose (*Viburnum opulus* 'Roseum'), with large snowball blooms composed wholly of sterile florets. Though still popular because of its ease of culture and hardiness, it is very susceptible to insect attack. For this reason, the Japanese Snowball (*V. plicatum*) was considered a desirable alternative. Introduced in 1814, it also bears large snowball blooms of infertile florets along the length of its horizontal branches, but it is not as hardy as the Guelder-rose. Most of the other Viburnums were introduced in the late nineteenth and early twentieth centuries from Asia. Although they are considered choice shrubs, none has so many desirable characteristics as the homegrown Highbush Cranberry: beautiful flowers, hardiness, ease of culture, disease resistance, attractive fall foliage, and ornamental and useful fruits.

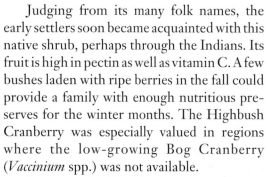

Viburnum trilobum

Judging from its many folk names, the early settlers soon became acquainted with this native shrub, perhaps through the Indians. Its fruit is high in pectin as well as vitamin C. A few bushes laden with ripe berries in the fall could provide a family with enough nutritious preserves for the winter months. The Highbush Cranberry was especially valued in regions where the low-growing Bog Cranberry (*Vaccinium* spp.) was not available.

In 1728 the Highbush Cranberry was among the native offerings of John Bartram's newly established plant nursery. It was probably from this source that Jefferson acquired plants for his Monticello gardens, where he scattered them among other native shrubs such as the Clove Currant and the Rosebay Rhododendron. Despite the introduction of so many other Viburnums, the native kind is still found thriving in vintage shrubberies from the late nineteenth and early twentieth centuries. I first saw it growing on the Bennington College campus (a former estate) in the 1950s.

The Highbush Cranberry has always been highly regarded by the most tasteful gardeners. "It is beautiful," Elizabeth Lawrence told her newspaper column readers in the *Charlotte Observer*, "when the corymbs of white flowers

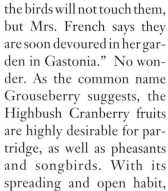

are in bloom, and again in the fall when bunches of red berries hang from the branches. According to the books the fruits hang all winter, as the birds will not touch them, but Mrs. French says they are soon devoured in her garden in Gastonia." No wonder. As the common name Grouseberry suggests, the Highbush Cranberry fruits are highly desirable for partridge, as well as pheasants and songbirds. With its spreading and open habit, there is no finer show than a bush laden with fruits in the fall and local birds enjoying them.

The Highbush Cranberry is at the top of the list for creating wildlife habitats and edible landscapes with heirloom-type plants. It could be planted as an informal hedge or as a specimen plant, handsome all through the growing season, underplanted with spring-flowering bulbs or overplanted with an attractive groundcover such as Lily-of-the-valley or Lungwort.

To Grow: The Highbush Cranberry will grow in almost any soil, in sun or partial shade, but it will thrive in slightly moist, enriched soil. Plant it as you would any shrub, digging a hole large enough to accommodate the roots and draping these on a little mound of soil to ensure good drainage. A top dressing of rotted manure or compost once a year is sufficient, along with a few handfuls of high-phosphate fertilizer if desired. Prune the bush as necessary in the late winter to retain its shape. Hardwood cuttings can be made during the fall.

Collector's Choice:

Viburnum trilobum, Highbush Cranberry. 167; 31; 151; 140 (all plants).

Viola tricolor

Violaceae

1600-1699   Zones 4-10   Naturalized

Johnny-jump-up

Bird's-eye, Field Pansy, Godfathers-and-godmothers, Heartsease, Herb Constancy, Herb Trinity, Jack-jump-up-and-kiss-me, Johnnies, Kiss-her-in-the-buttery, Kit-run-about, Kit-run-in-the-fields, Ladies'-delight, Live-in-idleness, Love-in-idleness, Loving-me, Meet-me-in-the-entry, Three-faces-under-a-hood, Wild Pansy

---

Type: Short-Lived Perennial/Biennial Flower/Herb
Height: 6-12"   Bloom: Spring-Fall
Site: Sun/Partial Shade/Shade

Viola tricolor is a native of Europe naturalized over much of the temperate world. The five-petaled flowers are quite small — one-quarter to one and one-quarter inches wide — with the top four petals large and overlapping and the lower one elongated to form a spur. The whole flower resembles a miniature heart whose face is variable in color — purple-red, violet-blue, yellow, or creamy white, with pencil-thin veins or whiskers radiating from a golden center. The plant can grow as high as one foot, though it is usually shorter, and has narrow, deeply lobed green leaves. This species is considered an important parent of the larger-flowered Garden Pansy. Both flowers are often referred to as Pansies, a corruption of the French common

Viola tricolor

name, *pensée*, meaning "thoughts" or "reflections."

Despite its diminutive size and humble status as a wildflower, *V. tricolor* is infused with great significance in herbal literature and in the minds of generations of people who regarded it with great affection (as reflected in its many delightful and witty names). Heartsease refers to its powers as a heart stimulant, both in the literal and figurative sense. "Fetch me that flower," Oberon orders Puck in Shakespeare's *A Midsummer Night's Dream*, "the herb I showed thee once/The juice of it on sleeping eyelids laid/Will make a man or woman madly dote/Upon the next live creature that it sees." Woe to Queen Titania, who is made to fall in love with an ass.

In the New World, *V. tricolor* was known primarily as Johnny-jump-up, a purely American contribution to its colorful collection of common names, playing on the plant's habit of scattering its seeds like a catapult when the pods break open, causing new plants to spring up where you least expect them — in the grass, between stones or cracks of cement, under stairs, and, of course, all over the garden. It was traditionally used in tussie-mussies, favored for its small blooms and associations with love, but its petals can also be candied or pressed for floral art. At one time, *V. tricolor* was recognized as a medicine in the U.S. Pharmacopoeia, used as an ointment for skin irritations and taken internally for bronchitis. There was no mention of its legendary uses as a heart stimulant.

It has long been observed that children seem to have a special liking for the Johnny-jump-up, drawn, perhaps, to its appealing little face, its uncomplicated beauty. Many years ago, my daughter raised a generation of 'King Henry' seedlings — violet, sky blue, and gold. She planted them in a Tulip bed we shared, established on the site of an old coal shed, where the soil was deep and fertile. Our plan was simple: we divided fifty bulbs between us and planted our allotment on either side of a central path bordered with 'King Henry'. That was in 1976. Since then I have raised many lovely large-flowered Pansies, long disappeared from the garden, but 'King Henry' and its descendants of variable countenance (crossed with nearby yellow Violas) remain among the Tulips — a fitting remembrance of my daughter's first flower garden.

Several strains of Violas (besides the wild version) are worth having, among them 'Helen Mount' in the traditional colors. It has been around for decades, as has 'King Henry', but the latter is rare now, so be sure to save its seeds and plant it away from other types to try and keep the strain pure. (Follow the suggestions for seed saving in Part I, p. 18). Plant Johnny-jump-ups in containers, as a groundcover near shrubs, in a shady border as an edging plant, or along a garden path, wherever it may lead.

To Grow: Plants can be set about six inches apart in ordinary, well-drained soil, in shade or sun, in early spring or (in warmer regions) winter. Light shade will prolong their bloom; which falls off as soon as the hot weather sets in. To grow the plants from seeds, refrigerate the seeds for one day, then sow them in a cold frame or any reserved piece of weed-free ground with fine soil. Germination takes eight to twelve days at 70°F. (21°C.). Be sure to cover the seeds with about one-eighth inch of soil, since they need darkness to germinate. The seedlings can be overwintered with no protection, then planted in their permanent location in very early spring. Johnny-jump-ups love cool weather and will bloom their heads off in appreciation. In Zones 9 and 10, they will bloom from late winter into the spring.

To prevent straggly plants, shear them halfway back four weeks after they have started blooming. This will encourage a second flowering in late summer or fall, and enough seeds will be dispersed to promote new seedlings. If you find a different face among a population you want to keep pure, dig up the offender with a ball of dirt and replant it elsewhere, watering it well. If you protect these little Pansies from wind and scorching sun, they will always be happy.

Collector's Choice:

Viola tricolor 'Helen Mount', Johnny-jump-up; 7". 109(p); 96; 42; 101; 62 (all seeds).

'King Henry'; 5-6". 101(s).

Candied Violets

Pick the flowers on a sunny day when they are fully opened and dry. Remove the stems and lay the flower heads on double sheets of waxed paper. Carefully brush one side of the heads or petals, then the other, with an egg white beaten with a little water. Be careful not to slop too much of the mixture onto the flowers. Remove the flowers to dry paper and sprinkle them on both sides with granulated sugar. Turn them periodically, changing the paper as necessary, until they are dry to the touch. Store the candied flowers in wax paper-lined boxes in a single layer. Use them within two weeks or so. They make beautiful cake decorations. Just place them in patterns on top of the frosting, then lightly press them in.

PART III

Sources & Resources

"No one can garden alone."

—ELIZABETH LAWRENCE

USDA Hardiness Zone Map

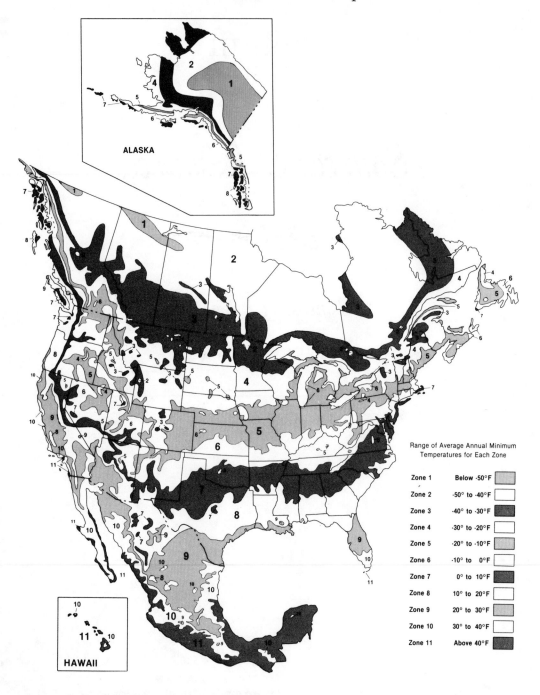

Range of Average Annual Minimum
Temperatures for Each Zone

Zone 1	Below -50°F
Zone 2	-50° to -40°F
Zone 3	-40° to -30°F
Zone 4	-30° to -20°F
Zone 5	-20° to -10°F
Zone 6	-10° to 0°F
Zone 7	0° to 10°F
Zone 8	10° to 20°F
Zone 9	20° to 30°F
Zone 10	30° to 40°F
Zone 11	Above 40°F

ALASKA

HAWAII

Mail-Order Sources for Seeds and Plants

The following retail mail-order sources for seeds and plants in the United States and Canada are organized geographically and keyed to the numbers found in the "Collector's Choice" sections in the Part II plant portraits.

General catalogs usually provide good plant descriptions and cultural information; small and specialty catalogs differ widely in the information they provide, but most of them make up for any deficiencies in this area by their interesting offerings and quite distinct personalities. The wild plant sources claim to sell only nursery-propagated material, according to the Andersen Horticultural Library's Source List, from which most of the following sources were drawn. Many of the specialty sources maintain display gardens of special interest to heirloom gardeners.

Note: Every effort has been made to verify each plant and seed source, some of which have changed their offerings during the course of writing this book. Unfortunately, seed companies and nurseries also sometimes change hands or go out of business. I have listed several sources where possible to avoid disappointment, but bear in mind that catalogs may change their listings annually.

Many companies charge for their catalogs; these prices change frequently and so are not listed here. Check with the individual companies for current catalog prices.

ARIZONA

1. Southwestern Native Seeds
   P.O. Box 50503
   Tucson, AZ 85703

CALIFORNIA

2. Country Bloomers Nursery
   20091 East Chapman Avenue
   Orange, CA 92669
   (714) 633-7222

3. The Country Garden
   Box 3539
   Oakland, CA 94609-0539
   (415) 658-8777

A great little specialty catalog, a tribute to former owner, Joe Seals: annuals, perennials; seeds only; very choice.

4. Greenmantle
   3010 Ettersburg Road
   Barberville, CA 95440
   (707) 986-7504

5. Heirloom Gardens
   P.O. Box 138
   Guerneville, CA 95446
   (707) 869-0967

Vague, but contains some interesting offerings; old strains, old-style plants.

6. J.L. Hudson, Seedsman
   P.O. Box 1058
   Redwood City, CA 94064

Great source for unusual seeds; odd and informative listings.

7. Las Pilitas Nursery
   Star Route Box 23X
   Santa Margarita, CA 93453
   (805) 438-5992

8. Theodore Payne Foundation
   10459 Tuxford Street
   Sun Valley, CA 91352
   (818) 768-1802

9. Clyde Robin Seed Co., Inc.
   P.O. Box 2366
   Castro Valley, CA 94545
   (415) 581-3468

10. Rose Acres
    6641 Crystal Boulevard
    Diamond Springs, CA 95619
    (916) 626-1722

11. Roses of Yesterday and Today
    802 Brown's Valley Road
    Watsonville, CA 95076
    (408) 724-3537

Entertaining, informative listings; lovely presentation.

12. William R.P. Welch
    Garzas Road
    Carmel Valley, CA 93924
    (408) 659-4537

A mimeographed listing for the knowledgeable tender Daffodil collector.

COLORADO

13. Colorado Alpines, Inc.
    P.O. Box 2708
    Avon, CO 81620
    (303) 949-6464

14. High Country Rosarium
    1717 Downing Street
    Denver, CO 80218
    (303) 832-4026

CONNECTICUT

15. Catnip Acres Herb Farm
    67 Christian Street
    Oxford, CT 06483

Interesting listings, but not for the novice; virtually no information, so you'd better know what you're ordering.

16. Logee's Greenhouses
55 North Street
Danielson, CT 06239
(203) 774-8038

Long famous for its choice greenhouse and tender plant collection.

17. Piedmont Gardens Nursery
517 Piedmont Street
Waterbury, CT 06706
(203) 754-8534

18. Select Seeds
81 Stickney Hill Road
Union, CT 06076

Excellent source for heirlooms; choice selections, dated, with miscellaneous information; attractive format.

19. Shepherd's Garden Seeds
30 Irene Street
Torrington, CT 06790
(203) 482-3638
California Address:
6116 Hwy. 9
Felton, CA 95018

Varied offerings of vegetables and flowers; very appealing.

20. White Flower Farm
Litchfield, CT 06759
(203) 496-1661

Long synonymous with elegance; besides the gorgeous photos, there's much valuable cultural information.

DELAWARE

20A. Winterthur Museum and
Gardens
100 Enterprise Place
Dover, DE 19901
(800) 767-0500

FLORIDA

21. Salter Tree Farm
Route 2, Box 1332
Madison, FL 32340
(904) 973-6312

GEORGIA

22. The Flowery Branch
Box 1330
Flowery Branch, GA 30542

23. Thomasville Nurseries, Inc.
P.O. Box 7
Thomasville, GA 31799
(913) 226-5568

Middle-aged Roses, native Azaleas, and other listings for the South; well presented.

IDAHO

24. High Altitude Gardens
P.O. Box 4238
Ketchum, ID 83340
(208) 726-3221

ILLINOIS

25. Blue Dahlia Gardens
c/o G. Kenneth Furrer
San Jose, IL 62682
(309) 274-3210

26. Midwest Wildflowers
Box 64
Rockton, IL 61072
(815) 624-7040

27. Arthur Weiler, Inc.
1280 Wincanton Drive
Deerfield, IL 60015
(312) 746-2393

INDIANA

28. Holly Hills, Inc.
1216 Hillsdale Road
Evansville, IN 47711
(812) 867-3367

29. Soules Garden
5809 Rahke Road
Indianapolis, IN 46217
(317) 786-7839

IOWA

30. Cascade Forestry Nursery
Route 1
Cascade, IA 52033
(319) 852-3042

31. Henry Field's Seed & Nursery
Shenandoah, IA 51602
(605) 665-4491

Carries old favorites; good descriptions and plant information.

32. Heard Gardens, Ltd.
5355 Merle Hay Road
Johnston, IA 50131
(515) 276-4533

*A **must** source for Lilac enthusiasts.*

33. Inter-State Nurseries
P.O. Box 208
Hamburg, IA 51640
(800) 325-4180

34. Earl May Seed & Nursery
Shenandoah, IA 51603
(800) 831-4193

Mainly bulbs; seeds are for lawns; old favorites included; unpretentious.

35. Nature's Way
R.R. 1, Box 62
Woodburn, IA 50275
(515) 342-6246

Wildflower specialists; helpful listings.

KENTUCKY

36. Dabney Herbs
Box 22061
Louisville, KY 40222
(502) 893-5198

LOUISIANA

37. Louisiana Nursery
Route 7, Box 43
Opelousas, LA 70570
(318) 948-3696

Magnolia specialists, but much else in the way of "garden aristocrats".

38. Sisters' Bulb Farm
Route 2, Box 170
Gibsland, LA 71028

Very short, but choice listing of species, natural hybrids, and pre-1940 Daffodils.

MAINE

39. Daystar
Route 2, Box 250
Litchfield, ME 04350
(207) 724-3369

40. Eastern Plant Specialties
Box 226
Georgetown Is., ME 04548
(207) 371-2888

41. Fedco Trees
Box 340
Palermo, ME 04354
(207) 766-3320

42. Johnny's Selected Seeds
Foss Hill Road
Albion, ME 04910
(207) 437-9294

General, mainly vegetables, but some old favorite flowers.

43. Merry Gardens
Camden, ME 04843

Specialists for indoor plants and herbs, for the specialist grower, so no growing information; available separately.

MARYLAND

44. Kurt Bluemel, Inc.
2740 Greene Lane
Baldwin, MD 21013
(301) 557-7229

Grass specialist, but catalog includes much else, including fine moisture-loving plants and perennials.

45. Carroll Gardens
P.O. Box 310
444 East Main Street
Westminster, MD 21157
(301) 848-5422

46-7. Lilypons Water Gardens
6800 Lilypons Road
Lilypons, MD 21717
(301) 874-5133

MASSACHUSETTS

48. Briarwood Gardens
RFD 1
14 Gully Lane
East Sandwich, MA 02537
(508) 888-2146

49. Cricket Hill Herb Farm Ltd.
Glen Street
Rowley, MA 01969
(617) 948-2818

50. Peter Dejager Bulb Company
P.O. Box 2010
188 Asbury Street
South Hamilton, MA 01982
(508) 468-4707

51. John D. Lyon, Inc.
143 Alewife Brook Parkway
Cambridge, MA 02140
(617) 876-3705

52. Messelaar Bulb Co., Inc.
P.O. Box 269
Route 1A, County Road
Ipswich, MA 01938
(508) 356-3737

MICHIGAN

53. Ensata Gardens
9823 East Michigan Avenue
Galesburg, MI 49053
(616) 665-7500

Japanese Iris specialists; good cultural information, introduction dates; call in June to find out peak bloom for their gardens.

54. Reath's Nursery
P.O. Box 521
100 Central Boulevard
Vulcan, MI 49892
(906) 563-9321

55. Southmeadow Fruit Gardens
Lakeside, MI 49116
(616) 469-2865

MINNESOTA

56. Ambergate Gardens
8015 Krey Avenue
Waconia, MN 55387
(612) 443-2248

57. Anderson Iris Gardens
22179 Keather Avenue North
Forest Lake, MN 55025
(612) 433-5268

58. Bergeson Nursery
Fertile, MN 56540
(218) 945-6988

59. Borbeleta Gardens, Inc.
15980 Canby Avenue
Faribault, MN 55021
(507) 334-2807

60. Brand Peony Farm
Box 842
St. Cloud, MN 56302

All you could want in the Peony line: dates of introduction, basic cultural information, and a very fine selection of heirloom types.

61. Busse Gardens
Route 2, Box 238
635 East 7th Street
Cokato, MN 55321
(612) 286-2654

62. Camelot North Greenhouses
& Nursery
R.R. 2, Box 398
Pequot Lakes, MN 56472
(218) 568-8922

63. Cooper's Garden
212 West County Road C
Roseville, MN 55113
(612) 484-7878

64. Double D-Lite Gardens
3008 64th Avenue North
Brooklyn Center, MN 55429
(612) 566-4573

65. Environmental Collaborative
P.O. Box 539
Osseo, MN 55369

66. Farmer Seed & Nursery
818 Northwest 4th Street
Faribault, MN 55021
(507) 334-1623

67. Ferndale Nursery &
Greenhouses
P.O. Box 27
Askov, MN 55704
(612) 838-3636

68. Landscape Alternatives, Inc.
1465 North Pascal Street
St. Paul, MN 55108
(612) 647-9571

69. Maroushek Gardens
120 East 11th Street
Hastings, MN 55033
(612) 437-9754

70. The New Peony Farm
Box 18235
St. Paul, MN 55118

Straightforward listing, but includes dates of introduction and some basic information; historic cultivars.

71. Noweta Gardens
900 Whitewater Avenue
St. Charles, MN 55972
(507) 932-4859

72. Orchid Gardens
2232 139th Avenue Northwest
Andover, MN 55304
(612) 755-0205

73. Prairie Moon Nursery
Route 3, Box 163
Winona, MN 55987
(507) 452-5231

Specialists in native plants and seeds; good cultural information; excellent presentation.

74. Rice Creek Gardens
1315 66th Avenue Northeast
Minneapolis, MN 55432
(612) 574-1197

75. Riverdale Iris Gardens
P.O. Box 524
Rockford, MN 55373
(612) 477-4859

76. Savory's Gardens, Inc.
5300 Whiting Avenue
Edina, MN 55435
(612) 941-8755

77. Shady Acres Nursery
7777 Hwy. 212
Chaska, MN 55318
(612) 466-3391

78. Shady Oaks Nursery
700 19th Avenue Northeast
Waseca, MN 56093

79. Swedberg Nurseries, Inc.
P.O. Box 418
Battle Lake, MN 56515
(218) 864-5526

80. Tischler Peony Garden
1021 East Division Street
Faribault, MN 55021
(507) 334-7242

81. Wedge Nursery
Route 2, Box 114
Albert Lea, MN 56007
(507) 373-5225

*Tops for Lilacs; descriptive listing of **own root** Lilacs; founded 1878.*

82. Worel's Iris Gardens
10930 Holly Lane North
Osseo, MN 55369
(612) 420-4876

MISSOURI

83. Manchester Gardens
614 Nandale Lane
Manchester, MO 63021
(314) 227-5930

Iris specialist; old and new, some dated; complete collection of Dykes Medal winners; bare descriptions; a few really historic Iris.

84. Gilbert H. Wild & Son, Inc.
Sarcoxie, MO 64862

MONTANA

85. Alpen Gardens
173 Lawrence Lane
Kalispell, MT 59901
(406) 257-2540

86. Valley Nursery
P.O. Box 4845
2801 North Montana Avenue
Helena, MT 59604
(406) 442-8460

NEBRASKA

87. Fragrant Path
P.O. Box 328
Fort Calhoun, NE 68023

Delightful selection of scented and unscented plants from seeds; chatty descriptions.

88. Hildenbrandt's Iris Garden
HCR 84, Box 4
Lexington, NE 68850
(308) 224-4334

89. Schliefert Iris Gardens
Murdock, NE 68407
(402) 234-4172

No-frills listing of Iris, old and new, many hard to find; Dykes Medal winners since 1927 are offered and on display in their gardens; a feast of Iris for the heirloom grower.

NEW HAMPSHIRE

90. Loew's Own-Root Roses
6 Sheffield Road
Nashua, NH 03062
(603) 888-2214

Specialists in Roses, old and new, for cold climates; very high-class selection; gardens to see — call ahead.

NEW JERSEY

91. Cummins Garden
22 Robertsville Road
Marlboro, NJ 07746
(201) 536-2591

92. Thompson & Morgan
P.O. Box 1308
Jackson, NJ 08527
(201) 363-2225

Some heirloom strains among large collection of flowers; excellent cultural information, especially those included with order; sometimes a discrepancy between listings and availability of seeds.

93. Well-Sweep Herb Farm
317 Mountain Bethel Road
Port Murray, NJ 07865
(201) 852-5390

Justly famous for its herb plant offerings; no descriptions; herb garden tours by reservation.

New Mexico

94. Bernardo Beach Native Plant
Farm
1 Sanchez Road
Veguito, NM 87062
(505) 345-6248

95. Plants of the Southwest
1812 2nd Street
Santa Fe, NM 87501
(505) 983-1548

Emphasis on natural landscaping; packed with information, some of it odd: "Eliminate seed companies. The best things in life are free."

New York

96. Harris Seeds
961 Lyell Avenue
Rochester, NY 14606
(716) 458-2882

Emphasis on vegetables, but some old favorite flowers still carried.

97. Kelly Nurseries
P.O. Box 800
Dansville, NY 14437
(800) 325-4180

Many shrubs; excellent information.

98. Plumtree Nursery
387 Springtown Road
New Paltz, NY 12561
(914) 255-0417

A few out-of-the-ordinary offerings, including the ornamental Currant.

99. Roslyn Nursery
211 Burrs Lane
Dix Hills, NY 11746
(516) 643-9347

100. Arthur H. Steffen, Inc.
P.O. Box 184
1259 Fairport Road
Fairport, NY 14450
(716) 377-1665

101. Stokes Seeds, Inc.
Box 548
Buffalo, NY 14240
(416) 688-4300

Old reliable seed house, repository of some old favorites; Canadian listing the same — see under Canada.

North Carolina

102. Camellia Forest Nursery
125 Carolina Forest Road
Chapel Hill, NC 27516
(919) 967-5529

Camellia specialists, but catalog contains much else of interest, including many shrubs and native species.

103. Cardinal Nursery
Route 1, Box 316
State Road, NC 28676
(919) 874-2027

Rhododendron specialist for eastern gardeners; descriptive listing.

104. Holbrook Farm and Nursery
Route 2, Box 223B
Fletcher, NC 28732
(704) 891-7790

105. Montrose Nursery
P.O. Box 957
Hillsborough, NC 27278
(919) 732-7787

106. Niche Gardens
Route 1, Box 290
Chapel Hill, NC 27514
(919) 967-0078

107. Sandy Mush Herb Nursery
Route 2, Surrett Cove Road
Leicester, NC 28748
(704) 683-2014

Comprehensive plant listings, no descriptions; shorter seed list; like most herb specialists, basic knowledge is assumed.

108. We-Du Nurseries
Route 5, Box 724
Marion, NC 28752
(704) 738-8300

Ohio

109. Bluestone Perennials
7211 Middle Ridge Road
Madison, OH 44057
(216) 428-7535

110. Companion Plants
7247 North Coolville Ridge
Road
Athens, OH 45701
(614) 592-4643

Better presentation than most herb catalogs: cultural information, plant descriptions, herbal uses, and an index.

111. Garden Place
P.O. Box 388
6780 Heisley Road,
Mentor, OH 44060
(216) 255-3705

112. Girard Nurseries
P.O. Box 428
Geneva, OH 44041
(216) 466-2881

Azaleas, Rhododendrons, and choice shrubs; excellent descriptions and information.

113. Historical Roses
1657 West Jackson Street
Painesville, OH 44077
(216) 357-7270

114. Mellinger's Inc.
2310 West South Range Rd.
North Lima, OH 44452
(216) 549-9861

115. Rocknoll Nursery
9210 U.S. Route 50
Hillsboro, OH 45133
(513) 393-1278

116. Sunnybrook Farms
P. O. Box 6
448 Mayfield Road
Chesterland, OH 44026
(216) 729-7232

117. William Tricker, Inc.
P.O. Box 31267
7125 Tanglewood Drive
Independence, OH 44131
(216) 524-3491

OREGON

118. Bovees Nursery
1737 Southwest Coronado
Portland, OR 97219
(503) 244-9341

*"In Search of the Uncommon":
Rhododendrons, Azaleas (including
natives), and other plants; good
descriptions and adequate information.*

119. Caprice Farm Nursery
15425 Southwest Pleasant
Hill Road
Sherwood, OR 97140
(503) 625-7241

120. Forestfarm
990 Tetherow Road
Williams, OR 97544
(503) 846-6963

121. Goodwin Creek Gardens
P.O. Box 83
Williams, OR 97544
(503) 846-7357

122. Gossler Farms Nursery
1200 Weaver Road
Springfield, OR 97478

123. Greer Gardens
1280 Goodpasture Island Rd.
Eugene, OR 97401
(503) 686-8266

*"Justly Famous for the Rare and
Unusual," which includes shrubs,
vines, and Rhododendrons; splendid
catalog, well worth the price; lots of
information and valuable commentary.*

124. Richard D. Havens
P.O. Box 218
Hubbard, OR 97032

125. Maplethorpe
11296 Sunnyview Northeast
Salem, OR 97301
(503) 362-5121

126. Nichols Garden Nursery
1190 North Pacific Hwy.
Albany, OR 97321
(503) 928-9280

*A very busy catalog of mixed offerings,
including herbs and some heirloom
flower strains; sufficient information
and descriptions.*

127-28. Northwest Biological
Enterprises
23351 Southwest Bosky Dell
Lane
West Linn, OR 97068
(503) 638-6029

129. Siskiyou Rare Plant Nursery
2825 Cummings Road
Medford, OR 97501
(503) 772-6846

130. Swan Island Dahlias
Box 800
Canby, OR 97013
(503) 266-7711

*A **must** for Dahlia fanciers; photos,
basic information.*

131. Whitman Farms
1420 Beaumont Northwest
Salem, OR 97403
(503) 364-3076

PENNSYLVANIA

132. Appalachian Gardens
Box 82
Waynesboro, PA 17268
(717) 762-4312

133. W. Atlee Burpee & Co.
300 Park Avenue
Warminster, PA 18974
(215) 674-4915

*A part of our horticultural heritage;
some old favorites along with the new.*

134. Eisler Nurseries
Route 422, Box 465
Prospect, PA 16052
(412) 865-2830

135. Charles H. Mueller
Star Route, Box 21
River Road
New Hope, PA 18938
(215) 862-2033

136. Ter-El Nursery
P.O. Box 112
Orefield, PA 18069

SOUTH CAROLINA

137. George W. Park Seed Co.
Cokesbury Road
Greenwood, SC 29647

*Well known for its wide selection,
among them some old favorites.*

138. Wayside Gardens
1 Garden Lane
Hodges, SC 29695-0001
(800) 845-1124

*Very fine perennials, well described; ask
for separate Rose catalog — lovely.*

139. Woodlander's Inc.
1128 Colleton Avenue
Aiken, SC 29801
(803) 648-7522

*Excellent source for native plants;
guaranteed nursery-propagated; basic
information.*

TENNESSEE

140. Hidden Springs Nursery
Route 14, Box 159
Cookeville, TN 38501
(615) 268-9889

141. Natural Gardens
113 Jasper Lane
Oak Ridge, TN 37838

142. Sunlight Gardens
Route 1, Box 600A
Hillvale Road
Anderson, TN 37705
(615) 494-8237

TEXAS

143. Green Horizons
218 Quinlan, Suite 571
Kerrville, TX 78028
(512) 257-5141

144. Yucca Do Nursery
P.O. Box 655
Waller, TX 77484

VERMONT

145. Mary Mattison Van Schaik
RFD Box 181
Cavendish, VT 05142
(802) 226-7338

VIRGINIA

146. Daffodil Mart
Route 3, Box 794
Gloucester, VA 23061
(804) 693-3966

An important source for historic Daffodils; other interesting brochures available on "Daffodils for Show and Garden"; Open Garden weekends in the spring by appointment.

147-48. The Thomas Jefferson
Center for Historic Plants
Monticello
Box 316
Charlottesville, VA 22902
(804) 979-5283

Becoming a very important source for historic seed strains; scant descriptions; plants available at the center.

149. Andre Viette Farm and
Nursery
Route 1, Box 16
Fishersville, VA 22939
(703) 943-2315

Fine collection of perennials, many heirloom types, basic information.

149A. Edible Landscaping
Route 2, Box 77
Afton, VA 22920
(804) 361-9134

Delightful listing that includes a few heirloom-type Roses and "the American Black Currant . . . the most exciting new flavor" — i.e., the native Clove Currant.

WASHINGTON

150. B & D Lilies
330 P Street
Port Townsend, WA 98368
(206) 385-1738

Tops for Lilies; gorgeous catalog, informative for both beginners and experienced growers.

151. Bear Creek Nursery
P.O. Box 411
Bear Creek Road
Northport, WA 99157

Specializes in natural landscapes, edible perennials — Daylilies, Elderberries, Hops — and much else; very informative; well presented.

152. Fancy Fronds
1911 4th Avenue West
Seattle, WA 98119
(206) 284-5332

153-54. Lamb Nurseries
East 101 Sharp Avenue
Spokane, WA 99202
(509) 328-7956

WEST VIRGINIA

155. Wrenwood of Berkeley
Springs
Route 4, Box 361
Berkeley Springs, WV 25411
(304) 258-3071

WISCONSIN

156. Brehm's Wondercreek
Nursery
N6050 South Crystal Lake
Road
Beaver Dam, WI 53916
(414) 885-4300

157. Clifford's Perennial & Vine
Route 2, Box 320
East Troy, WI 53120
(414) 642-7156

158. Country Wetlands Nursery
Box 126
Muskego, WI 53150
(414) 679-1268

159. J T Dahlias (John
Thiermann)
P.O. Box 20967
Greenfield, WI 53220
(414) 327-1759

160. J. W. Jung Seed Co.
Randolph, WI 53957
(414) 326-3121

A fixture of American gardening, endearing in its quirkiness; old favorites carried from year to year, as are the illustrations.

161. Little Valley Farm
Route 3, Box 544
Spring Green, WI 53588
(608) 935-3324

162. McClure & Zimmerman
P.O. Box 368
108 West Winnebago
Friesland, WI 53935
(414) 326-4220

Bulb specialists; catalog highly recommended for the novice; fine listings; informative, well presented.

163. McKay Nursery Co.
Waterloo, WI 53594
(414) 478-2121

164. Milaeger's Gardens
4838 Douglas Avenue
Racine, WI 53402
(414) 639-2371

165. Waushara Gardens
Plainfield, WI 54966
(715) 335-4462

CANADA

166. Aimers Seeds
81 Temperance Street
Aurora, ON L4G 2R1
(416) 833-5282

Most famous for wildflower seeds and mixes, but catalog lists much else, including heirloom perennials and bulbs.

167. Aubin Nurseries, Ltd.
Box 1089
Carman, MB R0G 0J0
(204) 745-6703

168. The Butchart Gardens
Box 4010, Station A
Victoria, BC V8X 3X4

Very appealing, uncomplicated listing; heirloom strains of annuals and perennials from seeds; garden is famous for colorful plantings.

169. Corn Hill Nursery Ltd.
R. R. 5
Peticodiac, NB E0A 2H0
(506) 756-3635

Fine listing of shrubs and perennials; well presented; not everything is shipped, but arrangements can be made; visitors are invited to extensive display gardens, where nearly every species (including many hardy heirloom Roses) grown at the nursery is found in the garden.

170. Cruickshank's Inc.
1015 Mount Pleasant Road
Toronto, ON M4P 2MI
(416) 488-8292

Bulb specialists; also carries perennials and some seeds, all first-rate; excellent presentation.

171. Wm. Dam Seeds
Box 8400
Dundas, ON L9H 6MI
(416) 628-6641

Small Dutch firm; general, but carries some old favorites.

172-73. Dominion Seeds
Georgetown, ON L7G 4A2
(416) 877-7802

General, but carries some old favorites; lots of information.

174. Honeywood Lilies
Box 63
Parkside, SK S0J 2A0
(306) 747-3296

Small catalog, but highly respected among Lily enthusiasts.

175. Hortico, Inc.
R.R. 1, Robson Road
Waterdown, ON L0R 2H0
(416) 689-6984

A wholesale nursery that sells small quantities retail; listed as mail-order source.

176. Pickering Nurseries, Inc.
670 Kingston Road
Pickering, ON L1V 1A6
(416) 839-2111

Tops for Old Roses; basic information.

177. Richters
Goodwood, ON L0C 1A0
(416) 640-6677

Probably the largest selection of herb seeds in North America; some plants; descriptions confined to herbal use, basic cultural information.

178. Riverside Gardens
R.R. 5
Saskatoon, SK S7K 3J8
(306) 374-0494

179. Stokes Seeds
Box 10
St. Catharines, ON L2R6R6
(416) 688-4300

Canadian base for Stokes; same listing as for U.S. (see p. 215).

180. McConnell Nurseries
Port Burwell, ON N0J 1T0
(519) 874-4800

Many old favorite perennials.

Additional Sources for Heirlooms

Abundant Life Seed Foundation
1029 Lawrence, Box 772
Port Townsend, WA 98368
(206) 385-5660

Nonprofit educational foundation developed for raising and collecting open-pollinated cultivars, flowers, herbs, and wildflowers.

Antique Rose Emporium
Route 5, Box 143
Brenham, TX 77833
(409) 836-9051

*Historical and cultural information; **own-root** plants.*

Canyon Creek Nursery
3527 Dry Creek Road
Oroville, CA 95965

Perennials.

DeGiorgi Co., Inc.
1409 3rd Street, Box 413
Council Bluffs, IA 51502
(712) 323-2372

General.

Far North Gardens
16785 Harrison
Livonia, MI 48154
(313) 422-0747

Perennials.

Good Seed Co.
Box 702
Tonasket, WA 98855

Open-pollinated herbs and flowers.

Heritage Rose Gardens
40350 Wilderness Road
Branscomb, CA 95417
(707) 984-6959

Specializes in Teas, Chinas, Ramblers, and Climbers.

Perennial Pleasures Nursery
Box 147
East Hardwick, VT 05836

Flowers and herbs.

Primrose Path
R.D. 2, Box 118
Scottdale, PA 15683

Perennials.

John Scheepers, Inc.
63 Wall Street
New York, NY 10005

Bulbs.

Seeds Blüm
Idaho City Stage
Boise, ID 83706

Vegetables, flowers, and herbs.

R.H. Shumway
P.O. Box 1
Shenandoah, IA 51683

General, with old favorites.

General and Specialty Sourcebook and Listings

Andersen Horticultural Library
Source List

Minnesota Landscape
Arboretum
3675 Arboretum Drive, Box 39
Chanhassen, MN 55317

More than 1,200 seed and plant sources for more than 40,000 plants; keep in mind that some listings may be obsolete.

The Canadian Plant Sourcebook

93 Fentiman Avenue
Ottawa, ON K15 0T7, Canada
(613) 235-0755

Combined Rose List

Beverly R. Dobson
215 Harriman Road
Irvington, NY 10533

Write for price; every Rose in cultivation and where to find it. Bev Dobson's Rose Letter issued bimonthly; updated information on nursery sources; news of the rose world.

Gardening by Mail, 3rd Edition
by Barbara Barton
(Boston: Houghton Mifflin, 1990)

1,500 nurseries and seed companies; hundreds of societies, libraries, and books; a classic and invaluable resource; available from most trade bookstores.

New England Wild Flower
Society, Inc.
Garden in the Woods
Hemenway Road
Framingham, MA 01701

Over 200 North American wildflowers, shrubs, and other flora hardy for Zones 4-6, with a descriptive listing of nurseries; write for price.

List of Historic Seeds & Plants
Scott G. Kunst
Old House Gardens
536 3rd Street
Ann Arbor, MI 48183

Valuable source for those involved with garden restoration or creating authentic period gardens.

Commercial Plant and Seed Search Sources

Sherry J. Vance/L.J. Vance
L.H. Bailey Hortorium
462 Mann Library
Cornell University
Ithaca, NY 14853
(607) 255-2131

Fee for information is $2.00 for each plant searched up to a maximum of five names at a time, preferably fewer. Send check or money order payable to L.H. Hortorium.

Plant Finders of America
186 Fayette Circle
Fort Wright, KY 41811

"Plants Wanted"
American Horticultural Society
Box 8185
Mount Vernon, VA 22121

Noncommercial Seed Sources and Exchanges

A knowledge of seed-saving techniques is very useful for participation in the following exchanges.

The Flower & Herb Exchange
R.R. 3, Box 239
Decorah, IA 52101

This is an outgrowth of the now-famous Seed Savers Exchange for food plants and is patterned on the same principles of sharing heirloom seeds with members. The 1990 Flower and Herb Exchange listed 182 members offering 678 heirloom flowers or herbs "whose simple beauty is seldom found in modern catalogs." Membership fee is $5.00.

Heritage Seed Program
R.R. 3
Uxbridge, ON   L8C 1K8
Canada

A very energetic program under the direction of Heather Apple. First-rate publication issued three times a year; December issue contains listing of all seeds offered to members; concentrates on vegetables and fruits but includes some ornamentals as well.

J.L. Hudson
P.O. Box 1058
Redwood City, CA 94064

Seed exchange open to anyone who would like to collect seeds from the wild or from unusual plants in your garden; ask for "Seed Exchange" pamphlet, which includes directions for seed saving.

National Gardening Association
180 Flynn Avenue
Burlington, VT 05401
(802) 863-1308

Offers an active seed exchange through its magazine, National Gardening.

Seed Savers Exchange
R.R. 3, Box 239
Decorah, IA 52101

The original seed exchange; for food crops (vegetable and fruit). I list it because some heirloom ornamentals are food, too, such as the Scarlet Runner and White Runner Beans. Perhaps a member has discovered the now-vanished 'Painted Lady' bicolored flower type.

Plant Societies and Preservation Organizations

With few exceptions, most plant societies are *not* devoted to preserving or finding heirloom plants, but there are enthusiasts in most groups. These are an excellent source for rare seeds or plants, available only to members. I have listed only those societies with whose work I am familiar. For a complete listing, see Barbara J. Barton's *Gardening by Mail*, 3rd Edition (Houghton Mifflin, 1990).

The American Daffodil Society
1686 Grey Fox Trails
Milford, OH 45150

Active group; quarterly journal; good source for heirloom Daffodil collectors.

The American Dahlia Society
10 Roland Place
Wayne, NJ 07470

Maybe some member is growing my 'Old Railroad Yellow' Dahlia; keen and knowledgeable membership.

American Rhododendron Society
Box 1380
Gloucester, VA 23061
(804) 693-4433

Various membership options; quarterly journal.

Canadian Chrysanthemum & Dahlia Society
17 Grandard Boulevard
Scarborough, ON M1L 3H8, Canada

Very active; Dahlias are a very popular flower in Canada; knowledgeable membership.

Canadian Gladiolus Society
1274 129A Street
Ocean Park (Surrey), BC V4A 3Y4, Canada
(604) 536-8200

Formed in 1921, the oldest of the world's national or international Glad organizations; a 100-plus-page annual publication includes a comprehensive rating of Glad cultivars, including "antique" types.

Canadian Rose Society
686 Pharmacy Avenue
Scarborough, ON M1L 3H8, Canada

Very enthusiastic Rose growers, some with interest in Old Garden Roses.

The Garden Conservancy
Main Street, Box 219
Cold Spring, NY 10516
(914) 265-2029

Formed in 1989 under the sponsorship of the Tides Foundation to preserve fine gardens by transferring them from private to public ownership. It is worth quoting from its brochure for its relevance to the whole issue of preserving ornamentals, a subject that has not yet been seriously addressed: "Left untended when their creators can no longer maintain them, gardens quickly succumb to nature's ravages.... While Americans have rallied to protect our wilderness lands, historic buildings, and endangered plants and animals, no single advocacy group has arisen to preserve our rich heritage of garden works of art." Gardens are selected for sponsorship by the Conservancy on the basis of their aesthetic, horticultural, and design value.

The Hardy Plant Society
539 Woodland Avenue
Media, PA 19063

Offers seed lists to members.

The Heritage Rose Group (Northeast chapter)
R.D. 1, Box 299
Clinton Corners, NY 12514

Founded in 1975, this organization is described as "a fellowship of those who care about Old Roses." Members receive Heritage Roses quarterly; very informative and entertaining. If you are interested in Old Roses, this is the group to join. The above address will get you membership information; there are seven regional groups.

Historic Iris Preservation Society
12219 Zilles Road
Blackstone, VA 23824

An outgrowth of the American Iris Society and the only group devoted solely to preserving heirloom plants, in this case all categories of Iris, the only qualification being their having been introduced at least thirty years ago. Extremely knowledgeable and enthusiastic members; issues a twice-yearly publication.

International Lilac Society (Walter W. Oakes)
Box 315
Rumford, ME 04276
(207) 562-7453

Founded to stimulate interest in Lilacs and promote their use in public and private landscaping; a very lively group of professional and nonprofessional Lilac enthusiasts; holds an annual convention. A great deal of information available to members on the culture, propagation, selection, and identification of Lilacs. A special and very worthy project is to assist nurseries in making the most desirable Lilacs available, many of them heirloom types. Lilac Newsletter sent to members several times a year.

New England Wild Flower Society, Inc.
Hemenway Road
Framingham, MA 01701

Actively supports wildflower preservation and propagation by commercial nurseries as an alternative to the collection of plants from the wild. A range of activities for members, including participation in plant sales, field trips, courses for children and adults; very worthwhile and worthy (see Garden in the Woods under "Gardens to Visit," p. 223).

North American Lily Society, Inc.
P.O. Box 272
Owatonna, MN 55060

Founded in 1964 to promote the culture of Lilies; quarterly bulletin and a bound yearbook, as well as participation in a Lily seed exchange, are offered to members. Write to this address (Executive Secretary) for information on ordering the classic booklet, Let's Grow Lilies.

Southern Garden History Society
   (Mrs. Zachary T. Bynum)
Old Salem, Inc.
Drawer F, Salem Station
Winston-Salem, NC 27108
(919) 723-3688

A group of individuals and institutions working toward restoring and gathering more history on southern gardens. Publishes the bulletin Magnolia; meets annually, in different areas of the South. It is the first regional garden history society in the United States, wholly a volunteer effort, with 500 members; membership open to anyone. The following states are within the group's interest: Alabama, Arkansas, District of Columbia, Florida, Georgia, Kentucky, Louisiana, Maryland, Mississippi, North Carolina, South Carolina, Tennessee, Texas, Virginia, and West Virginia; see Old Salem under "Gardens to Visit," p. 224.

Research Sources

If you are interested in researching heirloom plants for period gardens, historic landscapes, and the like, the following sources should get you off to a good start.

Association for Preservation Technology Bulletin
   (APT)
Box 8178
Fredericksburg, VA 22404
(703) 373-1621

Send $10.00 for a copy of vol. 21, no. 2 (1989), with an article by Scott Kunst and Arthur O. Tucker, "Where Have All the Flowers Gone?" You will learn about origination lists, which contain the names and dates of introduction of all known cultivars of a certain plant; lists addresses and contacts to obtain these.

Thomas A. Brown
524 6th Street, Apt. E
Petaluma, CA 94952

A landscape architect who embarked on an extraordinary project in 1982, the result of which is California Nurseries and Their Catalogues: 1850-1900 (available for about $25.00, but inquire first). To date he has verified the introduction into California of some 7,000 species and cultivars from this period, 1,100 of them Rose varieties.

Historic Hudson Valley
150 White Plains Road
Tarrytown, NY 10591
(914) 631-8200

Maintains a number of restorations in the Hudson Valley; write for further information; excellent bibliography available.

George Stritikus
Alabama Cooperative Extension Service
4576 South Court Street
Montgomery, AL 36105

County agent in Alabama, with an extensive knowledge about period gardens and plants in his area; has compiled List of Recommended Period Plant Materials for Alabama Gardens and a synopsis of "Alabama Landscapes." An excellent source.

Gardens to Visit

Visiting someone else's garden — no matter how large and grand or small and humble — can give you a new perspective on your own. The following fall into both categories, as well as in between, and illustrate themes stressed throughout this book regarding native flora, herbs, and various types of heirloom plants and their place in the garden.

CALIFORNIA

Los Angeles State and County Arboretum
301 North Baldwin Avenue
Arcadia, CA 91006
(213) 446-8251

Hours: 9-5 daily except Dec. 25
Admission: Fee, except on third Tuesday of every month

More than 5,000 plants, old favorites and new; historic area includes an 1885 Queen Anne cottage and an old-fashioned Rose garden.

Empire Mine State Historic Park
10791 East Empire Street
Grass Valley, CA 95945
(916) 273-8522

Hours: 10-5 daily
Admission: Fee

About 950 old-type Roses are planted in the formal gardens and on the landscaped grounds of a former mining center, which includes the Empire Cottage (English manor home), Gardener's House, and Greenhouse. The original Rose Garden, developed in the early 1900s, has been restored and organized into 11 basic groups according to their dates of discovery. The walking tour begins with the French Rose and moves on to the Damasks, Albas, Centifolias, and so on, to include types introduced before 1929, such as our Granny's favorite, 'Paul's Scarlet Climber' (1916).

Mission San Diego de Alcala
10818 San Diego Mission Road
San Diego, CA 92108-2498
(619) 281-8449

Hours: 9-5 daily
Admission: No fee

Mission gardens in California are dated from 1769, when the first of 21 Spanish missions was founded. Typical flowers include Jonquils, the Madonna Lily, Hollyhocks, and Roses in a charming setting with several courtyards.

LOUISIANA

Rosedown Plantation & Gardens
P.O. Box 1816
St. Francisville, LA 70775
(504) 635-3332

Hours: Mar.-Oct., 9-5 daily; Nov.-Feb., 10-4 daily; closed Dec. 24 and 25
Admission: Fee

Restoration of the 30-acre site was begun in the 1950s under private ownership. The 1830s gardens include the Herb Garden and Medicinal Garden. The tour also includes the 16-room mansion.

MARYLAND

William Paca House and Garden
1 Martin Street
Annapolis, MD 21401
(301) 269-0601

Hours: Mon.-Sat., 10-4; Sun., Nov.-Apr., noon-4; May-Oct., noon-5; closed Thanksgiving Day and Dec. 25 (hours are for garden only)
Admission: Fee

William Paca was a signer of the Declaration of Independence whose Colonial house and grounds were preserved from destruction in 1965 when the site was being considered for a high-rise office complex. The formal hedged gardens are beautifully restored and include herbs, flowers, and shrubs such as Columbine, Loosestrife, Calendula, Southernwood, Mountain-laurel, and Roses.

MASSACHUSETTS

Garden in the Woods
New England Wild Flower Society, Inc.
Hemenway Road
Framingham, MA 01701

Hours: Apr. 15-Oct., Tues.-Sun., 9-4
Admission: Fee

Plunked in the middle of a wall-to-wall suburb of flowerless lawns and foundation plantings, the garden comprises 45 acres of rolling hills, ponds, and trails beautifully planted to native flora and wildflowers in striking combinations, blooming from spring through fall. Visitors can buy plants, including such desirable heirloom natives as Flame Azalea, Maidenhair Fern, and Virginia-bluebells.

Old Sturbridge Village
Sturbridge, MA 01566
(508) 347-3362

Hours: Apr.-Oct., 9-5 daily; Nov.-March, Tues.-Sun., 10-4; closed Mon. during the winter, Dec. 25, and Jan. 1
Admission: Fee

Established in 1946, Old Sturbridge Village has helped to set the standard for such restorations, in this case an early 19th-century New England village on 200 acres. The village includes charming dooryard and formal gardens, one of which features the Child's Arbor, with climbing vines as described in Joseph Breck's 1833 children's book. Period plants of interest include Golden-glow, Jerusalem-cross, Garden Balsam, Bee-balm, Everlasting Pea, and Hop Vine. A compact Herb Garden displays 300 varieties of herbs, which are well labeled. Guides are very helpful and knowledgeable. Note the meticulous staking job on many flowers.

The Arnold Arboretum
Jamaica Plain, MA 02130
(617) 524-1718; 524-1717

Hours: Sunrise to sunset daily
Admission: No fee, donations accepted

Established in 1872, this is the oldest public arboretum in America, with 7,000 varieties of ornamental shrubs and trees on 265-plus acres. A visit here is a must for the shrub enthusiast. Flowers and foliage vary from week to week, beginning in the spring with Lilacs (the famous Lilac Walk), followed by masses of blooming Azaleas, and ending with brilliant autumn foliage. This very important resource includes classes and student programs.

NEW HAMPSHIRE

Moffatt-Ladd House and Garden
154 Market Street
Portsmouth, NH 03801
(603) 436-8221

Hours: June 15-Oct. 15, Mon.-Sat., 10-4; Sun., 2-5
Admission: Fee

The house was built in 1763, and the gardens were designed in 1862. Both are now maintained by the National Society of the Colonial Dames of America. The garden, on two and a half acres, features brick walks, Rose arbors, an herb garden, and old-fashioned perennials.

NEW YORK

Wave Hill
675 West 252nd Street
Bronx, NY 10471
(212) 549-2055

Hours: 10-4:30 daily
Admission: No fee on weekdays; fee on weekends

A 28-acre Hudson River estate with turn-of-the-century (1890s) gardens that include many old-fashioned perennials and herbs.

The Cloisters
The Metropolitan Museum of Art
Fort Tryon Park
New York, NY 10040
(212) 923-3700

Hours: Mar.-Oct., Tues.-Sun., 9:30-5:15; Nov.-Feb., Tues.-Sun, 9:30-4:45; closed Mon., Thanksgiving Day, Dec. 25, and Jan. 1
Admission: Fee, includes admission to Met Museum main building

Three gardens at the Cloisters display ancient herbs and flowers — among them the Madonna Lily, Florentine Iris, Damask and French Roses, and Betony — in a very peaceful setting to study these and other heirloom-type plants. In-depth tours for garden groups are available Tuesday through Sunday by reservation from May through June and September through October. For the general public, garden tours are available Tuesday through Sunday at 1 P.M. during the same months. No advance reservations are necessary. Contact the Cloisters Education Department for group arrangements and fees (phone number above, plus extension 126).

NORTH CAROLINA

Old Salem, Inc.
Drawer F, Salem Station
Winston-Salem, NC 27108

Hours: Mon.-Sat., 8:30-4:40; closed Sun. and Dec. 25
Admission: Fee

A restored Moravian community on 40 acres. Buildings date from 1760 to 1840 with authentic plantings on small home plots: Hop Vine, Roses, Lilacs, and many of the herbs and flowers listed in Christian Reuter's records — altogether about 1,000 types. Group garden tours can be arranged by writing to the Tour Coordinator at the above address; telephone (919) 721-7344; in North Carolina, telephone (800) 441-5305.

PENNSYLVANIA

Bartram's Garden
54th Street and Lindbergh Boulevard
Philadelphia, PA 19143
(215) 729-5281

Hours: Dawn to dusk daily (garden hours only)
Admission: Fee for house only

John Bartram, "curious gardener" extraordinaire and 18th-century plant explorer and botanist, established his plant nursery in 1728. You can see the Seed House where he stored native plants before shipping them to Europe. The 17-acre garden displays many of the plants he and his son William collected and grew, including many shrubs and flowers. The restored stone house is of interest, too.

TEXAS

San Antonio Botanical Center
555 Funston Place
San Antonio, TX 78209
(512) 821-5115

Hours: Tues.-Sun., 9-6; closed Mon. and Dec. 25
Admission: Fee

The 33-acre site includes the Old-Fashioned Garden of annuals and perennials and the Herb Garden with plants used by the Texas settlers.

VIRGINIA

The Anne Spencer House & Garden
1313 Pierce Street
Lynchburg, VA 24505
(804) 845-1313

Hours: Garden open daily; house by appointment
Admission: Fee for house only

Very charming restored garden of Harlem Renaissance poet Anne Spencer, born in 1882. With little means at her disposal and working with a small area behind her house (45 by 125 feet), she brilliantly created the illusion of space. There are many period shrubs, vines, and flowers, as well as middle-aged Roses such as 'Blaze' (1932) and 'Betty Prior'. The house and garden were placed on the National Register of Historic Places in 1976 after the poet's death. Well worth the visit.

Monticello
Charlottesville, VA 22902
(804) 979-5283

Hours: Mar.-Oct., 8-5 daily; Nov.-Feb., 9-4 daily; closed Dec. 25
Admission: Fee

Years of work by the Garden Club of Virginia and the Committee of the Thomas Jefferson Memorial Foundation have restored Jefferson's gardens according to plans dating from about 1807. The gardens include many native shrubs, as well as period annuals and perennials such as Roses, Primroses, Pinks, and Poppies. Plants for sale at the Jefferson Center's Plant Shop include Hollyhocks propagated from naturalized stands at the estate. Future plans include the propagation and distribution of many more heirlooms from the 18th to the early 20th centuries.

Colonial Williamsburg
P.O. Box Drawer C
Williamsburg, VA 23187
(804) 229-1000

Hours: Mar.-Nov., plus last 2 weeks in Dec. (including Dec. 25), 9-5 daily; walking tours of the gardens, Mon.-Fri., 10:30-2:30

Admission: No charge to the Historic Area gardens

The site and gardens are so well publicized that there is no need to describe them except to point out that visitors should watch for the following plants of interest: Canterbury-bells, Cornflowers (Bachelor's - button), Morning-glories, Feverfew, Golden-Marguerite, Sneezewort, and the Tawny and Lemon Daylilies, among the flowers, and Mountain-laurel, Tatarian Honeysuckle, native Rhododendrons, and Old Roses among the shrubs. There is much to see in the formal gardens of this ultimate in 18th-century restorations.

Canada

British Columbia

The Butchart Gardens, Ltd.
Box 4010, Station A
Victoria, BC V8X 3X4
(604) 652-4422

Hours & Admission: May vary; call for current information

The garden as spectacle. Jenny Butchart, the wife of a cement manufacturer (with the factory on the grounds of the estate), set out to prettify the place, including the creation of the now-famous Sunken Garden on the site of an old limestone quarry. Now these gardens are spread out over 50 acres, with mass plantings of bright period annuals and perennials from the early 20th century, among them Godetia, Nicotiana, Nasturtiums, Annual Phlox, and much more. Complete with light shows and a tea shop.

Newfoundland

The Memorial University Botanical Garden
Mount Scio Road
St. John's, NF AIC 5S7
(709) 737-8590

Hours: May 1-Nov. 30, Wed.-Sun., 10-5:30; closed Mon. and Tues.; closed Dec. 1-Apr. 30, visits by appointment only

Admission: No fee, donations appreciated

This is a gem of a botanical garden, developed over 20 years by Bernard S. Jackson. Of special interest is the Heritage Garden of perennials, all grown from actual plants found in Newfoundland gardens and grown before 1940. Among the most spectacular finds is the Fair Maids of France (*Ranunculus aconitifolius* 'Flore Pleno'), a charming double-flowered white Buttercup, traced back 150 years to a Norwegian whaling captain. This is probably the same flower that Sir Peyton ordered by the dozen for Lady Skipwirth in 18th-century Virginia.

Guided tours by appointment.

Nova Scotia

Annapolis Royal Historic Garden
P.O. Box 278
Annapolis Royal, NS B0S 1A0
(902) 532-5104

Hours: 9 A.M. to dusk, late May to late October
Admission: Fee

Ten acres of theme gardens on an historic site, representing English, Acadian, and Indian heritage. Of special interest are the 3,000 Roses of all types and classes from old to new, the impressive Rose Maze, the Herb Garden, the Victorian Garden of mainly annual flowers, and the Governor's Garden, dating from the early to mid 18th century.

Ontario

The Katie Osborne Lilac Garden
Royal Botanical Gardens, Box 399
Hamilton, ON L8N 3H8

Hours: 9:30–7:30 daily
Admission: Fee

The world's largest collection of Lilacs, 770 different varieties, presided over for the past 30 years by Charles Holetich, former president and active member of the International Lilac Society. This is a great place to study heirloom Lilacs.

Bibliography

Entries marked with an asterisk (*) are particularly recommended for their gardening information.

Abraham, George. *The Green Thumb Garden Handbook.* Englewood Cliffs, NJ: Prentice-Hall, Inc., 1961.

American Cottage Gardens. BBG Record/Plants & Gardens. Vol. 46, no. 1 (1990).

American Garden Heritage. BBG Record/Plants & Gardens. Vol. 23, no. 3, (1968).

American Gardens: A Traveler's Guide. Brooklyn Botanic Gardens. (BBG) Record/Plants & Gardens. Vol. 42, no. 3, (1986).

Andersen, A.W. *How We Got Our Flowers.* New York: Dover, 1966 (reprint of 1951 edition).

Andersen Horticultural Library's Source List of Plants and Seeds, comp. Richard T. Isaacson. Chanhassen, MN: Andersen Horticultural Library, 1989.

*Art, Henry W. *A Garden of Wildflowers.* Pownal, VT: Garden Way Publishing, 1986.

The Audubon Society Field Guide to North American Wildflowers, Eastern Region. New York: Alfred A. Knopf, 1979.

Bailey, L.H. *Gardener's Handbook.* New York: Macmillan, 1942.

Berrall, Julia, S. *The Garden.* New York: Viking, 1966.

Betts, Edwin M., and Hazlehurst Bolton Perkins. *Thomas Jefferson's Flower Garden at Monticello.* Rev. ed. Charlottesville: University Press of Virginia, 1986.

Bridgeman, Thomas. *The Kitchen Gardener's Instructor,* 1857; excerpts reproduced in facsimile in *The Herb Grower Magazine* 14, no. 4 (1962), 24-27.

Bubel, Nancy. *The New Seed-Starters Handbook.* Emmaus, PA: Rodale Press, 1988.

Buchanan, Rita. *A Weaver's Garden.* Loveland, CO: Interweave Press, 1987.

Christopher, Thomas. *In Search of Lost Roses.* New York: Summit Books, 1989.

Clarkson, Rosetta E. *Herbs: Their Culture and Uses.* New York: Macmillan, 1942.

*Crockett, James Underwood, and editors. *Annuals.* (The Time-Life Encyclopedia of Gardening). New York: Time-Life Books, 1971.

* ——*Bulbs.* (The Time-Life Encyclopedia of Gardening). New York: Time-Life Books, 1971.

* ——*Perennials.* (The Time-Life Encyclopedia of Gardening). New York: Time-Life Books, 1972.

* ——*Roses.* (The Time-Life Encyclopedia of Gardening). New York: Time-Life Books, 1975.

* ——*Wildflower Gardening.* (The Time-Life Encyclopedia of Gardening). New York: Time-Life Books. 1977.

Culpeper, Nicholas. *Culpeper's Complete Herbal.* London: W. Foulsham & Co., Ltd. (facsimile reprint, n.d.)

Dobson, Beverly R. *The Combined Rose List.* Irvington, NY: Dobson, 1990.

Dowden, Anne Ophelia. *This Noble Harvest.* New York: Wm. Collins, 1979.

Fairchild, David. *The World Grows Round My Door.* New York: Scribner's, 1947.

Favretti, Rudy J. *Early New England Gardens: 1620-1840.* Sturbridge, MA: Old Sturbridge Village, 1966.

Favretti, Rudy J., and Joy Putnam Favretti. *Landscapes and Gardens for Historic Buildings.* Nashville, TN: American Association for State and Local History, 1978.

*Fell, Derek. *Annuals: How to Select, Grow and Enjoy.* Los Angeles: HP Books, 1983.

Fish, Margery. *A Flower for Every Day.* London: Faber & Faber, 1965.

——*Cottage Garden Flowers.* London: W.H. & L. Collingridge, Ltd., 1961.

Flowering Shrubs. BBG Record/Plants & Gardens. Vol. 37, no. 1 (1981).

Foster, Gertrude B. *Herbs, Our Heritage.* Falls Village, CT: The Herb Grower Press, n.d.

Foster, Gertrude B., and Philip Foster, with Cathleen Maxwell. *Herbs for a Nosegay.* Falls Village, CT: The Herb Grower Press, 1966.

*Foster, Gertrude B., and Rosemary F. Louden. *Park's Success with Herbs.* Greenwood, SC: George W. Park Seed Co., Inc., 1980.

Fox, Helen Morgenthau. *Gardening with Herbs for Flavor and Fragrance.* New York: Macmillan, 1933.

Freeman, Margaret B. *Herbs for the Medieval Household.* New York: Metropolitan Museum of Art, 1943.

Friend, Rev. Hilderic. *Flowers and Flower Lore.* Vols. 1 and 2. London: George Allen & Co., Ltd., 1883.

Gardner, Jo Ann. *The Old-Fashioned Fruit Garden.* Halifax, NS: Nimbus Publishing, 1989.

——"Overwintering Annuals." *Horticulture Magazine*, October 1988.

——"Restoring Heritage Flowers." *Atlantic Advocate Magazine*, July 1990.

Genders, Roy. *The Cottage Garden and the Old-Fashioned Flowers.* London: Pelham Books, 1984.

Gerard, John. *Gerard's Herball, The Essence thereof distilled by Marcus Woodward from the Edition of Th. Johnson, 1636.* London: Bracken Books, 1985.

Gray, Asa. *Gray's School and Field Book of Botany.* New York: Ivison, Blakeman & Co., 1887.

Grieve, Mrs. M. *A Modern Herbal. Vols. 1 and 2.* New York: Dover, 1971 (reprint of 1931 Harcourt, Brace edition).

Ground Covers and Vines. BBG Record/Plants & Gardens. Vol. 34, no. 2, (1978).

Growing Annual Flowering Plants. Washington, DC: USDA Farmer's Bulletin, no. 1171 (1939).

Halifax Seed Company catalogs. Halifax, NS: 1926, 1930, 1945.

*Harper, Pamela, and Frederick McGourty. *Perennials: How to Select, Grow and Enjoy.* Los Angeles: HP Books, 1985.

Peter Henderson & Co. Flower seed listing. New York: 1891.

Hibberd, Shirley. *The Amateur's Flower Garden.* Portland, OR: Timber Press, 1986 (reprint of 1871 edition).

*Hill, Lewis, and Nancy Hill. *Successful Perennial Gardening.* Pownal, VT: Garden Way Publishing, 1988.

Hollingsworth, Buckner. *Flower Chronicles.* New Brunswick, NJ: Rutgers University Press, 1958.

——*Her Garden Was Her Delight.* New York: Macmillan, 1962.

Hortus Third. Comp. and ed. by the Staff of the Liberty Hyde Bailey Hortorium. New York: Macmillan, 1976.

Hottes, Alfred C. *A Little Book of Climbing Plants.* New York: A.T. De La Mare Co., 1933.

——*The Book of Shrubs.* New York: Dodd, Mead & Co., 1958.

——"How to Save Your Own Vegetable Seeds." Uxbridge, ON: Heritage Seed Program, 1990.

Huxley, Anthony. *Huxley's Encyclopedia of Gardening.* New York: Universe Books, 1982.

Hyams, Edward, with Jan de Graff. *Lilies.* London: Thomas Nelson & Sons, Ltd., 1967.

Ingwersen, Will. *Classic Garden Plants.* London: Hamlyn Pub. Group, Ltd., 1975.

Jabs, Carolyn. *The Heirloom Gardener.* San Francisco: Sierra Club Books, 1984.

Jackson, Bernard S. "Newfoundland's Heirloom Flower Garden." *Garden*, November/December 1986.

——"Oxen Pond Botanic Park." *Garden*, November/December 1981.

Jekyll, Gertrude. *Annuals and Biennials.* London: Country Life, 1916.

——*Colour Schemes in the Flower Garden.* London: Country Life, 1911.

——*A Gardener's Testament.* London: Antique Collector's Club, 1982 (first published by Country Life, 1937).

Johnson, Marjorie P., and Montague Free. *The Concise Encyclopedia of Favorite Flowers.* New York: Doubleday, 1953.

King, Mrs. Francis. *From a New Garden.* New York: Alfred A. Knopf, 1930.

Klimas, John E., and James A. Cunningham. *Wildflowers of Eastern America.* New York: Alfred A. Knopf, 1974.

Krauss, Helen K. *Geraniums for Home and Garden.* New York: Macmillan, 1955.

Kunst, Scott G. "Daffodils: The Glory of the Post-Victorian Garden." *Old House Journal*, September/October 1989.

Kunst, Scott G., and Arthur O. Tucker. "Where Have All the Flowers Gone?" *The Journal of Preservation Technology Bulletin.* Vol. 21, no. 2 (1989).

Lacy, Allen, ed. *The American Gardener: A Sampler.* New York: Farrar, Straus & Giroux, 1988.

Lawrence, Elizabeth. *Through the Garden Gate.* Chapel Hill: University of North Carolina Press, 1990.

Leighton, Ann. *American Gardens in the 19th Century: "For Comfort and Affluence."* Amherst, MA: University of Massachusetts Press, 1987.

——*American Gardens in the 19th Century: "For Use or for Delight."* Amherst, MA: University of Massachusetts Press, 1987.

——*Early American Gardens: For Meate or Medicine.* Amherst, MA: University of Massachusetts Press, 1986.

Marranca, Bonnie, ed. *American Garden Writing.* New York: PAJ Publishers, 1988.

Martin, Tovah. *Once Upon a Windowsill.* Portland, OR: Timber Press, 1988.

Michael, Pamela. *All the Good Things Around Us.* New York: Holt, Rinehart & Winston, 1980.

Mitchell, Henry. *The Essential Earthman.* Bloomington: University of Indiana Press, 1981.

Newcomb, Peggy C. *Popular Annuals of Eastern*

North America 1865-1914. Washington, DC: Dumbarton Oaks, 1985.

Nuese, Josephine. *The Country Garden.* New York: Scribner's, 1970.

One Hundred Finest Trees and Shrubs for Temperate Climates. BBG Record/Plants & Gardens. Vol. 13, no. 3 (1957).

Painter, Gilian. "Herbal Irises." *The Herb Grower Magazine.* Spring 1983.

Peterson, Roger Tory, and Margaret McKenny. *A Field Guide to Wild Flowers of Northeastern and North-central North America.* Boston: Houghton Mifflin, 1968.

*Phillips, Harry R. *Growing and Propagating Wild Flowers.* Chapel Hill: University of North Carolina Press, 1985.

*Phillips, Rodger, and Martin Rix. *The Random House Book of Shrubs.* New York: Random House, 1989.

Plowden, C. Chicheley. *A Manual of Plant Names.* New York: Philosophical Library, 1970.

Reader's Digest Magic and Medicine of Plants. Pleasantville, NY: Reader's Digest Association, 1986.

Reynolds, Joan, and John Tampion. *Double Flowers: A Scientific Study.* New York: Van Nostrand Reinhold, 1983.

Rockwell, F.F., and Esther C. Grayson. *The Complete Book of Bulbs.* Philadelphia: J.B. Lippincott, 1977.

Rockwell, F.F. and Esther C. Grayson. *The Complete Book of Roses.* New York: Doubleday, 1958.

Rockwell, F.F., Esther C. Grayson, and Jan de Graaf. *The Complete Book of Lilies.* New York: Doubleday, 1961.

Rodale's Illustrated Encyclopedia of Herbs. Emmaus, PA: Rodale Press, 1987.

Roots (Journal of the Historic Iris Preservation Society) 2, no. 2 (Fall 1989).
—— 3, no. 1 (Spring 1990).
—— 3, no. 2 (Fall 1990).

Sanecki, Kay N. *The Complete Book of Herbs.* New York: Macmillan, 1974.

Sanford, S.N.F. "New England Herbs." Boston: New England Museum of Natural History, 1937.

*Scott, George Harmon. *Bulbs: How to Select, Grow and Enjoy.* Los Angeles: HP Books, 1982.

Seals, Joseph. "Heirloom Blooms." *National Gardening Magazine,* August 1986.

Seymour, E.L.D., ed. *The Wise Garden Encyclopedia.* New York: Wm. H. Wise & Co., 1954.

Shohan, Lily. "How to Win a Trophy." *Heritage Roses.* 15, no. 3 (1989).

Slate, George L. *Lilies for American Gardens.* New York: Scribner's, 1947.

Snyder, Leon C. *Trees and Shrubs for Northern Gardens.* Minneapolis: University of Minnesota Press, 1980.

Steele Bros. Catalog (flower seed list). Toronto: 1878.

Strayer, Nannette M. "Wakefield." *The American Herb Grower Magazine* 1, no. 5, (December 1947-48).

Stritikus, George R. *List of Recommended Period Plant Materials for Alabama Gardens.* Montgomery, AL: 1986.

Stuart, David, and James Sutherland. *Plants from the Past.* New York: Viking, 1987.

Thomson, Richard. *Old Roses for Modern Gardens.* New York: Van Nostrand Reinhold, 1959.

Traill, Catharine Parr. *The Canadian Settler's Guide.* Toronto: McClelland & Stewart, Ltd., 1969 (reprint of 1855 edition).

Tucker, Arthur O. *Antique Plant Newsletter* 1, no. 1, (1989).
——*Antique Plants: Old Cultivars of Ornamentals for Today's Gardens.* Private collection of Dr. Arthur O. Tucker, n.d..

Von Baeyer, Edwinna. *Rhetoric and Roses: A History of Canadian Gardening.* Markham, ON: Fitzhenry & Whiteside, 1984.

Webster, Helen Noyes. *Herbs: How to Grow Them and How to Use Them.* Boston: Ralph T. Hale & Co., 1942.

Western Garden Book. Menlo Park, CA: Sunset Books, 1977.

Whiteside, Katherine. *Antique Flowers: A Guide to Using Old-Fashioned Species in Contemporary Gardens.* New York: Villard, 1989.

Wilder, Louise Beebe. *The Fragrant Garden.* New York: Dover, 1974 (reprint of *The Fragrant Path,* Macmillan, 1932).
——*The Garden in Color.* New York: Macmillan, 1937.

Williamson, John. *Perennial Gardens.* New York: Harper & Row, 1988.

Woodcock, H., and W. Stearn. *Lilies of the World.* London: Country Life, 1950.

Wyman, Donald. *Shrubs and Vines for American Gardens.* New York: Macmillan, 1969.
——*Wyman's Gardening Encyclopedia.* New York: Macmillan, 1971.

List of Common Names

A

American Virgin's-bower *Clematis virginiana*
Amur Daylily *Hemerocallis middendorfii*
Anemone Clematis *Clematis montana rubens*
Angel's-tears *Narcissus triandus albus*
Annual Clary Sage *Salvia viridis (S. horminum)*
Apothecary Rose *Rosa gallica officinalis*
Autumn Lily *Hosta plantaginea*
Azalea *Rhododendron* spp.
Azure Monkshood *Aconitum carmichaelii*

B

Bachelor's-button *Centaurea cyanus*
Balsam *Impatiens balsamina*
Beautiful Clarkia *Clarkia pulchella*
Bee-balm *Monarda didyma*
Bellflower *Campanula* spp.
Bergamot *Monarda* spp.
Bethlehem-sage *Pulmonaria saccharata*
Betony *Stachys officinalis*
Black-eyed-Susan *Rudbeckia hirta*
Black Hollyhock *Alcea rosea nigra*
Bleeding-heart *Dicentra* spp.
Blue Plantain Lily *Hosta ventricosa*
Blue Flag Iris *Iris versicolor*
Blue Lungwort *Pulmonaria angustifolia*
Border Phlox *Phlox paniculata*
Boston-ivy *Parthenocissus tricuspidata*
Bouncing-bet *Saponaria officinalis*
Breeder's Glad *Gladiolus* x *gandavensis*
Butterfly Weed *Asclepias tuberosa*

C

Cabbage Rose *Rosa*, Centifolia group
Canada Lily *Lilium canadense*
Canterbury-bells *Campanula medium*
Carolina Rhododendron *Rhododendron carolinianum*
Catawba Rhododendron *Rhododendron catawbiense*
China Aster *Callistephus chinensis*
Chives *Allium schoenoprasum*
Christmas-cowslip *Pulmonaria montana (P. rubens)*
Clarkia *Clarkia* spp.
Clary *Salvia sclarea*
Clematis *Clematis* spp.

Climbing Hydrangea *Hydrangea anomala petiolaris*
Clove Currant *Ribes odoratum*
Clustered Bellflower *Campanula glomerata*
Columbine *Aquilegia* spp.
Colville Glad *Gladiolus* x *colvillei*
Common Monthly Rose *Rosa*, China group
Corfu Lily *Hosta plantaginea*
Corn-flag *Gladiolus* spp.
Cornflower *Centaurea cyanus*
Corn Poppy *Papaver rhoeas*
Cosmos *Cosmos bipinnatus*
Cottage Rose *Rosa*, Alba group
Cowslip *Primula veris (P. officinalis)*
Creeping Bellflower *Campanula rapunculoides*
Crested Iris *Iris cristata*

D

Daffodil *Narcissus* spp.
Dahlia *Dahlia* hybrids
Dame's-rocket *Hesperis matronalis*
Danesblood *Campanula glomerata*
Double Campernelle *Narcissus* x *odorus plenus*
Drummond Phlox *Phlox drummondii*
Dwarf Nasturtium *Tropaeolum minus*

E

Eastern Columbine *Aquilegia canadensis*
Eglantine Rose *Rosa eglanteria*
Elderberry *Sambucus canadensis*
Elecampane *Inula helenium*
European Columbine *Aquilegia vulgaris*
Everblooming Honeysuckle *Lonicera* x *heckrottii*
Everlasting Pea *Lathyrus latifolius*

F

False Honeysuckle *Rhododendron canadense*
Father Hugo's Rose *Rosa hugonis*
Fern-leaf Geranium *Pelargonium denticulatum* 'Filicifolium'
Fern-leaved Peony *Paeonia tenuifolia* 'Flora Plena'
Feverfew *Chrysanthemum parthenium*
Flame Azalea *Rhododendron calendulaceum*
Florentine Iris *Iris* x *germanica* 'Florentina'
Flowering Tobacco *Nicotiana alata*

Forget-me-not   *Myosotis* spp.
Fortune's Plantain Lily   *Hosta fortunei*
Foxglove   *Digitalis purpurea*
French Marigold   *Tagetes patula*
French Rose   *Rosa gallica officinalis*
Fringed Bleeding-heart   *Dicentra eximia*
Funkia   *Hosta* spp.

G

Garden Forget-me-not   *Myosotis sylvatica*
Garden Sage   *Salvia officinalis*
Garlic Chives   *Allium tuberosum*
Glad   *Gladiolus* hybrids
Glossy Abelia   *Abelia* × *grandiflora*
Godetia   *Clarkia amoena*
Goldband Lily   *Lilium auratum*
Golden Currant   *Ribes aureum*
Golden-feather   *Chrysanthemum parthenium*
   'Aureum'
Golden-glow   *Rudbeckia laciniata* 'Hortensia'
Golden-Marguerite   *Anthemis tinctoria*
Goutweed   *Aegopodium podagraria*
Grandma's Peony   *Paeonia officinalis* 'Rubra Plena'
Grass-leaf Daylily   *Hemerocallis minor*
Great-flowered Betony   *Stachys grandiflora*
   (*S. macrantha*)
Great Yellow Monkshood   *Aconitum lycoctonum*

H

Hall's Honeysuckle   *Lonicera japonica* 'Halliana'
Hardy Glad   *Gladiolus byzantinus*
Harebell   *Campanula rotundifolia*
Herb-scented Geranium   *Pelargonium tomentosum*
Highbush Cranberry   *Viburnum trilobum*
Hollyhock   *Alcea rosea*
Hollyhock Mallow   *Malva alcea fastigiata*
Honeysuckle   *Lonicera* spp.
Hoop-petticoat Daffodil   *Narcissus bulbocodium*
Hop Vine   *Humulus lupulus*
Horsemint   *Monarda punctata*
Hosta   *Hosta* spp.

I

Imperial Morning-glory   *Ipomoea nil*
Iris   *Iris* spp.

J

Jackman Clematis   *Clematis* × *jackmanii*
Japanese Iris   *Iris kaempferi*
Japanese Primrose   *Primula japonica*
Jerusalem-cross   *Lychnis chalcedonica*

Johnny-jump-up   *Viola tricolor*
Jonquil   *Narcissus* spp.

L

Lamb's-ears   *Stachys byzantina*
Lemon Geranium   *Pelargonium crispum*
Lemon Yellow Daylily   *Hemerocallis lilioasphodelus*
Leopard Lily   *Lilium pardalinum*
Lewis Mock Orange   *Philadelphus lewisii*
Lilac   *Syringa vulgaris*
Lily   *Lilium* spp.
Lily-of-the-valley   *Convallaria majalis*
Loosestrife   *Lythrum* spp.
Lovage   *Levisticum officinale*
Lungwort   *Pulmonaria officinalis*
Lupine   *Lupinus* spp. and hybrids

M

Madonna Lily   *Lilium candidum*
Maidenhair Fern   *Adiantum pedatum*
Marigold   *Tagetes* spp.
Mock Orange   *Philadelphus coronarius*
Monkshood   *Aconitum* spp.
Moonflower   *Ipomoea alba*
Morning-glory   *Ipomoea purpurea*
Moss Phlox   *Phlox subulata*
Mountain-bluet   *Centaurea montana*
Mountain-laurel   *Kalmia latifolia*
Musk Mallow   *Malva moschata*

N

Narrow-leaved Plantain Lily   *Hosta lancifolia*
Nasturtium   *Tropaeolum majus*
Nicotiana   *Nicotiana alata*

O

Oak-leaved Geranium   *Pelargonium quercifolium*
Old-fashioned Bleeding-heart   *Dicentra spectabilis*
Old Pheasant's-eye   *Narcissus poeticus recurvus*
Orange Daylily   *Hemerocallis fulva*
Orange Geranium   *Pelargonium* × *citrosum*
Oregon Holly-grape   *Mahonia aquifolium*
Oriental Poppy   *Papaver orientale*

P

Peach-leaved Bellflower   *Campanula persicifolia*
Peegee Hydrangea   *Hydrangea paniculata*
   'Grandiflora'
Peony   *Paeonia* spp.
Peony Poppy   *Papaver somniferum*
Persian Musk Rose   *Rosa moschata nastarana*

Petunia   *Petunia* x *hybrida*
Phlox   *Phlox* spp.
Pink-shell Azalea   *Rhododendron vaseyi*
Plantain Lily   *Hosta* spp.
Poppy   *Papaver* spp.
Pot-marigold   *Calendula officinalis*
Purple Foxglove   *Digitalis purpurea*
Purple Loosestrife   *Lythrum* spp.

R
Red-bell Clematis   *Clematis texensis*
Redleaf Rose   *Rosa rubrifolia (R. glauca)*
Regal Lily   *Lilium regale*
Rhododendron   *Rhododendron* spp.
Rhodora   *Rhododendron canadense*
Ribbon Grass   *Phalaris arundinacea picta*
Rocky Mountain Garland   *Clarkia unguiculata*
Rosa Mundi   *Rosa gallica versicolor*
Rose   *Rosa* spp.
Rosebay Rhododendron   *Rhododendron maximum*
Rose Campion   *Lychnis coronaria*
Rose Geranium   *Pelargonium graveolens*
Rose-scented Geranium   *Pelargonium capitatum*
Rose-shell Azalea   *Rhododendron roseum*
    (R. prinophyllum)
Rubrum Lily   *Lilium speciosum* 'Rubrum'

S
Sage   *Salvia* spp.
Scarlet Honeysuckle   *Lonicera sempervirens*
Scarlet Runner Bean   *Phaseolus coccineus*
Scented Geranium   *Pelargonium* spp.
Scottish Bluebell   *Campanula rapunculoides;*
    C. rotundifolia
Siberian Iris   *Iris sibirica*
Siebold Plantain Lily   *Hosta sieboldiana*
Signet Marigold   *Tagetes tenuifolia*
Silver-bells   *Narcissus triandus albus*
Single Campernelle   *Narcissus* x *odorus*
Single Jonquil   *Narcissus jonquilla*
Sneezewort   *Achillea ptarmica*

Southern Blue Flag Iris   *Iris virginica*
Southernwood   *Artemisia abrotanum*
Summer Damask Rose   *Rosa,* Damask group
Swamp Azalea   *Rhododendron viscosum*
Sweet-alyssum   *Lobularia maritima*
Sweet Autumn Clematis   *Clematis paniculata*
Sweetbriar Rose   *Rosa eglanteria*
Sweet Cicely   *Myrrhis odorata*
Sweet Flag Iris   *Iris pallida* 'Dalmatica'
Sweet Pea   *Lathyrus odoratus*
Sweet-William   *Dianthus barbatus*

T
Tatarian Honeysuckle   *Lonicera tatarica*
Tawny Daylily   *Hemerocallis fulva*
Tiger Lily   *Lilium lancifolium*
Turk's-cap Lily   *Lilium superbum*
Traveler's-joy   *Clematis vitalba*
True Forget-me-not   *Myosotis scorpioides*
    (M. palustris)

V
Virginal Mock Orange   *Philadelphus* x *virginalis*
Virginia-bluebells   *Mertensia virginica*
Virginia Creeper   *Parthenocissus quinquefolia*

W
Western Bleeding-heart   *Dicentra formosa*
White Runner Bean   *Phaseolus coccineus* 'Albus'
Wild-bergamot   *Monarda fistulosa*
Wild Lupine   *Lupinus polyphyllus*
Wild Mallow   *Malva sylvestris*
Winter Currant   *Ribes sanguineum*

Y
Yellow Flag Iris   *Iris pseudacorus*
Yellow Lantern Clematis   *Clematis tangutica*

Z
Zebrina Mallow   *Malva sylvestris* 'Zebrina'

Index

A

Abelia × grandiflora, 35-36
Achillea ptarmica, 36-37
Aconitum spp., 37-39
   napellus, 11
Adam-and-Eve. *See* Lungwort
Adiantum pedatum, 13, *32*, 39-40.
   See also Maidenhair Fern
Aegopodium podagraria, 40-41
Alcea rosea, 11, 42-44. *See also*
   Hollyhock
Allium schoenoprasum, 11, *31*, 44-
   45. *See also* Chives
Allium tuberosum, 44-45
American Columbine, 47-49. *See*
   also Eastern Columbine
American Cranberry Bush. *See*
   Highbush Cranberry
American Elder. *See* Elderberry
American-ivy. *See* Virginia
   creeper
American-laurel. *See* Mountain-
   laurel
American Maidenhair. *See* Maid-
   enhair Fern
Ancient and antique types of heir-
   loom ornamentals, 6
Annual Bluebeard. *See* Annual
   Clary Sage
Annual Clary Sage, 189-191
Annuals
   in early settler's cottage
    garden, 11
   in native flora garden, 13
   wintering, 20
   See also specific annuals
Anthemis tinctoria, 17, 46-47
Apothecary rose, 11
Aquilegia canadensis, 12, 13, *28*,
   47-49
Aquilegia vulgaris, 11, 47-49. *See*
   also Columbine
Arbor, child's, 14, *16*
Artemisia abrotanum, 11, 49-50.

   See also Southernwood
Asclepias tuberosa, 13, *27*, 50-51.
   See also Butterfly Weed
Autumn Lily. *See* Hosta
Azalea, 12, 171-174

B

Bachelor's-button, 10, 11, 17, 58-
   59
Balsam, 15, 95-96
Bartram, John, 11
Beales, Peter, 4-5
Bearded Iris, 16, 17. *See also* Iris
Beautiful Clarkia, 61-63
Bee-balm, 12, 13, *25*, 132-134
Bellflower, 17, 55-57. *See also*
   Peach-leaved Bellflower
Bergamot. *See* Bee-balm
Bethlehem-sage. *See* Lungwort
Betony, 195-197
Biennials, 9
   in early settler's cottage
    garden, 11
   in native flora garden, 13
   See also specific biennials
Billy-buttons. *See* Wild Mallow
Bindweed. *See* Morning-glory
Bird's-eye. *See* Johnny-jump-up
Bishop's-weed. *See* Goutweed
Bitter-Indian. *See* Nasturtium
Black-eyed-Susan, 13, 187-188
Bleeding-heart, 12, 15, 75-77. *See*
   also Wild Bleeding-heart
Blew Bindweed. *See* Morning-
   glory
Blew-bottle. *See* Bachelor's-
   button
Bloody-butcher. *See* Lungwort
Bloody-fingers. *See* Purple Fox-
   glove
Blue Barberry. *See* Oregon Holly-
   grape
Blue-cowslip. *See* Lungwort
Blue Flag Iris, 13, 17. *See also* Iris

Blue Funnel Flower. *See* Virginia-
   bluebells
Blue Lungwort, 13. *See also*
   Lungwort
Blue Mallow. *See* Wild Mallow
Blue Monarda. *See* Wild-
   bergamot
Blue-pipe. *See* Lilac
Blue-rocket. *See* Monkshood
Boerner, Gene, 4-5
Bouncing-bet, 13
Bouquets, rose, 186
Boys-and-girls. *See* Lungwort
Bride's-bouquet. *See* Sneezewort
British Myrrh. *See* Sweet Cicely
Buffalo Currant. *See* Clove Cur-
   rant; Golden Currant
Bulbs
   propagating and preserving, 22
   storing, 23-24
Bunch Pink. *See* Sweet-William
Bush Balsam. *See* Balsam
Butterfly Flower. *See* Butterfly
   Weed
Butterfly Milkweed. *See* Butterfly
   Weed
Butterfly Weed, 12, 13, *27*, 50-51

C

Cabbage rose, 11
Calendula, 10, 11, 17, 51-53
Calendula officinalis, 11, 51-53. *See*
   also Calendula
Calico Bush. *See* Mountain-laurel
Callistephus chinensis, 53-55
Campanula spp., 55-57. *See also*
   Bellflower
   medium, 11
   persicifolia, 11. *See also* Peach-
    leaved Bellflower
Canadian Columbine. *See* Eastern
   Columbine
Candelabra Primrose. *See*
   Japanese Primrose

glove

Fairy's-hat. *See* Purple Foxglove

Fairy's-thimble. *See* Purple Foxglove

Farewell-to-spring. *See* Godetia

Featherfoil. *See* Feverfew

Fence, quiggly, 10, *12*

Fernleaf Bleeding-heart. *See* Fringed Bleeding-heart

Fether-few. *See* Feverfew

Feverfew, 10, 11, 17, 59-61

Field Pansy. *See* Johnny-jump-up

Fine-leaved Willow-herb. *See* Purple Loosestrife

Fire bean. *See* Scarlet Runner Bean

Five-finger Fern. *See* Maidenhair Fern

Five-leaved-ivy. *See* Virginia creeper

Flame Azalea, 13, *27. See also* Azalea

Flibberty-gibbet. *See* Wild Mallow

Flirtwort. *See* Feverfew

Florentine Iris, 10, 11. *See also* Iris

Floribunda hybrid rose, *30*

Flower-of-Bristol. *See* Rose Campion

Folk's-glove. *See* Purple Foxglove

Forget-me-not, 13, 134-136

Foxglove, 17. *See also* Purple Foxglove

Fragrance, 8

Fragrant-balm. *See* Bee-balm

Fragrant Plantain. *See* Hosta

French Grass. *See* Ribbon Grass

French Mallow. *See* Wild Mallow

French Marigold, 14, 200-202

Friar's-cap. *See* Monkshood

Fringed Bleeding-heart, 75-77

Fulvous Daylily. *See* Orange Daylily

Funkia. *See* Hosta

G

Garden Balsam. *See* Balsam

Gardener's-garters. *See* Ribbon Grass

Garden Forget-me-not. *See* Forget-me-not

Garden-honeysuckle. *See* European Columbine

Garden Lupine, 118-121

Garden Mallow. *See* Hollyhock

Garden-rocket. *See* Dame's-rocket

Gardens, 223-226

color in, *25-32*

cottage, 8

early settler's, 10-11

eclectic, 16-18

native flora, 11-14

old-fashioned mix, 14-15

preserving, 18-22

Puritan, 10

rock, 12-13

Garden Sage, 11, 189-191. *See also* Sage

Garlic Chives, 44-45

German Aster. *See* China Aster

Giant-chervil. *See* Sweet Cicely

Glad, 16, 17, 80-83

Gladiolus spp., 80-83

byzantinus, 17

x *colvillei* 'Albus', 17

hybrids, 80-83

Glossy Abelia, 35-36

Gloves-of-Our-Lady. *See* Purple Foxglove

Godetia, 13, 61-63

Godetia amoena. See Clarkia amoena

Godetia grandiflora. See Clarkia amoena

Godfathers-and-godmothers. *See* Johnny-jump-up

Goldband Lily, 14-15. *See also* Lily

Golden Anthemis. *See* Golden-Marguerite

Golden Currants, 11, 12, 13, 174-177

Golden-glow, *26*, 187-188

Golden-Marguerite, 17, 46-47

Goutweed, 13, 40-41

Grandma's Peony, 10, 11. *See also* Peony

Granny's-bonnet. *See* European Columbine

Great-flowered Betony, 195-197

Ground-ash. *See* Goutweed

Ground-elder. *See* Goutweed

Grouseberry. *See* Highbush Cranberry

Growing zones. *See* Hardiness zones

H

Hand-pollination, 19

Hardiness, 23

Hardiness zones, 7-8

map, *210*

Hardwood stem cuttings, 21

Hardy Glad, 17

Heartsease. *See* Johnny-jump-up

Heirloom ornamentals, defined, 6

Helen's Flower. *See* Elecampane

Helmet Flower. *See* Monkshood

Hemerocallis flava. See Hemerocallis lilioasphodelus

Hemerocallis fulva, 11, 83-86. *See also* Tawny Daylily

Hemerocallis lilioasphodelus, 11, 83-86

Herb Constancy. *See* Johnny-jump-up

Herb Peter. *See* Cowslip

Herbs, 10

Herb Trinity. *See* Johnny-jump-up

Hesperis matronalis, 11, 86-88. *See also* Dame's-rocket

Highbush Cranberry, 13, 205-206

High Mallow. *See* Wild Mallow

Holly Barberry. *See* Oregon Holly-grape

Holly-grape. *See* Oregon Holly-grape

Hollyhock, 10, 11, 42-44

Hollyhock Mallow, 126-128

Holly Mahonia. *See* Oregon Holly-grape

Holyoke. *See* Hollyhock

Honeysuckle, 116-118. *See also*

Honeysuckle (continued)
Scarlet Honeysuckle
Hop Vine, 10, 11, 91-93
Horseheal. See Elecampane
Horsemint, 12, 13, 132-134
Hosta, 15, 88-91
in old-fashioned mix garden, 14
Hosta spp., 88-91
fortunei, 15
plantaginea, 15
sieboldiana 'Elegans', 15
ventricosa, 15
Humulus lupulus, 11, 91-93. See
also Hop Vine
Hundreds-and-thousands. See
Lungwort
Hurt-sickle. See Bachelor's-
button
Hydrangea anomala petiolaris, 93-
94
Hydrangea paniculata, 93-94

I
Impatiens balsamina, 15, 95-96
Indian-cress. See Nasturtium
Indian Nasturtium. See Nastur-
tium
Indian-paintbrush. See Butterfly
Weed
Inula helenium, 96-98
Ipomoea alba, 15, 98-100. See also
Moonflower; Morning-glory
Ipomoea nil 'Scarlet O'Hara', 98-
100
Ipomoea purpurea, 32, 98-100
Iris, 16, 100-104
Iris spp., 100-104
cristata, 13. See also Crested Iris
x germanica 'Florentina', 11. See
also Florentine Iris
pallida, 18
sibirica, 18. See also Siberian Iris
virginica, 13
Ivybush. See Mountain-laurel

J
Jack-jump-up-and-kiss-me. See
Johnny-jump-up
Jackman Clematis, 15

Jacob-and-Rachel. See Lungwort
Jam
Currant, 177
Rose Hip, 186
Japan Day-lily. See Hosta
Japanese Primrose, 167-169
Jefferson, Thomas, 11, 13
Jerusalem-cowslip. See Lungwort
Jerusalem-cross, 10, 11, 17, 28,
121-123
Jerusalem Mallow Pie, Drora's,
130
Jerusalem-sage. See Lungwort
Johnnies. See Johnny-jump-up
Johnny-jump-up, 10, 11, 26, 207-
208
Jonquil. See Daffodil
Joseph-and-Mary. See Lungwort
Joseph Sage. See Annual Clary
Sage

K
Kalmia latifolia, 13, 29, 104-106.
See also Mountain-laurel
Key Flower. See Cowslip
Key-of-heaven. See Cowslip
The-King-in-splendour. See
Great-flowered Betony
Kiss-her-in-the-buttery. See
Johnny-jump-up
Kit-run-about. See Johnny-jump-
up
Kit-run-in-the-fields. See Johnny-
jump-up

L
Ladies-delight. See Johnny-jump-
up
Lad's-love. See Southernwood
Lady Pea. See Lathyrus odoratus
Lady's-balsam. See Balsam
Lady's-garters. See Ribbon Grass
Lady's-heart. See Bleeding-heart
Lady's-laces. See Ribbon Grass
Lady's-locket. See Bleeding-heart
Lady's-ribands. See Ribbon Grass
Lady's-slipper. See Balsam
Lamb's-ears, 15, 195-197
Lamb's-lugs. See Lamb's-ears

Lamb's-tongues. See Lamb's-ears
Lampflower. See Rose Campion
Lark's-heel. See Nasturtium
Lathyrus latifolius, 11, 106-108.
See also Everlasting Pea
Lathyrus odoratus, 15, 31, 106-108.
See also Sweet Pea
Latin names, 7, 230-32
Lauren, Verna, 5
Layering, 21-22
Laylock. See Lilac
Lemon Daylily. See Lemon
Yellow Daylily
Lemon Lily, 11. See also Lemon
Yellow Daylily
Lemon Yellow Daylily, 83-86
Leopard Lily, 12, 13
Levisticum officinale, 108-110
Lilac, 10, 11, 197-200
Lilac Funkia. See Hosta
Lilium spp., 110-114
auratum, 15
candidum, 11. See also Madonna
Lily
pardalinum, 12, 13
regale, 18, 26. See also Regal
Lily
speciosum 'Rubrum', 15
superbum, 13
Lily, 15, 16, 17, 110-114
Lily Asphodel. See Lemon Yellow
Daylily
Lily-convally. See Lily-of-the-
valley
Lily-of-the-valley, 10, 11, 66-68
Liriconfancy. See Lily-of-the-
valley
Live-in-idleness. See Johnny-
jump-up
Lobularia maritima, 15, 114-116.
See also Sweet-alyssum
London-pride. See Jerusalem-
cross
Lonicera spp., 116-118
sempervirens, 11. See also Scarlet
Honeysuckle
Lovage, 108-110
Love-in-idleness. See Johnny-
jump-up

The Lovers Plant. *See* Southern-
wood
Loving-me. *See* Johnny-jump-up
Lungwort, 11, 169-171. *See also*
Blue Lungwort
Lupine, 13, 18
cultivars, Russell Hybrid, 8, 17,
118-121
See also Wild Lupine
Lupinus, 18
Lupinus polyphyllus, 13, *32*, 118-
121
Lychnis chalcedonica, 11, *28*, 121-
123. *See also* Jerusalem-cross
Lychnis coronaria, 121-123
Lylack. *See* Lilac
Lythrum spp., 123-125

M

Madonna Lily, 10, 11, 17
Mahonia aquifolium, 13, *32*, 125-
126
Maidenhair Fern, 12, 13, *32*, 39-
40
Maid's-ruin. *See* Southernwood
Maltese-cross. *See* Jerusalem-
cross
Malva alcea fastigiata, 126-128
Malva moschata, 11, 126-128. *See
also* Musk Mallow
Malva sylvestris, 128-130. *See also*
Musk Mallow
Marigold, 14, 15, 200-202
Mary-and-Martha. *See* Lungwort
Marygold. *See* Pot-marigold
Mary's-milk-drops. *See* Lungwort
Mayflower. *See* Cowslip
May-lily. *See* Lily-of-the-valley
Meetinghouses. *See* Eastern
Columbine
Meet-me-in-the-entry. *See*
Johnny-jump-up
Merrigould. *See* Pot-marigold
Mertensia virginica, 130-132
Mexican Aster. *See* Cosmos
Middle-aged types of heirloom
ornamentals, 6
Milk Willow-herb. *See* Purple
Loosestrife

Missouri Currant. *See* Clove
Currant; Golden Currant
M'Mahon, Bernard, 11
Mock Orange, 10, 11, 161-163
Modern Roses, 184-186
Monarda didyma, 13, *25*, 132-134.
See also Bee-balm
Monarda fistulosa, 11, 132-134. *See
also* Wild-bergamot
Monarda punctata, 12, 13, 132-134
Monkshood, 11, 37-39
Moonflower, 14, 15, 98-100
Moonvine. *See* Moonflower
Morning-glory, 14, *32*, 98-100
Moss Phlox, 12, 13, *31*. *See also*
Phlox
Mother-of-the-evening. *See*
Dame's-rocket
Mountain-bluebottle. *See*
Mountain-bluet
Mountain-bluet, 17, 18, 58-59
Mountain-cowslip. *See* Virginia-
bluebells
Mountain-grape. *See* Oregon
Holly-grape
Mountain-laurel, 11, 12, 13, *29*,
104-106
Mountain Viburnum. *See*
Highbush Cranberry
Mullein-pink. *See* Rose Campion
Muskatel Sage. *See* Clary
Musk Mallow, 10, 11, 17, 126-
128
Myosotis spp., 134-136
Myrrhis odorata, 136-137. *See also*
Sweet Cicely

N

Narcissus spp., 137-142. *See also*
Sweet Cicely
bulbocodium, 15
poeticus 'Actaea', *26*
poeticus recurvus, 15
triandus albus, 15
Nasturtium, 14, 15, 203-205
Native flora garden, 11-14
Nicotiana, 14, 15, 17, 142-144
Nicotiana alata, 15, 142-144. *See
also* Nicotiana

Nonesuch. *See* Rose Campion
Northern Maidenhair. *See*
Maidenhair Fern
Nosebleed. *See* Sneezewort

O

Old Cluster Hop. *See* Hop Vine
Old English Lovage. *See* Lovage
Old-fashioned Bleeding-heart,
29. See also Bleeding-heart
Old-fashioned mix, 14-15
Old Garden Roses (OGRs), 177-
183. *See also* Roses
Old-man. *See* Southernwood
Old-man's-love. *See* Southern-
wood
Old-man Wormwood. *See*
Southernwood
Old White Day-lily. *See* Hosta
Open-pollinated (OP) plant, 6
Orange-blossom. *See* Mock
Orange
Orange Daylily, 83-86
Oregon-grape. *See* Oregon
Holly-grape
Oregon Holly-grape, 13, *32*, 125-
126
Oriental Garlic. *See* Garlic Chives
Oriental Poppy, 17, 18. *See also*
Poppy
Oswego-tea. *See* Bee-balm
Our-Lady's-tears. *See* Lily-of-
the-valley
Outlandish-rose. *See* Hollyhock
Ox-eye Chamomile. *See* Golden-
Marguerite

P

Paeonia spp., 144-147
officinalis, 11. *See also*
Grandma's Peony
Painted Pea Lady. *See* Lathyrus
odoratus
Painted Sage. *See* Annual Clary
Sage
Palsywort. *See* Cowslip
Pancake Plant. *See* Wild Mallow
Papaver spp., 147-150. *See also*
Poppy

Tropaeolum majus (continued)
    See also Nasturtium
Tropaeolum minus, 203-205
True Forget-me-not. *See* Forget-
    me-not
Turkey-corn. *See* Fringed
    Bleeding-heart
Turk's-cap. *See* Monkshood
Turk's-cap Lily, 13

U

U.S. Department of Agriculture's
    (USDA) Hardiness Zones, 7-
    8
    map, *210*

V

Variants, 8
Variety, 6
Velvet-dock. *See* Elecampane
Venus's-shell. *See* Monkshood
Viburnum trilobum, 13, 205-206
Vines
    in early settler's cottage
        garden, 10, 11
    in native flora garden, 13, 14
    in old-fashioned mix garden, 15
Viola tricolor, 11, *26*, 207-208. *See*
    also Johnny-jump-up

Virginia-bluebells, 12, 17, 130-
    132
Virginia-cowslip. *See* Virginia-
    bluebells
Virginia Creeper, 13, 150-152
Virgin's-glove. *See* Purple
    Foxglove

W

Washington Lupine. *See* Wild
    Lupine
Western Bleeding-heart, 75-77
White Dutch Runner Bean. *See*
    White Runner Bean
White Lily. *See* Madonna Lily
White-pipe. *See* Mock Orange
White Runner Bean, 15
Wild-bergamot, 10, 11, 132-134
Wild Bleeding-heart, 12, 13. *See*
    also Fringed Bleeding-heart
Wild-hop. *See* Betony
Wild Lupine, *32*, 118-121
Wild Mallow, 128-130
    Drora's Jerusalem Mallow Pie,
        130
Wild Pansy. *See* Johnny-jump-up
Wild-sunflower. *See* Elecampane
Wine, Cowslip, 169
Winged Lythrum. *See* Purple
    Loosestrife

Winking-Mary-budde. *See* Pot-
    marigold
Winter Currant, 14, 174-177. *See*
    also Redflower Currant
Witches'-glove. *See* Purple
    Foxglove
Wolfsbane. *See* Monkshood
Wood Betony. *See* Betony
Woodbine. *See* Virginia creeper
Woodland Forget-me-not. *See*
    Forget-me-not
Woolly Betony. *See* Lamb's-ears
Woolly Stachys. *See* Lamb's-ears
Woundwort. *See* Betony; Lamb's-
    ears
Wyman, Donald, 7

Y

Yellow Dahlia, *27*
Yellow Daylily. *See* Lemon
    Yellow Daylily
Yellow Flag Iris, 13, 17. *See also*
    Iris
Yellow-larkspur. *See* Nasturtium
Yellow Tuberose. *See* Lemon
    Yellow Daylily
Yerger, Meg, 5
Youth-before-old-age. *See*
    Goutweed